• KINGFISHER •

WORLD HISTORY

ATLAS

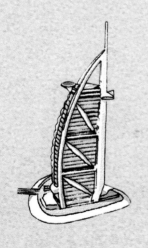

• KINGFISHER •

WORLD HISTORY
ATLAS

SIMON ADAMS

KINGFISHER
LONDON & NEW YORK

CONTENTS

ANCIENT
WORLD

Illustrated by Katherine Baxter

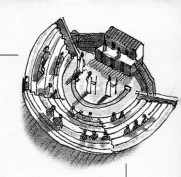

CONTENTS

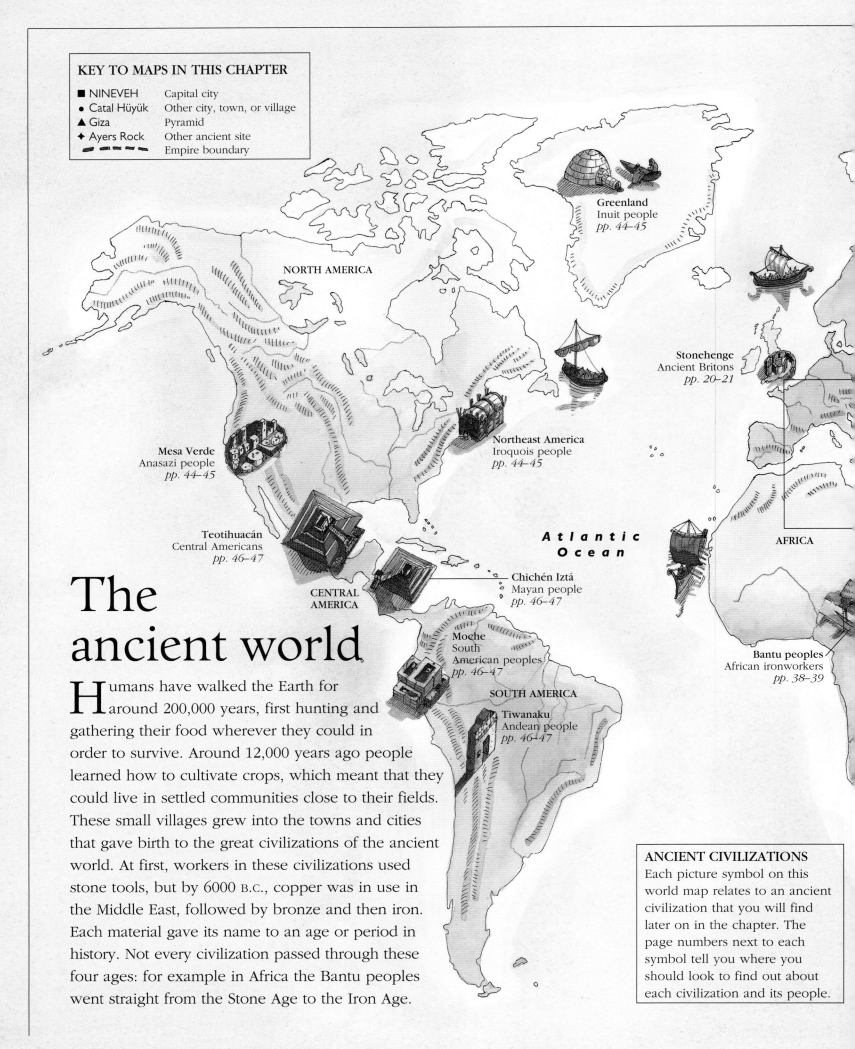

NORTH AMERICA

Greenland
Inuit people
pp. 44–45

Stonehenge
Ancient Britons
pp. 20–21

Mesa Verde
Anasazi people
pp. 44–45

Northeast America
Iroquois people
pp. 44–45

Teotihuacán
Central Americans
pp. 46–47

Chichén Iztá
Mayan people
pp. 46–47

CENTRAL
AMERICA

Atlantic Ocean

AFRICA

Bantu peoples
African ironworkers
pp. 38–39

Moche
South
American peoples
pp. 46–47

SOUTH AMERICA

Tiwanaku
Andean people
pp. 46–47

The ancient world

Humans have walked the Earth for around 200,000 years, first hunting and gathering their food wherever they could in order to survive. Around 12,000 years ago people learned how to cultivate crops, which meant that they could live in settled communities close to their fields. These small villages grew into the towns and cities that gave birth to the great civilizations of the ancient world. At first, workers in these civilizations used stone tools, but by 6000 B.C., copper was in use in the Middle East, followed by bronze and then iron. Each material gave its name to an age or period in history. Not every civilization passed through these four ages: for example in Africa the Bantu peoples went straight from the Stone Age to the Iron Age.

ANCIENT CIVILIZATIONS
Each picture symbol on this world map relates to an ancient civilization that you will find later on in the chapter. The page numbers next to each symbol tell you where you should look to find out about each civilization and its people.

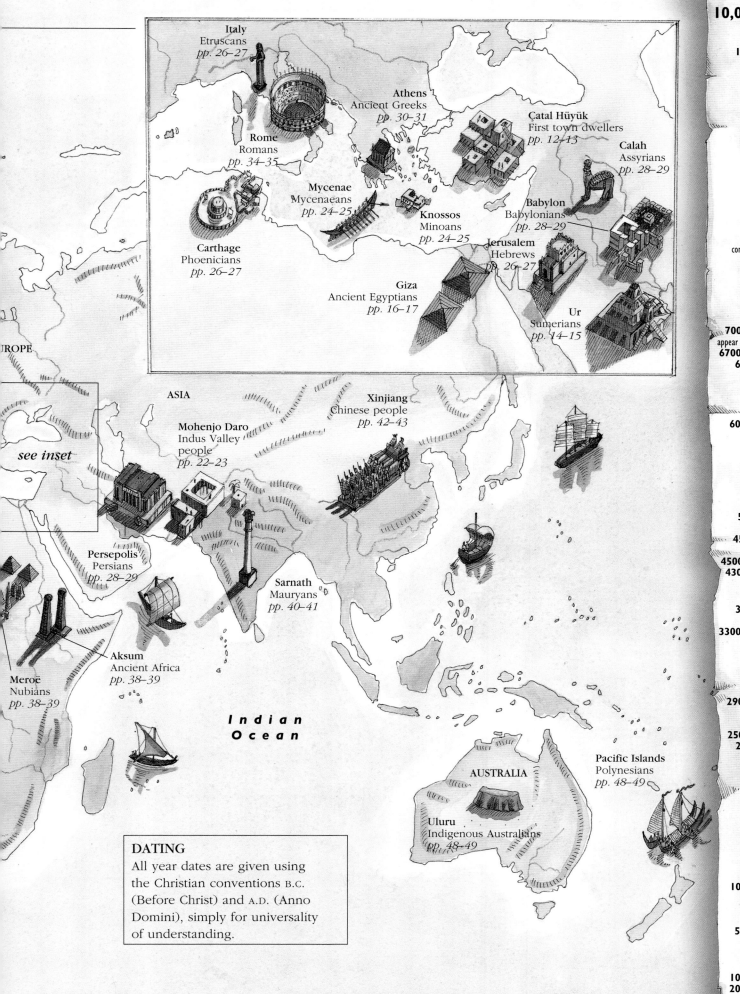

Italy
Etruscans
pp. 26–27

Athens
Ancient Greeks
pp. 30–31

Çatal Hüyük
First town dwellers
pp. 12–13

Calah
Assyrians
pp. 28–29

Rome
Romans
pp. 34–35

Mycenae
Mycenaeans
pp. 24–25

Knossos
Minoans
pp. 24–25

Babylon
Babylonians
pp. 28–29

Carthage
Phoenicians
pp. 26–27

Jerusalem
Hebrews
pp. 26–27

Giza
Ancient Egyptians
pp. 16–17

Ur
Sumerians
pp. 14–15

EUROPE

ASIA

Xinjiang
Chinese people
pp. 42–43

Mohenjo Daro
Indus Valley
people
pp. 22–23

see inset

Persepolis
Persians
pp. 28–29

Sarnath
Mauryans
pp. 40–41

Aksum
Ancient Africa
pp. 38–39

Meroë
Nubians
pp. 38–39

Indian
Ocean

Pacific Islands
Polynesians
pp. 48–49

AUSTRALIA

Uluru
Indigenous Australians
pp. 48–49

DATING

All year dates are given using
the Christian conventions B.C.
(Before Christ) and A.D. (Anno
Domini), simply for universality
of understanding.

The ancient world:
How we know about the past

Although we cannot travel back in time to speak to the people who lived in the ancient world, we can discover a lot about them based on the objects that they left behind. Buildings, aqueducts and roads, everyday objects, such as pots, tools, coins, and writing implements, and luxury items, such as jewelry and gold ornaments, have all survived to tell their tales. Some buildings, like the Forum in Rome, are still partially standing, while other buildings and smaller objects had been buried for hundreds of years and only recently have been uncovered by archaeologists. All these remains tell us a great deal about the peoples in the ancient world and the lives that they led. From them, we can piece together a picture of what it was like to live in ancient Rome or China, to march with Alexander the Great's army, or to sail the Pacific Ocean, colonizing new islands.

Royal music
This silver lyre—a stringed musical instrument—was made in Ur, modern-day southern Iraq, around 4,500 years ago. It was found in the Royal Cemetery—a lavish burial site where the kings of Ur were buried with their servants. Its incredible craftsmanship and its place of discovery suggest that it was played at the royal court and was buried with the king so that he could continue to enjoy it in the afterlife.

The Forum
The Forum was the political, judicial, and commercial center of Rome and the huge Roman Empire. There, senators met to discuss the important issues of the day and judges tried legal cases. Most of the Forum is now in ruins, but enough of its fine buildings, arches, and monuments survive for us to see just how impressive it must have been when Rome and its armies dominated the Western world.

Cuneiform writing

Priests in the cities of Sumer developed the world's first writing around 3400 B.C. It consisted of simple pictures, and each one represented a word or an idea. By 2900 B.C., this had developed into cuneiform—a writing system that used wedge-shaped marks (*cuneus* is Latin for wedge) that were made by pressing a reed stylus into wet clay.

Hieroglyphics

Around 3300 B.C. the ancient Egyptians began to use a form of writing known as hieroglyphs. This was more complex than Sumerian picture writing and used around 700 different signs to represent different ideas, words, and even individual letters. The hieroglyphs above date from the first century B.C.

Mayan writing

Zapotec scribes in the Americas developed their own unique form of hieroglyphic picture writing around 800 B.C. Later the Maya used these to develop their own advanced literary language with a "glyph" for every syllable. Many glyphs have been translated only recently.

Hands-on history

Archaeologists study the evidence that is left behind by previous generations. They examine a site or an object, looking for clues that might tell them how old it is, who made it, and why it was found where it was. Even the tiniest scrap of evidence can provide a vital clue, and archaeology can be a long process. Here, an archaeologist is examining a Roman mosaic that was uncovered during the construction of a road in Israel.

Chinese coins

We use coins every day, but each coin is a piece of history with its own story to tell. Coins show rulers of the time and important symbols, and we can tell a lot about trade based on where they are found. The Chinese have been using coins since the 400s B.C. These were made with a hole in the middle so that they could be kept on a string.

Karaoglan •

A N A T O L I A

Çatal Hüyük ·
The mud brick buildings of Çatal Hüyük housed 6,000 people between 6700 and 5700 B.C. Many of the houses were decorated with wall paintings and sculptures.

Lake Tuz

Çatal Hüyük

Mersin

Tarsus

Taurus Mountains

Farmers tending wild sheep

Tell Judaidah

Wheat and barley

Growing crops
Grains were first cultivated in the Levant around 8000 B.C.

Ugarit

Weaving textiles from flax

Philia
Cyprus

Khirokitia

L E V A N T

Fishing
Fishermen on the Tigris and Euphrates rivers built boats out of reeds and rushes to catch the plentiful fish.

M E S O P

Byblos

M e d i t e r r a n e a n S e a

Tell Ramad

S y r i a n   D e s e r t

Jericho

Jericho ·
The first permanent settlement in Jericho was built in 8500 B.C. By 8000 B.C., it was walled, housing at least 1,500 people.

The first towns

Around 8000 B.C. people in the Levant made one of the most important discoveries in history. They learned how to cultivate wild grains such as wheat and barley. This was the beginning of farming, and it meant that people could live in one place that was close to their crops. As a result, permanent settlements were built here and throughout the Fertile Crescent—the arc of fertile land stretching from southern Levant to Mesopotamia and the Persian Gulf. The first farmers built villages and, later, walled towns such as Jericho and Çatal Hüyük. In towns not everyone was a farmer. Townspeople learned new skills, such as making pottery and smelting copper, and began to trade. This helped their towns prosper and expand.

10,000 B.C.
10,000 Farmers in the Levant first build wooden huts with stone foundations

9500 B.C.

9000 B.C.
9000 Wild sheep herds are first kept by farmers in the Taurus and Zagros mountains

8500 B.C.

8000 B.C.
8000 Barley and wheat are cultivated in the Levant, allowing settled farming communities to develop
8000 The walled city of Jericho has 1,500 inhabitants

7500 B.C.
7500 Flax is first used for textiles

7000 B.C.
7000 Settled farming communities flourish throughout the Fertile Crescent
7000 Goats, sheep, and later pigs are domesticated in the Taurus Mountains
6700 Çatal Hüyük, with 6,000 inhabitants, is the largest town

6500 B.C.
6500 Pottery comes into general use

6200 Copper smelting begins in Çatal Hüyük

6000 B.C.
6000 Cattle are first domesticated
6000 Kiln-fired pottery develops in Hassuna

5500 B.C.
5500 Irrigation allows farming communities to flourish in the arid soil of Mesopotamia

5000 B.C.
5000 The first towns and temples are built in Mesopotamia

4500 B.C.
4500 The plow, sail, and potter's wheel are in common use in Mesopotamia
4300 Copper working for tools and weapons begins in Mesopotamia
4000 Sheep are bred for wool

4000 B.C.

The development of farming

The first peoples were hunter-gatherers who found food by killing wild animals and collecting wild fruits, nuts, and grains. In the Levant wild crops were so plentiful that by about 10,000 B.C. people did not need to move around in order to find food. Slowly they learned how to plant and grow wild grains so that the crops would produce more food and be easier to harvest. Early farmers domesticated sheep, goats, pigs, and cattle, and by 6000 B.C., they could feed a large, settled urban population.

Plows helping farmers cultivate the land

Pottery
Potters in Hassuna learned how to fire pottery in a kiln around 6000 B.C.

Smelting copper
Smelting copper to make weapons and tools reached southern Mesopotamia before 4000 B.C.

Irrigating the land
Farmers began building canals and irrigation ditches in Mesopotamia around 5500 B.C.

Local industries
A pottery industry that used local clay built up in Susa and nearby towns in the 4000s B.C.

Temples
The people of southern Mesopotamia built large temples and grain storehouses in Uruk and other towns after 5000 B.C.

Eridu
Eridu, the oldest town in southern Mesopotamia, had a population of around 5,000 in 4000 B.C. It traded pottery and other goods with Arabia.

Yanik Tepe
Lake Urmia
Tepe Gawra
Hassuna
Umm Dabaghiyeh
Tigris
Samarra
Tell Al-Sawwan
Choga Mami
MESOPOTAMIA
Tepe Guran
Susa
Tell 'Uqair
Nippur
Ali Kosh
Euphrates
Uruk
Tel Awayli
Eridu
Persian Gulf
Zagros Mountains

0   200km
0   100 miles

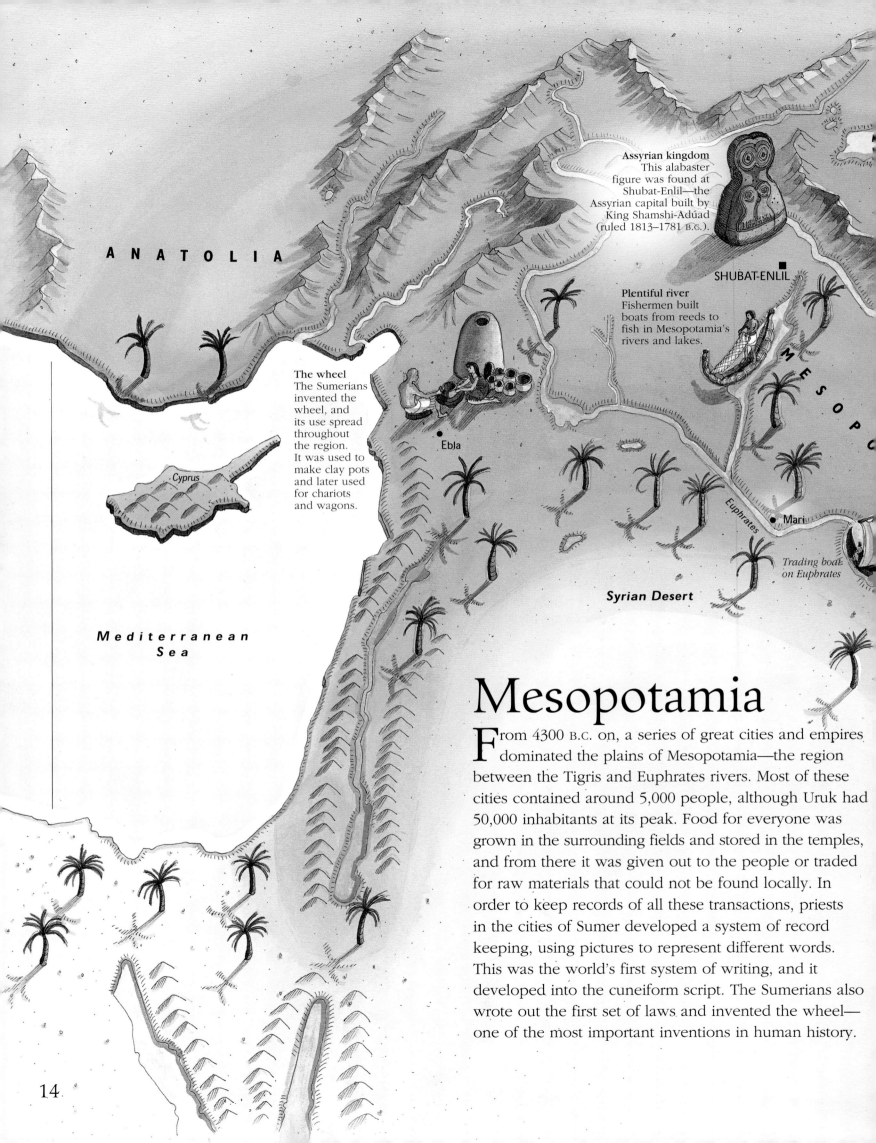

Assyrian kingdom
This alabaster figure was found at Shubat-Enlil—the Assyrian capital built by King Shamshi-Aduad (ruled 1813–1781 B.C.).

■ SHUBAT-ENLIL

Plentiful river
Fishermen built boats from reeds to fish in Mesopotamia's rivers and lakes.

A N A T O L I A

The wheel
The Sumerians invented the wheel, and its use spread throughout the region. It was used to make clay pots and later used for chariots and wagons.

Cyprus

• Ebla

M E S O P O

Euphrates

• Mari

Trading boat on Euphrates

Syrian Desert

Mediterranean Sea

Mesopotamia

From 4300 B.C. on, a series of great cities and empires dominated the plains of Mesopotamia—the region between the Tigris and Euphrates rivers. Most of these cities contained around 5,000 people, although Uruk had 50,000 inhabitants at its peak. Food for everyone was grown in the surrounding fields and stored in the temples, and from there it was given out to the people or traded for raw materials that could not be found locally. In order to keep records of all these transactions, priests in the cities of Sumer developed a system of record keeping, using pictures to represent different words. This was the world's first system of writing, and it developed into the cuneiform script. The Sumerians also wrote out the first set of laws and invented the wheel— one of the most important inventions in human history.

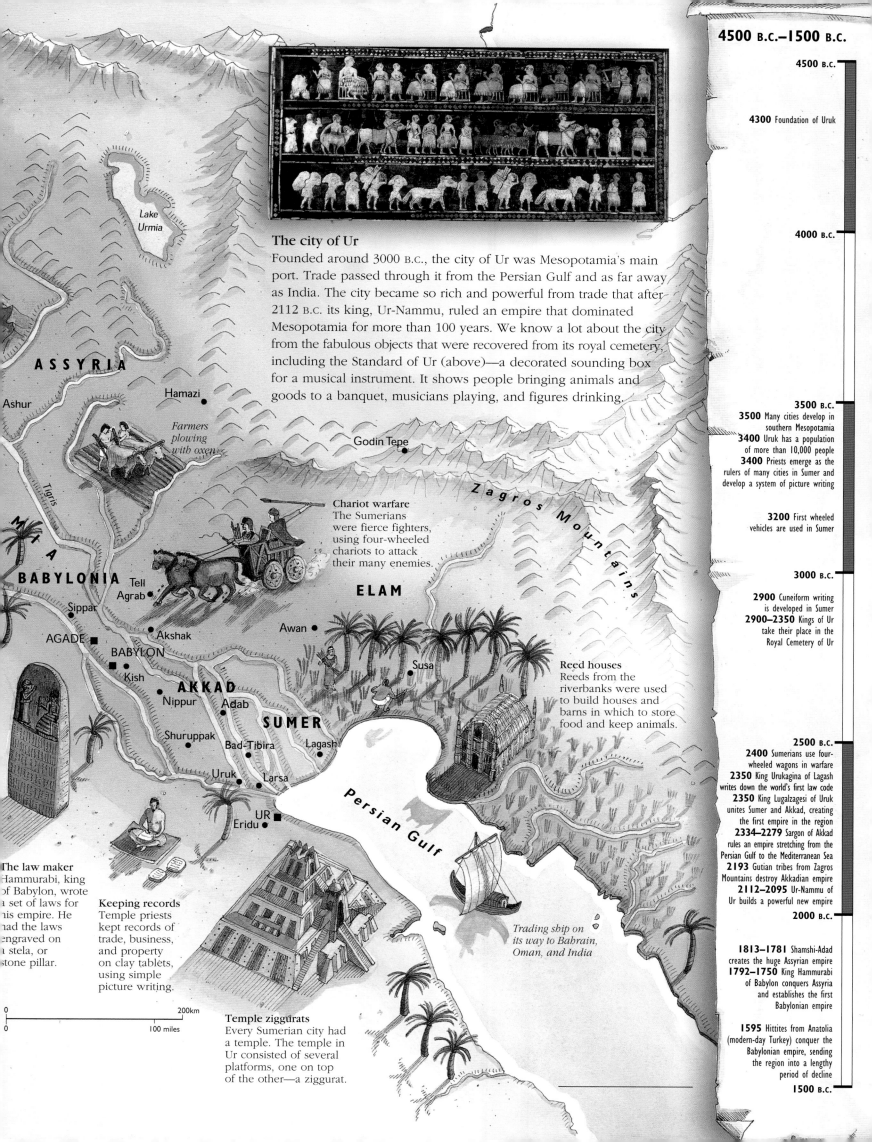

The city of Ur

Founded around 3000 B.C., the city of Ur was Mesopotamia's main port. Trade passed through it from the Persian Gulf and as far away as India. The city became so rich and powerful from trade that after 2112 B.C. its king, Ur-Nammu, ruled an empire that dominated Mesopotamia for more than 100 years. We know a lot about the city from the fabulous objects that were recovered from its royal cemetery, including the Standard of Ur (above)—a decorated sounding box for a musical instrument. It shows people bringing animals and goods to a banquet, musicians playing, and figures drinking.

ASSYRIA

Lake Urmia

Ashur

Hamazi

Farmers plowing with oxen

Godin Tepe

Tigris

Zagros Mountains

Chariot warfare
The Sumerians were fierce fighters, using four-wheeled chariots to attack their many enemies.

BABYLONIA

Tell Agrab

Sippar

AGADE

BABYLON

Kish

AKKAD

Nippur

Adab

ELAM

Awan

Susa

SUMER

Shuruppak

Bad-Tibira

Lagash

Uruk

Larsa

UR

Eridu

Reed houses
Reeds from the riverbanks were used to build houses and barns in which to store food and keep animals.

Persian Gulf

The law maker
Hammurabi, king of Babylon, wrote a set of laws for his empire. He had the laws engraved on a stela, or stone pillar.

Keeping records
Temple priests kept records of trade, business, and property on clay tablets, using simple picture writing.

Trading ship on its way to Bahrain, Oman, and India

0   200km
0   100 miles

Temple ziggurats
Every Sumerian city had a temple. The temple in Ur consisted of several platforms, one on top of the other—a ziggurat.

4500 B.C.

4300 Foundation of Uruk

4000 B.C.

3500 B.C.
3500 Many cities develop in southern Mesopotamia
3400 Uruk has a population of more than 10,000 people
3400 Priests emerge as the rulers of many cities in Sumer and develop a system of picture writing

3200 First wheeled vehicles are used in Sumer

3000 B.C.

2900 Cuneiform writing is developed in Sumer
2900–2350 Kings of Ur take their place in the Royal Cemetery of Ur

2500 B.C.
2400 Sumerians use four-wheeled wagons in warfare
2350 King Urukagina of Lagash writes down the world's first law code
2350 King Lugalzagesi of Uruk unites Sumer and Akkad, creating the first empire in the region
2334–2279 Sargon of Akkad rules an empire stretching from the Persian Gulf to the Mediterranean Sea
2193 Gutian tribes from Zagros Mountains destroy Akkadian empire
2112–2095 Ur-Nammu of Ur builds a powerful new empire

2000 B.C.

1813–1781 Shamshi-Adad creates the huge Assyrian empire
1792–1750 King Hammurabi of Babylon conquers Assyria and establishes the first Babylonian empire

1595 Hittites from Anatolia (modern-day Turkey) conquer the Babylonian empire, sending the region into a lengthy period of decline

1500 B.C.

Ancient Egypt

For more than 3,000 years the Egyptians, ruled by kings called pharaohs, established a remarkable civilization along the banks of the Nile river—Egypt's main highway. People and goods traveled along it, and it supplied fresh water for humans and animals and irrigated the crops. Surplus food, linen, and papyrus were traded throughout the region in return for silver, copper, tin, timber, horses, and human slaves, making Egypt a wealthy and powerful nation. The Egyptians were one of the first people to invent a system of picture writing, known as hieroglyphs. They were also skilled builders, constructing magnificent stone palaces, temples, and pyramid-shaped tombs—many of which still survive today.

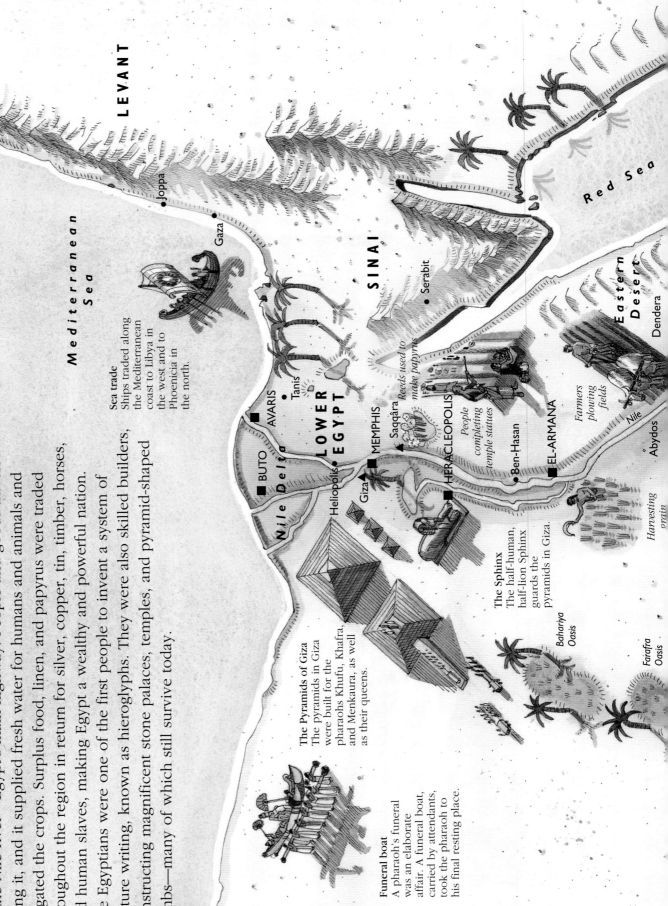

LEVANT

Mediterranean Sea

• Joppa

• Gaza

Sea trade
Ships traded along the Mediterranean coast to Libya in the west and to Phoenicia in the north.

Nile Delta

■ BUTO

■ AVARIS

• Tanis

LOWER EGYPT

Heliopolis •

Giza ▲

■ MEMPHIS

Saqqâra ▲

HERACLEOPOLIS ■

SINAI

• Serabit

Red Sea

Eastern Desert

Reeds used to make papyrus

People completing temple statues

• Ben-Hasan

■ EL-ARMANA

Farmers plowing fields

Nile

Dendera

Abydos

Harvesting grain

Bahariya Oasis

Farafra Oasis

The Pyramids of Giza
The pyramids in Giza were built for the pharaohs Khufu, Khafra, and Menkaura, as well as their queens.

The Sphinx
The half-human, half-lion Sphinx guards the pyramids in Giza.

Funeral boat
A pharaoh's funeral was an elaborate affair. A funeral boat, carried by attendants, took the pharaoh to his final resting place.

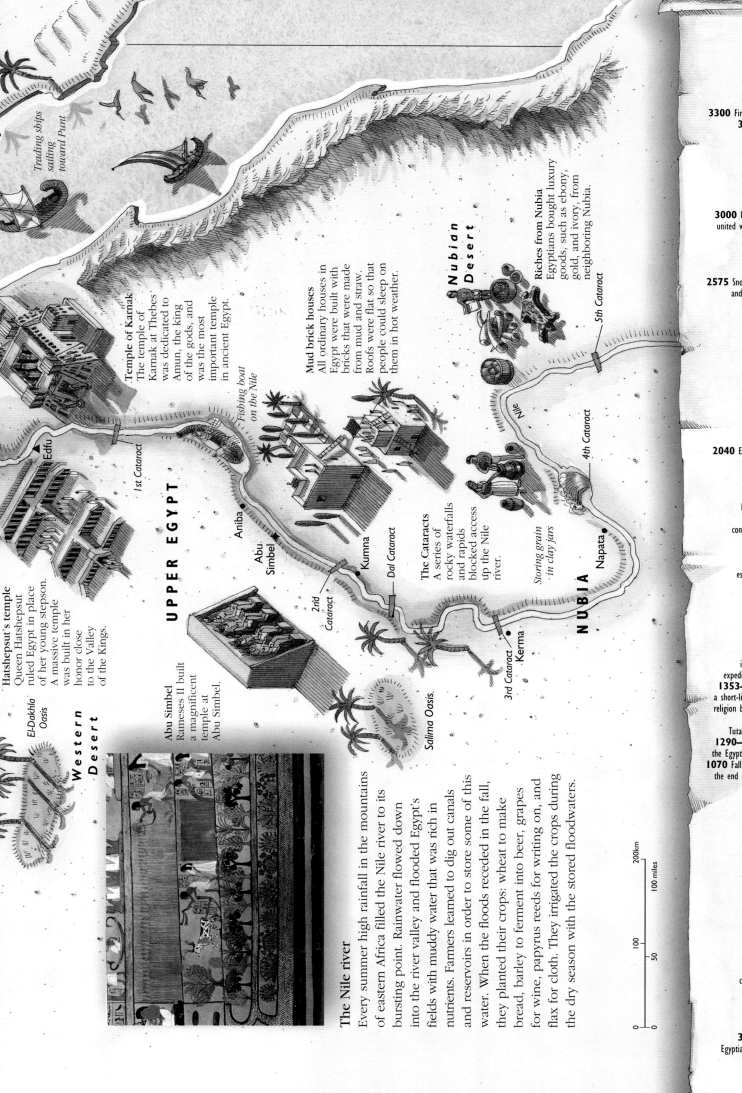

Trading ships sailing toward Punt

Temple of Karnak
The temple of Karnak at Thebes was dedicated to Amun, the king of the gods, and was the most important temple in ancient Egypt.

Fishing boat on the Nile

Mud brick houses
All ordinary houses in Egypt were built with bricks that were made from mud and straw. Roofs were flat so that people could sleep on them in hot weather.

Nubian Desert

Riches from Nubia
Egyptians bought luxury goods, such as ebony, gold, and ivory, from neighboring Nubia.

5th Cataract

Edfu

1st Cataract

U P P E R   E G Y P T

Aniba

Abu Simbel

2nd Cataract

Kumna

Dal Cataract

The Cataracts
A series of rocky waterfalls and rapids blocked access up the Nile river.

4th Cataract

Nile

Storing grain in clay jars

N U B I A
Napata

Hatshepsut's temple
Queen Hatshepsut ruled Egypt in place of her young stepson. A massive temple was built in her honor close to the Valley of the Kings.

El-Dakhla Oasis

Abu Simbel
Rameses II built a magnificent temple at Abu Simbel.

Salima Oasis

3rd Cataract
Kerma

W e s t e r n   D e s e r t

The Nile river

Every summer high rainfall in the mountains of eastern Africa filled the Nile river to its bursting point. Rainwater flowed down into the river valley and flooded Egypt's fields with muddy water that was rich in nutrients. Farmers learned to dig out canals and reservoirs in order to store some of this water. When the floods receded in the fall, they planted their crops: wheat to make bread, barley to ferment into beer, grapes for wine, papyrus reeds for writing on, and flax for cloth. They irrigated the crops during the dry season with the stored floodwaters.

200km

100 miles

100

50

3500 B.C.
3500 Farming flourishes in the Nile Valley

3300 First Egyptian towns are built
3300–3000 Hieroglyphic script is developed

3000 B.C.
3000 Upper and Lower Egypt are united with the capital at Memphis
2920 First dynasty of kings begins to rule
2630 First step pyramid is built at Saqqâra
2575 Snofru founds the 4th dynasty and establishes a powerful Old Kingdom based at Memphis
2550 Khufu builds the Great Pyramid in Giza

2500 B.C.

2134 Old Kingdom ends as Egypt divides into two rival kingdoms
2040 Egypt is reunified under the 11th dynasty, establishing the Middle Kingdom

2000 B.C.
1640–1550 The Hyksos people from the Levant conquer and rule Lower Egypt

1550 Ahmose founds the 18th dynasty and establishes the New Kingdom

1500 B.C.
1473–1458 Hatshepsut is queen and sends a naval expedition to Punt in east Africa
1353–1335 Akhenaten creates a short-lived monotheistic (one-god) religion based on Aten, the sun-god
1333–1323 Reign of Tutankhamen, the boy pharaoh
1290–1224 Rameses II extends the Egyptian empire into the Levant
1070 Fall of the 21st dynasty marks the end of effective Egyptian power

1000 B.C.

671–651 The Assyrians occupy Egypt

525–523 The Persians briefly conquer Egypt

500 B.C.

323 Alexander the Great conquers Egypt, establishing a new Ptolemaic dynasty

30 Death of Cleopatra, last Egyptian pharaoh; Egypt becomes part of the Roman Empire

0

Ancient Egypt:
Preparing for the afterlife

The ancient Egyptians had a strong belief in the afterlife, since they dreaded the day that their own world might come to an end. They developed an elaborate method of embalming and mummifying bodies so that they would last forever. Important people, such as the pharaoh (king), were buried along with their belongings inside a great pyramid. Later the pharaohs were buried in tombs in the Valley of the Kings. Although most of these pyramids and tombs have been robbed of their contents, a few have survived intact, giving us a good idea about the Egyptian way of life and death more than 3,000 years ago.

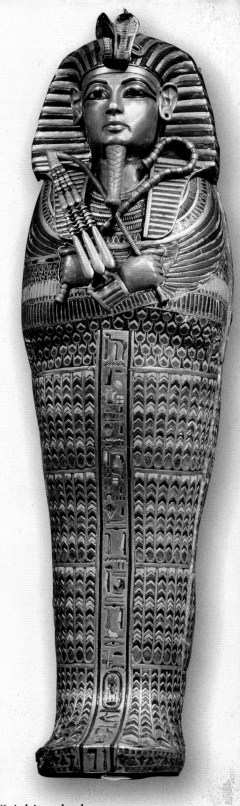

Mummification

After death the body was taken to a place known as the Beautiful House to be preserved. Embalmers removed the internal organs, leaving the heart so that it could be weighed in the afterlife. The body was then covered with the crystals of the chemical natron, in order to dry it out and prevent decay. After around 40 days the body was ready for the next stage. It was stuffed with dry materials, such as sawdust or leaves, and tightly wrapped up in linen bandages. Finally, it was put into a stone or wooden coffin. Lowly people were buried in graveyards, but important people, such as the boy pharaoh Tutankhamen (right; ruled 1333–1323 B.C.) were placed into an elaborate container. This was made up of layers—each one beautifully decorated inside with gods of the underworld, and outside with hieroglyphs and magic symbols. Once it was safely in its coffin, the body was ready for the afterlife.

Weighing the heart

The Egyptians believed in an underworld called Duat, which contained lakes of fire and poisonous snakes. Spells to ward off these dangers, and others, were written on the coffin. The biggest danger was in the Hall of Two Truths, where a person's heart was weighed against past deeds (left). There the dead person was asked about their life. If they told the truth, they were allowed to pass into the afterlife.

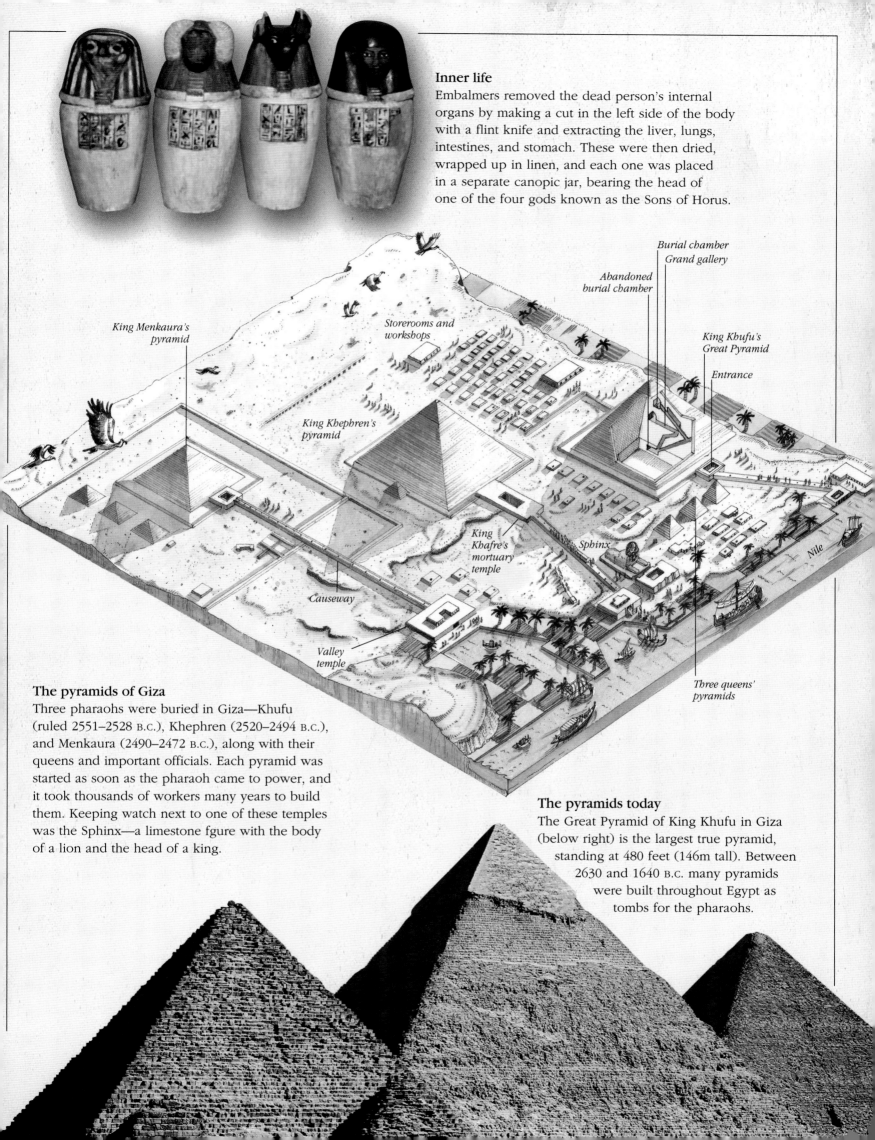

Inner life

Embalmers removed the dead person's internal organs by making a cut in the left side of the body with a flint knife and extracting the liver, lungs, intestines, and stomach. These were then dried, wrapped up in linen, and each one was placed in a separate canopic jar, bearing the head of one of the four gods known as the Sons of Horus.

Burial chamber
Grand gallery

Abandoned burial chamber

King Khufu's Great Pyramid

Entrance

King Menkaura's pyramid

Storerooms and workshops

King Khephren's pyramid

King Khafre's mortuary temple

Sphinx

Nile

Causeway

Valley temple

Three queens' pyramids

The pyramids of Giza

Three pharaohs were buried in Giza—Khufu (ruled 2551–2528 B.C.), Khephren (2520–2494 B.C.), and Menkaura (2490–2472 B.C.), along with their queens and important officials. Each pyramid was started as soon as the pharaoh came to power, and it took thousands of workers many years to build them. Keeping watch next to one of these temples was the Sphinx—a limestone fgure with the body of a lion and the head of a king.

The pyramids today

The Great Pyramid of King Khufu in Giza (below right) is the largest true pyramid, standing at 480 feet (146m tall). Between 2630 and 1640 B.C. many pyramids were built throughout Egypt as tombs for the pharaohs.

Ancient Europe

Farming began in southeastern Europe during the Neolithic Age—around 6000 B.C.—and slowly spread throughout Europe over the next 2,000 years. Farming allowed people to settle down and build houses and villages to live in, but the real advance came with the use of copper, bronze, and then iron. These metals could be made into tools and weapons, as well as items such as jewelry and other ornamental or ceremonial objects. In many places chiefs and other important people were buried in megalithic (giant stone) tombs with beautiful offerings to the gods next to them. People built massive circles and rows of standing stones and circular earth structures known as henges. Some of these line up with the Sun and stars at certain times of the year, indicating a detailed knowledge of the calendar and astronomy.

Ancient sites
The key on page 8 tells you that places that are marked with a diamond are not cities, towns, or villages but other types of ancient sites. On this map these sites are stone circles, rows of standing stones, or stone tombs. An example is ✦ Stonehenge.

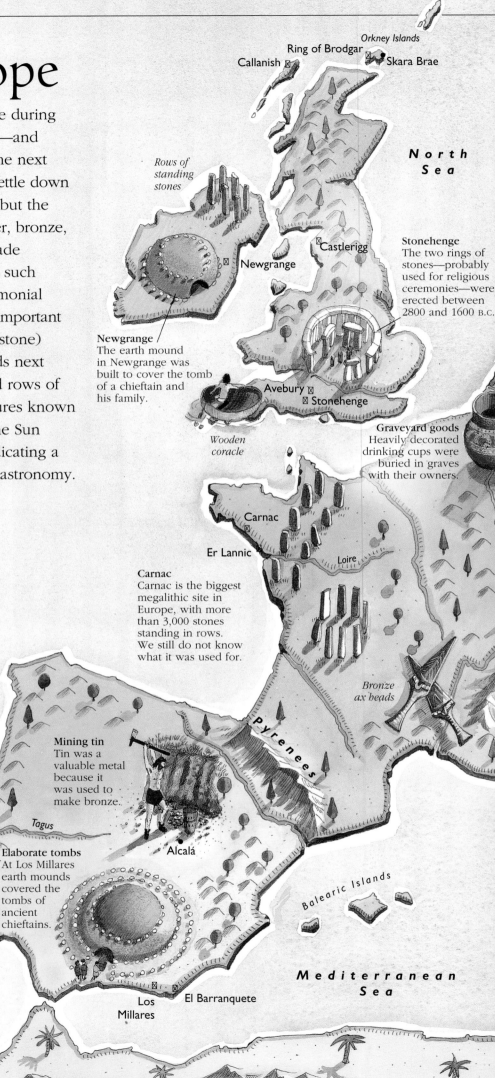

Ring of Brodgar

Orkney Islands

Callanish

Skara Brae

North Sea

Rows of standing stones

Castlerigg

Newgrange

Stonehenge
The two rings of stones—probably used for religious ceremonies—were erected between 2800 and 1600 B.C.

Newgrange
The earth mound in Newgrange was built to cover the tomb of a chieftain and his family.

Avebury

Stonehenge

Wooden coracle

Graveyard goods
Heavily decorated drinking cups were buried in graves with their owners.

Carnac

Er Lannic

Loire

Carnac
Carnac is the biggest megalithic site in Europe, with more than 3,000 stones standing in rows. We still do not know what it was used for.

Bronze ax heads

Pyrenees

Mining tin
Tin was a valuable metal because it was used to make bronze.

Tagus

Alcalá

Elaborate tombs
At Los Millares earth mounds covered the tombs of ancient chieftains.

Atlantic Ocean

Balearic Islands

Los Millares

El Barranquete

Mediterranean Sea

0	500	1000km
0	250	500 miles

SCANDINAVIA

Rickeby

Ålborg

Trundholm

Kivic

Bronze Age burial mound

Collecting amber for jewelry

Celtic weapons
The Celts made elaborate shields and other items out of bronze.

Elbe

Rhine

☒ Leubingen

Helmsdorf

Lake villages
Bronze Age peoples often built villages off the shores of a lake for defense.

Vasserburg

Longhouse for people and animals

Barca

Carpathian Mountains

Cutting down trees for timber and fuel

Danube

Alps

House raised up on wooden pillars

Making bronze
Smiths mixed together hot tin and copper in a mold to make bronze—a stronger metal.

Corsica

Sardinia

Adriatic Sea

Milking goats

Black Sea

Aegean Sea

Greek cargo ship

Sicily

Stentinello

Life at home

Wood was plentiful, so most people in Europe lived in wooden longhouses. The ruins of these houses are very rare, and we know very little about what they were like inside. The exception is on the treeless Orkney Islands, where, around 3000 B.C. at Skara Brae, the people built an entire village out of stone. Their houses were covered with stone and turf and contained stone cupboards, fireplaces, beds, and boxes.

6000 B.C.–500 B.C.

6000 B.C.

6000 Farming is established in southeastern Europe during the Neolithic Age

5500 B.C.

5000 B.C.

5000 Farming spreads around the Mediterranean

4500 B.C.

4500 Copper smelting begins in southeastern Europe—start of the Copper Age
4500 Plows are first used on farms in southeastern Europe
4300 First megalithic tombs are built

4000 B.C.

4000 Horses are first domesticated in Europe

3500 B.C.

3200 First wheeled vehicles are in use in the Balkans

3000 B.C.

3000 Skara Brae stone village is built in the Orkney Islands
3000 Megalithic stone circles and rows, as well as earth-mound burial tombs, are first built in western Europe
2800 Work begins on the construction of Stonehenge

2500 B.C.

2500 Tin is first added to copper in central Europe to make bronze—start of the Bronze Age in Europe

2000 B.C.

2000 Hill forts and lake villages are built in central Europe
2000 Metal ores and amber are now traded across all of Europe

1500 B.C.

1200 Early Hallstatt culture in central Europe

1000 B.C.

1000 Iron is first used in Greece—start of the Iron Age in Europe
750 early Celtic cultures begin to spread in Europe
700 Iron is in widespread use throughout Europe

500 B.C.

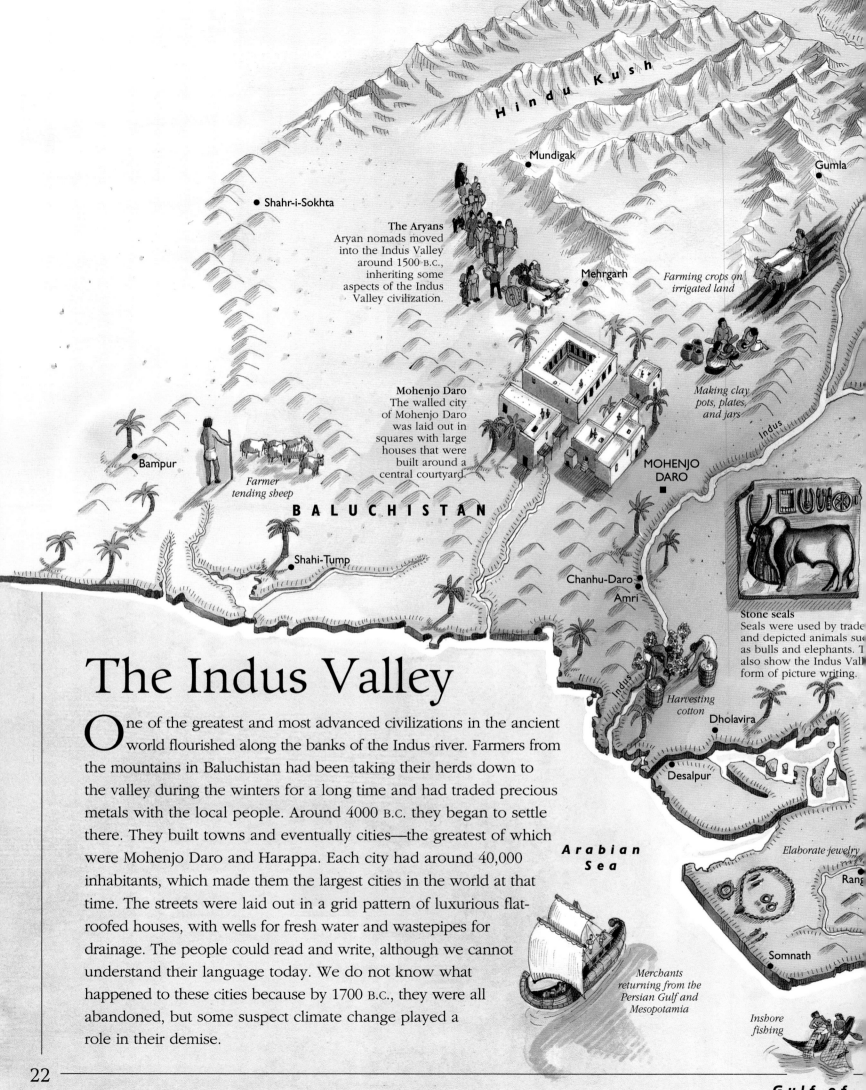

Hindu Kush

Mundigak

Gumla

Shahr-i-Sokhta

The Aryans
Aryan nomads moved into the Indus Valley around 1500 B.C., inheriting some aspects of the Indus Valley civilization.

Mehrgarh

Farming crops on irrigated land

Making clay pots, plates, and jars

Mohenjo Daro
The walled city of Mohenjo Daro was laid out in squares with large houses that were built around a central courtyard.

Bampur

Farmer tending sheep

B A L U C H I S T A N

MOHENJO DARO

Indus

Stone seals
Seals were used by trade and depicted animals su as bulls and elephants. T also show the Indus Vall form of picture writing.

Shahi-Tump

Chanhu-Daro
Amri

Indus

Harvesting cotton

Dholavira

Desalpur

The Indus Valley

One of the greatest and most advanced civilizations in the ancient world flourished along the banks of the Indus river. Farmers from the mountains in Baluchistan had been taking their herds down to the valley during the winters for a long time and had traded precious metals with the local people. Around 4000 B.C. they began to settle there. They built towns and eventually cities—the greatest of which were Mohenjo Daro and Harappa. Each city had around 40,000 inhabitants, which made them the largest cities in the world at that time. The streets were laid out in a grid pattern of luxurious flat-roofed houses, with wells for fresh water and wastepipes for drainage. The people could read and write, although we cannot understand their language today. We do not know what happened to these cities because by 1700 B.C., they were all abandoned, but some suspect climate change played a role in their demise.

A r a b i a n S e a

Elaborate jewelry

Rang

Somnath

Merchants returning from the Persian Gulf and Mesopotamia

Inshore fishing

Gulf of Khabhat

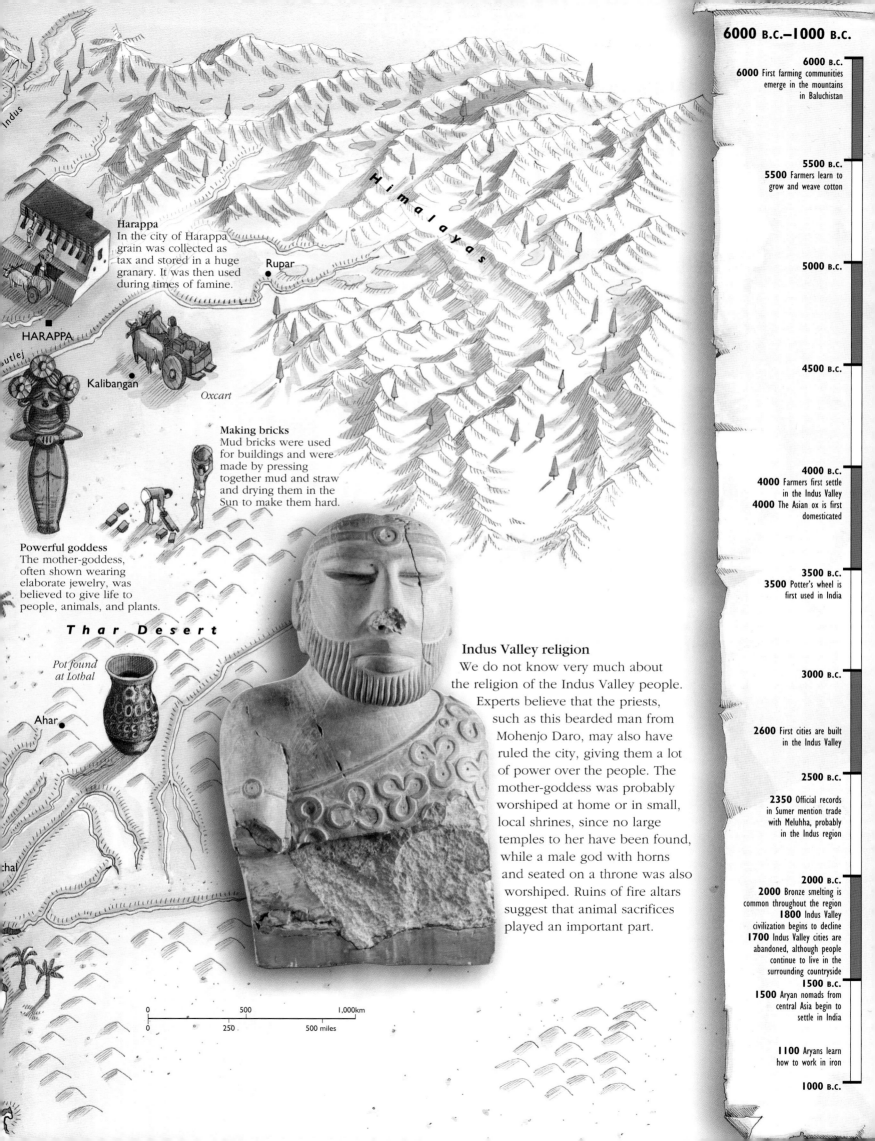

Harappa
In the city of Harappa grain was collected as tax and stored in a huge granary. It was then used during times of famine.

HARAPPA

Rupar

Kalibangan

Oxcart

Sutlej

Making bricks
Mud bricks were used for buildings and were made by pressing together mud and straw and drying them in the Sun to make them hard.

Powerful goddess
The mother-goddess, often shown wearing elaborate jewelry, was believed to give life to people, animals, and plants.

T h a r   D e s e r t

Pot found at Lothal

Ahar

Indus

Himalayas

Indus Valley religion
We do not know very much about the religion of the Indus Valley people. Experts believe that the priests, such as this bearded man from Mohenjo Daro, may also have ruled the city, giving them a lot of power over the people. The mother-goddess was probably worshiped at home or in small, local shrines, since no large temples to her have been found, while a male god with horns and seated on a throne was also worshiped. Ruins of fire altars suggest that animal sacrifices played an important part.

0   500   1,000km
0   250   500 miles

6000 B.C.
6000 First farming communities emerge in the mountains in Baluchistan

5500 B.C.
5500 Farmers learn to grow and weave cotton

5000 B.C.

4500 B.C.

4000 B.C.
4000 Farmers first settle in the Indus Valley
4000 The Asian ox is first domesticated

3500 B.C.
3500 Potter's wheel is first used in India

3000 B.C.

2600 First cities are built in the Indus Valley

2500 B.C.

2350 Official records in Sumer mention trade with Meluhha, probably in the Indus region

2000 B.C.
2000 Bronze smelting is common throughout the region
1800 Indus Valley civilization begins to decline
1700 Indus Valley cities are abandoned, although people continue to live in the surrounding countryside

1500 B.C.
1500 Aryan nomads from central Asia begin to settle in India

1100 Aryans learn how to work in iron

1000 B.C.

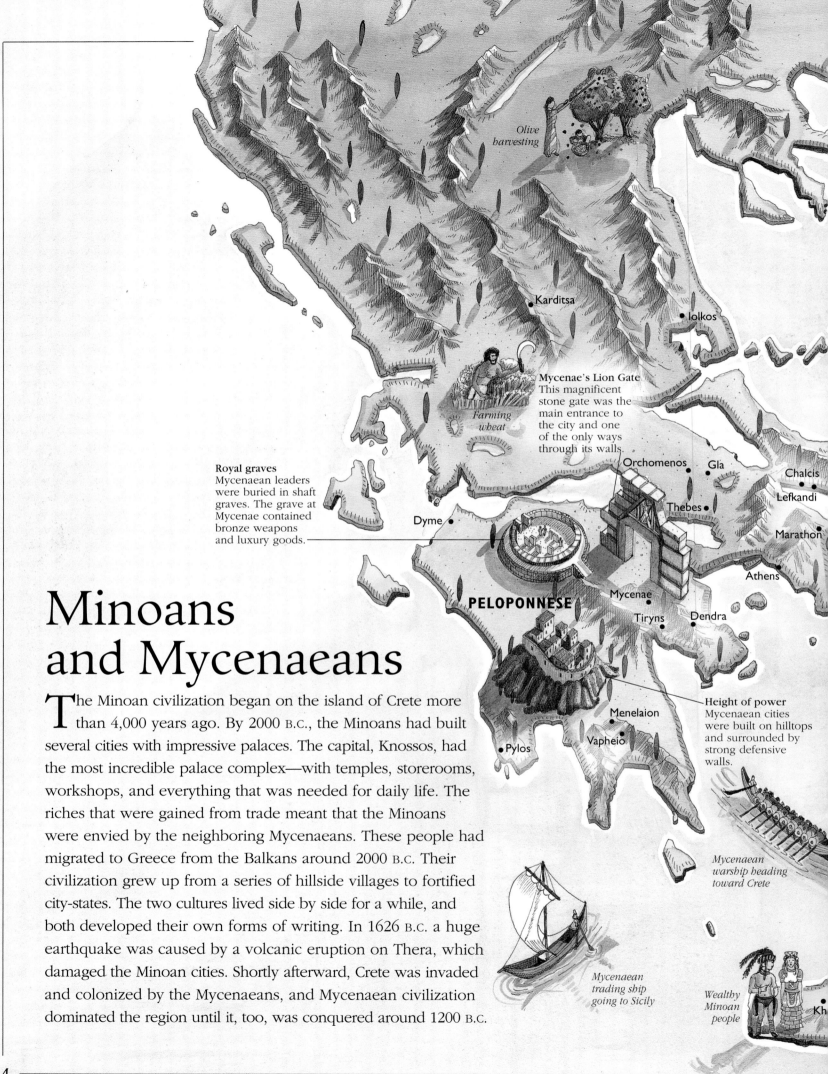

Olive harvesting

• Karditsa

• Iolkos

Mycenae's Lion Gate
This magnificent stone gate was the main entrance to the city and one of the only ways through its walls.

Farming wheat

Royal graves
Mycenaean leaders were buried in shaft graves. The grave at Mycenae contained bronze weapons and luxury goods.

Orchomenos   Gla

Chalcis

Lefkandi

Dyme •

Thebes

Marathon

Athens

Mycenae

PELOPONNESE

Tiryns   Dendra

Menelaion

Height of power
Mycenaean cities were built on hilltops and surrounded by strong defensive walls.

Vapheio

• Pylos

Mycenaean warship heading toward Crete

Minoans and Mycenaeans

The Minoan civilization began on the island of Crete more than 4,000 years ago. By 2000 B.C., the Minoans had built several cities with impressive palaces. The capital, Knossos, had the most incredible palace complex—with temples, storerooms, workshops, and everything that was needed for daily life. The riches that were gained from trade meant that the Minoans were envied by the neighboring Mycenaeans. These people had migrated to Greece from the Balkans around 2000 B.C. Their civilization grew up from a series of hillside villages to fortified city-states. The two cultures lived side by side for a while, and both developed their own forms of writing. In 1626 B.C. a huge earthquake was caused by a volcanic eruption on Thera, which damaged the Minoan cities. Shortly afterward, Crete was invaded and colonized by the Mycenaeans, and Mycenaean civilization dominated the region until it, too, was conquered around 1200 B.C.

Mycenaean trading ship going to Sicily

Wealthy Minoan people

Kh

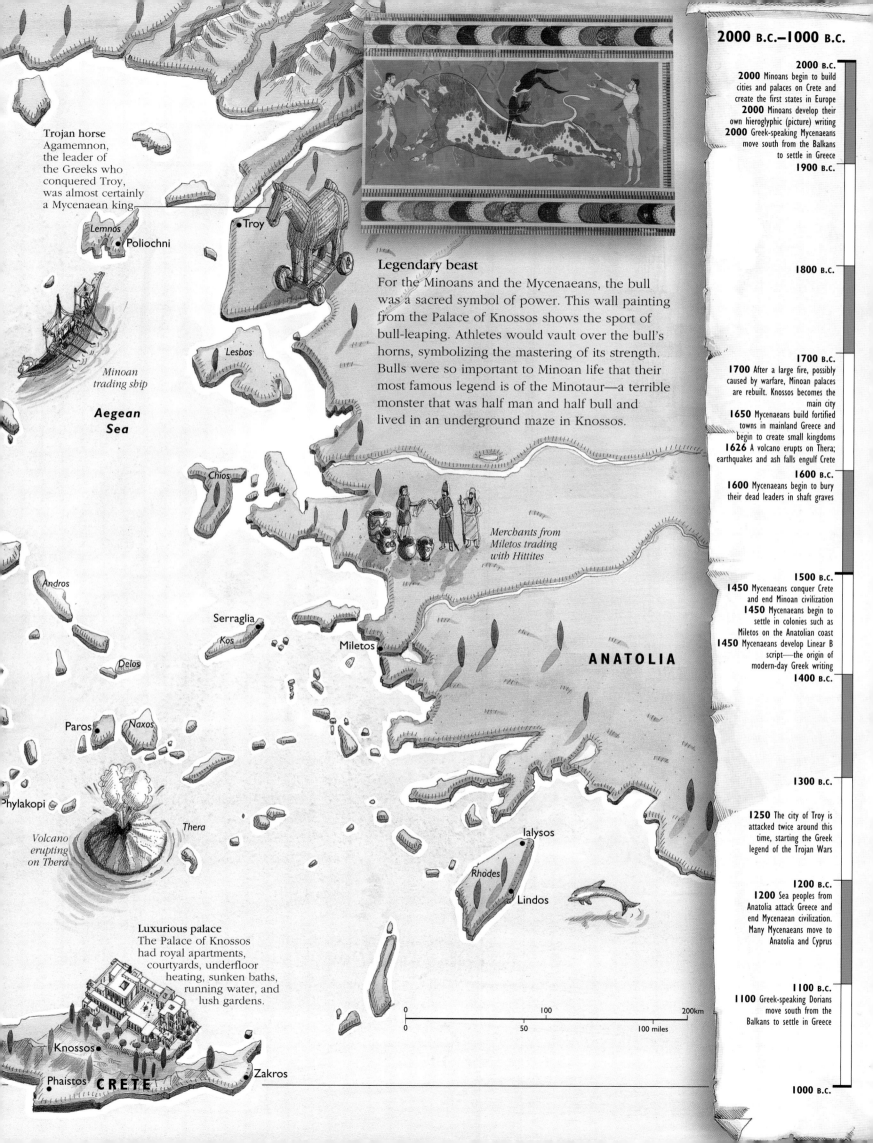

Trojan horse
Agamemnon,
the leader of
the Greeks who
conquered Troy,
was almost certainly
a Mycenaean king.

Lemnos
• Poliochni

• Troy

*Minoan
trading ship*

**Aegean
Sea**

Lesbos

Legendary beast

For the Minoans and the Mycenaeans, the bull
was a sacred symbol of power. This wall painting
from the Palace of Knossos shows the sport of
bull-leaping. Athletes would vault over the bull's
horns, symbolizing the mastering of its strength.
Bulls were so important to Minoan life that their
most famous legend is of the Minotaur—a terrible
monster that was half man and half bull and
lived in an underground maze in Knossos.

Chios

*Merchants from
Miletos trading
with Hittites*

Andros

ANATOLIA

Serraglia
Kos

Miletos •

Delos

Paros *Naxos*

Phylakopi •

*Volcano
erupting
on Thera*

Thera

Ialysos •

Rhodes

Lindos •

Luxurious palace

The Palace of Knossos
had royal apartments,
courtyards, underfloor
heating, sunken baths,
running water, and
lush gardens.

Knossos •

0 ——— 100 ——— 200km
0 —— 50 —— 100 miles

Phaistos • **CRETE** • Zakros

2000 B.C.
2000 Minoans begin to build
cities and palaces on Crete and
create the first states in Europe
2000 Minoans develop their
own hieroglyphic (picture) writing
2000 Greek-speaking Mycenaeans
move south from the Balkans
to settle in Greece

1900 B.C.

1800 B.C.

1700 B.C.
1700 After a large fire, possibly
caused by warfare, Minoan palaces
are rebuilt. Knossos becomes the
main city
1650 Mycenaeans build fortified
towns in mainland Greece and
begin to create small kingdoms
1626 A volcano erupts on Thera;
earthquakes and ash falls engulf Crete

1600 B.C.
1600 Mycenaeans begin to bury
their dead leaders in shaft graves

1500 B.C.
1450 Mycenaeans conquer Crete
and end Minoan civilization
1450 Mycenaeans begin to
settle in colonies such as
Miletos on the Anatolian coast
1450 Mycenaeans develop Linear B
script—the origin of
modern-day Greek writing

1400 B.C.

1300 B.C.

1250 The city of Troy is
attacked twice around this
time, starting the Greek
legend of the Trojan Wars

1200 B.C.
1200 Sea peoples from
Anatolia attack Greece and
end Mycenaean civilization.
Many Mycenaeans move to
Anatolia and Cyprus

1100 B.C.
1100 Greek-speaking Dorians
move south from the
Balkans to settle in Greece

1000 B.C.

BRITAIN

FRANCE

Atlantic Ocean

Hannibal
In 218 B.C. the Carthaginian general Hannibal crossed the Alps to surprise his Roman enemies during the Second Punic War.

Phoenician ship sailing to Britain to trade for tin

Mining tin

Pyrenees

Massilia

A L P S

ITALY

Adriatic Sea

The Etruscans
The Etruscans—the major force in central Italy—ruled Rome before it became a republic in 509 B.C.

Corsica

ROME

Rome
Rome was originally a series of hilltop villages that gradually joined together to become a single city.

SPAIN

Mediterranean Sea

Mining silver

●Palma

Balearic Islands

Sardinia

Sulcis

Gades

Cartagena

Tingis (Tangier)   *Trading highly prized Phoenician cloths*

Cartenna

Sicily

Lixus

Trading ship traveling along African coast

CARTHAGE

Carthage harbor
The Phoenicians established the trading post of Carthage in 814 B.C. It soon grew to become the most powerful nation in the Mediterranean.

Phoenician writing
The Phoenicians had an alphabet of 22 consonants. T Greeks added vowels, makin the alphabet that we use toda

Peoples of the Mediterranean

For the people living close to the Mediterranean, the sea either presented a barrier that they could not cross or a wonderful opportunity to get rich through trade and conquests. The Greeks established trading colonies around the Mediterranean, while the Phoenicians were more adventurous and sent trading expeditions out into the Atlantic Ocean. The two peoples fought often. They were later joined by the Carthaginians in North Africa, the Etruscans from Italy, and, eventually, the Romans, who dominated the Mediterranean Sea and most of its coastline by 100 B.C.

Human sacrifice
The Carthaginians worshiped the Sun and Moon gods, offering human sacrifices during times of danger.

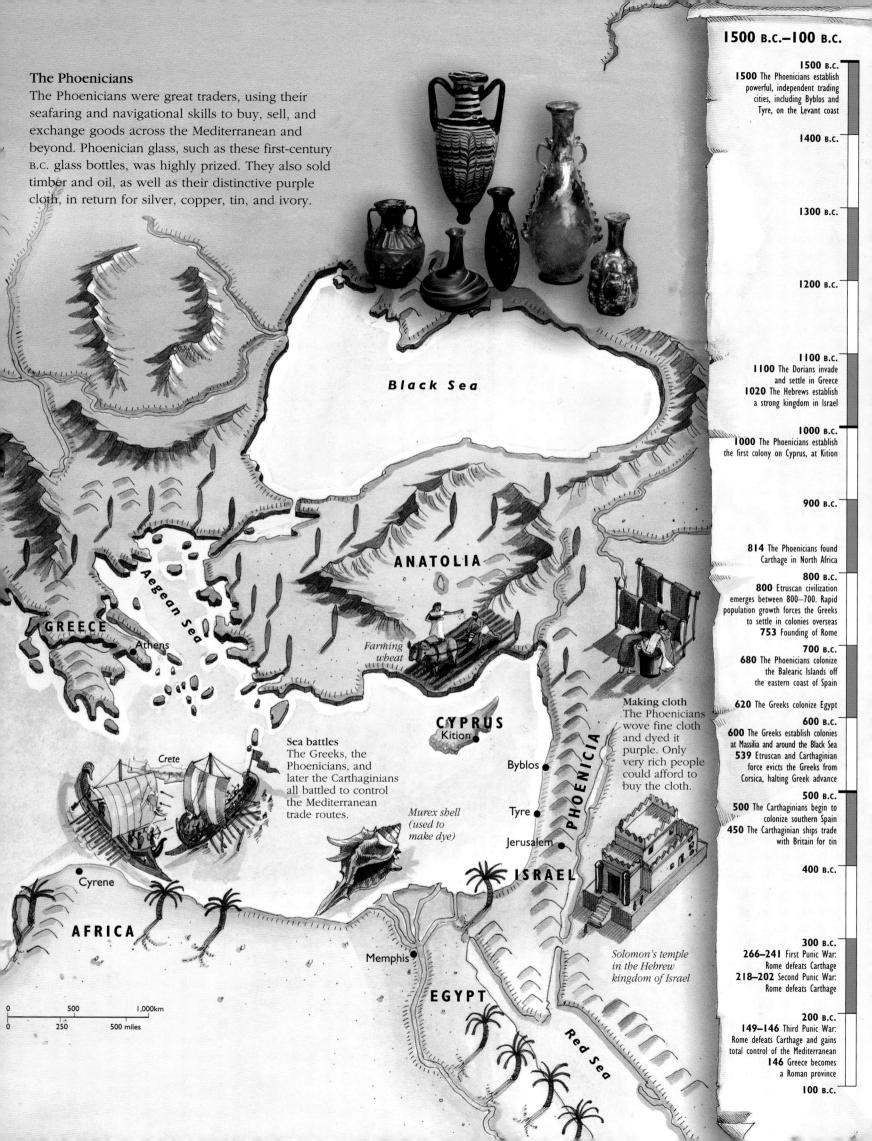

The Phoenicians

The Phoenicians were great traders, using their seafaring and navigational skills to buy, sell, and exchange goods across the Mediterranean and beyond. Phoenician glass, such as these first-century B.C. glass bottles, was highly prized. They also sold timber and oil, as well as their distinctive purple cloth, in return for silver, copper, tin, and ivory.

Black Sea

ANATOLIA

Farming wheat

GREECE

Athens

Aegean Sea

Sea battles
The Greeks, the Phoenicians, and later the Carthaginians all battled to control the Mediterranean trade routes.

Crete

Cyrene

AFRICA

CYPRUS
Kition

Murex shell (used to make dye)

Byblos

Tyre

Jerusalem

ISRAEL

PHOENICIA

Making cloth
The Phoenicians wove fine cloth and dyed it purple. Only very rich people could afford to buy the cloth.

Solomon's temple in the Hebrew kingdom of Israel

Memphis

EGYPT

Red Sea

0   500   1,000km
0   250   500 miles

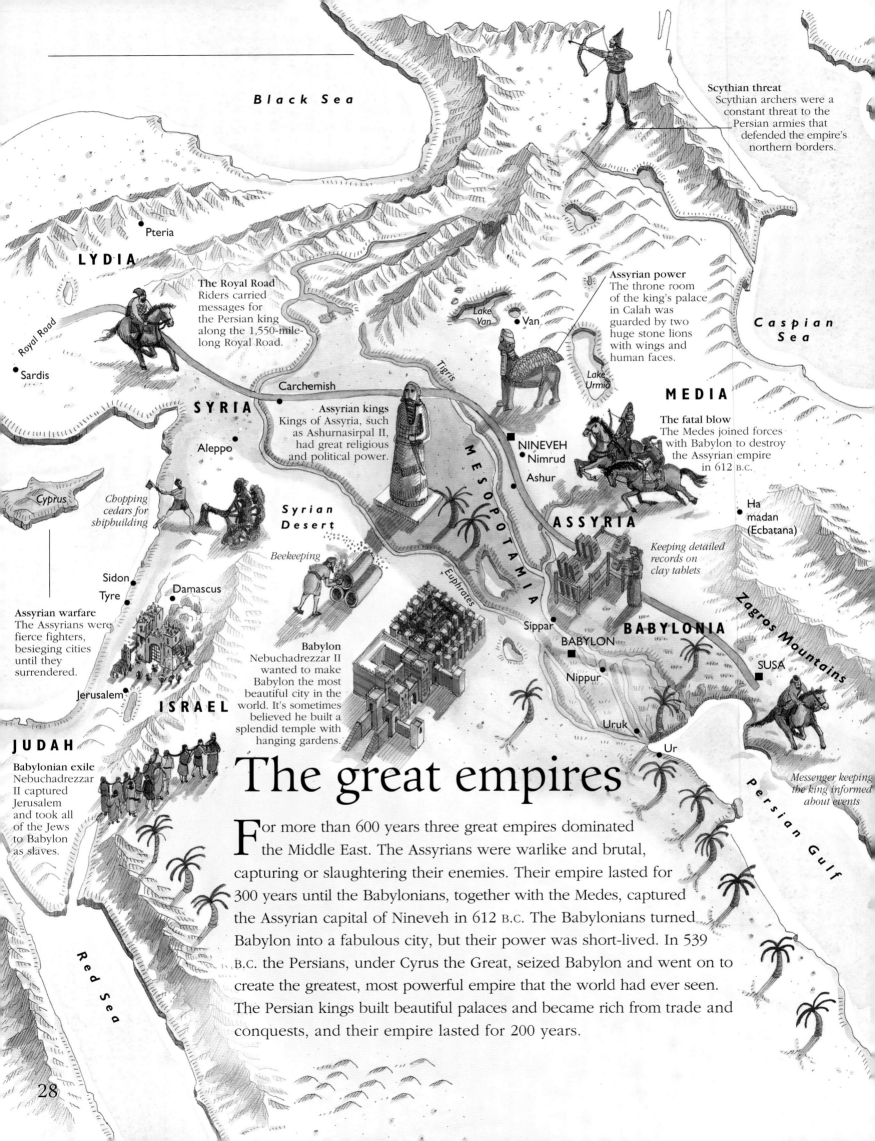

Black Sea

Scythian threat
Scythian archers were a constant threat to the Persian armies that defended the empire's northern borders.

• Pteria

LYDIA

The Royal Road
Riders carried messages for the Persian king along the 1,550-mile-long Royal Road.

Royal Road

• Sardis

SYRIA

Carchemish

Assyrian power
The throne room of the king's palace in Calah was guarded by two huge stone lions with wings and human faces.

Lake Van • Van

Caspian Sea

MEDIA

Tigris

Assyrian kings
Kings of Assyria, such as Ashurnasirpal II, had great religious and political power.

Lake Urmia

• Aleppo

M E S O P O T A M I A

■ NINEVEH
• Nimrud

Ashur

The fatal blow
The Medes joined forces with Babylon to destroy the Assyrian empire in 612 B.C.

Cyprus

Chopping cedars for shipbuilding

Syrian Desert

ASSYRIA

• Ha madan (Ecbatana)

Keeping detailed records on clay tablets

Beekeeping

Euphrates

Assyrian warfare
The Assyrians were fierce fighters, besieging cities until they surrendered.

Sidon •
Tyre •

Damascus •

• Sippar

BABYLON •

BABYLONIA

Zagros Mountains

• Nippur

■ SUSA

Jerusalem •

ISRAEL

Babylon
Nebuchadrezzar II wanted to make Babylon the most beautiful city in the world. It's sometimes believed he built a splendid temple with hanging gardens.

JUDAH

Babylonian exile
Nebuchadrezzar II captured Jerusalem and took all of the Jews to Babylon as slaves.

Uruk •

• Ur

Persian Gulf

Messenger keeping the king informed about events

The great empires

For more than 600 years three great empires dominated the Middle East. The Assyrians were warlike and brutal, capturing or slaughtering their enemies. Their empire lasted for 300 years until the Babylonians, together with the Medes, captured the Assyrian capital of Nineveh in 612 B.C. The Babylonians turned Babylon into a fabulous city, but their power was short-lived. In 539 B.C. the Persians, under Cyrus the Great, seized Babylon and went on to create the greatest, most powerful empire that the world had ever seen. The Persian kings built beautiful palaces and became rich from trade and conquests, and their empire lasted for 200 years.

Red Sea

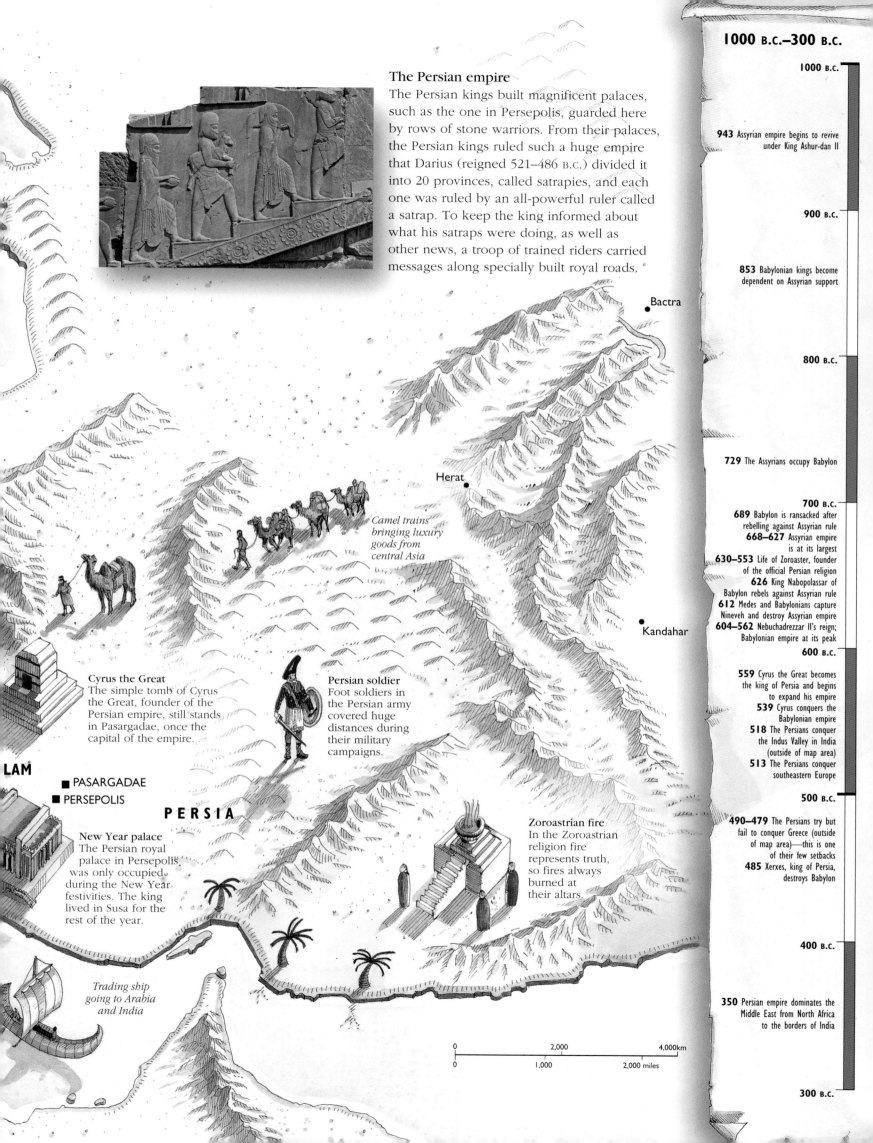

The Persian empire

The Persian kings built magnificent palaces, such as the one in Persepolis, guarded here by rows of stone warriors. From their palaces, the Persian kings ruled such a huge empire that Darius (reigned 521–486 B.C.) divided it into 20 provinces, called satrapies, and each one was ruled by an all-powerful ruler called a satrap. To keep the king informed about what his satraps were doing, as well as other news, a troop of trained riders carried messages along specially built royal roads.

Bactra

Herat

Camel trains bringing luxury goods from central Asia

Kandahar

Cyrus the Great
The simple tomb of Cyrus the Great, founder of the Persian empire, still stands in Pasargadae, once the capital of the empire.

Persian soldier
Foot soldiers in the Persian army covered huge distances during their military campaigns.

LAM

■ PASARGADAE
■ PERSEPOLIS

P E R S I A

New Year palace
The Persian royal palace in Persepolis was only occupied during the New Year festivities. The king lived in Susa for the rest of the year.

Zoroastrian fire
In the Zoroastrian religion fire represents truth, so fires always burned at their altars.

Trading ship going to Arabia and India

0   2,000   4,000km
0   1,000   2,000 miles

1000 B.C.–300 B.C.

1000 B.C.

943 Assyrian empire begins to revive under King Ashur-dan II

900 B.C.

853 Babylonian kings become dependent on Assyrian support

800 B.C.

729 The Assyrians occupy Babylon

700 B.C.
689 Babylon is ransacked after rebelling against Assyrian rule
668–627 Assyrian empire is at its largest
630–553 Life of Zoroaster, founder of the official Persian religion
626 King Nabopolassar of Babylon rebels against Assyrian rule
612 Medes and Babylonians capture Nineveh and destroy Assyrian empire
604–562 Nebuchadrezzar II's reign; Babylonian empire at its peak

600 B.C.

559 Cyrus the Great becomes the king of Persia and begins to expand his empire
539 Cyrus conquers the Babylonian empire
518 The Persians conquer the Indus Valley in India (outside of map area)
513 The Persians conquer southeastern Europe

500 B.C.

490–479 The Persians try but fail to conquer Greece (outside of map area)—this is one of their few setbacks
485 Xerxes, king of Persia, destroys Babylon

400 B.C.

350 Persian empire dominates the Middle East from North Africa to the borders of India

300 B.C.

MACEDON

Mount Olympus
The Greeks believed that their gods and goddesses lived on top of this holy mountain.

Mount Olympus ◆

EPIRUS

Corcyra •

Public speaking
Greek city-states were the first democracies. Politicians spoke to large crowds of citizens.

THESSALY

Painted pottery
Greek craftsmen produced decorated pots, showing the gods or scenes from their history.

Ambracia •

Horses were bred in Thessaly

Thermopylae •

AETOLIA

Priestess consulting the Oracle at Delphi

BOEOTIA

Kephallenia

Delphi •

Thebes •

Olympic athletes
The ancient Olympic Games were held once every four years. Winners of each men-only event received a wreath of laurel leaves.

ATTICA
Marathon •
Athens •

ACHAEA

Sykyon •
Megara •

Corinth •

Argos •

Olympia •
Mantinea •

Tegea •

Ancient Greece

Ancient Greece was the home of an impressive culture. It was the birthplace of democracy, and many Greek inventions and ideas in philosophy, theater, architecture, mathematics, and medicine still influence us today. Ancient Greece was made up of many independent city-states, which grew from the 900s B.C. Each one had its own laws and way of life. Each city had a marketplace in the center, and an acropolis, or fort, built on higher ground. City-states were competitive—they fought many wars and, although they formed alliances, they never united to become a country. Athens and Sparta were the most important city-states. Athens was a busy trading city, as well as the first democracy. Sparta was a military state, where all male citizens had to be warriors. Throughout the Greek world citizens built temples and theaters where they held festivals, involving plays, processions, and games.

ARCADIA
Sparta •

Acropolis
Originally a fort, the Acropolis in Athens was a giant complex of shrines and temples that dominated the city.

Warrior state
The city-state of Sparta was known for its tough soldiers, called hoplites.

Mediterranean Sea

Kydonia •

CRETE

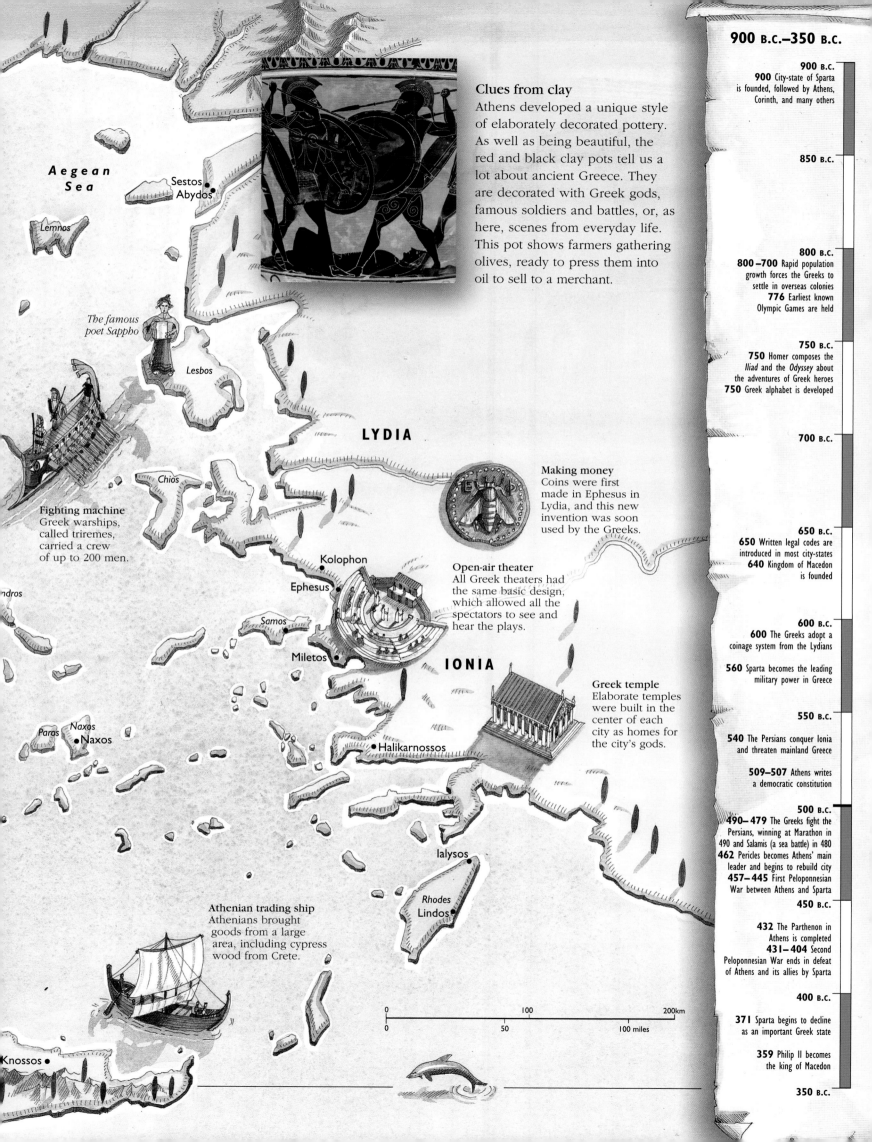

Aegean Sea

Sestos
Abydos

Lemnos

The famous poet Sappho

Lesbos

Clues from clay
Athens developed a unique style of elaborately decorated pottery. As well as being beautiful, the red and black clay pots tell us a lot about ancient Greece. They are decorated with Greek gods, famous soldiers and battles, or, as here, scenes from everyday life. This pot shows farmers gathering olives, ready to press them into oil to sell to a merchant.

LYDIA

Chios

Fighting machine
Greek warships, called triremes, carried a crew of up to 200 men.

ndros

Making money
Coins were first made in Ephesus in Lydia, and this new invention was soon used by the Greeks.

Kolophon

Open-air theater
All Greek theaters had the same basic design, which allowed all the spectators to see and hear the plays.

Ephesus

Samos

Miletos

IONIA

Greek temple
Elaborate temples were built in the center of each city as homes for the city's gods.

Paros Naxos
Naxos

Halikarnossos

Ialysos

Rhodes
Lindos

Athenian trading ship
Athenians brought goods from a large area, including cypress wood from Crete.

Knossos

0 — 100 — 200km
0 — 50 — 100 miles

900 B.C.–350 B.C.

900 B.C.
900 City-state of Sparta is founded, followed by Athens, Corinth, and many others

850 B.C.

800 B.C.
800–700 Rapid population growth forces the Greeks to settle in overseas colonies
776 Earliest known Olympic Games are held

750 B.C.
750 Homer composes the *Iliad* and the *Odyssey* about the adventures of Greek heroes
750 Greek alphabet is developed

700 B.C.

650 B.C.
650 Written legal codes are introduced in most city-states
640 Kingdom of Macedon is founded

600 B.C.
600 The Greeks adopt a coinage system from the Lydians
560 Sparta becomes the leading military power in Greece

550 B.C.
540 The Persians conquer Ionia and threaten mainland Greece
509–507 Athens writes a democratic constitution

500 B.C.
490–479 The Greeks fight the Persians, winning at Marathon in 490 and Salamis (a sea battle) in 480
462 Pericles becomes Athens' main leader and begins to rebuild city
457–445 First Peloponnesian War between Athens and Sparta

450 B.C.
432 The Parthenon in Athens is completed
431–404 Second Peloponnesian War ends in defeat of Athens and its allies by Sparta

400 B.C.
371 Sparta begins to decline as an important Greek state
359 Philip II becomes the king of Macedon

350 B.C.

Ancient Greece:
The Greek world

From around 800 B.C., the Greeks founded trading colonies around the shores of the Mediterranean and Black seas. Greece's population had been rising for a while, but there was limited fertile land for growing the crops that were needed to feed everyone. Spreading out overseas solved this problem and made the Greeks richer at the same time. Some colonies were very successful, trading iron ore, tin, slaves, and wheat in return for wine and other goods. They also spread Greek culture and language throughout a wide region. By the end of the 400s, they had declined in importance as other states, especially Carthage, threatened their livelihood. However, in 334 B.C. Greece's fortunes changed, when Alexander the Great invaded the Persian empire and made Greece the most important nation in the Middle East.

Greek culture

In their many colonies the Greeks built amphitheaters, such as this one in Miletos in southwest Anatolia (modern-day Turkey), in which to put on plays and sporting events. The success of these colonies spread Greek language, literature, law, religion, philosophy, art, and architecture far and wide throughout the Mediterranean world, especially in Sicily and the Etruscan states of northern Italy, and brought great wealth back to Greece itself.

Alexander the Great

Alexander the Great was born in Macedonia, northern Greece, in 356 B.C. He became king after the death of his father, Philip, in 336 B.C., and, after a series of epic marches and remarkable victories, he conquered the Persian empire. Although his empire fell apart after his death in 323 B.C., it left a lasting legacy of Greek cultural influence, known as Hellenism, that dominated the Mediterranean and the Middle East until the coming of Islam during the A.D. 600s. This coin shows Alexander wearing an elephant-scalp headdress to commemorate his victories in India.

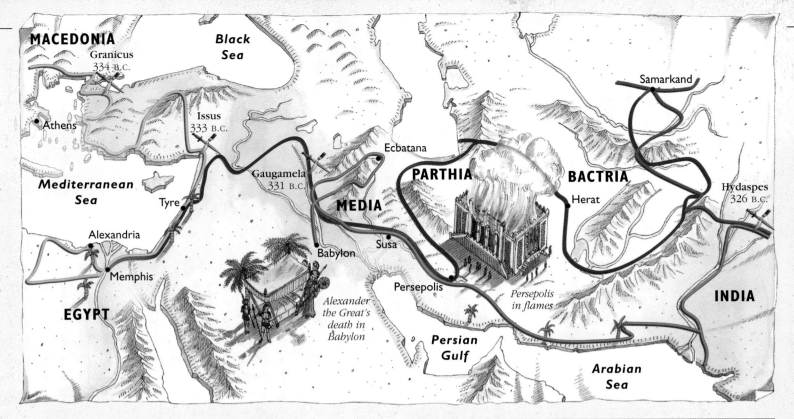

KEY TO MAP: lines show four stages in Alexander's march

⚔ Battle

| 334–331 B.C. | 329–326 B.C. |
| 331–329 B.C. | 326–323 B.C. |

Conquering the world

Alexander and his army crossed into Asia in 334 B.C. and defeated a Persian army by the Granicus river. He beat an even larger Persian army in Issus in 333 B.C. Having conquered Egypt, he headed into the heart of the Persian empire, defeating the Persians for the third time at Gaugamela. His march took him into central Asia—destroying the Persian capital, Persepolis, along the way—and then into India, where he achieved his final victory. He died in Babylon in 323 B.C., aged only 32.

Alexander's legacy

Alexander left an incredible legacy. His empire stretched from Egypt to India and into central Asia, and at least 20 cities bore his name. Alexandria in Egypt soon became one of the greatest cities in the ancient world. It boasted a massive library, which was said to contain all human knowledge at the time. In 2003 a huge new library (right) opened in Alexandria to commemorate this ancient library.

Alexander the Conqueror

Alexander was a superb military commander, leading his Macedonian troops into battle—often against overwhelming Persian strength. At the Battle of Issus in November 333 B.C., Alexander, seen here on horseback in the left of this mosaic, came face-to-face with the Persian emperor Darius, riding in a war chariot. After his army was defeated, Darius was forced to flee the battlefield, leaving behind most of his family and a huge amount of treasures.

Roman Empire

The Roman Empire began life as a series of small villages next to the Tiber river in central Italy. According to legend, Rome was founded in 753 B.C., and in 510 B.C. the city became a republic. Over the next 500 years, Rome conquered all of Italy, and then, after wars against Carthage, it conquered the lands that surrounded the Mediterranean Sea. Political instability led to the creation of an empire and a massive expansion of Roman power. The empire reached its greatest extent in A.D. 117 and enjoyed 300 years of relative peace and prosperity. Eventually, after civil wars and invasions, Rome became too weak to defend against invaders. By A.D. 476, the great empire had collapsed in the west.

CALEDONIA

North Sea

Hadrian's Wall

HIBERNIA

Military forts
The Romans built military forts and barracks at strategic sites throughout the empire.

BRITANNIA

Londinium

Sheep herder

GERMANIA

Legion in tortoise formation

Augusta Treverorum (Trier)

GAUL

Rhine

A straight, flat road to transport troops and goods

Lugdunum

Alps

Trade ship taking goods to Egypt

Country villa

ITALY

Cemenelum

Massilia (Marseille)

Corsica

ROME

HISPANIA

Pyrenees

Atlantic Ocean

Tarraco

Balearic Islands

Sardinia

Bringing water
Aqueducts were amazing feats of engineering and brought water to the cities.

Augusta

Farmer tending vines

Roman arena
Gladiator contests were held in Rome's arena, the Colosseum.

Carales

Cordoba

Wealth from trade
Trading ships carried valuable goods around the empire.

Carthago Nova (Cartagena)

Iol Caeserea

Mounted soldier patrolling the frontier

Carthage

Tingis (Tangier)

Violent sports
Many slaves that were captured in Africa were forced to fight as gladiators in Rome.

NUMIDIA

MAURETANIA

Atlas Mountains

Empires at war
Rome and Carthage fought three long wars, until Carthage's defeat in 146 B.C.

AFRICA

Roman baths

0   500   1,000km
0   250   500 miles

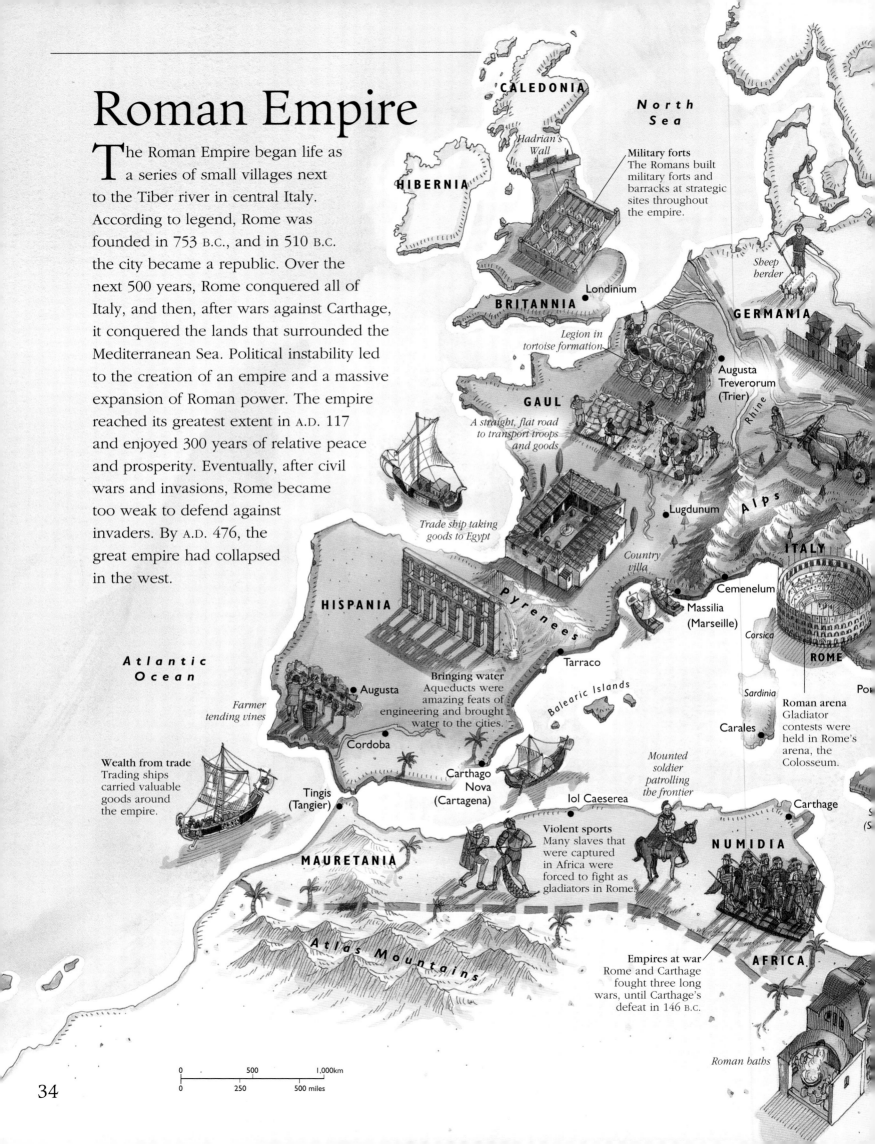

Water engineering

The Romans were great engineers. They built long aqueducts and viaducts, such as this one in Spain (Roman Hispania), to bring fresh water into their towns and cities for drinking and for supplying the many public baths. Baths were leisure complexes where people could bathe, exercise, meet friends, discuss current affairs, or just relax. They were heated by a hypocaust, or central heating system, that pushed hot air up under the floors and into cavities inside the walls.

Formidable barrier
The Roman Limes was a line of forts that were linked by wooden stakes stretching along the border with Germany.

Carpathian Mountains

Caucasus

Carnuntum

Aquincum

ner plowing s with oxen

DACIA

Viminacium

Danube

Black Sea

Salonae

DALMATIA

Adriatic Sea

Olive oil and wine

THRACIA

Byzantium (Constantinople)

Perinthus

Nicomedia

Thessalonica

Roman soldier

ASIA

Brundisium

MACEDONIA

Aegean Sea

Mount Vesuvius erupting in A.D. 79

Ephesus

Athens

Antiochia (Antioch)

SYRIA

Myra

Cyprus

yracuse

Trade ship taking goods to Egypt

Crete

Gortyn

Victory at sea
The Roman naval victory at Actium in 31 B.C. led to Rome's conquest of Egypt.

Jerusalem

Roman temple

Mediterranean Sea

Magna

Cyrene

Provincial governors

Alexandria

EGYPT

ARABIA

Nile

approximate extent of Roman empire in A.D. 117

Bread providers
Egypt provided much of the grain for the rest of the empire.

Red Sea

800 B.C.–A.D. 500

800 B.C.

753 Date, by legend, of the founding of Rome by Romulus and Remus

700 B.C.

600 B.C.

510 Roman republic is established

500 B.C.

400 B.C.
378 Servian Wall is built around Rome to protect the city

338 Rome begins to expand its power in central Italy

300 B.C.

264 Rome controls most of Italy
264–146 Three major wars are fought against Carthage for control of the Mediterranean, Spain, and North Africa

200 B.C.

146 Greece becomes a Roman province

100 B.C.

58–51 Julius Caesar conquers Gaul
44 Julius Caesar is assassinated
27 Octavian becomes the first emperor with the title of Augustus

0

A.D. 43 Conquest of Britannia

79 Mount Vesuvius erupts, destroying Pompeii

A.D. 100
117 Roman Empire is at its largest size

192–193 Civil war breaks out between rival emperors

A.D. 200

285 Emperor Diocletian divides the empire into two

A.D. 300
313 Emperor Constantine ends the persecution of Christians
330 Constantinople becomes the capital of the Roman Empire
364 Empire is formally split into eastern and western halves
A.D. 400
410 Invading Visigoths ransack Rome

476 Last western emperor is overthrown

A.D. 500

Roman Empire:
The city of Rome

The imperial city of Rome—the capital of the Roman Empire—was by far the most grand and important city in Europe. It was a huge but often rundown city. The first emperor, Augustus (ruled 27 B.C.–A.D. 14), decided to make it beautiful, clearing away narrow streets and building public baths, theaters, and temples. He set up police and a fire service to keep its citizens safe and dredged and widened the Tiber river to prevent its frequent floods. By the end of the A.D. first century, Rome was a showcase for its empire, designed to impress visitors and enemies with the might of the Roman Empire.

Ruling the empire
From 27 B.C. to A.D. 476, Rome was governed by emperors. Some, such as Augustus, were outstanding, while others were brutal dictators or madmen. Below the emperor was the Senate—an unelected group of around 600 rich men that were called senators (below), who passed laws, controlled the treasury, and appointed governors to the Roman provinces that were not run by the emperor himself.

Street life
The streets of Rome were packed with shops that sold every type of produce. Bread was made in the shops themselves (above), while traders brought in fresh food and other goods from outside the city on handcarts and stocked up their shops each night, to be ready to sell the next day. Every street had a local bar, where wine and other drinks were sold, as well as many workshops, where everything from furniture and pots to fine clothes and jewelry were made. Although the main streets were swept clean, most of the smaller streets were very dirty because people threw their garbage out of their windows. At night the city was pitch black because there was no street lighting.

Women were separated from men and watched events from their own terrace on top of the building

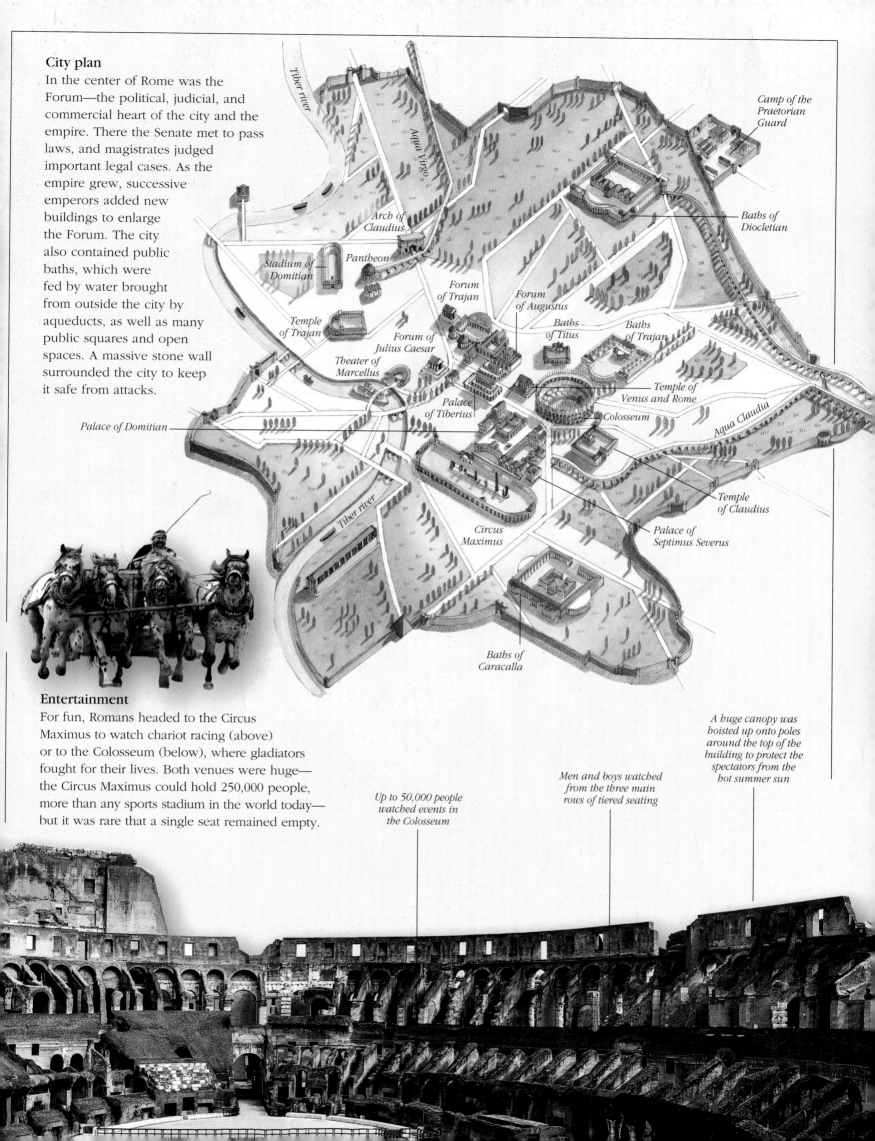

City plan

In the center of Rome was the Forum—the political, judicial, and commercial heart of the city and the empire. There the Senate met to pass laws, and magistrates judged important legal cases. As the empire grew, successive emperors added new buildings to enlarge the Forum. The city also contained public baths, which were fed by water brought from outside the city by aqueducts, as well as many public squares and open spaces. A massive stone wall surrounded the city to keep it safe from attacks.

Entertainment

For fun, Romans headed to the Circus Maximus to watch chariot racing (above) or to the Colosseum (below), where gladiators fought for their lives. Both venues were huge— the Circus Maximus could hold 250,000 people, more than any sports stadium in the world today— but it was rare that a single seat remained empty.

Tiber river

Aqua Virgo

Camp of the Praetorian Guard

Baths of Diocletian

Arch of Claudius

Stadium of Domitian

Pantheon

Forum of Trajan

Forum of Augustus

Baths of Titus

Baths of Trajan

Temple of Trajan

Forum of Julius Caesar

Theater of Marcellus

Palace of Tiberius

Temple of Venus and Rome

Colosseum

Aqua Claudia

Palace of Domitian

Temple of Claudius

Circus Maximus

Palace of Septimus Severus

Tiber river

Baths of Caracalla

Up to 50,000 people watched events in the Colosseum

Men and boys watched from the three main rows of tiered seating

A huge canopy was hoisted up onto poles around the top of the building to protect the spectators from the hot summer sun

Ancient Africa

Around 5,500 years ago the grassy plains of the Sahara began to dry out and turn into a desert, dividing Africa in half. Until the introduction of camels from Arabia around 100 B.C., there was very little communication across this sandy desert. Many great civilizations flourished south of the Sahara. The oldest of these was in Nubia, close to the top of the Nile river. At one time the Nubian kingdom was so powerful that it ruled all of Egypt, but its successor, Meroë, was eventually conquered by the Christian kingdom of Aksum—the forerunner of modern-day Ethiopia. In the west the people of Nok learned to work with iron and produced beautiful terra-cotta figures. The neighboring Bantu peoples were also skilled ironworkers, gradually spreading their language and technology east and south to everywhere except the far southern tip of Africa. In many places, however, Africans remained in the Stone Age, hunting and gathering their food from the forests and plains around them.

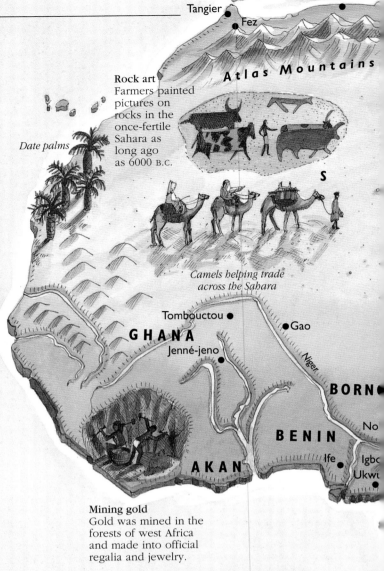

Rock art Farmers painted pictures on rocks in the once-fertile Sahara as long ago as 6000 B.C.

Date palms

Camels helping trade across the Sahara

Tombouctou ● ● Gao

GHANA

Jenné-jeno ●

BORN

BENIN No

AKAN Ife Igbo Ukwu

Mining gold Gold was mined in the forests of west Africa and made into official regalia and jewelry.

Atlantic Ocean

Nok culture

From around 500 B.C., Nok craftworkers produced beautiful terra cotta heads and figures—among the earliest surviving artworks from Africa south of the Sahara. They also learned to smelt iron ore to produce weapons and tools—a valuable skill when most of their enemies had only wooden spears and stones to use against them. Farther up the Niger River Valley was the city of Jenné-Jeno—the earliest-known town in sub-Saharan Africa, which became the hub of trade across the Sahara and where traders used camels to carry gold, silver, ivory, and salt across the desert.

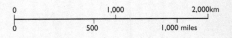

| 0 | | 1,000 | 2,000km |
| 0 | 500 | | 1,000 miles |

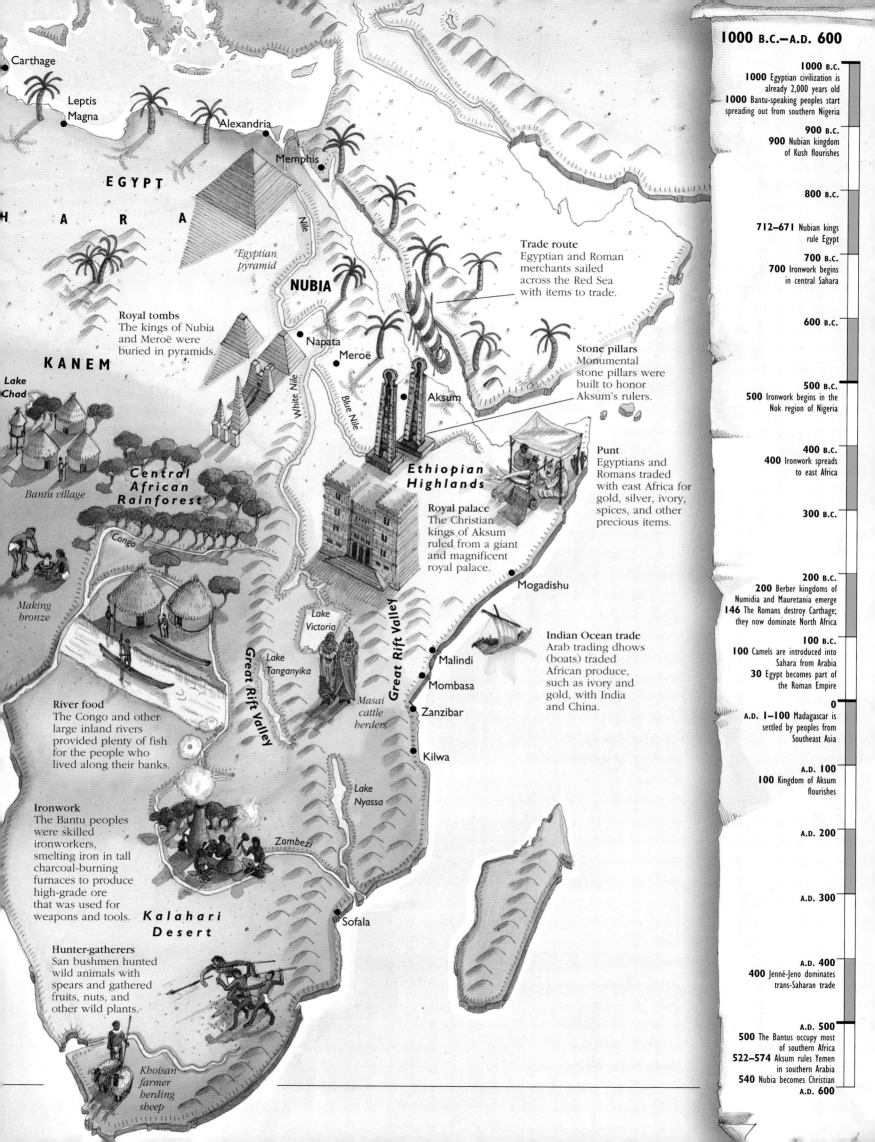

Carthage

Leptis Magna

Alexandria

Memphis

EGYPT

S A H A R A

Egyptian pyramid

NUBIA

Nile

Royal tombs
The kings of Nubia and Meroë were buried in pyramids.

KANEM

Lake Chad

Napata

Meroë

White Nile

Blue Nile

Aksum

Central African Rainforest

Bantu village

Congo

Making bronze

River food
The Congo and other large inland rivers provided plenty of fish for the people who lived along their banks.

Lake Victoria

Lake Tanganyika

Great Rift Valley

Masai cattle herders

Great Rift Valley

Ethiopian Highlands

Royal palace
The Christian kings of Aksum ruled from a giant and magnificent royal palace.

Mogadishu

Malindi

Mombasa

Zanzibar

Kilwa

Trade route
Egyptian and Roman merchants sailed across the Red Sea with items to trade.

Stone pillars
Monumental stone pillars were built to honor Aksum's rulers.

Punt
Egyptians and Romans traded with east Africa for gold, silver, ivory, spices, and other precious items.

Indian Ocean trade
Arab trading dhows (boats) traded African produce, such as ivory and gold, with India and China.

Lake Nyassa

Ironwork
The Bantu peoples were skilled ironworkers, smelting iron in tall charcoal-burning furnaces to produce high-grade ore that was used for weapons and tools.

Zambezi

Kalahari Desert

Sofala

Hunter-gatherers
San bushmen hunted wild animals with spears and gathered fruits, nuts, and other wild plants.

Khoisan farmer herding sheep

1000 B.C.–A.D. 600

1000 B.C.
1000 Egyptian civilization is already 2,000 years old
1000 Bantu-speaking peoples start spreading out from southern Nigeria

900 B.C.
900 Nubian kingdom of Kush flourishes

800 B.C.

712–671 Nubian kings rule Egypt

700 B.C.
700 Ironwork begins in central Sahara

600 B.C.

500 B.C.
500 Ironwork begins in the Nok region of Nigeria

400 B.C.
400 Ironwork spreads to east Africa

300 B.C.

200 B.C.
200 Berber kingdoms of Numidia and Mauretania emerge
146 The Romans destroy Carthage; they now dominate North Africa

100 B.C.
100 Camels are introduced into Sahara from Arabia
30 Egypt becomes part of the Roman Empire

0

A.D. 1–100 Madagascar is settled by peoples from Southeast Asia

A.D. 100
100 Kingdom of Aksum flourishes

A.D. 200

A.D. 300

A.D. 400
400 Jenné-Jeno dominates trans-Saharan trade

A.D. 500
500 The Bantus occupy most of southern Africa
522–574 Aksum rules Yemen in southern Arabia
540 Nubia becomes Christian

A.D. 600

Ancient India

The first ruler to unite most of India was Candragupta, founder of the Mauryan dynasty that lasted from 321 to 185 B.C. His grandson, Ashoka, was a bloodthirsty ruler who was so shocked by the death of more than 100,000 people at Kalinga in 261 B.C that he converted to Buddhism, a nonviolent religion. Buddhism became an important religion in India. After the Mauryans lost power, India broke up until first the Kushans and then the Guptas reunited the country. The Guptas were devout Hindus and supported the arts and sciences. During their time the great Hindu epics of the *Mahabharata* and *Ramayana* were completed and mathematicians invented the decimal system and the concept of zero.

Market city
The city of Taxila had been occupied by Persians, Greeks, Mauryans, and Kushans, and became a major trading center.

• Taxila

UTTARA PATHA

• **Candragupta**
After Alexander the Great left India in 330 B.C., Candragupta drove out the troops he had left behind and seized the land.

• Kandahar

Bull pulling carts of produce to the market

Watering the fields
Oxen were used to pull up huge barrels of water from deep wells to irrigate the fields.

Thar Desert

Indus

• Pattala

• Barbaricum

Growing rice in paddy fields

AVANTI

Great Stupa at Sanchi

• Sanchi

• Eran

Narmada

Mud houses with thatched

Buddha
The Buddha achieved enlightenment at Bodh Gaya around 528 B.C.

• Sarnath

• Bharhut

• Bodh Gaya

Buddhist propaganda
All over India, Ashoka carved statements about the correct way of life on stone pillars

Ganges

■ **PATALIPUTRA**

MAGADHA

Pataliputra
Pataliputra was the capital of Magadha and of the Mauryan empire. It was one of the largest cities in the ancient world.

VANGA

Ganges

• Tamluk

H i m a l a y a s

Bay of Bengal

Battle of Kalinga
After the bloody and brutal conquest of Kalinga in 261 B.C., Ashoka converted to Buddhism, which preaches nonviolence.

Buddhist center
Amaravati was the main center of Buddhism in southern India from the 200s B.C. until the A.D. 1300s.

Hinduism

Hinduism is the world's oldest religion. The word *Hindu* comes from the Persian word *sindhu*, or "river," because the religion began among the people who lived in the Indus River Valley cities of Mohenjo Daro and Harappa around 5,000 years ago. The Hindu scriptures were first written down around 900 B.C., by which time Hinduism was the major religion in India. There is no single belief in Hinduism, which has many gods. Their stories are written down in such epics as the *Ramayana*, a scene from which is shown above.

State irrigation
The Mauryans built a massive dam, reservoir, and irrigation project in Junagadh.

Deccan Plateau

Godavari

DAKSHINA PATHA

Krishna

Amaravati

Suvannagiri

Banyan trees shading travelers

Arabian Sea

Arikamedu

Anuradhapura

Sri Lanka

Indian riches
The trade in gold, diamonds, and pearls with merchants from Arabia and elsewhere made southern India rich.

Indian Ocean

800km

400 miles

400

200

400

200

0

0

Buddhism

Siddhártha Gautama (c. 563–483 B.C.) was born a wealthy prince in northern India. He was distressed by the poverty that he saw, and after his "enlightenment" in around 528 B.C., he developed the Buddhist religion of nonviolence and correct behavior. At first, Buddhism was one of many religions in India, but when King Ashoka converted to it in 260 B.C., the religion spread. Ashoka built the Great Stupa at Sanchi (above) to house the remains of the Buddha's body.

500 B.C.—A.D. 600

500 B.C.
500 Magadha is the main Hindu kingdom in northern India
500 The *Mahabharata* is first written down
483 Vijaya founds first kingdom in Sri Lanka
483 Death of Buddha

400 B.C.
364 Under the Nanda dynasty, Magadha dominates the Ganges Valley
327–325 Alexander the Great conquers the Indus River Valley
321 Candragupta Maurya seizes power in Magadha

300 B.C.
300 The *Ramayana* is written down
293 Candragupta Maurya abdicates in favor of Bindusara Maurya, who conquers southern India
268–233 Ashoka rules the Mauryan empire

200 B.C.
185 Mauryan empire is overthrown

100 B.C.

0

A.D. 50 The Kushans conquer northwest India

A.D. 100
130 Kushan empire is at its peak

A.D. 200
200 Hindu laws are first written down

A.D. 300
320–335 Candragupta I, founder of the Mauryan dynasty, rules
335–380 Samudragupta conquers Kushan empire
380 Candragupta II conquers western India
A.D. 400

A.D. 500
510 Gupta empire begins to decline, finally ending in 720

575 Indian mathematicians develop the decimal system and the concept of zero
A.D. 600

Ancient China

In 221 B.C. Zheng, the ruler of Qin in central China, defeated his rivals and united China. He took the title Qin Shi Huangdi, or "first sovereign Qin emperor." Ever since 1122 B.C., China had supposedly been united under the Zhou kings, but real power rested with the many provincial leaders, who often had more power than the king himself. Qin Shi Huangdi changed all this by setting up a strong state where all power remained with the emperor. He built the Great Wall to keep out invaders, as well as many roads and canals. But after his death a civil war broke out and the rulers of the Han dynasty came to power in 202 B.C. The Han expanded the empire south and east, but when they were overthrown in A.D. 220, China split into three kingdoms.

Buddhism

The Buddhist religion was introduced to China by monks from India—one of whom is shown here with Buddha himself— around A.D. 100. The peaceful teachings of Buddhism appealed to the Chinese people during the troubled years after the fall of the Han dynasty in A.D. 220, and it soon became one of China's three major religions, alongside Confucianism and Taoism. The monks traveled into China along the Silk Road—a series of trade routes that connected the major cities of China with central Asia, the eastern Mediterranean, and eventually Rome. Merchants traveled along the road carrying silk, jade, and, much later, fine porcelain.

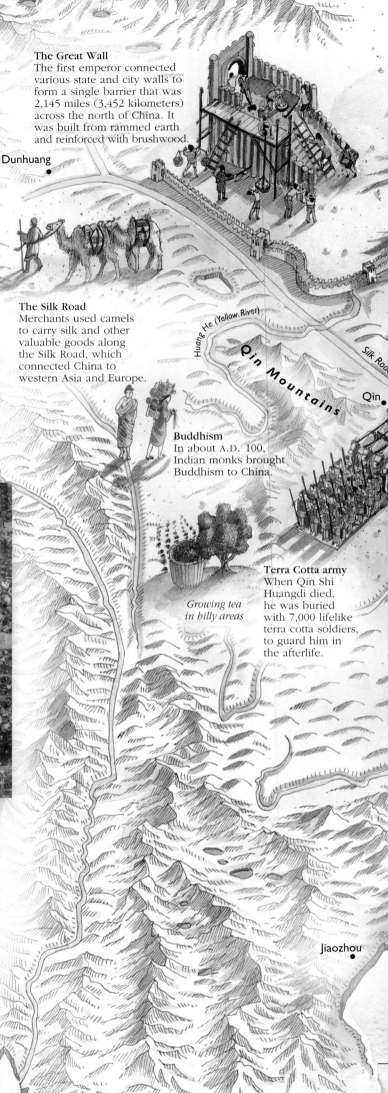

The Great Wall
The first emperor connected various state and city walls to form a single barrier that was 2,145 miles (3,452 kilometers) across the north of China. It was built from rammed earth and reinforced with brushwood.

Dunhuang

The Silk Road
Merchants used camels to carry silk and other valuable goods along the Silk Road, which connected China to western Asia and Europe.

Huang He (Yellow River)

Qin Mountains

Silk Road

Qin

Buddhism
In about A.D. 100, Indian monks brought Buddhism to China.

Growing tea in hilly areas

Terra Cotta army
When Qin Shi Huangdi died, he was buried with 7,000 lifelike terra cotta soldiers, to guard him in the afterlife.

Jiaozhou

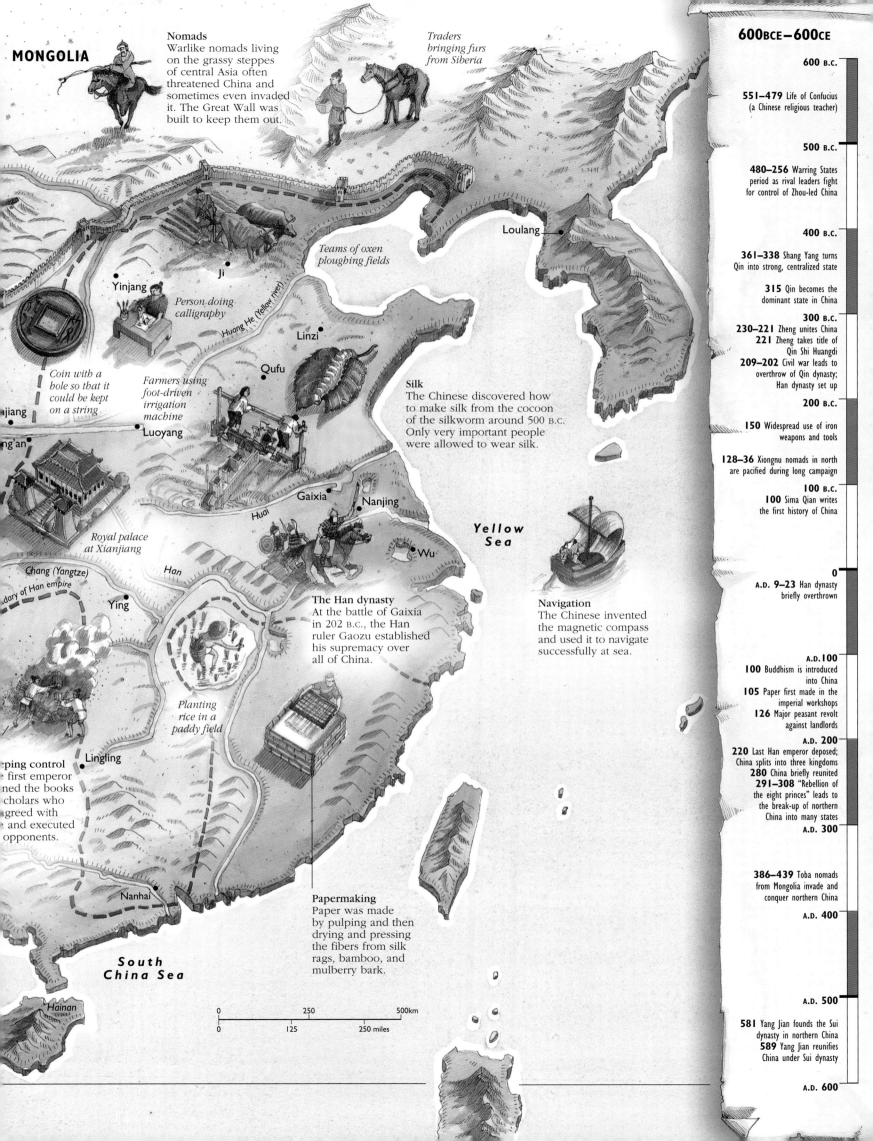

MONGOLIA

Nomads
Warlike nomads living on the grassy steppes of central Asia often threatened China and sometimes even invaded it. The Great Wall was built to keep them out.

Traders bringing furs from Siberia

Loulang

Teams of oxen ploughing fields

Ji

Yinjang

Person doing calligraphy

Huang He (Yellow river)

Linzi

Qufu

Coin with a hole so that it could be kept on a string

Farmers using foot-driven irrigation machine

jiang

Luoyang

ng'an

Silk
The Chinese discovered how to make silk from the cocoon of the silkworm around 500 B.C. Only very important people were allowed to wear silk.

Gaixia

Nanjing

Huai

Royal palace at Xianjiang

Wu

Yellow Sea

Chang (Yangtze)

dary of Han empire

Ying

Han

The Han dynasty
At the battle of Gaixia in 202 B.C., the Han ruler Gaozu established his supremacy over all of China.

Navigation
The Chinese invented the magnetic compass and used it to navigate successfully at sea.

Planting rice in a paddy field

ping control
first emperor
ned the books
cholars who
greed with
and executed
opponents.

Lingling

Nanhai

Papermaking
Paper was made by pulping and then drying and pressing the fibers from silk rags, bamboo, and mulberry bark.

South China Sea

Hainan

0	250	500km
0	125	250 miles

600BCE–600CE

600 B.C.

551–479 Life of Confucius (a Chinese religious teacher)

500 B.C.

480–256 Warring States period as rival leaders fight for control of Zhou-led China

400 B.C.

361–338 Shang Yang turns Qin into strong, centralized state

315 Qin becomes the dominant state in China

300 B.C.

230–221 Zheng unites China
221 Zheng takes title of Qin Shi Huangdi
209–202 Civil war leads to overthrow of Qin dynasty; Han dynasty set up

200 B.C.

150 Widespread use of iron weapons and tools

128–36 Xiongnu nomads in north are pacified during long campaign

100 B.C.
100 Sima Qian writes the first history of China

0

A.D. 9–23 Han dynasty briefly overthrown

A.D. 100
100 Buddhism is introduced into China
105 Paper first made in the imperial workshops
126 Major peasant revolt against landlords

A.D. 200
220 Last Han emperor deposed; China splits into three kingdoms
280 China briefly reunited
291–308 "Rebellion of the eight princes" leads to the break-up of northern China into many states

A.D. 300

386–439 Toba nomads from Mongolia invade and conquer northern China

A.D. 400

A.D. 500

581 Yang Jian founds the Sui dynasty in northern China
589 Yang Jian reunifies China under Sui dynasty

A.D. 600

North American peoples

The first people arrived in North America from Siberia over the land bridge that existed around 17,000 years ago. They slowly moved south, spreading out over the vast plains, woodlands, deserts, and mountains of the continent, living as hunter-gatherers as they went. From around 700 B.C., the Adena people of the Ohio River Valley began to cultivate wild plants for food and build sacred earthworks and burial mounds. The later Hopewell people, who spread out from the Ohio River Valley into the Mississippi River Valley, built towns, burial mounds, and a huge earthwork in the shape of a snake—although no one really knows why they did this. The people of the southwestern deserts began to settle down into farming communities by around A.D. 300, eventually building complex villages of adobe (dried mud) brick houses. In the far north of America the Inuit people learned how to live in very cold conditions, trapping wild animals for their fur, meat, and bones.

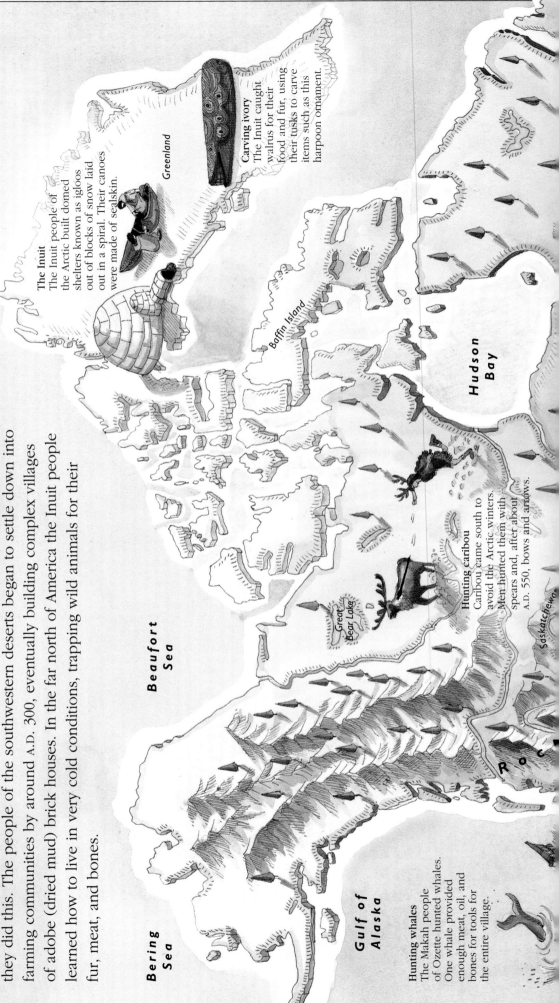

Greenland Sea

The Inuit
The Inuit people of the Arctic built domed shelters known as igloos out of blocks of snow laid out in a spiral. Their canoes were made of sealskin.

Carving ivory
The Inuit caught walrus for their food and fur, using their tusks to carve items such as this harpoon ornament.

Greenland

Baffin Island

Hudson Bay

Beaufort Sea

Great Bear Lake

Hunting caribou
Caribou came south to avoid the Arctic winters. Men hunted them with spears and, after about A.D. 550, bows and arrows.

Saskatchewan

R o c

Bering Sea

Gulf of Alaska

Hunting whales
The Makah people of Ozette hunted whales. One whale provided enough meat, oil, and bones for tools for the entire village.

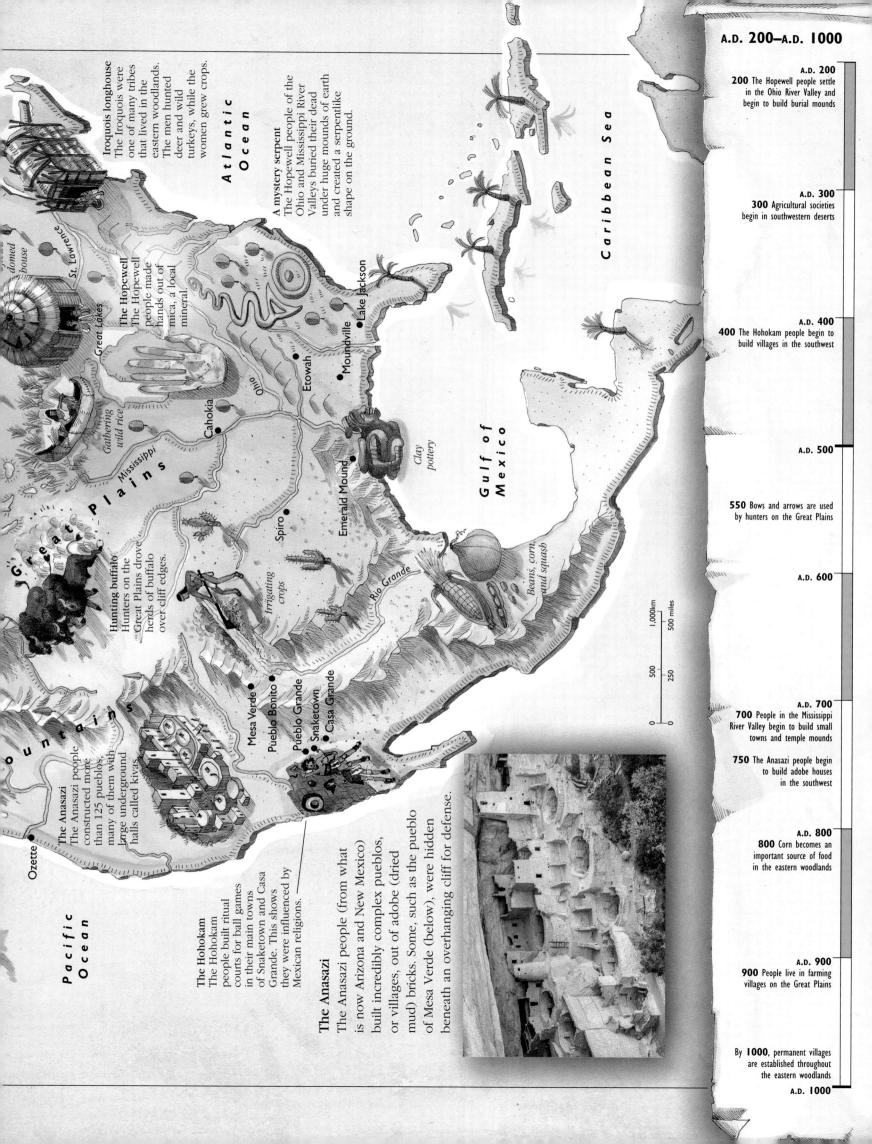

Iroquois longhouse
The Iroquois were one of many tribes that lived in the eastern woodlands. The men hunted deer and wild turkeys, while the women grew crops.

domed house

St. Lawrence

Great Lakes

Atlantic Ocean

A mystery serpent
The Hopewell people of the Ohio and Mississippi River Valleys buried their dead under huge mounds of earth and created a serpentlike shape on the ground.

The Hopewell
The Hopewell people made hands out of mica, a local mineral.

Gathering wild rice

Cahokia •

Ohio

Etowah •

Moundville •

• Lake Jackson

Caribbean Sea

Mississippi

Emerald Mound •

Spiro •

Great Plains

Clay pottery

Gulf of Mexico

Hunting buffalo
Hunters on the Great Plains drove herds of buffalo over cliff edges.

Irrigating crops

Rio Grande

Beans, corn, and squash

Mesa Verde •

Pueblo Bonito •

Pueblo Grande •

Snaketown •

Casa Grande •

Mountains

Ozette •

The Anasazi
The Anasazi people constructed more than 125 pueblos, many of them with large underground halls called kivas.

The Hohokam
The Hohokam people built ritual courts for ball games in their main towns of Snaketown and Casa Grande. This shows they were influenced by Mexican religions.

The Anasazi
The Anasazi people (from what is now Arizona and New Mexico) built incredibly complex pueblos, or villages, out of adobe (dried mud) bricks. Some, such as the pueblo of Mesa Verde (below), were hidden beneath an overhanging cliff for defense.

Pacific Ocean

1,000km

500 miles

500

250

500

0

0

A.D. 200
200 The Hopewell people settle in the Ohio River Valley and begin to build burial mounds

A.D. 300
300 Agricultural societies begin in southwestern deserts

A.D. 400
400 The Hohokam people begin to build villages in the southwest

A.D. 500

550 Bows and arrows are used by hunters on the Great Plains

A.D. 600

A.D. 700
700 People in the Mississippi River Valley begin to build small towns and temple mounds

750 The Anasazi people begin to build adobe houses in the southwest

A.D. 800
800 Corn becomes an important source of food in the eastern woodlands

A.D. 900
900 People live in farming villages on the Great Plains

By **1000**, permanent villages are established throughout the eastern woodlands

A.D. 1000

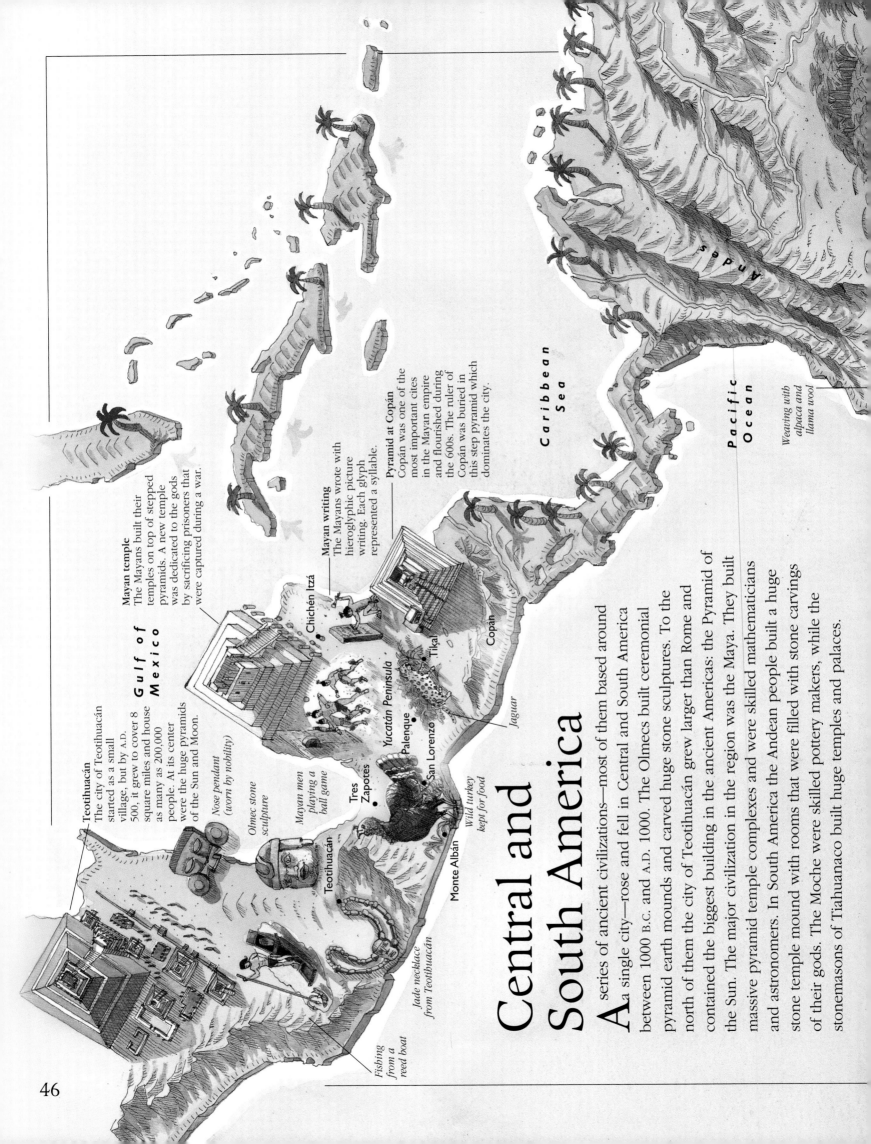

Central and South America

A series of ancient civilizations—most of them based around a single city—rose and fell in Central and South America between 1000 B.C. and A.D. 1000. The Olmecs built ceremonial pyramid earth mounds and carved huge stone sculptures. To the north of them the city of Teotihuacán grew larger than Rome and contained the biggest building in the ancient Americas: the Pyramid of the Sun. The major civilization in the region was the Maya. They built massive pyramid temple complexes and were skilled mathematicians and astronomers. In South America the Andean people built a huge stone temple mound with rooms that were filled with stone carvings of their gods. The Moche were skilled pottery makers, while the stonemasons of Tiahuanaco built huge temples and palaces.

Teotihuacán
The city of Teotihuacán started as a small village, but by A.D. 500, it grew to cover 8 square miles and house as many as 200,000 people. At its center were the huge pyramids of the Sun and Moon.

Nose pendant (worn by nobility)

Olmec stone sculpture

Mayan temple
The Mayans built their temples on top of stepped pyramids. A new temple was dedicated to the gods by sacrificing prisoners that were captured during a war.

Mayan writing
The Mayans wrote with hieroglyphic picture writing. Each glyph represented a syllable.

Pyramid at Copán
Copán was one of the most important cites in the Mayan empire and flourished during the 600s. The ruler of Copán was buried in this step pyramid which dominates the city.

Mayan men playing a ball game

Gulf of Mexico

Caribbean Sea

Pacific Ocean

Andes

Weaving with alpaca and llama wool

Chichén Itzá

Palenque

Yucatán Peninsula

Tikal

Copán

Monte Albán

San Lorenzo

Tres Zapotes

Teotihuacán

Jaguar

Wild turkey kept for food

Jade necklace from Teotihuacán

Fishing from a reed boat

Steep hillsides terraced and irrigated for farming

Fishing on Lake Titicaca

A n d e s

Lake Titicaca

Tiwanaku

Alto Rairez

Gold panning in Andean streams

Huarpa

Wari

Nazca

Pampa Ingenio

Corn grown in irrigated fields

San Pedro de Atacama

Nazca Lines
The Nazca people drew huge geometric shapes and outlines of animals, birds, and insects in the desert sands.

Tiwanaku
The highest city in the Andes controlled a large empire. At its heart was a precinct of temples and palaces, as well as the stone Gateway of the Sun.

Moche warrior graves

Cerro Vicus
Pampa Grande
Viracocha
Moche
Pañamarca

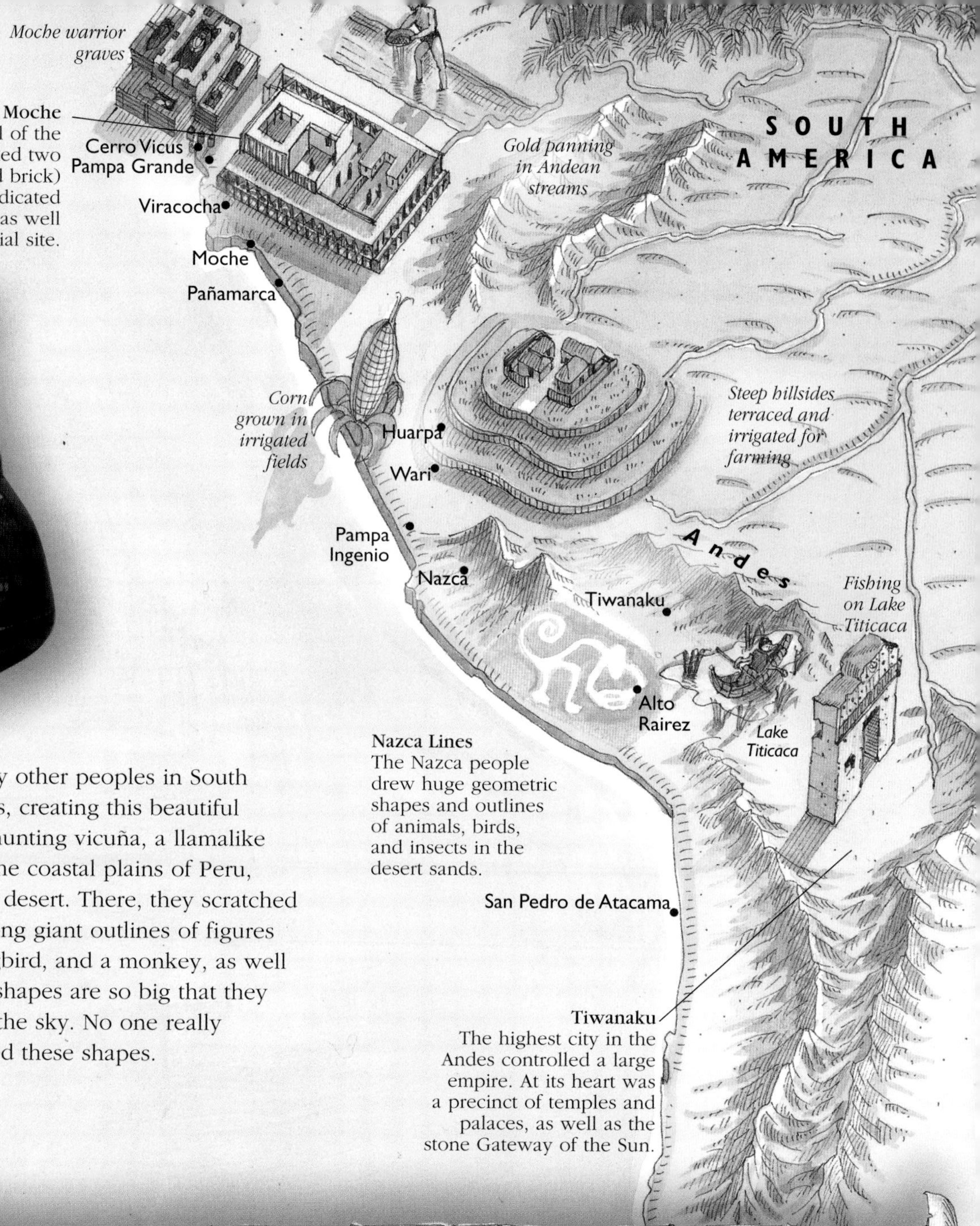

Moche
Moche—the capital of the Moche state—contained two huge adobe (mud brick) platforms that were dedicated to the Sun and Moon, as well as a vast royal burial site.

The Nazca
The Nazca people, like many other peoples in South America, were skilled potters, creating this beautiful painted vase showing men hunting vicuña, a llamalike animal. The Nazca lived in the coastal plains of Peru, much of which was hot, dry desert. There, they scratched shapes into the sand, including giant outlines of figures such as a spider, a hummingbird, and a monkey, as well as geometric shapes. These shapes are so big that they can only be fully seen from the sky. No one really knows why the Nazca created these shapes.

The Maya
The Maya settled in Central America from around 1000 B.C. They began to build temple pyramids on which to worship their gods, and by 350 B.C., they were creating powerful city-states such as Palenque, Tikal, and Copán. The Maya created the only complete picture writing system in the ancient Americas. It was a sophisticated system that could fully express their entire spoken language. They were also skilled mathematicians and studied the stars so that they could draw up a detailed calendar that told them when eclipses of the Sun and Moon occurred.

Mayan city-states dominated the region from A.D. 300 to 800, but then they went into decline for reasons that no one fully understands today. The exception was the northern city of Chichén Itzá, founded in around A.D. 850, which was dominated by the El Castillo pyramid, shown above. Eventually Chichén Itzá itself declined and was overrun by the Toltecs, which brought Mayan civilization to an end.

1000km
500 miles

500 B.C.–A.D. 1000

500 B.C.
500 Olmec civilization flourishes by the Gulf of Mexico
450 Monte Albán is the center of Zapotec culture

400 B.C.
400 Chavin de Huantar culture spreads throughout central Andes
350 First Maya city-state is built in the Yucatán Peninsula

300 B.C.
300 Olmec civilization declines

200 B.C.
200 City of Teotihuacán is founded
200 The Nazcas begin to draw lines in the Peruvian desert
150 The Maya first develop their picture writing around this time

100 B.C.
100 Moche state is created in northern Peru

0

A.D. 100
150 Pyramid of the Sun is built in Teotihuacán

A.D. 200
200 People in Huarpa begin to terrace and irrigate the Andes for agriculture

A.D. 300
300 Moche state is at its most powerful

A.D. 400
450 Tikal is the main Mayan city-state

A.D. 500
500 Wari state begins to create an empire in the central Andes

A.D. 600
600 Tiahuanaco empire dominates southern Andes region

A.D. 700
700 Wari empire overruns Moche
700 Teotihuacán is ransacked by armies from nearby rival city

A.D. 800
800 Mayan city-states begin to decline
850 Chichén Itzá, the last major Mayan city-state, is founded

A.D. 900
900 Center of Mayan civilization moves north to Chichén Itzá
950 The Toltecs migrate from Mexico and overrun the remaining Mayan city-states

A.D. 1000

Australia and Polynesia

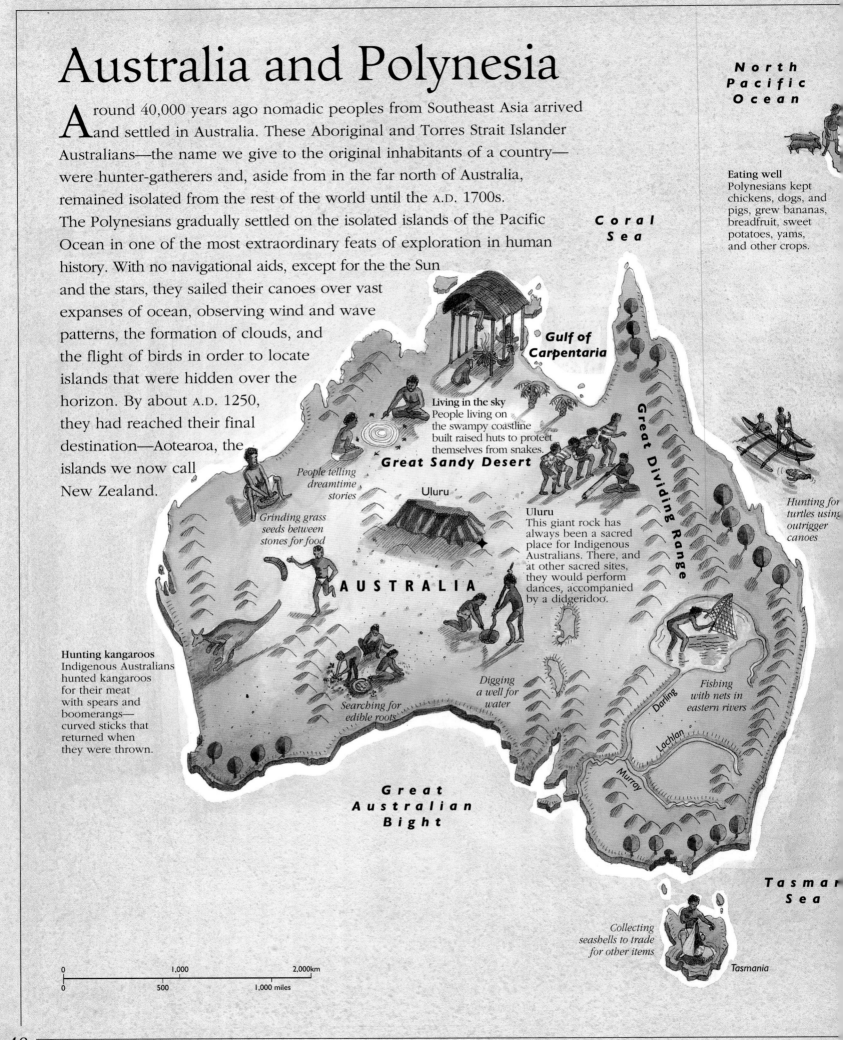

Around 40,000 years ago nomadic peoples from Southeast Asia arrived and settled in Australia. These Aboriginal and Torres Strait Islander Australians—the name we give to the original inhabitants of a country—were hunter-gatherers and, aside from in the far north of Australia, remained isolated from the rest of the world until the A.D. 1700s. The Polynesians gradually settled on the isolated islands of the Pacific Ocean in one of the most extraordinary feats of exploration in human history. With no navigational aids, except for the the Sun and the stars, they sailed their canoes over vast expanses of ocean, observing wind and wave patterns, the formation of clouds, and the flight of birds in order to locate islands that were hidden over the horizon. By about A.D. 1250, they had reached their final destination—Aotearoa, the islands we now call New Zealand.

North Pacific Ocean

Coral Sea

Eating well
Polynesians kept chickens, dogs, and pigs, grew bananas, breadfruit, sweet potatoes, yams, and other crops.

Gulf of Carpentaria

Living in the sky
People living on the swampy coastline built raised huts to protect themselves from snakes.

Great Sandy Desert

Uluru

People telling dreamtime stories

Grinding grass seeds between stones for food

Great Dividing Range

Hunting for turtles using outrigger canoes

Uluru
This giant rock has always been a sacred place for Indigenous Australians. There, and at other sacred sites, they would perform dances, accompanied by a didgeridoo.

AUSTRALIA

Hunting kangaroos
Indigenous Australians hunted kangaroos for their meat with spears and boomerangs—curved sticks that returned when they were thrown.

Searching for edible roots

Digging a well for water

Darling

Lachlan

Murray

Fishing with nets in eastern rivers

Great Australian Bight

Tasman Sea

Collecting seashells to trade for other items

Tasmania

| 0 | 1,000 | 2,000km |
| 0 | 500 | 1,000 miles |

Oceangoing canoes
The twin-hulled, oceangoing canoes were up to 100 ft. (30m) long and could carry up to 200 people, as well as supplies for the journey, animals, and seeds to plant on their new island home.

Gilbert Islands

Tuvalu

Sturdy ships
Polynesian canoes were made from dug-out tree trunks with sails made of palm leaf matting and had outriggers to stabilize them; the ropes were made from coconut fibers.

Solomon Islands

Samoa

Smaller canoes were used for fishing between the local islands

Vanuatu

Weaving baskets

Fiji

Catching coconuts from palm trees

Tonga

Cook Islands

Tahiti

New Caledonia

Harvesting yams

South Pacific Ocean

Long-distance voyages
Oceangoing canoes had to sail at least 1,550 mi. (2,500km) across the open sea to reach Aotearoa.

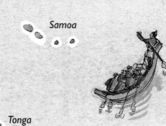

The Maori
The Polynesian settlers in Aotearoa became known as Maori. Their warriors fought each other using sharp-edged clubs that were made out of whalebone.

Carving wood
The Maori carved statues of Pukaki, one of their main ancestors, out of wood.

AOTEAROA

Hunting moa (a flightless bird)

Dreamtime
Indigenous Australians believe that their ancestors were heroes who walked the earth during Tjukurpa, or dreamtime. Some ancestors were human, some were animals and plants, and others were the Sun, stars, wind, and rain. They used certain paths that link the land and the people together. Indigenous peoples retell the stories of dreamtime from generation to generation, using paintings on rocks and walking along the sacred paths.

500 B.C.–A.D. 1000

500 B.C.

400 B.C.

500 Indigenous Australians are already well established in Australia and the Solomon Islands

300 B.C.

300 Polynesian culture develops in Fiji, Samoa, and Tonga

200 B.C.

200 The Polynesians sail east to the Cook Islands and Tahiti

100 B.C.

0

A.D. 100

A.D. 200

A.D. 300

300 The Polynesians reach distant Easter Island in the eastern Pacific Ocean (not shown on map area)

A.D. 400

400 The Polynesians sail north from the Marquesas Islands to settle in the Line Islands and Hawaii (not shown on map area)

A.D. 500

A.D. 600

A.D. 700

A.D. 800

A.D. 900

900s The Polynesians sail south to settle in Aotearoa (New Zealand), where they are known as Maori, and eventually to the Chatham Islands

A.D. 1000

MEDIEVAL WORLD

Illustrated by Kevin Maddison

CONTENTS

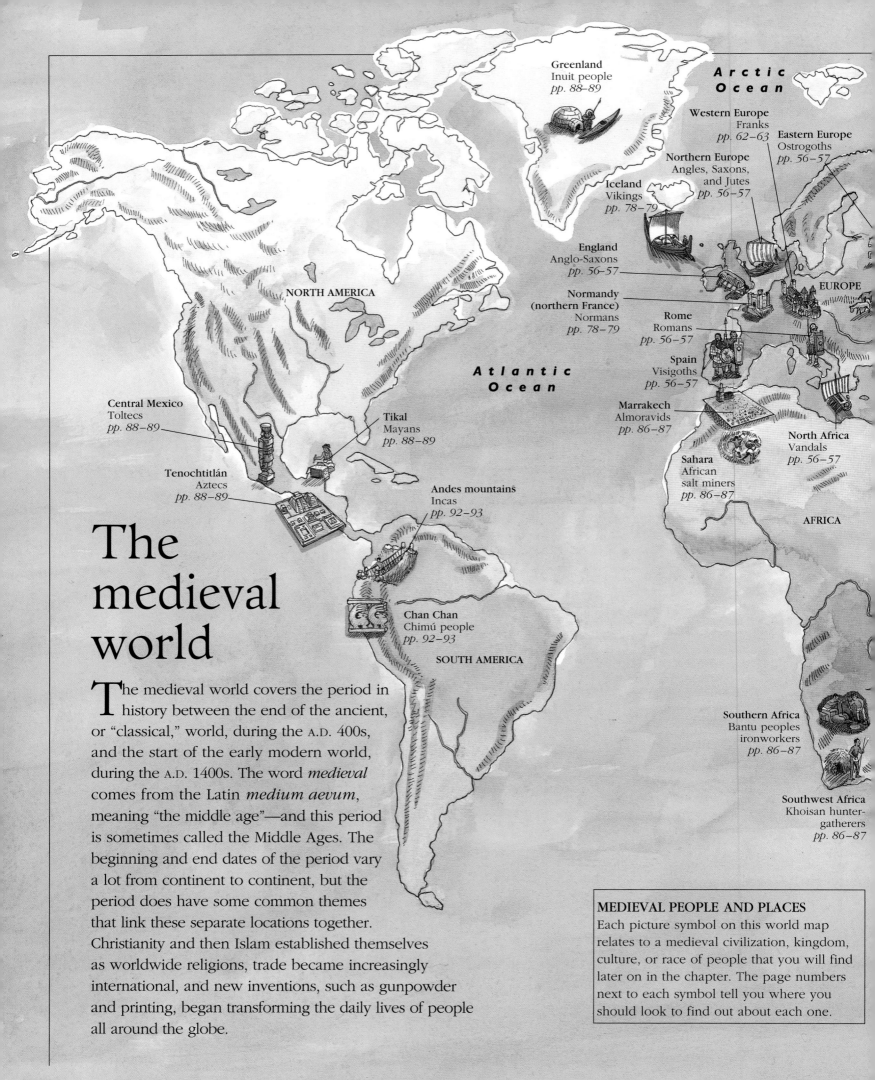

Greenland
Inuit people
pp. 88–89

Arctic Ocean

Western Europe
Franks
pp. 62–63

Eastern Europe
Ostrogoths
pp. 56–57

Northern Europe
Angles, Saxons,
and Jutes
pp. 56–57

Iceland
Vikings
pp. 78–79

England
Anglo-Saxons
pp. 56–57

Normandy
(northern France)
Normans
pp. 78–79

Rome
Romans
pp. 56–57

Spain
Visigoths
pp. 56–57

Marrakech
Almoravids
pp. 86–87

NORTH AMERICA

EUROPE

North Africa
Vandals
pp. 56–57

Sahara
African
salt miners
pp. 86–87

AFRICA

Central Mexico
Toltecs
pp. 88–89

Tikal
Mayans
pp. 88–89

Tenochtitlán
Aztecs
pp. 88–89

Atlantic Ocean

Andes mountains
Incas
pp. 92–93

The medieval world

Chan Chan
Chimú people
pp. 92–93

SOUTH AMERICA

The medieval world covers the period in history between the end of the ancient, or "classical," world, during the A.D. 400s, and the start of the early modern world, during the A.D. 1400s. The word *medieval* comes from the Latin *medium aevum*, meaning "the middle age"—and this period is sometimes called the Middle Ages. The beginning and end dates of the period vary a lot from continent to continent, but the period does have some common themes that link these separate locations together. Christianity and then Islam established themselves as worldwide religions, trade became increasingly international, and new inventions, such as gunpowder and printing, began transforming the daily lives of people all around the globe.

Southern Africa
Bantu peoples
ironworkers
pp. 86–87

Southwest Africa
Khoisan hunter-
gatherers
pp. 86–87

MEDIEVAL PEOPLE AND PLACES
Each picture symbol on this world map relates to a medieval civilization, kingdom, culture, or race of people that you will find later on in the chapter. The page numbers next to each symbol tell you where you should look to find out about each one.

Hungary
Magyar nomads
pp. 62–63

Anatolia
Seljuk Turks
pp. 58–59

ASIA

Mongol China
Mongols
pp. 84–85

Korea
Koreans
pp. 72–73

Middle East
Byzantines
pp. 58–59

China
Chinese
pp. 70–71

Japan
Japanese
pp. 72–73

Arabia
Arabs
pp. 58–59

*Pacific
Ocean*

Mecca
Muslims
pp. 64–65

India
Hindus
pp. 68–69

Southeast Asia
Khmer people
pp. 74–75

Indian Ocean

Tahiti
Polynesians
pp. 76–77

AUSTRALIA

Aotearoa
(New Zealand)
Maori
pp. 76–77

LOCATOR MAP

You will find a diagram like this along with every map in the chapter. This allows you to see exactly which part of the world the main map is showing you.

KEY TO MAPS IN THIS CHAPTER

CHINA	Main region or country
Anatolia	Other region
■ NARA	Capital city
• Tikal	City, town, or village
Rhine	River, lake, or island
Himalayas	Ocean, sea, desert, or mountain range
– – – –	Empire boundary

A.D. 500–A.D. 1500

A.D. 500
527 Emperor Justinian rules eastern Roman Empire and regains territory lost to barbarian control
550 Slav peoples settle in eastern Europe
589 China reunited under Sui and Tang dynasties after long period of conflict

A.D. 600
600 Frankish kingdom becomes the most powerful state in western Europe
610 Eastern Roman Empire becomes the Byzantine Empire
622 Muhammad flees from Mecca to Medina: the birth of Islam
632 Death of Muhammad: rapid expansion of Islam
680 Islam split between Sunni and Shia Muslims

A.D. 700
711 Arabs invade Spain
732 Invading Arab army defeated by the Franks at Poitiers in France
750 Abbasids rule Muslim world from Baghdad
793 Vikings raid western Europe for the first time

A.D. 800
800 Charlemagne crowned Emperor of the Romans by the Pope in Rome
802 Creation of Khmer Empire in Cambodia, Southeast Asia
850 Chinese first use gunpowder in warfare
850 Chimú Empire founded in South America
868 World's first book printed in China

A.D. 900
936 Korea emerges as a unified nation
962 Holy Roman Empire created in Germany and Italy

A.D. 1000
c. 1000 Polynesian navigators reach New Zealand
1000 Easter Islanders begin carving stone statues
1000 Vikings settle in North America
1054 Final split between the Roman and Orthodox churches
1066 Norman conquest of England
1095 First Crusade to win back the Holy Land from Muslim control

A.D. 1100
1171 England first rules Ireland
1175 Muslim conquest of northern India begins
1192 Military shogun government rules Japan

A.D. 1200
c. 1200 Great Zimbabwe founded
1206 Genghis Khan begins Mongol conquests
1220 Inca Empire founded
1241 Mongols invade eastern Europe
1250 Kingdom of Benin founded in West Africa
1279 Mongols conquer China
1280 Ottoman Empire founded
1291 Muslims expel crusaders from Holy Land

A.D. 1300
1325 Aztec Empire founded
1337 England and France begin the Hundred Years' War
1347 Black Death starts to overwhelm Europe
1354 Ottomans begin conquest of the Balkans
1361 Timur creates new Mongol Empire in central Asia
1368 Ming dynasty ends Mongol rule of China

A.D. 1400
1415 Portuguese establish their first European colony in Africa
1432 Portuguese begin exploring West African coast

A.D. 1500

The medieval world:
How we know about the past

The medieval world came to an end more than 500 years ago, but evidence from the period is all around us today. Medieval towns and castles, churches and cathedrals, temples and mosques, books and documents, ships and wagons, artifacts and jewelry, as well as many other things, still survive. These remains enable us to build up a good picture of what it was like to live and work all those years ago, while examining them can reveal how things were constructed in medieval times. We can also use documents from the period to reenact festivals, battles, and famous events.

Medieval towns

Many of the walled towns built during the medieval period still survive. Owing to careful restoration in the 1800s, Carcassonne in France (shown below) is a perfect example. Its castle, walls, gatehouses, and street plan are almost untouched since the town was fortified during the 1200s.

Town walls are 4,200 feet (1,280m) long and include three gatehouses and 21 towers.

Documents

Medieval books and paper documents are rare. The Chinese had printing presses, but European monks and scholars had to write each book out by hand, and they added beautiful illustrations.

Reconstructions

Wooden artifacts can easily rot away. Luckily, this Viking ship from Oseberg in Norway was buried in boggy clay soil, which preserved most of its timbers. This allowed archaeologists to have the ship rebuilt to its original design.

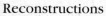

Excavations

This medieval ship (above) was found buried in a muddy river in Newport, Wales, U.K. Every piece of timber and scrap of evidence was examined to build up an almost complete picture of how wooden trading ships were designed and built during this period.

Artifacts

This limestone figure from Central America is of Chicomecoatl, the Mayan goddess of maize. It also shows us the clothing and jewelry that an ordinary Mayan woman of the period might have worn.

Reenactments

We cannot go back in time to fight a joust or win a battle, but we can reenact them using medieval accounts as our guide. These jousters are taking part in a medieval fair staged in Sarasota, Florida. Their costumes and weapons are modern re-creations of the medieval originals.

The fall of Roman Empire

The mighty Roman Empire had dominated Europe for more than 500 years, but during the A.D. 400s, it slowly fell apart, as waves of Germanic tribes from central Europe poured over its borders. The western half of the empire finally collapsed in A.D. 476, when the last western emperor, Augustulus, was overthrown. In its place came a series of tribal kingdoms that converted to Christianity and kept many of the old Roman institutions in place.

St. Patrick
In 432 St. Patrick arrived in Ireland to convert its people to Christianity.

Anglo-Saxons
Angles, Saxons, and Jutes from northern Germany and Denmark crossed the North Sea to settle in eastern Britain after 450.

Ireland

Britain

North Sea

Barbarians
There were many "barbarian" tribes in Germany, but most of them were helpful to the Romans.

Germany

Rhine

Gaul
Wooden houses

Sutton Hoo
Anglo-Saxon lords were buried in their ships surrounded by treasures such as this helmet from Sutton Hoo.

Alps

Theodoric
In 493 Theodoric, king of the Ostrogoths, conquered Rome and restored peace, keeping Roman civilization alive in Italy.

Buildings in Ravenna

• Ravenna

Kingdom of Odoacer

Atlantic Ocean

Ruined Roman villa

Suevic kingdom

Spain

Visigothic kingdom

WESTERN ROMAN EMPIRE

ROME

The Visigoths
The Visigoths came from the Balkans, and in 418 they settled in southwestern France as allies of Rome. They later conquered much of Spain.

Attacking Rome
Rome was ransacked by the Visigoths in 410 and then by the Vandals in 455.

Vandal kingdom

Carthage

North Africa

The Vandals
The Vandals from central Europe crossed over to North Africa and set up an independent kingdom in Carthage in 439.

Vandal pirates
Vandal pirates from North Africa attacked Roman ships in the Mediterranean, seizing valuable cargoes.

---- dotted line shows the extent of the Roman Empire in the A.D. 400s

The Slavs
No one knows where the Slavs came from, but during the 500s, they settled across eastern Europe, later converting to Christianity.

The Ostrogoths
The Ostrogoths settled in the Balkans and eventually conquered Italy itself. They often helped Rome against its enemies.

Balkans

Constantinople
The eastern empire was governed from Constantinople. The city's massive walls kept it free from attacks.

ube

■ CONSTANTINOPLE

Black Sea

EASTERN ROMAN EMPIRE

Anatolia

Athens

SASSANIAN EMPIRE

Mediterranean Sea

Arabs
The eastern borders of the Roman Empire were not threatened as often as those in the north, as the Arabs traded peacefully with the Romans. The Sassanian Persians, however, were a constant threat.

The legacy of Rome
The Roman Empire left behind many achievements. The Romans introduced the calendar of 365 days—with an extra day every four years—devised by Julius Caesar in 45 B.C. This system included the 12-month year, the seven-day week, and the names of our months. October is shown on this mosaic floor from the A.D. 200s. Other Roman legacies include the Catholic Church, the Latin language, a legal system, and a system of republican government that has been copied in modern France and the U.S.

0 — 500km
0 — 250 miles

A.D. 400–A.D. 700

A.D. 400
402 Capital of the western empire moves from Rome to the safer city of Ravenna
406 Vandals, Suevi, and Alans invade Gaul (France) and later Spain
410 Visigoths ransack Rome
418 Visigoths make peace with Rome and settle in Aquitaine (southwestern France)

429 Vandals cross from Spain to North Africa and conquer Carthage in 439
432 St. Patrick begins converting the Irish to Christianity

A.D. 450
450 Anglo-Saxons from northern Germany begin settling in Britain
455 Vandals ransack Rome

476 Odoacer, a barbarian general, removes the last western Roman emperor, Augustulus, from power and rules Italy

486 Clovis founds the Frankish kingdom in Gaul

493–526 Theodoric rules Ostrogothic kingdom in Italy

A.D. 500
507 Clovis drives the Visigoths out of Gaul and into Spain

527–565 Justinian rules eastern Roman Empire and reconquers much of the land lost to the barbarians

A.D. 550
550 Slavs settle in eastern Europe and the Balkans

570s Visigoths dominate most of Spain

A.D. 600
600 Frankish kingdom becomes the most powerful state in western Europe

626 Avar nomadic tribes threaten the eastern empire but fail to take Constantinople

639 After death of King Dagobert, a sequence of short-lived kings weakens the Frankish kingdom

A.D. 650

679 Pepin II leads the Frankish kingdom and expands Frankish power into Germany

A.D. 700

Byzantine architecture
The Byzantines developed a distinctive style of church architecture, using domes and mosaic walls. An example is the Basilica of St. Mark in Venice.

Missionaries
In 863 Byzantine missionaries, Saints Cyril and Methodius, set out to convert the pagan Slavs of eastern Europe to Christianity.

Frontier forts
Justinian built a series of forts along the Danube to protect his frontier against attacks by Slav raiders.

Craftsmen making a mosaic on a wall

•Venice

Ravenna •

Italy

Emperor Justinian
Justinian fought to regain Roman lands lost to the barbarians.

•Rome

Danube

Black Sea

Bulgaria

Byzantine priest

•Bari

Byzantine-style Christian church

Balathista•

Adrianople •

The Normans
In 1091 Norman knights from France conquered Byzantine lands in southern Italy and Sicily.

Mount Athos
Communities of religious men, such as the one on Mount Athos, sprang up across the Byzantine Empire.

Thessalonica•

Mount Athos

Constantinople
The Byzantine capital of Constantinople was founded in 324 by the Roman Emperor Constantine.

Nicaea •

Myriocephalum

Farmer taking a goat to the market

•Ephesus

Sicily

dotted line shows the extent of the Byzantine Empire in 1025

BYZANTINE EMPIRE

Crete

The Byzantine Empire

Despite the collapse of the western Roman Empire in A.D. 476, the eastern empire continued to prosper. During the reign of Justinian (527–565), it even managed to regain land that was lost to the barbarians. But the empire was threatened by enemies all along its lengthy borders, so Heraclius (reigned 610–641) completely restructured the empire and changed its official language from Latin to Greek. He created a new "Byzantine Empire"—named after its capital city, Byzantium—the old Greek name for Constantinople. This new empire survived against its many enemies until 1453, when Constantinople finally fell to the Ottoman Turks.

Mediterranean Sea

Muslim rule
Arab armies swept out of Arabia in 632, bringing their new religion, Islam. Islam replaced Christianity throughout the eastern half of the empire.

Egypt

Newly built mosque in Egypt

0		500km

| 0 | | 250 miles |

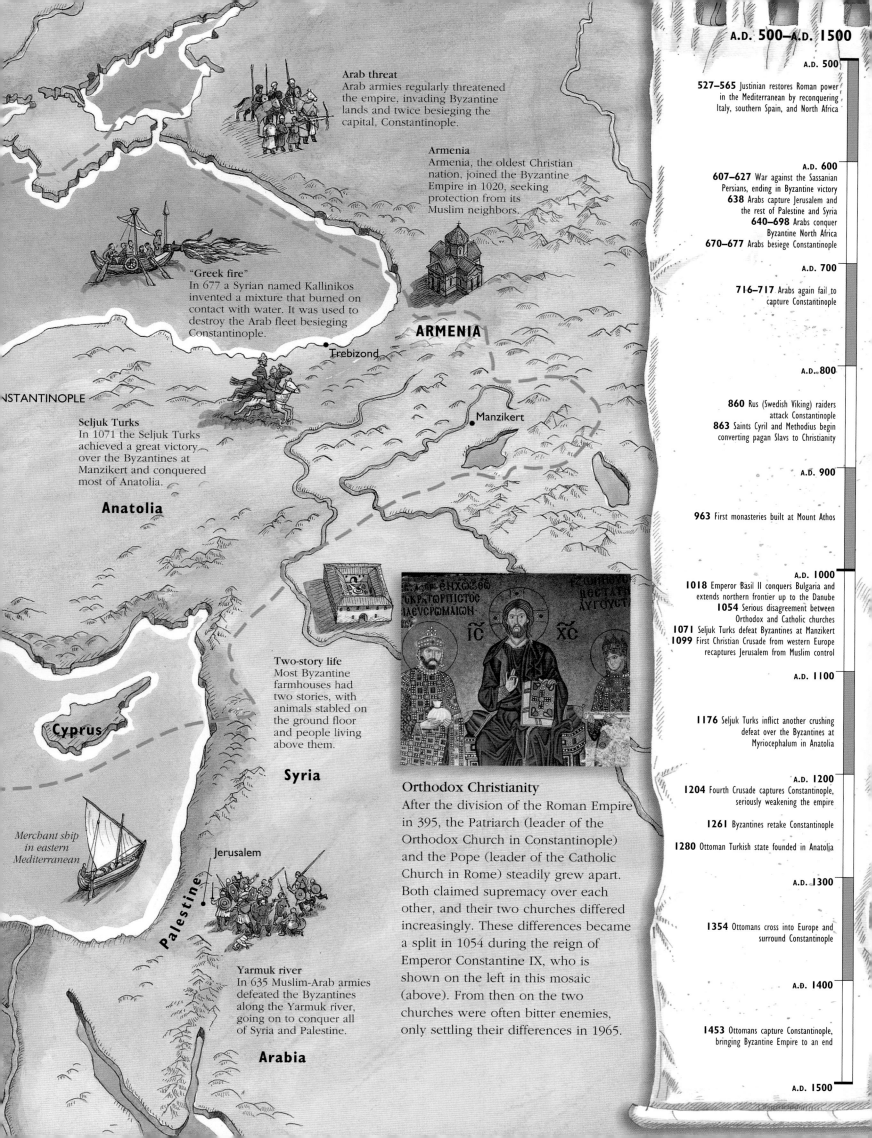

Arab threat
Arab armies regularly threatened the empire, invading Byzantine lands and twice besieging the capital, Constantinople.

Armenia
Armenia, the oldest Christian nation, joined the Byzantine Empire in 1020, seeking protection from its Muslim neighbors.

"Greek fire"
In 677 a Syrian named Kallinikos invented a mixture that burned on contact with water. It was used to destroy the Arab fleet besieging Constantinople.

ARMENIA

• Trebizond

NSTANTINOPLE

Seljuk Turks
In 1071 the Seljuk Turks achieved a great victory over the Byzantines at Manzikert and conquered most of Anatolia.

• Manzikert

Anatolia

Two-story life
Most Byzantine farmhouses had two stories, with animals stabled on the ground floor and people living above them.

Cyprus

Syria

Merchant ship in eastern Mediterranean

Jerusalem •

Palestine

Yarmuk river
In 635 Muslim-Arab armies defeated the Byzantines along the Yarmuk river, going on to conquer all of Syria and Palestine.

Arabia

Orthodox Christianity

After the division of the Roman Empire in 395, the Patriarch (leader of the Orthodox Church in Constantinople) and the Pope (leader of the Catholic Church in Rome) steadily grew apart. Both claimed supremacy over each other, and their two churches differed increasingly. These differences became a split in 1054 during the reign of Emperor Constantine IX, who is shown on the left in this mosaic (above). From then on the two churches were often bitter enemies, only settling their differences in 1965.

A.D. 500—A.D. 1500

A.D. 500

527–565 Justinian restores Roman power in the Mediterranean by reconquering Italy, southern Spain, and North Africa

A.D. 600

607–627 War against the Sassanian Persians, ending in Byzantine victory
638 Arabs capture Jerusalem and the rest of Palestine and Syria
640–698 Arabs conquer Byzantine North Africa
670–677 Arabs besiege Constantinople

A.D. 700

716–717 Arabs again fail to capture Constantinople

A.D. 800

860 Rus (Swedish Viking) raiders attack Constantinople
863 Saints Cyril and Methodius begin converting pagan Slavs to Christianity

A.D. 900

963 First monasteries built at Mount Athos

A.D. 1000

1018 Emperor Basil II conquers Bulgaria and extends northern frontier up to the Danube
1054 Serious disagreement between Orthodox and Catholic churches
1071 Seljuk Turks defeat Byzantines at Manzikert
1099 First Christian Crusade from western Europe recaptures Jerusalem from Muslim control

A.D. 1100

1176 Seljuk Turks inflict another crushing defeat over the Byzantines at Myriocephalum in Anatolia

A.D. 1200

1204 Fourth Crusade captures Constantinople, seriously weakening the empire

1261 Byzantines retake Constantinople

1280 Ottoman Turkish state founded in Anatolia

A.D. 1300

1354 Ottomans cross into Europe and surround Constantinople

A.D. 1400

1453 Ottomans capture Constantinople, bringing Byzantine Empire to an end

A.D. 1500

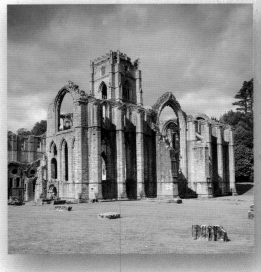

Monasteries

These are the remains of Fountains Abbey in Yorkshire, England—once part of a large monastic estate that was founded by 13 Benedictine monks in 1132. Monasteries were major centers of learning and scholarship across Europe, running schools to provide education for boys.

Pilgrimage

The pilgrimage was an important part of medieval Christianity. Both rich and poor walked to shrines, such as Canterbury in England; Santiago de Compostela in Spain; Rome; and even Jerusalem, in search of a miraculous cure or forgiveness for their sins. This stained-glass window from Canterbury cathedral shows pilgrims on their way to the shrine of St. Thomas à Becket.

Medieval Europe:
Christianity

Medieval Europe was entirely Christian, with the exception of southern Spain, and after the 1300s, the Balkans. In the west of Europe the Catholic Church played a major role in society, providing schools and hospitals and encouraging people to make pilgrimages to holy places or shrines containing relics of saints. The Catholic Church also dominated politics and owned large areas of land. The Pope, based in Rome, was the head of the Catholic Church. He was often more powerful than most emperors and kings, although disputes between him and these nonreligious leaders often led to bitter arguments and even war.

Christian education

The Christian Church played a major role in education across Europe, as priests and monks—such as those shown in this illuminated manuscript—were often the only people in the area who could read and write. Churches and cathedrals ran their own schools, and after the A.D. 1000s many cathedral schools set up universities to teach theology (the study of religious belief) and law.

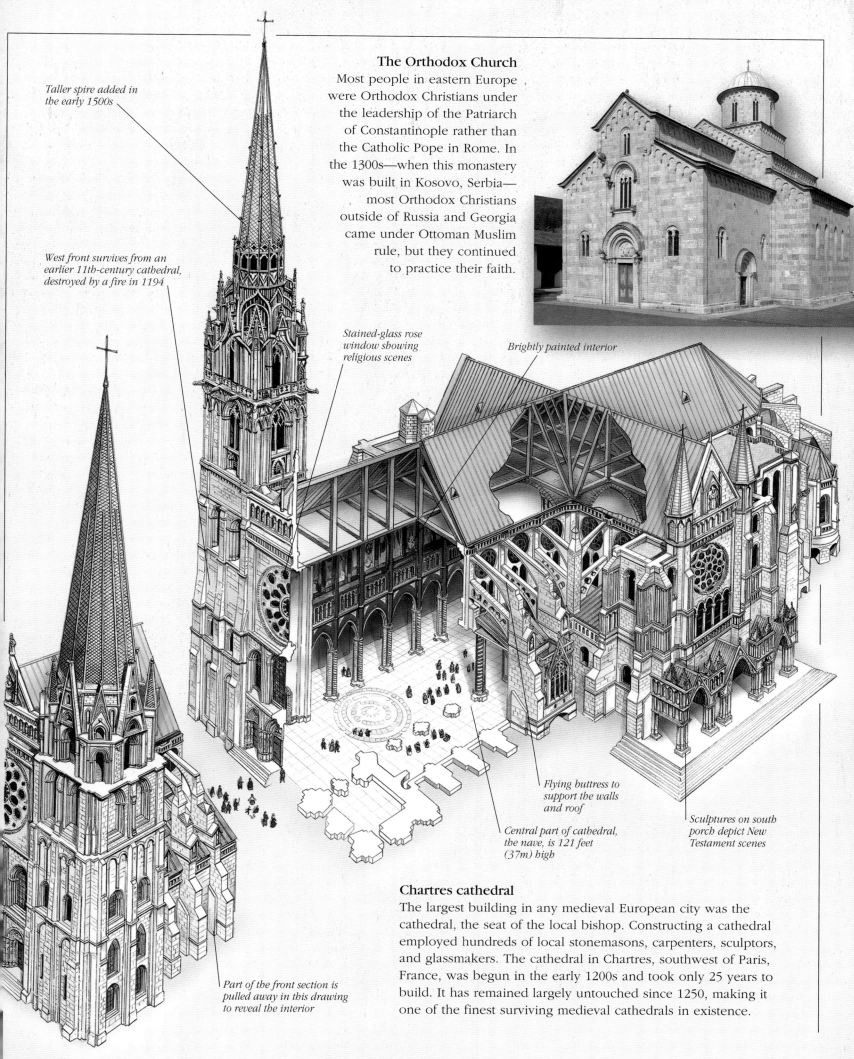

Taller spire added in the early 1500s

West front survives from an earlier 11th-century cathedral, destroyed by a fire in 1194

Stained-glass rose window showing religious scenes

Brightly painted interior

The Orthodox Church

Most people in eastern Europe were Orthodox Christians under the leadership of the Patriarch of Constantinople rather than the Catholic Pope in Rome. In the 1300s—when this monastery was built in Kosovo, Serbia—most Orthodox Christians outside of Russia and Georgia came under Ottoman Muslim rule, but they continued to practice their faith.

Flying buttress to support the walls and roof

Central part of cathedral, the nave, is 121 feet (37m) high

Sculptures on south porch depict New Testament scenes

Part of the front section is pulled away in this drawing to reveal the interior

Chartres cathedral

The largest building in any medieval European city was the cathedral, the seat of the local bishop. Constructing a cathedral employed hundreds of local stonemasons, carpenters, sculptors, and glassmakers. The cathedral in Chartres, southwest of Paris, France, was begun in the early 1200s and took only 25 years to build. It has remained largely untouched since 1250, making it one of the finest surviving medieval cathedrals in existence.

Charlemagne's Europe

In A.D. 711 Muslim armies from North Africa crossed into Europe and soon conquered Visigothic Spain. The Franks now ruled over the only surviving Germanic kingdom in Europe. Yet the Franks were weak because whenever a king died, it was their custom to divide up the kingdom among all the king's sons. So when Pepin III died in 768, his kingdom was divided between his sons Carloman and Charlemagne. Carloman died three years later, leaving Charlemagne in control. For 30 years, Charlemagne campaigned to extend his kingdom, establishing a new Roman Empire that covered much of western Europe.

0	500km
0	250 miles

Charlemagne's empire

Charlemagne governed his empire from his palace in Aachen (right). From there, he sent out a stream of orders and instructions that provided a model of how a good king should rule. He also set up systems of government for Europe that were to last for the next 700 years. Charlemagne could barely read or write, but he provided funds to support and encourage learning in his empire.

The Holy Roman Empire

On Christmas Day in 800, Charlemagne was crowned Emperor of the Romans by the Pope in Rome (above). He became a Christian successor to the emperors of ancient Rome. His empire broke up after his death, and in 911 the Saxon dynasty took power in East Francia (Germany). Otto I (ruled 936–973) expanded his kingdom by defeating the Magyars and the Slavs and by conquering Burgundy, Provence, and Italy. In 962 the Pope crowned Otto as Holy Roman Emperor.

Ireland

Viking wooden houses in Dublin

Wal

Offa's dyke
In the late 700s King Offa of Mercia built a huge dirt and timber rampart along his western boundary to keep out the hostile Welsh.

WESSE

Atlantic Ocean

Brittany

Poitiers
In 732 the leader of the Franks defeated a large Muslim army at Poitiers. From then on, the Muslims were in retreat in western Europe.

dotted line shows the extent of the Frankish kingdom in around 814

Charlemagne's royal seal

Covadonga

Trading ship

Christian church

Spain

Córdoba
Córdoba, the capital of Muslim Spain, was the biggest city in Europe during the time of Charlemagne, with a population of more than 100,000.

Córdoba

UMAYYAD CALIPHATE

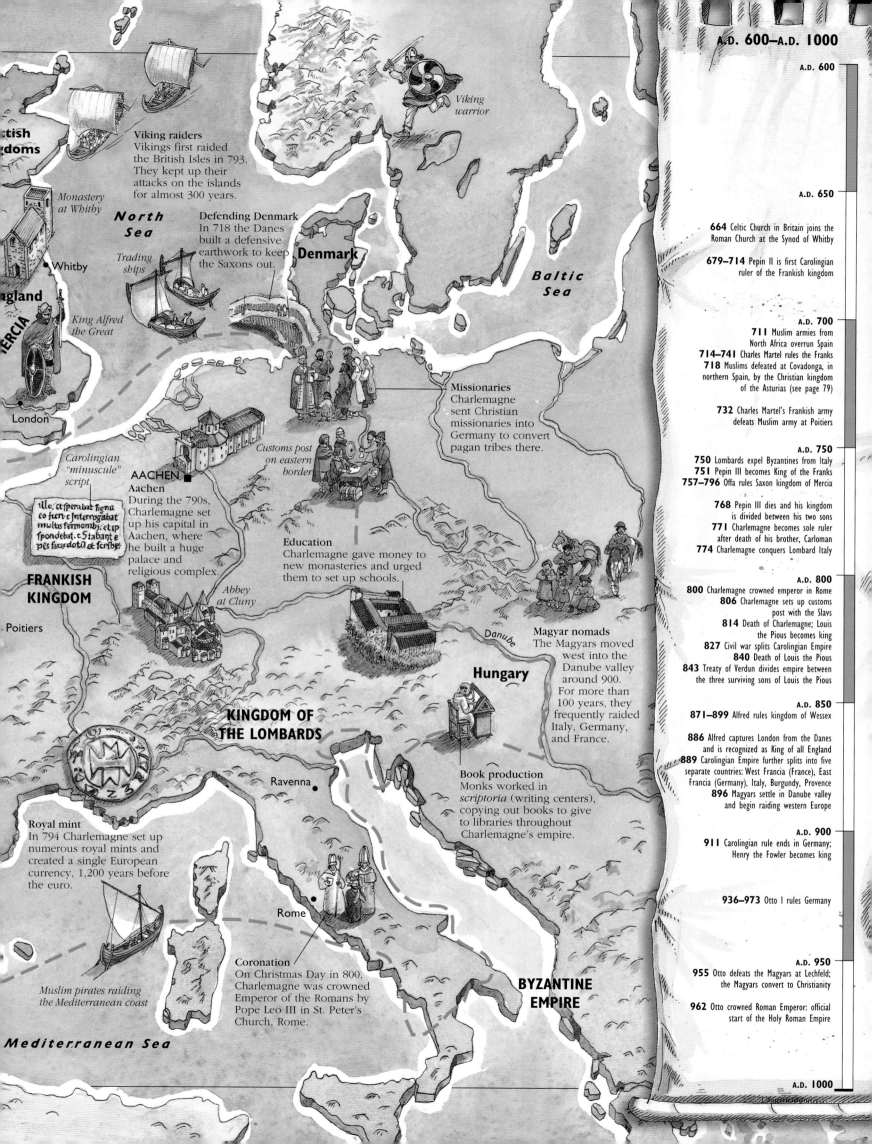

Viking raiders
Vikings first raided the British Isles in 793. They kept up their attacks on the islands for almost 300 years.

Viking warrior

Monastery at Whitby

North Sea

Defending Denmark
In 718 the Danes built a defensive earthwork to keep the Saxons out.

Trading ships

Denmark

Baltic Sea

• Whitby

England

MERCIA

King Alfred the Great

• London

Missionaries
Charlemagne sent Christian missionaries into Germany to convert pagan tribes there.

Carolingian "minuscule" script

illo. et sperabat figna eo fun e interrogabat multus sermonibz. et ip spondebat. e Stabant e pes sacerdotu et scribe

AACHEN
Aachen
During the 790s, Charlemagne set up his capital in Aachen, where he built a huge palace and religious complex.

Customs post on eastern border

Education
Charlemagne gave money to new monasteries and urged them to set up schools.

FRANKISH KINGDOM

Abbey at Cluny

• Poitiers

Danube

Magyar nomads
The Magyars moved west into the Danube valley around 900. For more than 100 years, they frequently raided Italy, Germany, and France.

Hungary

KINGDOM OF THE LOMBARDS

Book production
Monks worked in *scriptoria* (writing centers), copying out books to give to libraries throughout Charlemagne's empire.

Ravenna •

Royal mint
In 794 Charlemagne set up numerous royal mints and created a single European currency, 1,200 years before the euro.

Rome •

BYZANTINE EMPIRE

Muslim pirates raiding the Mediterranean coast

Coronation
On Christmas Day in 800, Charlemagne was crowned Emperor of the Romans by Pope Leo III in St. Peter's Church, Rome.

Mediterranean Sea

A.D. 600

A.D. 650

664 Celtic Church in Britain joins the Roman Church at the Synod of Whitby

679–714 Pepin II is first Carolingian ruler of the Frankish kingdom

A.D. 700

711 Muslim armies from North Africa overrun Spain
714–741 Charles Martel rules the Franks
718 Muslims defeated at Covadonga, in northern Spain, by the Christian kingdom of the Asturias (see page 79)

732 Charles Martel's Frankish army defeats Muslim army at Poitiers

A.D. 750

750 Lombards expel Byzantines from Italy
751 Pepin III becomes King of the Franks
757–796 Offa rules Saxon kingdom of Mercia

768 Pepin III dies and his kingdom is divided between his two sons
771 Charlemagne becomes sole ruler after death of his brother, Carloman
774 Charlemagne conquers Lombard Italy

A.D. 800

800 Charlemagne crowned emperor in Rome
806 Charlemagne sets up customs post with the Slavs
814 Death of Charlemagne; Louis the Pious becomes king
827 Civil war splits Carolingian Empire
840 Death of Louis the Pious
843 Treaty of Verdun divides empire between the three surviving sons of Louis the Pious

A.D. 850

871–899 Alfred rules kingdom of Wessex

886 Alfred captures London from the Danes and is recognized as King of all England
889 Carolingian Empire further splits into five separate countries: West Francia (France), East Francia (Germany), Italy, Burgundy, Provence
896 Magyars settle in Danube valley and begin raiding western Europe

A.D. 900

911 Carolingian rule ends in Germany; Henry the Fowler becomes king

936–973 Otto I rules Germany

A.D. 950

955 Otto defeats the Magyars at Lechfeld; the Magyars convert to Christianity

962 Otto crowned Roman Emperor; official start of the Holy Roman Empire

A.D. 1000

Battle of Poitiers
In 732 Arab armies invaded France, reaching as far north as Poitiers. There, they were defeated by a large Frankish army.

Poitiers

FRANKISH KINGDOM

Constantinople
Despite their many successes, the Arabs twice failed to capture Constantinople, the capital of the Byzantine Empire.

Constantinople

Anatolia

UMAYYAD CALIPHATE

Córdoba
From 756 to 1031 the Umayyads governed Spain from Córdoba, where they built a beautiful mosque. This mihrab from the mosque shows the direction of Mecca.

CÓRDOBA

Rome

Taurus Mountains

BYZANTINE EMPIRE

Syr

DAMAS

Carthage

IDRISID CALIPHATE

AGHLABID CALIPHATE

Palesti

Jerusa

Jerusalem
In 638 Arab armies captured Jerusalem and built the Dome of the Rock—the first major Islamic building outside Arabia.

Arabic
The Arab armies introduced a new language, Arabic, across their vast empire. Spoken Arabic varies from country to country, but written Arabic is the same everywhere.

Muslim raiders
Muslim pirates launched frequent raids across the Mediterranean, capturing Sicily, Sardinia, and other islands.

Libya

North Africa

Cairo

Egypt

Camel

Cairo
The Fatimid rulers of Egypt established a new city at Cairo in 969. It soon became one of the most important cities in the Arab world.

A Muslim praying toward Mecca

Felucca on the Nile river

The spread of Islam

In A.D. 610 Muhammad, a trader from Mecca in Arabia, began experiencing divine revelations that were later written down in the Koran, the Islamic holy book. By the time of his death in 632, the new religion of Islam dominated the Arabian peninsula. Arab armies then set out on a whirlwind campaign of conquest and conversion. They overwhelmed the Sassanian Empire of Persia and took Islam from the borders of India across Asia and North Africa into Spain and southern Europe. Islam brought political and religious unity to a vast region, but divisions soon opened up. Weakened by these divisions, the Islamic world lost some of its territory to Christian forces in Europe.

Baghdad
The Abbasids' capital of Baghdad became the center of the Islamic world in 763, a position it held for almost 200 years.

• Merv

Talas river
The Arab victory at the Talas river in 751 ended Chinese control over the peoples of central Asia and led to their conversion to Islam.

RMENIA

India

Battle of Karbala
Divisions inside Islam erupted at Karbala in 680, where Muhammad's grandson, Hussein, was killed.

Mosque with a tall minaret

Sind

...potamia

BAGHDAD

■

Karbala

Persia

Indus

Yemen

Bedouin tent in the desert

Arab dhow

Oman

Arabian Sea

Hijra
In 622 Muhammad and his followers fled from Mecca to Medina to escape persecution. This event—the *hijra*, or "flight"—marks the start of Islam.

Medina •

Arabia

Mecca
The pagan Kaaba shrine in Mecca was rededicated to Allah (God), by Muhammad, in 630. It is now the holiest site in Islam.

Mecca •

Armed Islam
Within 20 years of Muhammad's death, Arab armies had spread Islam from the boundary of India in the east to Libya in the west and threatened the Byzantine Empire in Europe.

| 0 | | 1,000km |
| 0 | | 500 miles |

Harvesting fruits

AKSUM

Governing Islam

The caliphs (successors) of Muhammad were both political and religious leaders. The first caliphs were elected, but in 661 the Umayyads set up a hereditary caliphate based in Damascus. By 715 the Umayyad government was the biggest the world had ever seen. In 750 the rival Abbasids took over. The Umayyads fled to Spain, while independent caliphates soon sprang up in North Africa. The Abbasids moved the capital to the new city of Baghdad, where they built many mosques—such as the impressive Al Kadhimiya, shown here.

A.D. 600

610 Muhammad experiences divine revelations
622 Muhammad flees Mecca; birth of Islam
630 Muhammad recaptures Mecca
632 Death of Muhammad
635 Arab armies defeat Byzantines at Yarmuk river, north of Jerusalem
640–698 Arabs conquer Byzantine North Africa
642 Arabs defeat Persian Sassanian Empire at Nehavend, east of Baghdad
661 Umayyads kill the caliph Ali and set up a dynastic (hereditary) caliphate; capital moves from Medina to Damascus
670–677 Arabs besiege Constantinople
680 Hussein, Ali's son, is killed by the Umayyads; Islam now splits into the minority Shia ("party of Ali") and the majority Sunnis ("tradition of Muhammad")

A.D. 700

711 Arab armies invade Spain
713 Arab armies cross Indus river into India
715 Islamic Umayyad caliphate is the largest empire the world has ever seen
716–717 Arabs again fail to capture Constantinople
732 Franks defeat Arab army at Poitiers in France
750 Abbasids seize control from Umayyads, who flee to Spain
751 Arabs defeat Chinese at the Talas river and begin converting the region to Islam
763 Muslim capital moves to Baghdad

786–809 Harun al-Rashid is caliph; Abbasid power at its peak
789 Idrisid emirs (Muslim rulers) rebel to set up caliphate in North Africa

A.D. 800

840–871 Muslim pirates establish permanent bases in France and southern Italy

868 Egypt and Palestine independent under Tulunid emirs
874 Saminid emirs of central Asia form an independent emirate

899 Major revolt against Abbasids breaks out in Arabia

A.D. 900

913 Buwayhids capture Persia

945 Buwayhids capture Baghdad and end Abbasid power

A.D. 1000

999–1030 Mahmud of Ghazni, an Afghan Muslim, invades northwest India

1038 Seljuk Turks from central Asia conquer Persia

1055 Seljuk Turks take Baghdad and become major force in Islamic world

A.D. 1100

The Arab world:
Islamic culture

In the centuries following the death of Muhammad and the Arab invasion of the Middle East, North Africa, and Spain, Muslim scientists, scholars, and engineers developed a culture that was unrivaled in the world at that time. They made huge advances in astronomy, medicine, and mathematics—giving the world algebra, trigonometry, and the decimal fraction—and translated many earlier Greek and Indian works into their own language, Arabic. They also developed a highly decorative architecture that made great use of landscape design and calligraphy (decorative writing).

Art and calligraphy

The Islamic faith discourages the depiction of Allah (God) and Muhammad. If Muslim artists do show Muhammad in books or paintings, they always cover his face with a veil. They also use beautiful calligraphy to write out and decorate the verses of the Koran, their holy book, as this 16th-century example shows.

Astronomy

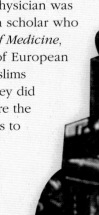

Muslim scholars were world leaders in astronomy, and most major Muslim cities had at least one observatory. Muslim astronomers also developed the astrolabe (left). This is a device that was used by navigators to measure the height of the Sun at noon so that they could work out their latitude—how far north or south they were.

Medicine

The most important Muslim physician was Ibn Sina (980–1037), a Persian scholar who wrote the 14-volume *Canon of Medicine*, which later formed the basis of European medicine until the 1600s. Muslims disapproved of surgery, but they did use it when necessary and were the first people to remove cataracts to restore eyesight.

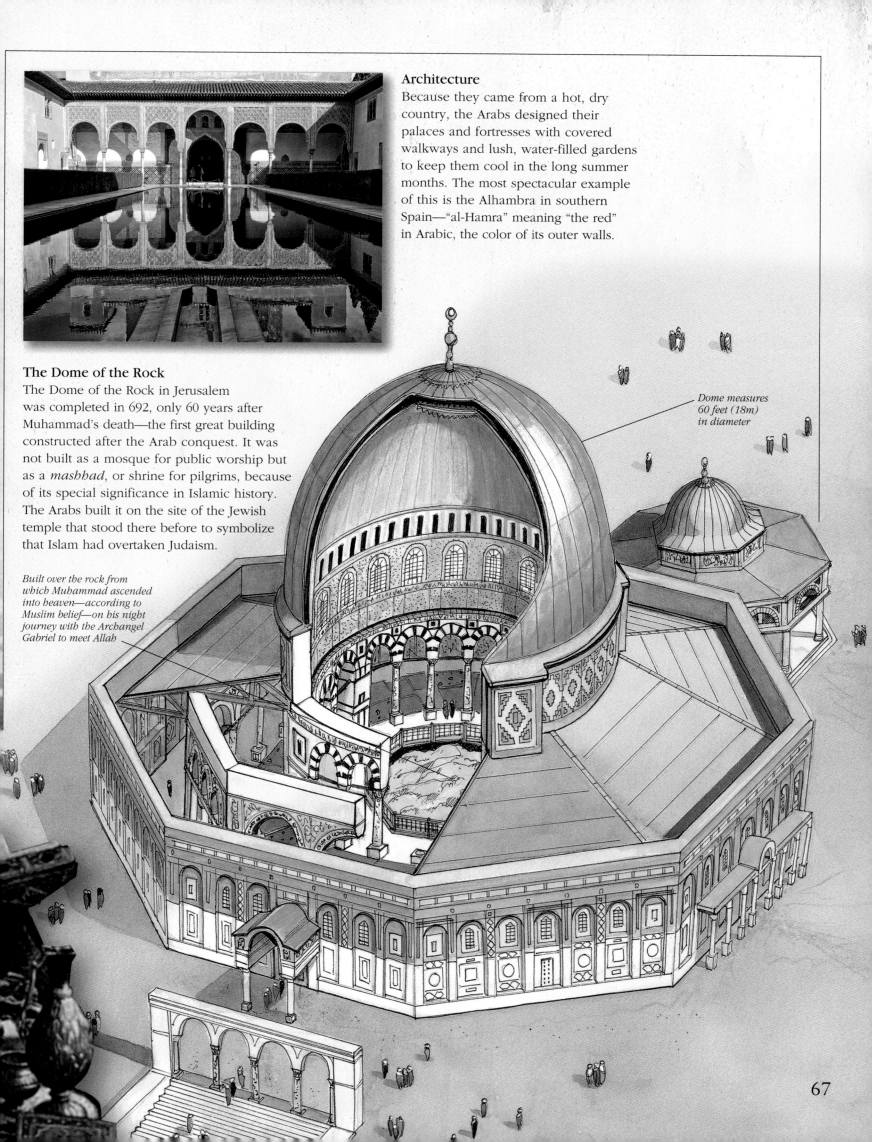

Architecture

Because they came from a hot, dry country, the Arabs designed their palaces and fortresses with covered walkways and lush, water-filled gardens to keep them cool in the long summer months. The most spectacular example of this is the Alhambra in southern Spain—"al-Hamra" meaning "the red" in Arabic, the color of its outer walls.

The Dome of the Rock

The Dome of the Rock in Jerusalem was completed in 692, only 60 years after Muhammad's death—the first great building constructed after the Arab conquest. It was not built as a mosque for public worship but as a *mashhad*, or shrine for pilgrims, because of its special significance in Islamic history. The Arabs built it on the site of the Jewish temple that stood there before to symbolize that Islam had overtaken Judaism.

Built over the rock from which Muhammad ascended into heaven—according to Muslim belief—on his night journey with the Archangel Gabriel to meet Allah

Dome measures 60 feet (18m) in diameter

Medieval India

The Hindu and Buddhist dominance of India came to an end in A.D. 711, when Arab armies brought Islam across the Indus river into western India. From then on, Muslims (followers of Islam) and Hindus waged a constant battle to control the Indian subcontinent. In 1175, in what is now Afghanistan, Muhammad of Ghur and his army broke through into the Ganges river valley in the north. This paved the way for more than 600 years of Muslim domination in India. After Muhammad's death in 1206, one of his most trusted generals, Qutb-ud-Din, established the independent Sultanate of Delhi. This sultanate controlled everything except the southern tip of the country by 1351.

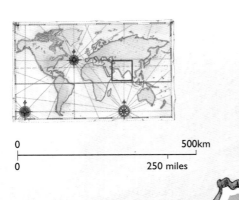

```
0                    500km
0          250 miles
```

Raiding party
The war-hungry Muslim ruler Mahmud of Ghazni launched 17 invasions of India after the year 999, raiding and destroying Hindu temples.

Ghur   Ghazni

Timur
In 1398 Timur the Lame, a Turkish nomad from central Asia, invaded India and ransacked Delhi.

Indus   **Multa**

Sind

Islam
Arab Muslims conquered Sind in 711, introducing Islam to the subcontinent. The new religion slowly spread east and south across India.

Making pots

Gujarat

Inshore fishing

Arabian

Sea

Hinduism
Although Muslims ruled much of India during this period, most people remained Hindu, with some keeping their Buddhist or Jain faith. Hindu kingdoms flourished in the south and east of the country, the Cholas of southern India even exporting Hinduism throughout Southeast Asia. This picture shows the 11th-century Brahmeswar Siva temple at Bhubaneswar, in eastern India. Hindu temples of this kind were incredibly wealthy, with large estates of land and donations from wealthy people eager to please the gods.

Punjab

Muslim Delhi
In 1206 Qutb-ud-Din set up the Sultanate of Delhi, an event that is commemorated by this minaret.

Tarain •

■ DELHI

Battles of Tarain
Victory by Muhammad of Ghur at the two battles of Tarain, in 1191–1192, led to the Muslim conquest of northern India.

Sowing crops

Kanauj •

Khajuraho •

Deccan

Muslim capital
The massive hilltop fortress and walled city of Daulatabad became the center of Muslim rule in India in 1339.

Ellore •
■ ULATABAD

• Manyakheta

Spinning cotton

■ VIJAYANAGAR

Vijayanagara
The city of Vijayanagara covered around 10 sq. mi. (25km²). During the 1300s, it was the capital of the largest Indian Hindu state.

Thanjavur •

Sri Lanka

A farmer plowing a field

Bihar

Nalanda •

Bengal

Bhubaneswar •

Ganges

The end of Buddhism
The destruction of the Buddhist university of Nalanda by the Ghurids, in 1199, marked the end of Buddhist influence in India.

Hindu pilgrims
Khajuraho was the most important religious site in the Chandella kingdom in northern India during the 800s to 1000s. Pilgrims flocked to the complex of 20 Hindu temples there.

Chinese trade
Fleets of Chinese junks traded with India. One took the Venetian traveler Marco Polo home via India in 1293.

Thanjavur
The Chola kingdom of southeast India became powerful in the 800s. Incredible riches filled the Hindu temples in Thanjavur, as wealthy Cholas gave gifts to the gods.

Bay of Bengal

Power of the Cholas
The Chola kingdom dominated southern India in the 900s and 1000s, sending out trading and raiding fleets as far afield as Bengal, Myanmar, and Indonesia.

A.D. 600
600s Gupta dynasty rules Bengal; rest of India ruled by regional Hindu kingdoms

A.D. 700
711 Arabs conquer Sind and later Multan, introducing Islam to India
720 Gupta dynasty loses power
730–1000 Powerful Hindu Gurjara-Pratiharas dynasty prevents Islam's advance into northern India

A.D. 800

850 Hindu Chola kingdom founded in southern India; Chola traders take Hinduism to Southeast Asia

A.D. 900

A.D. 1000
999–1030 Mahmud of Ghazni, a militant Afghan Muslim, raids India 17 times to plunder Hindu temples
1000 Cholas occupy Sri Lanka at height of their power
1030–1151 Ghaznavid emirs rule Sind, Multan, and Punjab; rest of country remains largely Hindu

A.D. 1100
1151 The governors of Ghur overthrow Ghaznavid Empire
1175 Muhammad of Ghur begins Muslim conquest of northern India
1191–1192 Ghurid victories at Tarain lead to Muslim conquest of northern India
1199 Buddhism declines in India after Ghurids destroy university at Nalanda

A.D. 1200
1206 After death of Muhammad of Ghur, Qutb-ud-Din sets up independent Muslim Sultanate of Delhi; Delhi becomes Muslim capital of India

A.D. 1300
1320–1413 Tughluk dynasty rules Delhi sultanate and expands south into the Deccan
1339 Muhammad ibn Tughluk, Sultan of Delhi, moves his capital south to Daulatabad in the Deccan
1351 Hindu kingdom of Vijayanagar begins to halt further Muslim expansion south
1398 Timur the Lame sacks Delhi, weakening Delhi sultanate's hold over northern India

A.D. 1400

1450 Sultanate of Delhi reduced to a small area around the city

1485 City of Vijayanagar rules most of southern India

A.D. 1500

Battle of the Talas river
In 751 China's expansion into central Asia was stopped by an Arab army at the Talas river. From then on, the peoples of this region became Muslim.

Gunpowder
The Chinese first used gunpowder in warfare around 850. By 969 they were using it to fire rockets at their enemies.

Altai Mountains

Tian Shan Mountains

Tingzhou

Kucha

Turfan

Karashahr

Kashgar

Taklimakan Desert

Gansu Corridor

Qilian Mountains

Hotan

Gilgit

The Silk Road
Caravans of camels bearing silk and other goods headed west along the Silk Road, an ancient trading route connecting China with western lands.

Frontier forts
The Chinese built forts around the Taklimakan Desert in the 650s to protect their western frontier from attacks.

Buddhist learning
The Buddhist monk Xuan Zang left for India in 629. He returned 16 years later with Buddhist texts that he had translated from Sanskrit.

these lines show the various routes taken along the Silk Road

TIBET

Himalayas

China

Since the end of the Han dynasty in A.D. 220, China had been divided among three warring kingdoms. In 589 Yang Jian reunited the country by force, and, as Emperor Wen, established the short-lived Sui dynasty. The succeeding Tang dynasty, which ruled from 618 to 907, introduced strong government and presided over great achievements in technology and the arts, especially poetry. The collapse of the Tang dynasty saw China fall apart again during the "Ten Kingdoms and Five Dynasties" period, but in 960 the country was reunited by the Song dynasty. The Song were the most effective governors in Chinese history, and under their rule, China became rich and its people grew prosperous.

Printing
During the 700s, the Chinese perfected the technique of printing words and pictures onto paper using engraved blocks of wood. This enabled them to print multiple copies of bank notes, documents, and then whole books. An example is the *Diamond Sutra* (above), the world's first printed book, which dates from 868. At first the printers had to engrave whole pages onto the blocks—but around the year 1000 they invented "movable type," allowing them to set individual earthenware letters to make up words and sentences.

Invasion from the north
In 1127 the Jurchen from Manchuria seized much of northern China, keeping control until the Mongols conquered their empire 100 years later.

The Great Wall
The Great Wall was regularly strengthened to keep out invaders from the north—but it did not always succeed in doing so!

G o b i   D e s e r t

Traders bringing furs from the north

• Beijing

Fields being irrigated

KOREA

Barges carrying grain and other products to Changan

The Grand Canal
In the early 600s the Chinese built a massive internal waterway linking Yue to Beijing via Luoyang.

Yellow River • Kaifeng
CHANGAN   Luoyang

Changan
The Tang capital of Changan had more than one million inhabitants in 750. It was the world's biggest city at that time.

Granaries
Wen, the first Sui emperor, had granaries built to store grain—in case of a food shortage.

Chang (Yangtze)

Growing rice

CHINA

Yue
Hangzhou

Government
Taizong, the second Tang emperor, created a strong, central administration and introduced a tough entrance exam for new public servants.

Oxen being used to plow fields

Porcelain
The first true porcelain was made in eastern China during the Tang period. In the West we call this pottery "china."

Typical Chinese house

Tea
Buddhist monks brought tea bushes into China from the lower slopes of the Himalayas in India. Tea soon became a national drink.

Printing block for making books and documents

Guangzhou

Death of an emperor
The last Song emperor drowned in a naval battle with the Mongols off the island of Yashan, near Guangzhou, in 1279.

A.D. 500

589 General Yang Jian reunites China, and as Emperor Wen, founds Sui dynasty

A.D. 600
604–617 Wen's successor, Yang, tries to conquer Korea and fails; peasants revolt against him
606–609 Grand Canal is constructed
617 Li Yuan captures Sui capital of Luoyang
618 Li Yuan becomes first Tang emperor, as Gaozu
626 Gaozu deposed (removed from power) by his son Taizong, one of China's most capable rulers

640–659 Chinese expand into central Asia

A.D. 700
700s Block printing is invented

751 Arab victory over Chinese at Talas river ends Chinese control of central Asia

791 Tibetans seize western China after their military victory at Tingzhou

A.D. 800

825 Chamber locks first installed on Chinese canals

c. 850 Gunpowder first used in warfare

859–884 Peasant revolts weaken Tang government

A.D. 900
907 Tang Empire collapses
907–960 China divided between the Five Dynasties state and the Ten Kingdoms

960 Song Taizu becomes emperor of the Five Dynasties and begins reuniting China
979 Song Taizu's brother Song Taizong reunites China and founds Song dynasty; start of Northern Song period

A.D. 1000
c. 1000 Printing by movable type invented

1090 Water-driven mechanical clock constructed for Song court

A.D. 1100
1117–1124 Jurchen people of Manchuria conquer Liao state north of China and set up Jin Empire
1127 Jin invade and capture Song capital of Kaifeng; Song retreat south and establish new capital at Hangzhou— start of Southern Song period

1150 Chinese navigators begin using magnetic compass

A.D. 1200
1200 Chinese build ships with watertight bulkheads to make them safer at sea
1200 Water-powered textile machinery first used
1226 Mongols overrun western China
1234 Mongols conquer northern China and begin attacking the Southern Song Empire

1279 Mongols conquer Southern Song Empire

A.D. 1300

Japan and Korea

The histories of Korea and Japan are both entangled with that of their powerful neighbor, China. The Korean kingdom of Silla managed to throw the Chinese off the Korean peninsula in A.D. 676 and eventually unify the country under the ruling Koryo dynasty by 936. Both Korea and Japan tried to create strong, centralized states—as China had done—but in Japan powerful families undermined the authority of the emperor. One such family, the Fujiwaras, effectively became the rulers of the country in 858. However, as the emperor withdrew from public life, rival warlords and samurai (warrior knights) fought each other for control.

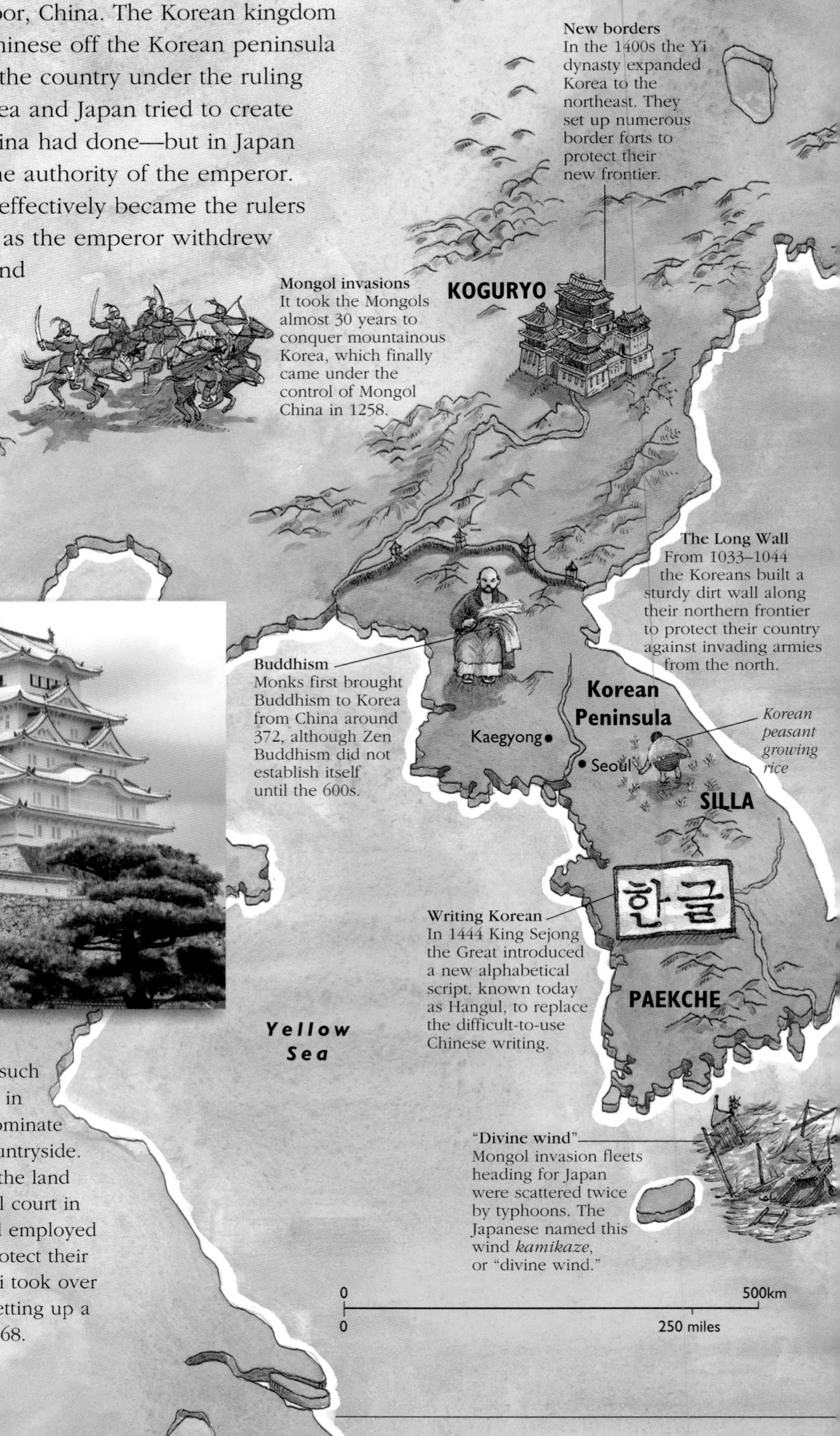

New borders
In the 1400s the Yi dynasty expanded Korea to the northeast. They set up numerous border forts to protect their new frontier.

KOGURYO

Mongol invasions
It took the Mongols almost 30 years to conquer mountainous Korea, which finally came under the control of Mongol China in 1258.

The Long Wall
From 1033–1044 the Koreans built a sturdy dirt wall along their northern frontier to protect their country against invading armies from the north.

Buddhism
Monks first brought Buddhism to Korea from China around 372, although Zen Buddhism did not establish itself until the 600s.

Korean Peninsula

Kaegyong●

● Seoul

Korean peasant growing rice

SILLA

Writing Korean
In 1444 King Sejong the Great introduced a new alphabetical script, known today as Hangul, to replace the difficult-to-use Chinese writing.

한글

PAEKCHE

Yellow Sea

Medieval Japan
Powerful Japanese lords built castles—such as the 14th-century White Heron castle in Himeji, shown here—from which to dominate and often terrorize the surrounding countryside. These lords became the real power in the land after the emperor withdrew to his royal court in 794. They had huge private estates and employed private armies of samurai knights to protect their interests. During the 1100s, the samurai took over in Japan, seizing control in 1192 and setting up a military dictatorship that lasted until 1868.

"Divine wind"
Mongol invasion fleets heading for Japan were scattered twice by typhoons. The Japanese named this wind *kamikaze*, or "divine wind."

0 ———————————— 500km

0 ———————————— 250 miles

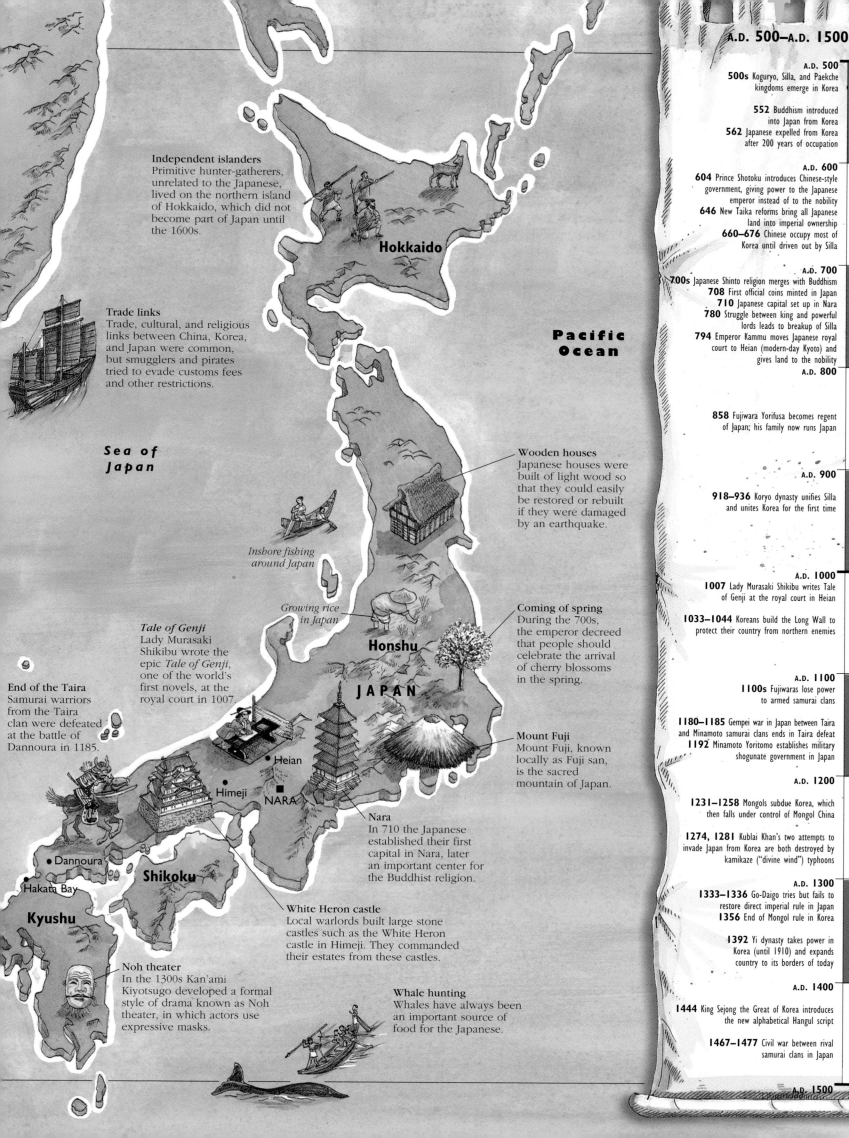

Independent islanders
Primitive hunter-gatherers, unrelated to the Japanese, lived on the northern island of Hokkaido, which did not become part of Japan until the 1600s.

Hokkaido

Pacific Ocean

Trade links
Trade, cultural, and religious links between China, Korea, and Japan were common, but smugglers and pirates tried to evade customs fees and other restrictions.

Sea of Japan

Inshore fishing around Japan

Wooden houses
Japanese houses were built of light wood so that they could easily be restored or rebuilt if they were damaged by an earthquake.

Growing rice in Japan

Honshu

JAPAN

Tale of Genji
Lady Murasaki Shikibu wrote the epic *Tale of Genji*, one of the world's first novels, at the royal court in 1007.

End of the Taira
Samurai warriors from the Taira clan were defeated at the battle of Dannoura in 1185.

Coming of spring
During the 700s, the emperor decreed that people should celebrate the arrival of cherry blossoms in the spring.

• Heian

• Himeji

■ **NARA**

Mount Fuji
Mount Fuji, known locally as Fuji san, is the sacred mountain of Japan.

Nara
In 710 the Japanese established their first capital in Nara, later an important center for the Buddhist religion.

• Dannoura

Shikoku

• Hakata Bay

Kyushu

White Heron castle
Local warlords built large stone castles such as the White Heron castle in Himeji. They commanded their estates from these castles.

Noh theater
In the 1300s Kan'ami Kiyotsugo developed a formal style of drama known as Noh theater, in which actors use expressive masks.

Whale hunting
Whales have always been an important source of food for the Japanese.

A.D. 500
500s Koguryo, Silla, and Paekche kingdoms emerge in Korea
552 Buddhism introduced into Japan from Korea
562 Japanese expelled from Korea after 200 years of occupation
A.D. 600
604 Prince Shotoku introduces Chinese-style government, giving power to the Japanese emperor instead of to the nobility
646 New Taika reforms bring all Japanese land into imperial ownership
660–676 Chinese occupy most of Korea until driven out by Silla
A.D. 700
700s Japanese Shinto religion merges with Buddhism
708 First official coins minted in Japan
710 Japanese capital set up in Nara
780 Struggle between king and powerful lords leads to breakup of Silla
794 Emperor Kammu moves Japanese royal court to Heian (modern-day Kyoto) and gives land to the nobility
A.D. 800
858 Fujiwara Yorifusa becomes regent of Japan; his family now runs Japan
A.D. 900
918–936 Koryo dynasty unifies Silla and unites Korea for the first time
A.D. 1000
1007 Lady Murasaki Shikibu writes Tale of Genji at the royal court in Heian
1033–1044 Koreans build the Long Wall to protect their country from northern enemies
A.D. 1100
1100s Fujiwaras lose power to armed samurai clans
1180–1185 Gempei war in Japan between Taira and Minamoto samurai clans ends in Taira defeat
1192 Minamoto Yoritomo establishes military shogunate government in Japan
A.D. 1200
1231–1258 Mongols subdue Korea, which then falls under control of Mongol China
1274, 1281 Kublai Khan's two attempts to invade Japan from Korea are both destroyed by kamikaze ("divine wind") typhoons
A.D. 1300
1333–1336 Go-Daigo tries but fails to restore direct imperial rule in Japan
1356 End of Mongol rule in Korea
1392 Yi dynasty takes power in Korea (until 1910) and expands country to its borders of today
A.D. 1400
1444 King Sejong the Great of Korea introduces the new alphabetical Hangul script
1467–1477 Civil war between rival samurai clans in Japan
A.D. 1500

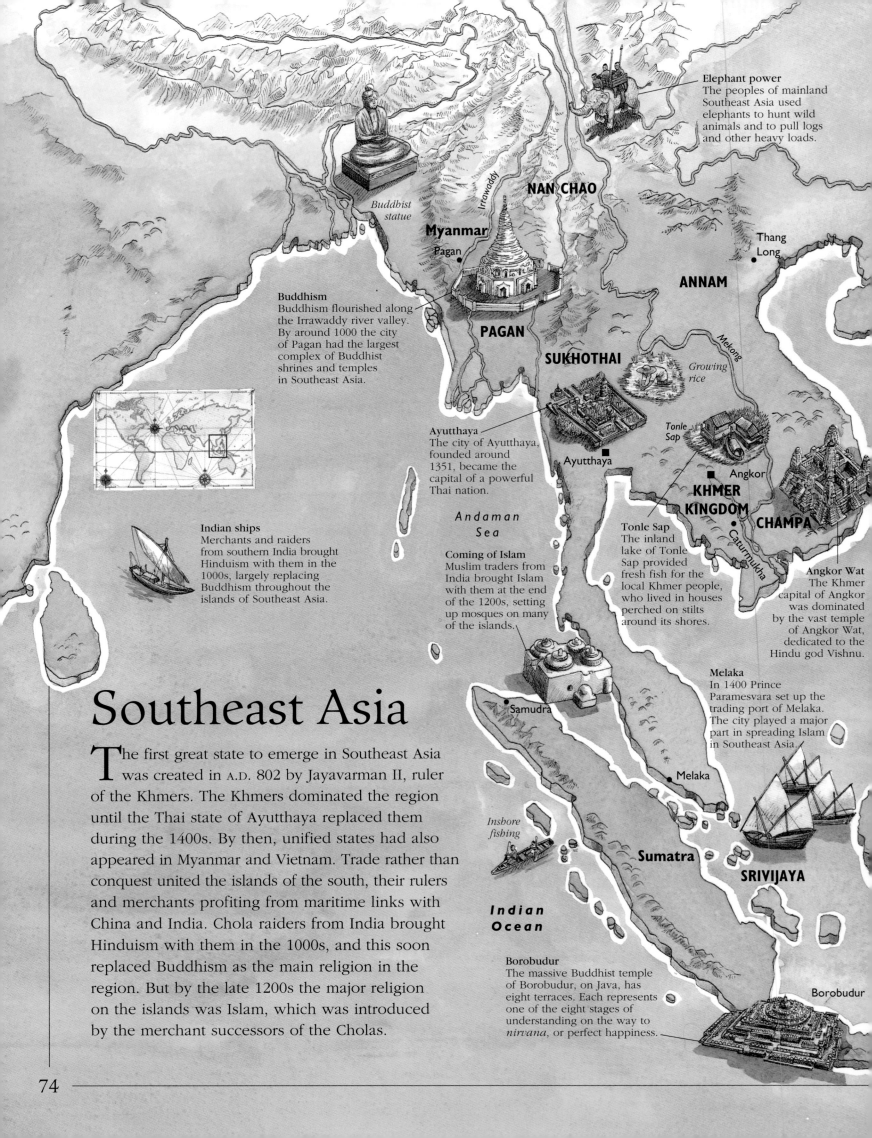

Elephant power
The peoples of mainland Southeast Asia used elephants to hunt wild animals and to pull logs and other heavy loads.

Buddhist statue

NAN CHAO

Myanmar
Pagan

Irrawaddy

Thang Long

ANNAM

PAGAN

Buddhism
Buddhism flourished along the Irrawaddy river valley. By around 1000 the city of Pagan had the largest complex of Buddhist shrines and temples in Southeast Asia.

SUKHOTHAI

Growing rice

Mekong

Tonle Sap

Ayutthaya
The city of Ayutthaya, founded around 1351, became the capital of a powerful Thai nation.

Ayutthaya

Angkor

KHMER KINGDOM

CHAMPA

Andaman Sea

Indian ships
Merchants and raiders from southern India brought Hinduism with them in the 1000s, largely replacing Buddhism throughout the islands of Southeast Asia.

Coming of Islam
Muslim traders from India brought Islam with them at the end of the 1200s, setting up mosques on many of the islands.

Tonle Sap
The inland lake of Tonle Sap provided fresh fish for the local Khmer people, who lived in houses perched on stilts around its shores.

Caturmukha

Angkor Wat
The Khmer capital of Angkor was dominated by the vast temple of Angkor Wat, dedicated to the Hindu god Vishnu.

Melaka
In 1400 Prince Paramesvara set up the trading port of Melaka. The city played a major part in spreading Islam in Southeast Asia.

Samudra

Southeast Asia

The first great state to emerge in Southeast Asia was created in A.D. 802 by Jayavarman II, ruler of the Khmers. The Khmers dominated the region until the Thai state of Ayutthaya replaced them during the 1400s. By then, unified states had also appeared in Myanmar and Vietnam. Trade rather than conquest united the islands of the south, their rulers and merchants profiting from maritime links with China and India. Chola raiders from India brought Hinduism with them in the 1000s, and this soon replaced Buddhism as the main religion in the region. But by the late 1200s the major religion on the islands was Islam, which was introduced by the merchant successors of the Cholas.

Melaka

Inshore fishing

Sumatra

SRIVIJAYA

Indian Ocean

Borobudur
The massive Buddhist temple of Borobudur, on Java, has eight terraces. Each represents one of the eight stages of understanding on the way to *nirvana*, or perfect happiness.

Borobudur

CHINA

South China Sea

Mongol ships
During the 1200s, the Mongols attacked the Burmese and Thai states and even sent an invasion fleet south to Java in 1292–1293.

Chinese trading junks
The Ming dynasty of China encouraged trade with Southeast Asia. Fleets of junks carried spices and other precious goods.

Brunei

Borneo

Indigenous peoples

The Khmers

The Khmer people lived in the Mekong river valley, establishing their first unified nation around A.D. 400. In 802 Jayavarman II, a minor king, proclaimed himself *devaraja* ("god-king") and ruled all the Khmer peoples from his capital of Angkor. The Khmers had strong trading links with India, so they adopted the Hindu religion and Indian styles of architecture. In 1113 Suryavarman II began building the massive temple complex of Angkor Wat (shown above) outside the capital.

Java   **Bali**

0 ———— 1,000km

0 ———— 500 miles

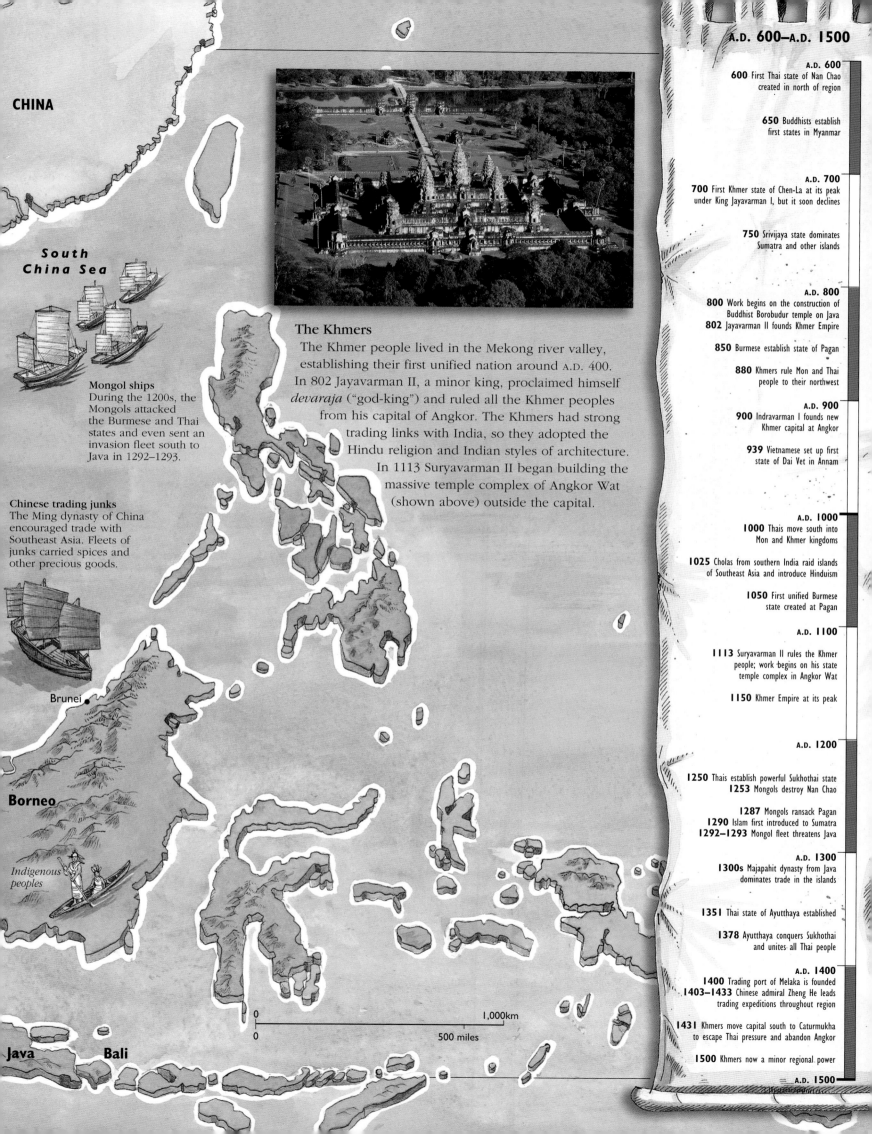

A.D. 600–A.D. 1500

A.D. 600

600 First Thai state of Nan Chao created in north of region

650 Buddhists establish first states in Myanmar

A.D. 700

700 First Khmer state of Chen-La at its peak under King Jayavarman I, but it soon declines

750 Srivijaya state dominates Sumatra and other islands

A.D. 800

800 Work begins on the construction of Buddhist Borobudur temple on Java
802 Jayavarman II founds Khmer Empire

850 Burmese establish state of Pagan

880 Khmers rule Mon and Thai people to their northwest

A.D. 900

900 Indravarman I founds new Khmer capital at Angkor

939 Vietnamese set up first state of Dai Vet in Annam

A.D. 1000

1000 Thais move south into Mon and Khmer kingdoms

1025 Cholas from southern India raid islands of Southeast Asia and introduce Hinduism

1050 First unified Burmese state created at Pagan

A.D. 1100

1113 Suryavarman II rules the Khmer people; work begins on his state temple complex in Angkor Wat

1150 Khmer Empire at its peak

A.D. 1200

1250 Thais establish powerful Sukhothai state
1253 Mongols destroy Nan Chao

1287 Mongols ransack Pagan
1290 Islam first introduced to Sumatra
1292–1293 Mongol fleet threatens Java

A.D. 1300

1300s Majapahit dynasty from Java dominates trade in the islands

1351 Thai state of Ayutthaya established

1378 Ayutthaya conquers Sukhothai and unites all Thai people

A.D. 1400

1400 Trading port of Melaka is founded
1403–1433 Chinese admiral Zheng He leads trading expeditions throughout region

1431 Khmers move capital south to Caturmukha to escape Thai pressure and abandon Angkor

1500 Khmers now a minor regional power

A.D. 1500

The Pacific

For more than 1,000 years, intrepid Polynesian navigators from Tahiti, and elsewhere in the central Pacific Ocean, had sailed out to colonize the more remote islands. By around A.D. 1250 to 1300 they had reached Aotearoa, which we now call New Zealand. Its two large islands were far colder and wetter than their homelands farther north, and they had to learn to cultivate new crops and build better shelters. They hunted the moa, a large flightless bird, for its meat and grew sweet potatoes and other crops. On many of the Pacific islands, the Polynesians built ceremonial platforms out of coral, called *marae*, where their priests conducted religious and social ceremonies.

South Pacific Ocean

Hawaii

Heiau
The *heiau* of Hawaii are very similar to the *marae* found on other Polynesian islands. They had raised platforms on which the priests stood to conduct religious ceremonies.

Line Islands

Basket weaving
Women wove baskets, bowls, and other items from the leaves of the coconut palm.

Atoll fishing
Throughout the region, Polynesians caught fish by standing on the semisubmerged coral atolls and attacking fish with spears.

Tuvalu

Society Islands

Samoa

Thatched home

Cook Islands

Fiji

Tonga

Fishing equipment
Fishermen carved pearl shells to make hooks. They twisted coconut fibers to create lines and nets.

Hillside terraces
On hilly islands, such as Hawaii and the Cook Islands, farmers built terraces on the steep hillsides in which to grow crops such as taro and other root vegetables.

Musical instruments

Kermadec

Tasman Sea

Combat
Maori warriors fought each other with spears or clubs made of whalebone or greenstone, a type of jade.

Inshore fishing
Fishermen caught their fish from a simple canoe stabilized by a special frame called an outrigger.

Sails being made from palm leaves

Oceangoing canoe
The Polynesians traveled thousands of miles in twin-hulled canoes. These canoes could carry up to 200 people as well as all their supplies for the long voyage.

Maori tattoos
A Maori chief, or *rangatiri*, had his face tattooed as a mark of his importance. His clothes were made out of flax and kiwi feathers.

Maori warrior hunting a moa

Aotearoa

Chatham Islands

A.D. 500
by **500** Polynesians have reached the Hawaiian Islands, their most northerly settlement in the Pacific

A.D. 600
600 Ceremonial marae, or platforms, common throughout the Pacific islands

A.D. 700
700 Rapa Nui peoples begin to build ceremonial ahu, or platforms

A.D. 800

A.D. 900
c. **900** Polynesians settle in remote Pitcairn Islands

A.D. 1000
1000 Rapa Nui peoples begin carving giant statues

A.D. 1100

A.D. 1200
1200 Tribal chiefdoms develop throughout Polynesia
1250 Polynesians begin settling in Aotearoa (New Zealand)

A.D. 1300

A.D. 1400
1400 Polynesians reach Chatham Islands, their last settlement in the Pacific

c. **1500** Conflict between rival Maori tribes leads to construction of pas (fortified settlements) in Aotearoa

A.D. 1500

Rapa Nui

Polynesian navigators reached the remote Rapa Nui (Easter Island) in the eastern Pacific in around A.D. 300. In around A.D. 1000 the 7,000 or so inhabitants of the island began to carve huge stone statues in the island's three main quarries. They used hammers made out of basalt rock because they had no iron. Once they were finished, the Polynesians hauled these massive statues across the island on wooden sleds, using palm trunks as levers and rollers to help them, and erected the statues on platforms in their ceremonial *ahu*—the equivalent of the *marae* platforms that were found elsewhere in the Pacific.

Leaf plates
Polynesians lived off seafood, yams, and fruits, eating their food from plates made of leaves.

Marquesas Islands

Tahiti

Marae
A *marae* was used for religious and ceremonial purposes. It consisted of a flat court paved with coral and a series of raised platforms. Upright slabs marked where the priests and officials stood.

Rope being made from coconut palm fibers

Pitcairn Islands

Outrigger canoe

Island statues
Rapa Nui peoples carved and erected more than 1,000 stone statues—probably to honor their ancestors. Some of these statues had inlaid eyes of white coral and red obsidian, a dark volcanic glass.

Rapa Nui (Easter Island)

South Pacific Ocean

Humpback whale

```
0                              2,000km
0                    1,000 miles
```

Greenland

Greenland
Norsemen set up colonies along the coast of Greenland. To survive in the harsh climate, they farmed sheep and cattle and traded furs and other items with the local Inuit people.

Figure of a Viking god

Local houses
Viking settlers used local materials to build houses—stone and turf in Iceland and Scotland, where wood was scarce, and timber in woodland areas such as England.

Iceland

Kingigtorssuaq
Sandnes

Norse people

Ivigtut
Brattahlid

Herjolfsnes

Atlantic

Ocean

L'Anse aux Meadows
Norsemen from Greenland were the first Europeans to reach the Americas, setting up a small settlement in Vinland (Newfoundland) around the year 1000.

Markland

L'Anse aux Meadows

Vinland

The Vikings

In 793 Norsemen launched an attack on the monastery of Lindisfarne, off the east coast of England, in search of booty. Further raids followed, terrorizing coastal regions of western Europe for more than 200 years. At first the Vikings—as these Norsemen, Danes, and Swedes are known—went in search of plunder, but later they took large armies abroad to conquer new lands. Yet the Vikings were not just robbers. They were also skilled navigators capable of crossing the North Atlantic and settling in newly discovered lands or sailing down the rivers of Russia in search of new markets. Their threat ended in the 1000s as their leaders became Christian and Denmark and Norway emerged as unified nations.

Viking religion

The Vikings believed in many different gods and goddesses. The main three were Odin, god of war and wisdom; Thor, god of thunder and patron of peasants and warriors; and Freyr, god of fertility and birth. This memorial stone (left) depicts a scene from the saga of Thor. According to this religion, soldiers who died in battle lived in Valhalla, the Viking heaven, where they held great feasts and celebrations. Valkyries (female warriors) searched the battlefields for dead heroes who could join the gods.

Rune stones
The Vikings celebrated battles and heroes by erecting stones that were carved with pictures and words in their runic alphabet.

Funeral ships
Viking chieftains were buried in their ships with all they would need for the afterlife. Some ships were covered with mounds of dirt.

Sailing to Iceland
Between 870 and 930, more than 10,000 Norsemen made the seven-day crossing of the North Atlantic to settle in Iceland.

Woolly sheep

Viking log home

Longhorn cow

Gotland
Paviken in Gotland was the major Viking commercial center in the Baltic, trading amber and furs for silks, spices, and silver from as far away as Constantinople and Baghdad.

Norway

Sweden

Novgorod

Gotland

Silver brooch

Baltic Sea

Smolensk

Rus traders
Swedish traders sailed down the Dnieper and Volga rivers to the Black and Caspian seas. The locals called these Vikings "Rus."

Scotland

Lindisfarne monastery raided by Vikings

g port blin

Lindisfarne

York

England

Danelaw

Dublin

Wales

Wessex

North Sea

Denmark

Hamburg

Viking forts
During the 980s, King Harald Bluetooth built four huge circular forts in Denmark.

Kyiv

Viking trade
Vikings erected rune stones along their trade routes, which covered a wide area. Arab silver coins have been found in Sweden.

Louvain

Rhine

CAROLINGIAN EMPIRE

Rouen

Normans
In 911 the French king allowed Danes to settle around Rouen in France.

Nantes

Loire

Viking warriors

Arles

Pisa

Black Sea

Viking sword

Constantinople

Santiago de Compostela

KINGDOM OF THE STURIAS AND LEÓN

UMAYYAD EMIRATE

Narbonne

sbon

Seville

arve

IDRISID CALIPHATE

Plunder
Vikings raided Mediterranean ports for booty, sailing up the rivers to attack inland towns.

North Africa

BYZANTINE EMPIRE

Mediterranean Sea

0   1,000km

0   500 miles

A.D. 700

A.D. 750

793 Norse raiders attack Lindisfarne monastery on coast of England, the first of many raids against the British Isles
799 First Norse raids on Frankish coast; Charlemagne sets up coastal defenses to protect his empire

A.D. 800

830s Start of large-scale raids against British Isles and Carolingian Empire

841 Norsemen establish a trading base in Dublin
845 The Franks buy off the raiders by paying them Danegeld (protection money)

A.D. 850

859–862 Viking raiders attack Mediterranean ports
862 Rus create first Russian state around Novgorod
865 Danish Great Army invades England
870 Norsemen settle in Iceland

878 Alfred, King of Wessex, defeats Danes and restricts them to the eastern Danelaw region of Britain

A.D. 900

911 Charles the Simple of France allows Danes to settle around Rouen, leading to the creation of Normandy

A.D. 950

954 Viking kingdom of York falls to English king

965 Harald Bluetooth of Denmark is first Viking king to be baptized a Christian

980 Danes renew their raids on England
986 Erik the Red founds Norse settlements in Greenland

A.D. 1000

1000 Norse settlement established at L'Anse aux Meadows on North American coast

1014 Danes conquer England
1016–1035 King Canute rules vast kingdom of Denmark, Norway, and England

A.D. 1050

1066 The Normans (the Danes that settled in Normandy) conquer England

A.D. 1100

Medieval Europe

Medieval Europe was dominated by two great institutions: the feudal system and the Catholic Church. Feudalism began in France during the A.D. 700s and eventually spread throughout Europe. Kings granted estates to their leading noblemen in return for military service. Knights fought for these noblemen and received smaller estates of land, farmed by serfs (peasants) in return for military protection. This structure was bound together by oaths of loyalty. The Catholic Church was the sole religious authority in western Europe but also claimed increasing control over secular (nonreligious) rulers, leading to constant struggles with powerful emperors and kings.

The Crusades

In 1095 Pope Urban II (right, above throne) issued a call to European leaders to win back the Holy Land from Muslim control because the Seljuk Turks were disrupting pilgrimage routes through Asia to the sacred Christian sites. A series of crusades (military expeditions) set out from Europe over the next 200 years, capturing Jerusalem in 1099 and ruling the Holy Land until the crusaders were driven out in 1291.

The Black Death

In the 1330s the bubonic plague broke out in eastern Asia, spreading to the Black Sea in 1346. Rats on ships, infested with parasitic fleas, carried the plague to European ports in 1347, and it soon spread across the continent. By the time the plague died out in 1351, around 24 million people—one third of Europe's population—had died, causing many social and economic problems. Towns and farms lost their workers, prices fell, and wages rose as labor became scarce.

Scottish independence Robert the Bruce's victory against the English at Bannockburn, in 1314, led to Scottish independence by 1328.

Bannockburn

SCOTLAND

North Sea

IRELAND

Tower of London After his victory at Hastings, William built a royal home and fort beside the Thames river.

WALES

Concentric castle on the Welsh border

ENGLAND

LONDON

Hastings

Battle of Hastings In 1066 the Normans invaded England and defeated Harold II.

Agincourt

English longbowman

Normandy

Paris **Champagn**

Poitiers

FRANCE

Vineyard in Gascony

Clermont

The feudal system Across Europe serfs (peasants), dependent on their lords, worked the land in return for shelter and protection.

Avignon

Santiago de Compostela

León

LEÓN

Spanish windmill

CASTILE

PORTUGAL

Pilgrimage Christian pilgrims walked hundreds of miles to pray at holy places such as Rome, Jerusalem, and Santiago de Compostela.

ARAGON

Lisbon

Muslim rule The Muslim Moors controlled a small region in Granada, southern Spain.

Spain

Crusaders setting out for the Holy Land in the Near East

GRANADA

Granada

International trade Venice and Genoa dominated trade in the Mediterranean, importing goods from as far away as central Asia and China.

0   500km
0   250 miles

SWEDEN

Neva

Novgorod •

Sturdy Hanseatic cog (ship) used to transport goods

Fir Trees

The Hanseatic League
Thirty-seven northern German and Baltic towns formed a league that dominated trade in northern Europe.

Trade settlements
Hanseatic traders set up *kontors* (foreign depots) where their merchants could live and trade securely.

• Hamburg   • Lübeck

Salted fish from the Baltic

HOLY ROMAN EMPIRE

Germany

The Hapsburgs
The Hapsburg family conquered Austria in 1282. They dominated the Holy Roman Empire from 1274 until its end in 1806.

European assault
In 1241 the Mongols wiped out vast European armies in Poland and Hungary. They withdrew when their leader Ogedai died, saving Europe from conquest.

LITHUANIA

POLAND

Kyiv •

Orthodox Christianity
The peoples of the Balkans and Russia were Orthodox Christians.

Banking
In the 1400s the Fugger family of Augsburg and the Medicis of Florence ran banks that lent money to local rulers and merchants.

• Augsburg

Wooden house in Kyiv

Austria

C a r p a t h i a n s

Alps

HUNGARY

The Ottomans
The Ottomans from central Turkey defeated the Serbs at the Battle of Kosovo in 1389. They went on to conquer the rest of the Balkans.

Universities
The first university in Europe was set up in Bologna, Italy, in 1088.

• Venice

B a l k a n s

Genoa

• Bologna
• Florence

Black Sea

Kosovo

Orthodox monastery
Mount Athos in Greece was the most important Orthodox Christian monastery.

Rome •

The papacy
The Pope was the head of the Catholic Church. He was also an important political figure and owned a lot of land in Italy and France.

NAPLES

Constantinople •

Gallipoli •

Mount Athos

BYZANTINE EMPIRE

SICILY

Mediterranean Sea

A.D. 1000–A.D. 1500

A.D. 1000

A.D. 1050
1054 Final split between Roman Catholic and Orthodox churches
1066 Duke William of Normandy invades England and seizes throne
1073 Pope Gregory VII increases authority of the papacy over secular kings
1095 Pope Urban II calls for First Crusade against Muslim rule in the Holy Land

A.D. 1100

1143 Portugal gains its independence from Spanish kingdom of León

A.D. 1150
1154 Henry II of England rules huge Angevin Empire, which stretches from Scotland down to Spanish kingdoms

1171 English begin to rule Ireland

A.D. 1200
1212 Christian troops win an important battle against Muslim Moors in Spain
1230 Kingdoms of Castile and León unite in Spain
1230 Towns of Lübeck and Hamburg form Hanseatic League
1241 Mongol invasion of Europe called off after Mongol leader dies

A.D. 1250

1274 Rudolph I becomes first Hapsburg ruler of Holy Roman Empire

1282 Hapsburgs rule Austria
1284 English King Edward I ends Welsh independence

A.D. 1300
1309–1377 Papacy moves to Avignon in France; major split in Catholic Church
1314 English defeated by Scots at Bannockburn
1337–1453 Hundred Years' War between England and France—caused by English claims on the French throne
1347–1351 Black Death devastates Europe

A.D. 1350
1354 Ottomans seize Gallipoli, their first foothold in Europe

1368 Lithuanians become Christian
1378–1417 Election of rival popes leads to Great Schism (split) in Catholic Church
1380 Hans Fugger sets up bank in Augsburg

A.D. 1400
1414 Medicis of Florence, Italy, become papal bankers
1415 English archers win major battle against the French in Agincourt

1429 Joan of Arc drives English out of France

A.D. 1450

A.D. 1500

Medieval Europe:
Castles and villages

During the medieval period, most people in Europe lived in small villages that were owned by the lord of the manor. Often, they died in the same village that they were born in and rarely traveled much farther than the local market town. Most people were serfs, which means that they were landless peasants who worked on the lord of the manor's lands in return for shelter and protection. The great lords of the country—the dukes and earls—lived in huge stone castles, heavily fortified against attacks by rival lords or invading armies. The first castles were built in France during the 800s.

A medieval village
This photograph shows Riquewihr, in France. A medieval village such as this was ruled by the lord of the manor, a knight who had been given the manor (estate) and all of its houses and fields by his lord. The lord of the manor served as the judge at the local manorial court.

Knights in armor
A knight was a mounted warrior who had been granted a fief (estate) by a rich and powerful nobleman in return for loyalty and military service. Knights were trained to ride and fight from an early age, learning their skills in jousts and tournaments. They followed an elaborate code of chivalry, which dictated their behavior both on and off the battlefield.

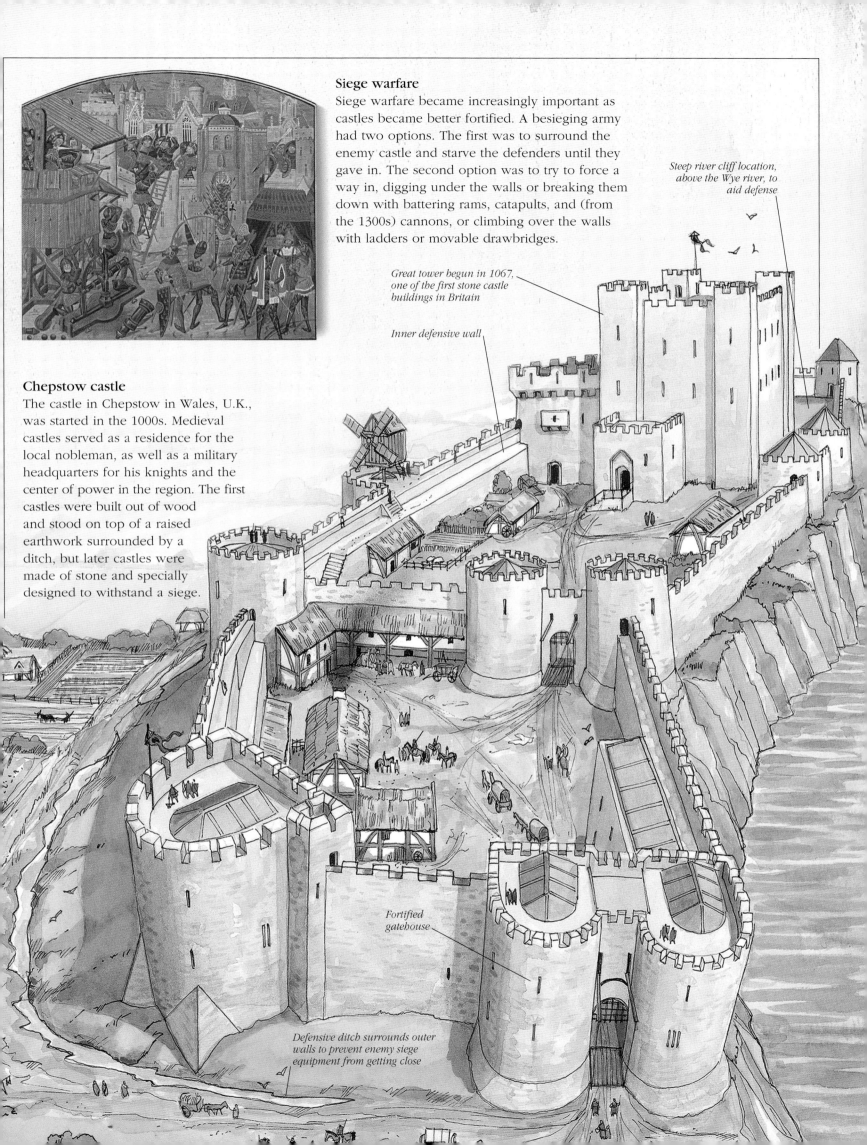

Siege warfare

Siege warfare became increasingly important as castles became better fortified. A besieging army had two options. The first was to surround the enemy castle and starve the defenders until they gave in. The second option was to try to force a way in, digging under the walls or breaking them down with battering rams, catapults, and (from the 1300s) cannons, or climbing over the walls with ladders or movable drawbridges.

Steep river cliff location, above the Wye river, to aid defense

Great tower begun in 1067, one of the first stone castle buildings in Britain

Inner defensive wall

Chepstow castle

The castle in Chepstow in Wales, U.K., was started in the 1000s. Medieval castles served as a residence for the local nobleman, as well as a military headquarters for his knights and the center of power in the region. The first castles were built out of wood and stood on top of a raised earthwork surrounded by a ditch, but later castles were made of stone and specially designed to withstand a siege.

Fortified gatehouse

Defensive ditch surrounds outer walls to prevent enemy siege equipment from getting close

On horseback
Mongol warriors were skilled archers, accurately firing volleys of arrows more than 655 ft. (200m) on horseback.

Frozen invasion
In the winter of 1238–1239 the Mongols invaded Russia, using its frozen rivers as highways. This was the only successful winter invasion of Russia in history.

• Novgorod

Russian Principalities

POLAND

Legnica
• Kraków

European assault
In 1241 the Mongols wiped out huge European armies in Poland and then Hungary.

Kyiv

HUNGARY
• Mohi

Mongol horses could run for up to 60 mi. (95km) a day

The Golden Horde
The Mongol state that ruled southern Russia was known as the Khanate of the Golden Horde, probably after the color of the first khan's tent.

Kara-khitai
• Otrar

BYZANTINE EMPIRE

Black Sea

Caspian Sea

• Tbilisi

Timur
The last great Mongol leader, Timur, was a Turkish-speaking Muslim nomad.

Tashkent

■ SAMARQAND

Khwarizm Shahdom

• Kabul

Mongol defeat
In 1260, with nowhere for their horses to graze in the desert, the Mongols were stopped by the Mamluks of Egypt in 'Ain Jalut.

• Damascus
• 'Ain Jalut

Siege engines
The Mongols paid foreign engineers to build siege engines that were capable of destroying city walls—as they did in Baghdad in 1258.

• Baghdad

Abbasid Caliphate

• Esfahan

Samarqand
Timur brought skilled workers from across the Middle East to build mosques and public buildings in his capital, Samarqand.

H i m

Towers of skulls
In Esfahan, Timur killed 70,000 people so that he could build towers out of their skulls.

SULTANATE OF DELHI

The Mongols

In A.D. 1206 the young son of a minor Mongol chief united the warring Mongol tribes behind him. These warring people named him Genghis Khan, meaning "the Great" Khan. By the time of his death in 1227, he had conquered an empire that covered most of central Asia. His successors continued these conquests so that the Mongols soon ruled the biggest empire in world history. Yet the Mongols had no experience of government and could not even read or write. After the death of Ogodei, the second Great Khan, in 1241, the Mongol Empire split into smaller "khanates." Timur attempted to recreate the empire in the late 1300s, but this was not to last. The Mongol Empire soon lost its power and territory.

- - - - -
dotted line shows the extent of the Mongol Empire at its height in around 1280

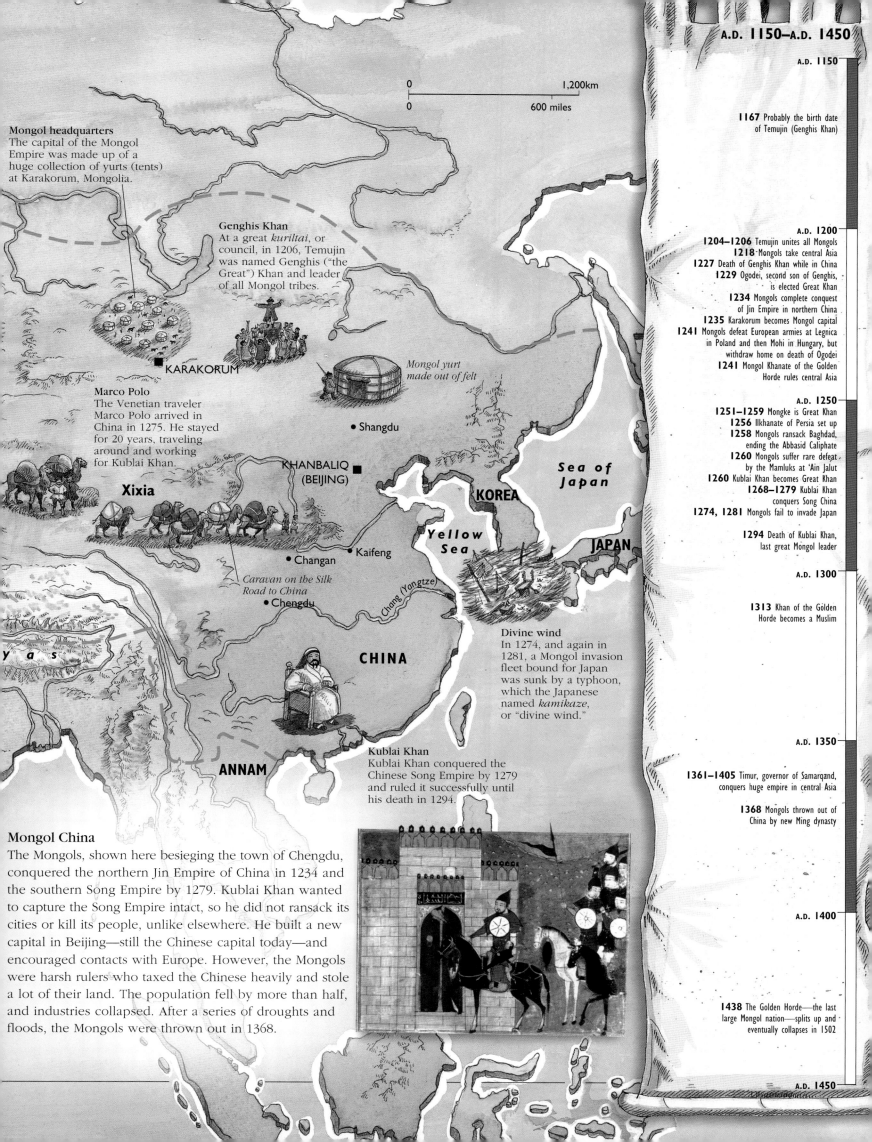

Mongol headquarters
The capital of the Mongol Empire was made up of a huge collection of yurts (tents) at Karakorum, Mongolia.

Genghis Khan
At a great *kuriltai*, or council, in 1206, Temujin was named Genghis ("the Great") Khan and leader of all Mongol tribes.

Mongol yurt made out of felt

Marco Polo
The Venetian traveler Marco Polo arrived in China in 1275. He stayed for 20 years, traveling around and working for Kublai Khan.

KARAKORUM

• Shangdu

KHANBALIQ (BEIJING)

Xixia

KOREA

Sea of Japan

Yellow Sea

• Kaifeng

• Changan

Caravan on the Silk Road to China

• Chengdu

Chang (Yangtze)

JAPAN

Divine wind
In 1274, and again in 1281, a Mongol invasion fleet bound for Japan was sunk by a typhoon, which the Japanese named *kamikaze*, or "divine wind."

CHINA

ANNAM

Kublai Khan
Kublai Khan conquered the Chinese Song Empire by 1279 and ruled it successfully until his death in 1294.

Mongol China

The Mongols, shown here besieging the town of Chengdu, conquered the northern Jin Empire of China in 1234 and the southern Song Empire by 1279. Kublai Khan wanted to capture the Song Empire intact, so he did not ransack its cities or kill its people, unlike elsewhere. He built a new capital in Beijing—still the Chinese capital today—and encouraged contacts with Europe. However, the Mongols were harsh rulers who taxed the Chinese heavily and stole a lot of their land. The population fell by more than half, and industries collapsed. After a series of droughts and floods, the Mongols were thrown out in 1368.

A.D. 1150

1167 Probably the birth date of Temujin (Genghis Khan)

A.D. 1200
1204–1206 Temujin unites all Mongols
1218 Mongols take central Asia
1227 Death of Genghis Khan while in China
1229 Ogodei, second son of Genghis, is elected Great Khan
1234 Mongols complete conquest of Jin Empire in northern China
1235 Karakorum becomes Mongol capital
1241 Mongols defeat European armies at Legnica in Poland and then Mohi in Hungary, but withdraw home on death of Ogodei
1241 Mongol Khanate of the Golden Horde rules central Asia

A.D. 1250
1251–1259 Mongke is Great Khan
1256 Ilkhanate of Persia set up
1258 Mongols ransack Baghdad, ending the Abbasid Caliphate
1260 Mongols suffer rare defeat by the Mamluks at 'Ain Jalut
1260 Kublai Khan becomes Great Khan
1268–1279 Kublai Khan conquers Song China
1274, 1281 Mongols fail to invade Japan

1294 Death of Kublai Khan, last great Mongol leader

A.D. 1300

1313 Khan of the Golden Horde becomes a Muslim

A.D. 1350

1361–1405 Timur, governor of Samarqand, conquers huge empire in central Asia

1368 Mongols thrown out of China by new Ming dynasty

A.D. 1400

1438 The Golden Horde—the last large Mongol nation—splits up and eventually collapses in 1502

A.D. 1450

African kingdoms

Trade in gold, ivory, salt, cattle—and also slaves—brought great wealth to the interior (noncoastal parts) of Africa. This led to the creation of several wealthy trading nations such as Ghana, Mali, and Great Zimbabwe. The West African states grew rich on trade across the Sahara with the Muslim world and Europe to their north. On the east coast, Muslim merchants set up independent trading cities that prospered by doing business across the Indian Ocean—with the Arabian peninsula, India, and China. Arab merchants introduced Islam to west Africa and coastal east Africa, while Christianity flourished in both Aksum and Ethiopia in the east of the continent.

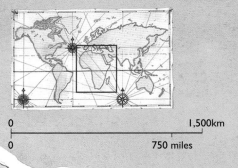

Portuguese exploration
After 1432 Portuguese navigators began to explore the west coast of Africa—in search of trade and wealth.

PORTUGAL
SPAIN
MOROCCO
MARRAKECH

The Almoravids
In 1056 the nomadic Almoravids began to conquer northwest Africa, building their capital city at Marrakech.

Sahara

Salt mining in the western Sahara

Camel caravan on the trans-Saharan trade route

Trading markets
Tombouctou was the main market in West Africa. Gold, ivory, and slaves were exchanged for luxuries from the north.

MALI
Tombouctou

Mansa Musa
Mansa Musa was a wealthy king who ruled Mali from 1312 to 1337. In 1324 he went on the *hajj*, or pilgrimage to Mecca.

GHANA
Jenne

KANEM-BORNU

Hausa States

BENIN

Mosque at trading city of Jenne

Farming

Ife • Igbo-Ukwu
• Benin

Islam in west Africa
Arab merchants from the north brought Islam into west Africa after A.D. 750, making it the main religion in the area by 1000.

Gold mining
Gold was mined throughout the coastal forests of west Africa. It was made into royal jewelry or traded north in return for other precious goods.

Ife people
The Yoruba people of Ife in west Africa made beautiful terra cotta sculptures of their rulers and other heroes.

0   1,500km
0   750 miles

Atlantic Ocean

African trade

East African trade was dominated by a series of independent coastal cities, from Mogadishu in the north down to Sofala. These east African cities would later become the Swahili coast, and their ancient peoples were descendants of Arab, Omani, Yemeni, and Persian traders who had settled on the coast after 1000, bringing Islam with them. The rulers of these cities acted as middlemen between traders from the African interior and the Arab and Persian merchants who traded across the Indian Ocean. The vast range of these trading contacts can be seen by the presence of this giraffe in Beijing in 1414, a gift from the ruler of Malindi to the Ming emperor of China.

Cape of Good Hope

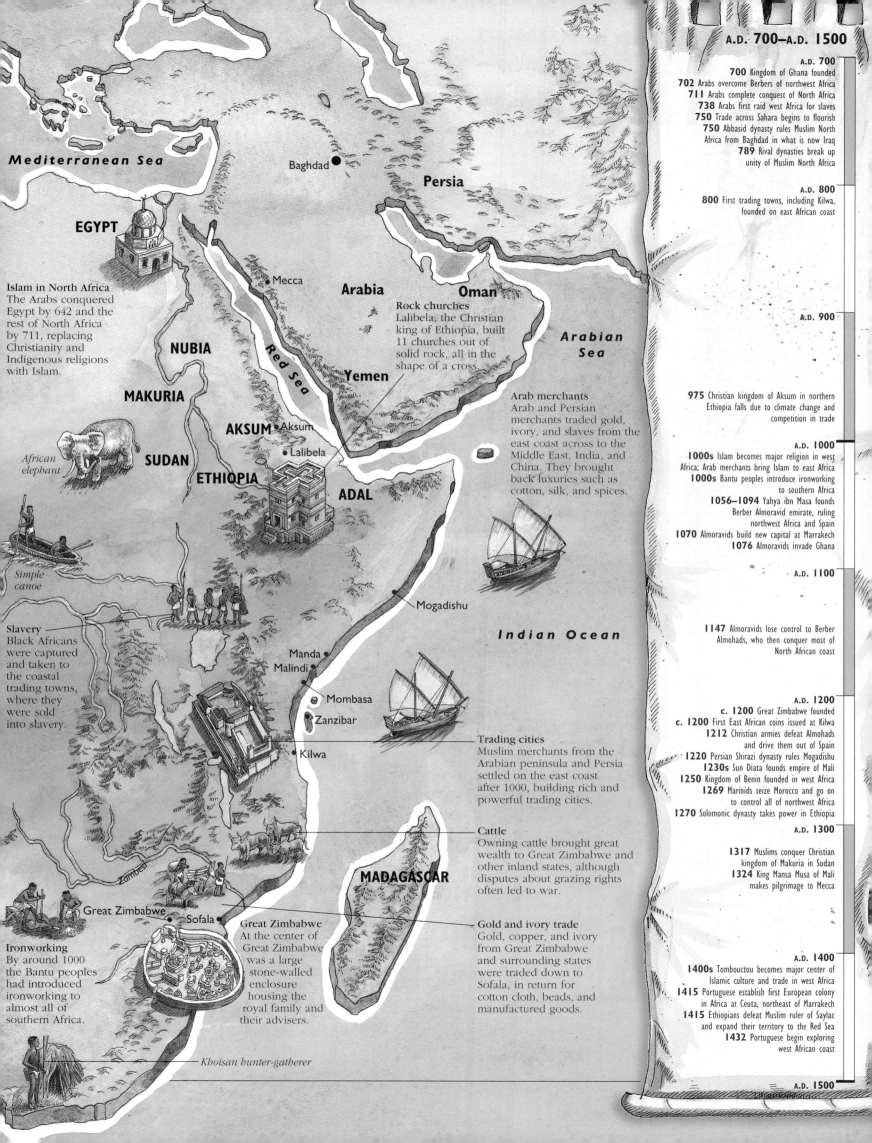

Mediterranean Sea

EGYPT

Baghdad

Persia

Mecca

Arabia

Oman

Red Sea

Yemen

Arabian Sea

Islam in North Africa
The Arabs conquered Egypt by 642 and the rest of North Africa by 711, replacing Christianity and Indigenous religions with Islam.

NUBIA

MAKURIA

Rock churches
Lalibela, the Christian king of Ethiopia, built 11 churches out of solid rock, all in the shape of a cross.

African elephant

SUDAN

AKSUM • Aksum

• Lalibela

ETHIOPIA

ADAL

Arab merchants
Arab and Persian merchants traded gold, ivory, and slaves from the east coast across to the Middle East, India, and China. They brought back luxuries such as cotton, silk, and spices.

Simple canoe

Slavery
Black Africans were captured and taken to the coastal trading towns, where they were sold into slavery.

Mogadishu

Indian Ocean

Manda
Malindi

Mombasa

Zanzibar

Kilwa

Trading cities
Muslim merchants from the Arabian peninsula and Persia settled on the east coast after 1000, building rich and powerful trading cities.

Cattle
Owning cattle brought great wealth to Great Zimbabwe and other inland states, although disputes about grazing rights often led to war.

MADAGASCAR

Zambezi

Great Zimbabwe • Sofala

Great Zimbabwe
At the center of Great Zimbabwe was a large stone-walled enclosure housing the royal family and their advisers.

Gold and ivory trade
Gold, copper, and ivory from Great Zimbabwe and surrounding states were traded down to Sofala, in return for cotton cloth, beads, and manufactured goods.

Ironworking
By around 1000 the Bantu peoples had introduced ironworking to almost all of southern Africa.

Khoisan hunter-gatherer

A.D. 700–A.D. 1500

A.D. 700
700 Kingdom of Ghana founded
702 Arabs overcome Berbers of northwest Africa
711 Arabs complete conquest of North Africa
738 Arabs first raid west Africa for slaves
750 Trade across Sahara begins to flourish
750 Abbasid dynasty rules Muslim North Africa from Baghdad in what is now Iraq
789 Rival dynasties break up unity of Muslim North Africa

A.D. 800
800 First trading towns, including Kilwa, founded on east African coast

A.D. 900

975 Christian kingdom of Aksum in northern Ethiopia falls due to climate change and competition in trade

A.D. 1000
1000s Islam becomes major religion in west Africa; Arab merchants bring Islam to east Africa
1000s Bantu peoples introduce ironworking to southern Africa
1056–1094 Yahya ibn Masa founds Berber Almoravid emirate, ruling northwest Africa and Spain
1070 Almoravids build new capital at Marrakech
1076 Almoravids invade Ghana

A.D. 1100

1147 Almoravids lose control to Berber Almohads, who then conquer most of North African coast

A.D. 1200
c. 1200 Great Zimbabwe founded
c. 1200 First East African coins issued at Kilwa
1212 Christian armies defeat Almohads and drive them out of Spain
1220 Persian Shirazi dynasty rules Mogadishu
1230s Sun Diata founds empire of Mali
1250 Kingdom of Benin founded in west Africa
1269 Marinids seize Morocco and go on to control all of northwest Africa
1270 Solomonic dynasty takes power in Ethiopia

A.D. 1300

1317 Muslims conquer Christian kingdom of Makuria in Sudan
1324 King Mansa Musa of Mali makes pilgrimage to Mecca

A.D. 1400
1400s Tombouctou becomes major center of Islamic culture and trade in west Africa
1415 Portuguese establish first European colony in Africa at Ceuta, northeast of Marrakech
1415 Ethiopians defeat Muslim ruler of Saylac and expand their territory to the Red Sea
1432 Portuguese begin exploring west African coast

A.D. 1500

Arctic Ocean

Polar traders
Inuit and Norsemen from Greenland traded ivory, furs, textiles, tools, food, and other items as far north as Ellesmere Island in the Arctic Ocean.

Trapping caribou
Indigenous American hunters set up their camps by river crossings. As caribou crossed the river, the hunters trapped and killed them for their fur, meat, and antlers.

Buffalo traps
Plains Indians killed buffalo by driving them over a cliff edge—a practice that lasted for more than 7,000 years.

Hunting whales off the Pacific coast

Pacific Ocean

Great Plains

Mississippi

Medicine Creek

Cahokia

Chaco Canyon
This D-shaped, four-story apartment building in Pueblo Bonito in the Chaco Canyon housed up to 1,200 people in 800 rooms.

Pueblo Bonito
Chaco Canyon

Cahokia
Cahokia was founded around A.D. 600. A huge dirt temple mound, used for religious purposes, dominated the city.

Shell carving
People in the southern Mississippi river valley carved shells with religious symbols to be used in ceremonies at temple mounds.

Farming the plains
Small farming villages on the Great Plains grew maize, squash, and other produce for food or to trade with nomadic hunters.

Native farmer in Mexico

Searching for seashells

Gulf of Mexico

Chichén Itzá
Chichén Itzá, founded in 850, survived as the Toltec capital of the Yucatán Peninsula until it was attacked in 1221.

Tenochtitlán
The Aztec capital city had a huge temple complex at its center.

Toltec statues
The Toltecs lived in the Valley of Mexico and their capital city was at Tula. They erected huge statues at the top of their large pyramid temple in Tula.

■TULA
TENOCHTITLÁN■

CHICHÉN ITZÁ■

Yucatán Peninsula

Mayan scribe writing on folded bark

Palenque
Tikal ●

Jaguar in the Mayan jungle

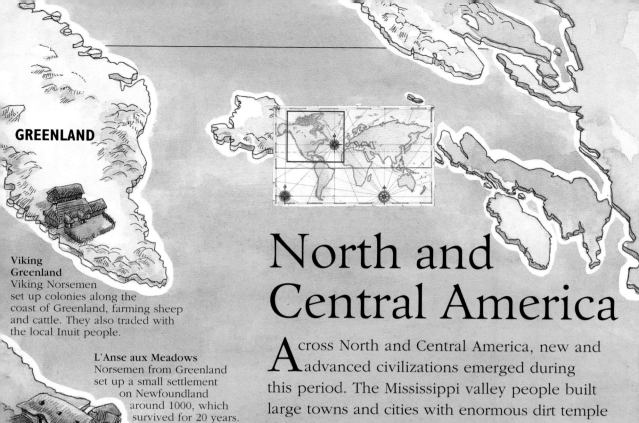

GREENLAND

Viking Greenland
Viking Norsemen set up colonies along the coast of Greenland, farming sheep and cattle. They also traded with the local Inuit people.

L'Anse aux Meadows
Norsemen from Greenland set up a small settlement on Newfoundland around 1000, which survived for 20 years.

• L'Anse aux Meadows

```
0 ———————————— 1,000km
0 ———————————— 500 miles
```

Atlantic Ocean

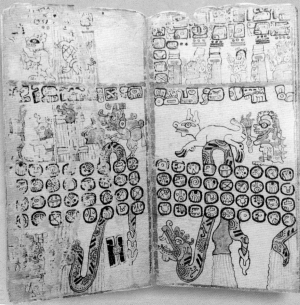

North and Central America

Across North and Central America, new and advanced civilizations emerged during this period. The Mississippi valley people built large towns and cities with enormous dirt temple mounds. Meanwhile, the people of the Chaco Canyon constructed huge apartment buildings, unmatched in size until larger ones were erected in New York City during the 1800s. Small farming villages sprang up in the eastern woodlands and on the Great Plains, while the people of the west coast lived settled lives fishing the abundant Pacific Ocean. To their south, the Maya and Toltec civilizations flourished in Central America until the Aztecs emerged to dominate the region during the 1400s.

The Maya

The Maya were the only people in the Americas to devise a complete writing system. Their complex script was made up of glyphs (pictures), which represented both entire words and individual sounds. They used these glyphs to record the names and deeds of their families and kings on walls, pillars, and other stone monuments in their cities. They also made codices, which were books that were made out of bark paper coated with gesso (plaster and glue) and folded like an accordion. Only four of these books now survive, giving us a picture of what life was like in the Mayan civilization.

A.D. 600–A.D. 1500

A.D. 600
600 Plains hunters now use bows and arrows to hunt wild game
c. 600 Cahokia founded in northern Mississippi valley

A.D. 700
700 Mississippi valley people begin building small towns with temple mounds
700 Farming villages flourish in the southwest regions of North America

A.D. 800
800 Hardier strains of maize and beans increase food production in Mississippi valley, allowing population to rise

850 Chichén Itzá, last Mayan state, is founded

A.D. 900
900 Toltecs found state with capital at Tula
900 Network of villages, linked by roads, begun at Chaco Canyon
900 Small farming villages spring up on the Great Plains
900 Hohokam farmers begin irrigating fields
986 Erik the Red founds Viking settlement in Greenland

A.D. 1000
1000 Permanent farming villages built throughout the eastern woodlands
1000 Viking settlement founded by Leif Erikson at L'Anse aux Meadows in Newfoundland
1000 Toltecs conquer Mayan states in Yucatán Peninsula
1000s Thule Inuits settle in Alaska and gradually move east, forcing out earlier Inuit inhabitants

A.D. 1100
1100 Towns with large ceremonial centers built in Mississippi region

1168 Tula is ransacked, and the Mexican Toltec state collapses

A.D. 1200
1200 Cahokia at height of its power, with more than 10,000 inhabitants
1200s Aztecs move into Valley of Mexico

1221 Chichén Itzá seized, ending Toltec rule in the Yucatán region

A.D. 1300
1300s Thule Inuits settle in Greenland
1300s Droughts cause decline of Chaco Canyon villages

1325 Aztecs found Tenochtitlán

A.D. 1400
1428–1440 Aztecs begin expanding empire under Itzcóatl

1450 Norse settlements in Greenland die out and are occupied by Thule Inuits

A.D. 1500

Central America:
The Aztecs

The Aztecs were the last and most powerful in a long line of peoples who lived in the fertile valley of Mexico in Central America. They were a warlike tribe who dominated the region after the 1200s, capturing enemy warriors in order to sacrifice them to their own sun god. The Aztecs were spectacular builders, creating huge cities and temple complexes. They kept elaborate records of their achievements painted on sheets of bark that were then folded into books.

The Aztec world
The Aztecs believed that the universe had been created and destroyed four times before the current "fifth creation" in which they lived. This huge stone, measuring 13 feet (4m) across, tells this story. The sun god is in the middle, with the four previous creations around him and then a band showing the 20 days of each Aztec calendar month.

Aztec religion
The main god of the Aztecs was Huitzilopochtli (above), the sun god and god of war. The Aztecs feared that one day the sun god would fail to rise into the sky and their world would come to an end. In order to keep the sun god alive, the Aztecs made human sacrifices to nourish the god with hearts and blood.

Daily life
Aztec houses were made out of adobe (mud brick) and often had only a single room. They were furnished with low tables and reed mats for beds. Aztec women cooked meals made out of maize tortillas wrapped around meat or vegetables such as beans, peppers, avocados, and tomatoes.

The Aztec capital: Tenochtitlán

The name Tenochtitlán means the "place of the high priest Tenoch." It was the capital of the Aztec Empire, and it was built on an island in the middle of a lake, connected to the shore by wide causeways. At the height of its power in the early 1500s, the city housed around 500,000 people and was much larger than most European cities of that time. Tenochtitlán is now buried beneath Mexico City.

Templo Mayor

In the center of Tenochtitlán was a walled precinct that was built for ceremonial and religious purposes. It was dominated by the Templo Mayor, a huge pyramid that stood 200 ft. (60m) high. At the top were two shrines dedicated to Tlaloc, the god of rain, and Huitzilopochtli, the sun god and god of war. There priests made offerings and human sacrifices to the gods, placing the skulls of the victims on the walls of the two shrines. Each Aztec ruler expanded the Templo Mayor, building a bigger and more impressive temple around and on top of the previous one.

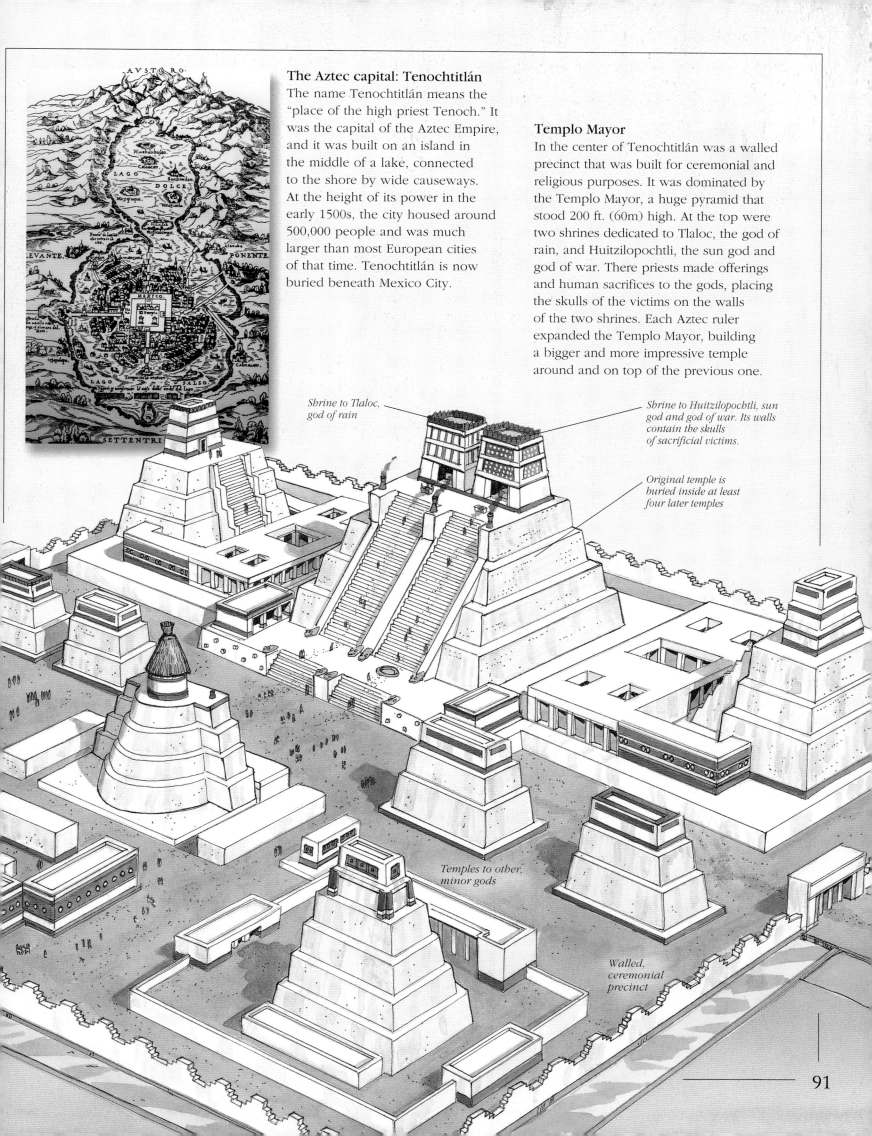

Shrine to Tlaloc, god of rain

Shrine to Huitzilopochtli, sun god and god of war. Its walls contain the skulls of sacrificial victims.

Original temple is buried inside at least four later temples

Temples to other, minor gods

Walled, ceremonial precinct

these lines show
the location of the
Incan roads

dotted line shows
the extent of the
Inca Empire in 1525

Incan scribes
The Incan scribes who
kept the quipus were
highly valued, as they
were the only people
who could "read" the
information that was
recorded in the
quipu strings.

Rope bridges
Rope suspension
bridges, made from
twisted vines and
wooden slats, were
hung across steep
ravines and wide
river valleys.

Terraced farming
Potatoes, beans, tomatoes,
squash, and other root
crops and vegetables were
grown on irrigated terraces
carved out of the steep
mountainside.

Alpacas
Alpacas were kept
for their fine wool,
which was made
into clothes, hats,
and rugs.

Textiles
All the South American
peoples were skilled
textile weavers, using
alpaca and other wools
to weave clothes, rugs,
and wall hangings.

Chan Chan
Ten walled compounds
dominated the center
of Chan Chan, the
Chimú capital. Repeated
designs were carved
onto the walls.

Stone finishing
Incan stonemasons
finished off the
stone walls of
important buildings
by polishing them
with wet sand.

Sacsayhuaman
The huge stone fort
of Sacsayhuaman
protected the Incan
capital, Cuzco. It could
easily house all the
people of the city
during times of crisis.

*Harvesting a
potato crop*

*Sowing
maize seeds*

*Reed boat on
Lake Titicaca*

Oracle to the gods
With its temple and
oracle, Pachacamac was
one of the major religious
centers and pilgrimage
sites in the region.

Machu Picchu
The mountaintop
city of Machu Picchu
was a religious
center and frontier
post. After the fall of
the Inca Empire, it
was not discovered
again until 1911.

Quito

Lambayeque
Valley

CHAN
CHAN

Moche
Valley

A n d e s

Pachacamac

Nazca

Machu
Picchu

Wari

CUZCO

La Paz

Tiwanaku

Lake Titicaca

Lake

Chimú
and Incas

Sometime around A.D. 1220, a semilegendary
figure named Maco Capac founded the Incan
state at Cuzco, high up in the Andes mountains,
in what is now southern Peru. The new state
was slow to expand, but in the mid-1400s it grew
rapidly, conquering the neighboring Chimú
Empire to its north and soon controlling 2,170
miles (3,500km) of Pacific coastline—from
modern-day Ecuador in the north to central
Chile in the south. The all-powerful Incan
emperor governed more than 12 million people,
keeping control through a powerful army and
a network of fine roads along which troops
could travel in an emergency. Efficient social
services took care of the sick and needy, while
everyone was expected to work hard to keep
themselves busy and out of trouble at all times.

A n d e s

Pacific Ocean

● Santiago

Imperial messengers
Runners stationed at rest houses along the main roads carried messages to and from the emperor in Cuzco. A team of runners could cover 150 miles (240km) a day.

Pack animals
Llamas, the main pack animals of the Incas, were used to carry heavy loads at high altitudes.

The Incan emperor
The emperor was worshiped as the son of the Sun—a living god. He was carried through his empire in style.

Roadside hostels
Rest houses called tambos, located one day's journey apart, were built along the main roads to house messengers and weary travelers.

Food supplies
Food and clothes stored in the tambos were given out to the elderly, sick, and disabled during times of need.

Fishing
Fresh fish that were caught offshore were carried by relays of runners to the emperor in Cuzco.

Incan walls
Stonemasons built walls using huge stones. The stones were so carefully shaped and fitted that a blade could not be placed between them.

1,000km

500 miles

0
0

Incan roads

The Incas were excellent builders, constructing a strategic network of roads that connected the farthest reaches of their massive empire to the imperial capital, Cuzco. The roads had rest houses called tambos, similar to the reconstruction shown here (left). The entire road system measured more than 12,400 miles (20,000km) long. These roads enabled the emperor to move his army quickly during times of trouble, as well as keep in touch with his regional governors through the imperial messenger system.

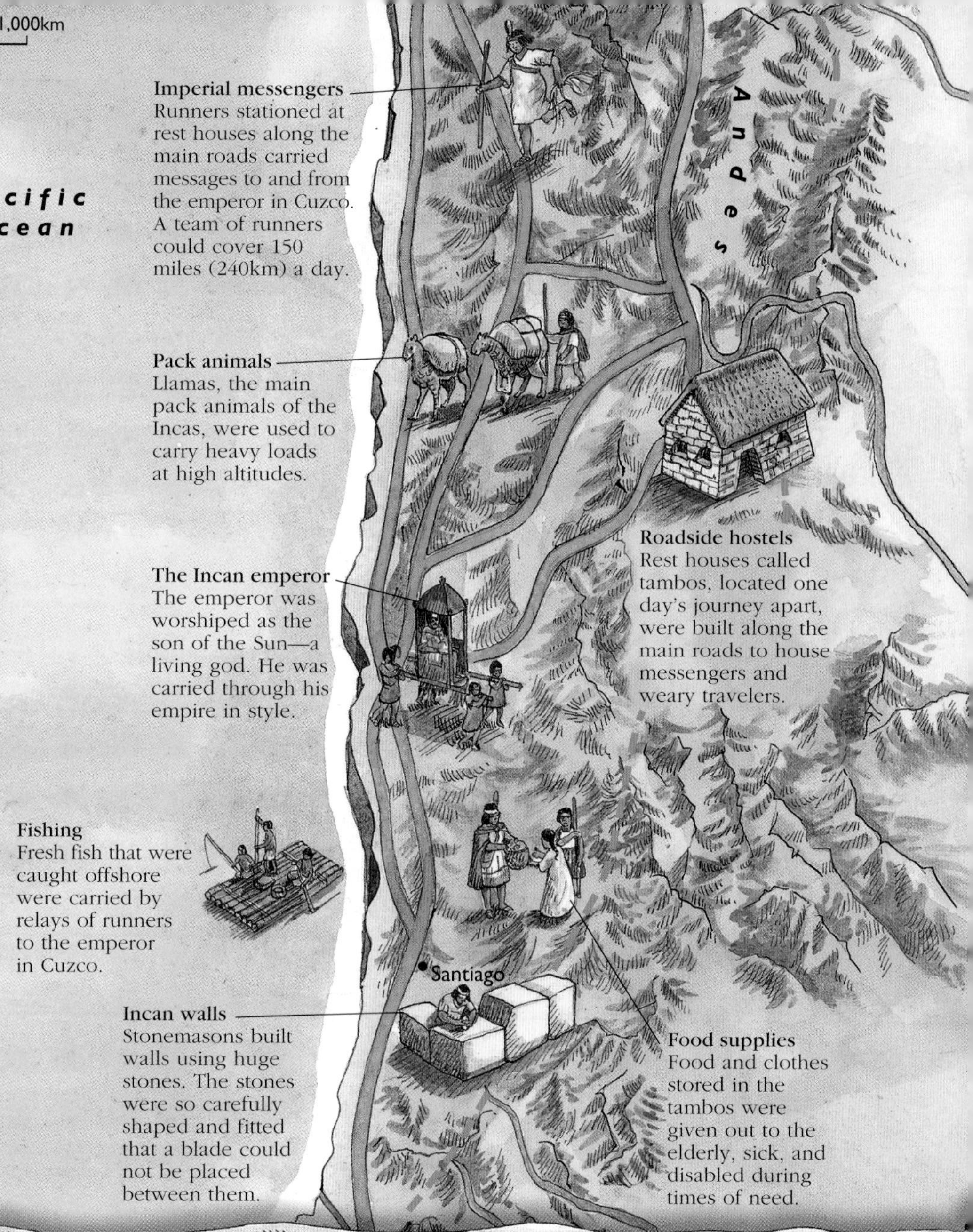

Strings of information

The Incas never developed a system of writing, but they figured out a way to record facts and figures using a system of knotted string known as the quipu. Various colored ropes with single, double, or triple knots tied into them hung from a main rope. The color, position, and number of each hanging rope and knot recorded information such as the size of the food harvest, the amount of tax money that had been collected, and the size of the population. This was very useful during times of war or emergency.

A.D. 800–A.D. 1500

A.D. 800

850 Chimú capital Chan Chan founded in the coastal Moche valley

A.D. 900

900 Sicán state founded in Lambayeque Valley in northern Peru

A.D. 1000

1000 The highland empires of Tiwanaku and Wari collapse

A.D. 1100

A.D. 1200

1200 Chimú Empire begins expanding along the coast

c. 1220 Manco Capac founds Incan state at Cuzco in the Peruvian Andes

A.D. 1300

1370 Chimús conquer Sicán state

A.D. 1400

1400 Yahua Huyacac expands Inca Empire into neighboring Andes valleys
1438–1471 Emperor Pachacutec rapidly expands Inca Empire northwest to the Pacific coast
1470 Incas conquer Chimú Empire
1471–1493 Tupac Yupanqui, son of Pachacutec, expands Inca Empire south

1494–1525 Under Huayna Capac, Inca Empire reaches its greatest size

A.D. 1500

EXPLORATION & EMPIRE

Illustrated by Mark Bergin

CONTENTS

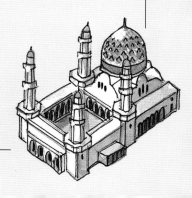

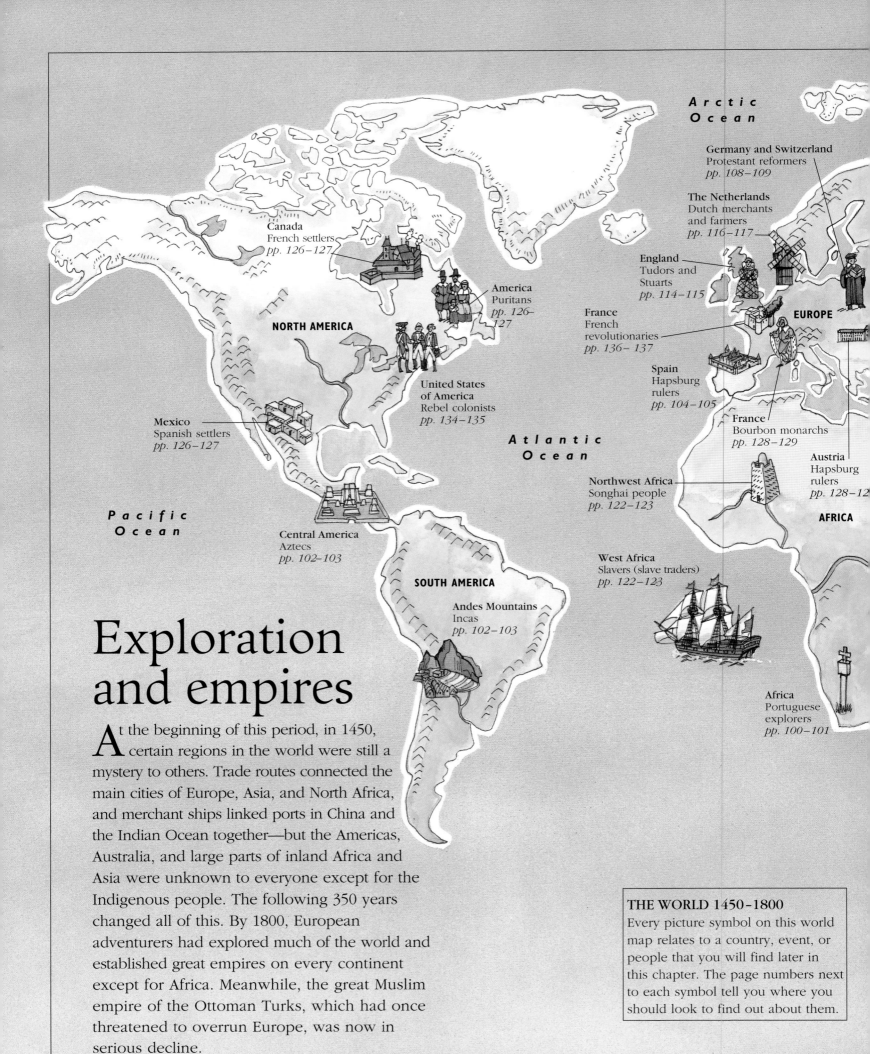

Canada
French settlers
pp. 126–127

America
Puritans
pp. 126–127

NORTH AMERICA

United States of America
Rebel colonists
pp. 134–135

Mexico
Spanish settlers
pp. 126–127

Atlantic Ocean

Pacific Ocean

Central America
Aztecs
pp. 102–103

SOUTH AMERICA

Andes Mountains
Incas
pp. 102–103

Arctic Ocean

Germany and Switzerland
Protestant reformers
pp. 108–109

The Netherlands
Dutch merchants and farmers
pp. 116–117

England
Tudors and Stuarts
pp. 114–115

EUROPE

France
French revolutionaries
pp. 136–137

Spain
Hapsburg rulers
pp. 104–105

France
Bourbon monarchs
pp. 128–129

Austria
Hapsburg rulers
pp. 128–12

Northwest Africa
Songhai people
pp. 122–123

AFRICA

West Africa
Slavers (slave traders)
pp. 122–123

Africa
Portuguese explorers
pp. 100–101

Exploration and empires

At the beginning of this period, in 1450, certain regions in the world were still a mystery to others. Trade routes connected the main cities of Europe, Asia, and North Africa, and merchant ships linked ports in China and the Indian Ocean together—but the Americas, Australia, and large parts of inland Africa and Asia were unknown to everyone except for the Indigenous people. The following 350 years changed all of this. By 1800, European adventurers had explored much of the world and established great empires on every continent except for Africa. Meanwhile, the great Muslim empire of the Ottoman Turks, which had once threatened to overrun Europe, was now in serious decline.

THE WORLD 1450–1800
Every picture symbol on this world map relates to a country, event, or people that you will find later in this chapter. The page numbers next to each symbol tell you where you should look to find out about them.

Russia
Russians
pp. 118–119

ASIA

Siberia
Russian merchants
pp. 120–121

Middle East
The Ottomans
pp. 110–111

China
The Manchus
pp. 120–121

Japan
Shoguns
pp. 120–121

India
The Moguls
pp. 112–113

Pacific Ocean
Spanish explorers
pp.100–101

Pacific Ocean

East Africa
Portuguese
traders
pp. 122–123

East Indies
European
traders
pp. 132–133

Indian Ocean

AUSTRALIA

Australia
British convicts
pp. 132–133

LOCATOR MAP

You will find a world map like this with every map in the chapter. This allows you to see exactly which part of the world the main map is showing you.

KEY TO MAPS IN THIS CHAPTER

JAPAN	Main region or country
Deccan	Other region or province
■ PARIS	Capital city
• Yorktown	City, town, or village
Zambezi	River, lake, or island
Andes	Ocean, sea, desert, or mountain range
— · — · —	National boundary
– – – – –	Empire boundary

The world 1450–1800:
What we know about the past

The world changed rapidly after 1450. Inventions that had been known to the Chinese for a long time, such as printing and gunpowder, transformed the world when Europeans discovered them for themselves and then exported them to other continents. New ship designs and navigational aids helped European adventurers explore and then conquer much of the globe. In some countries systems of government based on the rule of an emperor or king were gradually replaced with "democratic" rule by the people, although democracy of this type would not be widespread until the late 1800s. Not everyone was affected at the same time or at the same speed by these changes, but the world of 1800 was very different than the world of 1450.

Printing
In the German town of Mainz, in 1448, Johann Gutenberg developed a printing press that used movable type. This led to a revolution in learning because more and more people were able to obtain and read printed books and pamphlets on a wide range of subjects. It also allowed new or revolutionary ideas to circulate freely as they never had before. Gutenberg's first printed book was the Bible (above).

Democracy
The intellectual revolution of the 1700s—known as the Enlightenment—led many people to question how they were governed and to seek to govern themselves through a democracy. By 1800, democratically elected parliaments ruled some western European nations, as well as the United States of America. The picture above shows the United States' Declaration of Independence, which was signed in 1776.

Powerful monarchs
After 1640 a series of powerful kings ruled in Europe. They were known as "absolute monarchs" because they believed that they held complete power and did not have to answer to anyone else on Earth. One of the most powerful of these kings was Frederick the Great of Prussia (ruled 1740–1786), who ordered the construction of the Neues Palais (below) in Potsdam, outside of Berlin, in Germany.

The Neues Palais was built from 1763–1769 to celebrate Prussia's successes in the Seven Years' War (1756–1763) against Austria, France, and Russia.

The palace contains more than 200 rooms, including four state reception rooms

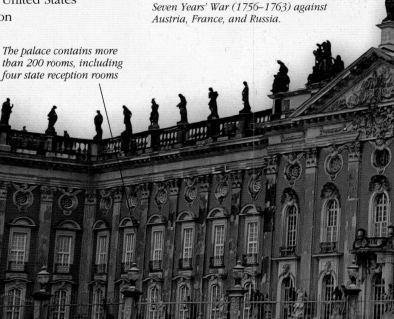

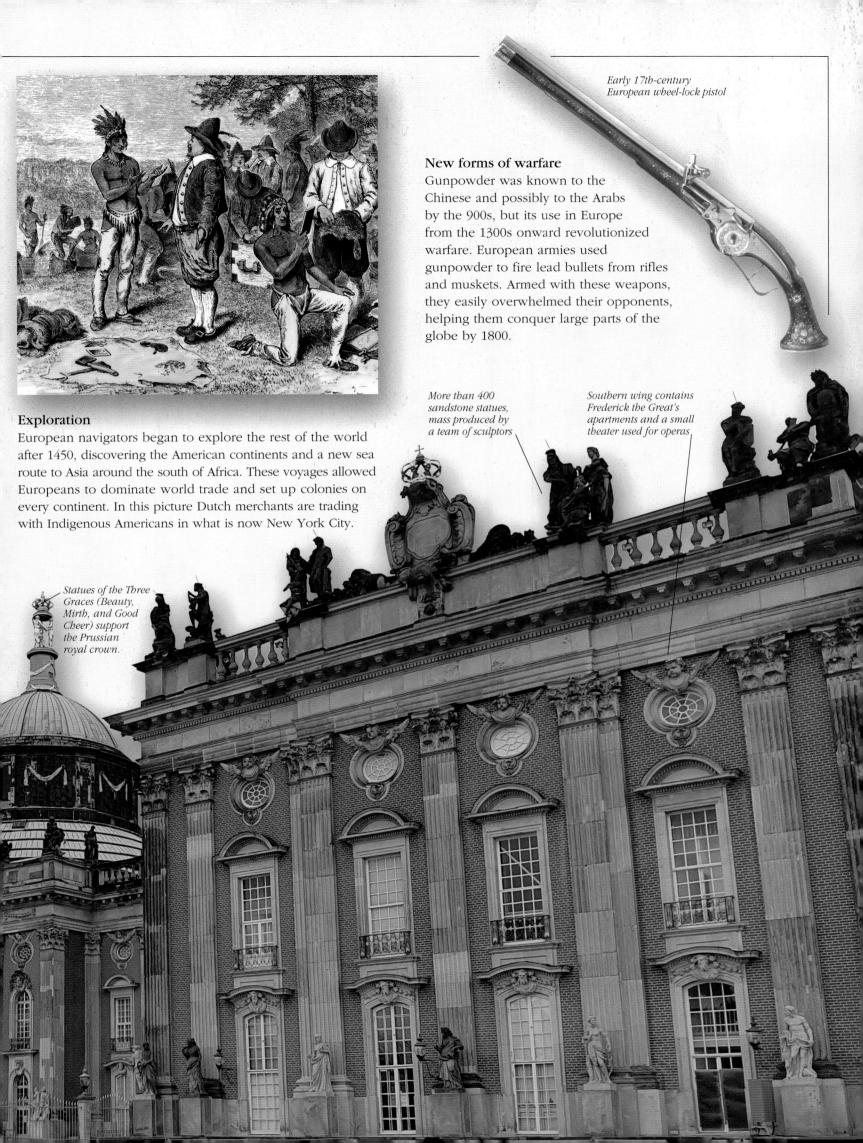

*Early 17th-century
European wheel-lock pistol*

New forms of warfare
Gunpowder was known to the
Chinese and possibly to the Arabs
by the 900s, but its use in Europe
from the 1300s onward revolutionized
warfare. European armies used
gunpowder to fire lead bullets from rifles
and muskets. Armed with these weapons,
they easily overwhelmed their opponents,
helping them conquer large parts of the
globe by 1800.

*More than 400
sandstone statues,
mass produced by
a team of sculptors*

*Southern wing contains
Frederick the Great's
apartments and a small
theater used for operas*

Exploration
European navigators began to explore the rest of the world
after 1450, discovering the American continents and a new sea
route to Asia around the south of Africa. These voyages allowed
Europeans to dominate world trade and set up colonies on
every continent. In this picture Dutch merchants are trading
with Indigenous Americans in what is now New York City.

*Statues of the Three
Graces (Beauty,
Mirth, and Good
Cheer) support
the Prussian
royal crown.*

Voyages of discovery

In the mid-1400s European sailors explored the oceans in search of trade, wealth, and conquests. The Portuguese led the way, exploring the coast of Africa and discovering a sea route to India and Asia. The Spanish sponsored (financially supported) Christopher Columbus to find a western sea route to Asia. Instead, he found the Americas. The English and French then looked for a northwest route to Asia around the north of North America, while the Dutch looked for a northeast route around Siberia. By 1600, Europeans ruled the seas.

KEY TO VOYAGES	
Bartolomeu Dias	1487–1488
Christopher Columbus: 1st voyage	1492–1493
John Cabot	1497
Vasco da Gama	1497–1498
Christopher Columbus: 3rd voyage	1498–1500
Ferdinand Magellan and Sebastián de Elcano	1519–1522
Martin Frobisher	1576
Francis Drake	1577–1580
Willem Barents	1596–1598

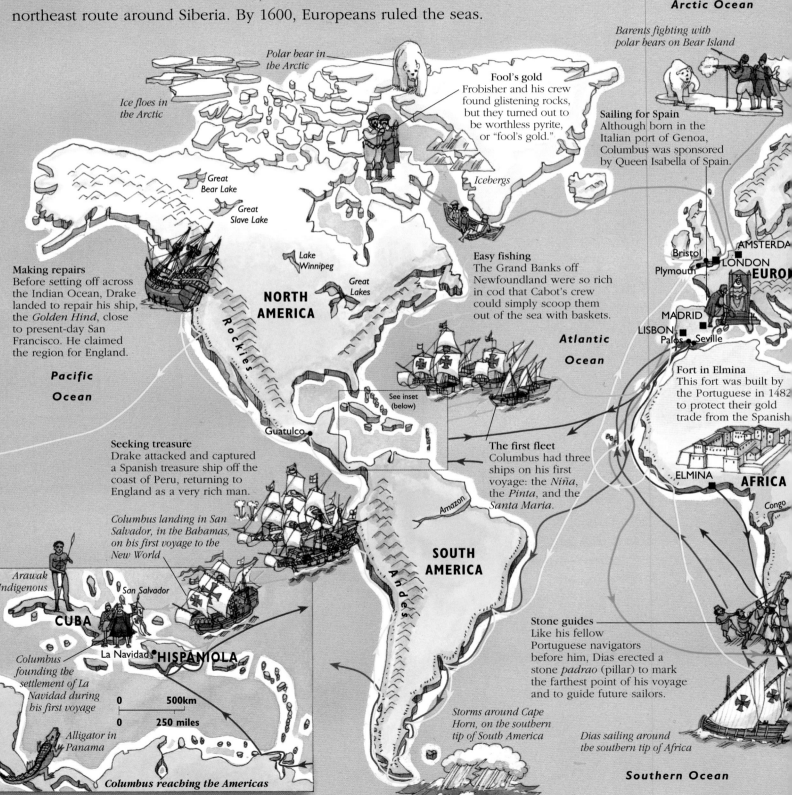

Barents fighting with polar bears on Bear Island

Fool's gold
Frobisher and his crew found glistening rocks, but they turned out to be worthless pyrite, or "fool's gold."

Sailing for Spain
Although born in the Italian port of Genoa, Columbus was sponsored by Queen Isabella of Spain.

Polar bear in the Arctic

Ice floes in the Arctic

Icebergs

Great Bear Lake

Great Slave Lake

Lake Winnipeg

Great Lakes

NORTH AMERICA

Rockies

Easy fishing
The Grand Banks off Newfoundland were so rich in cod that Cabot's crew could simply scoop them out of the sea with baskets.

Bristol

AMSTERDAM

Plymouth

LONDON

EUROPE

MADRID

LISBON

Palos · Seville

Atlantic Ocean

Making repairs
Before setting off across the Indian Ocean, Drake landed to repair his ship, the *Golden Hind*, close to present-day San Francisco. He claimed the region for England.

Pacific Ocean

See inset (below)

Guatulco

The first fleet
Columbus had three ships on his first voyage: the *Niña*, the *Pinta*, and the *Santa Maria*.

Fort in Elmina
This fort was built by the Portuguese in 1482 to protect their gold trade from the Spanish.

ELMINA

AFRICA

Seeking treasure
Drake attacked and captured a Spanish treasure ship off the coast of Peru, returning to England as a very rich man.

Columbus landing in San Salvador, in the Bahamas, on his first voyage to the New World

Amazon

SOUTH AMERICA

Andes

Congo

Stone guides
Like his fellow Portuguese navigators before him, Dias erected a stone *padrao* (pillar) to mark the farthest point of his voyage and to guide future sailors.

Storms around Cape Horn, on the southern tip of South America

Dias sailing around the southern tip of Africa

Southern Ocean

Arctic Ocean

Inset

Arawak Indigenous

San Salvador

CUBA

Columbus founding the settlement of La Navidad during his first voyage

La Navidad **HISPANIOLA**

0	500km
0	250 miles

Alligator in Panama

Columbus reaching the Americas

Navigation

The first European explorers had few instruments to help them and often sailed in the wrong direction. They did, however, use a magnetic compass (left) to follow a set course. To figure out their latitude (how far north or south they were) they used an astrolabe to measure the height of the Sun at noon and a quadrant or a cross-staff, both of which measured the height of a star. Navigators had no way of calculating their longitude (how far east or west they were) until the invention of the marine chronometer in 1759.

Ice-bound
In his search for the Northeast Passage to Asia, Barents's ship got stuck in the ice. He and his crew had to spend the winter of 1596 in a hut that they built on the shore.

Arctic Ocean

0 ———— 4,000km

0 ———— 2,000 miles

ASIA

Yenisey

Ural Mountains

Vasco da Gama in India
Da Gama reached India in 1498 and met the Hindu ruler of Calicut. He had little to exchange with the rich ruler and returned home with only a few spices.

Lake Baikal

Aral Sea

Caspian Sea

Yellow river

Himalayas

Chang (Yangtze)

Across the ocean
Magellan took four months to cross the Pacific Ocean, sighting a few uninhabited islands before landing in Guam in March 1521.

CALICUT

PHILIPPINES

Pacific Ocean

Guam

Cebu

Lake ictoria

MOMBASA
Arab sailing ships

Arab traders
Arab merchants controlled trade in the western Indian Ocean, shipping goods to and from the Persian Gulf, India, and Africa.

EAST INDIES

Death of Magellan
Magellan never completed his around-the-world voyage. He was killed in a skirmish on the island of Cebu, in the Philippines, in 1521.

Spice Islands

Indian Ocean

AUSTRALIA

Food of the Spice Islands (Moluccas), in the East Indies

Bay

Unwelcome visitor
Da Gama visited the busy trading port of Mombasa, but he fled when the local Muslim ruler attacked his two ships.

Lonely voyage home
Magellan began his voyage with five ships and a large crew. After his death, Sebastián de Elcano battled through storms to return home to Spain in 1522, with only one ship and 17 other men.

Southern Ocean

1450

1460 Death of Prince Henry "the Navigator," the first Portuguese sponsor (financial supporter) of voyages of discovery

1485–1486 Diogo Cão sails down the west African coast for Portugal
1487–1488 Dias becomes the first European to sail around the southern tip of Africa into the Indian Ocean
1492–1493 Columbus sails to the Americas
1493–1496 Columbus's second voyage, to the West Indies
1494 Treaty of Tordesillas divides the undiscovered world between Portugal and Spain
1497 Italian John Cabot sails to Newfoundland for the English king
1497–1498 Vasco da Gama opens up a new trade route from Europe across the Indian Ocean to India
1498–1500 Columbus's third voyage: he becomes the first European to land in South America

1500

1502–1504 Columbus's fourth voyage: he lands in Central America

1519–1521 Magellan becomes the first European to sail across the Pacific Ocean
1521–1522 Sebastián de Elcano completes Magellan's voyage as the first person to sail around the world

1527–1528 Pánfilo de Narváez explores the Gulf of Mexico for Spain

1534 Jacques Cartier searches for a Northwest Passage to Asia for the French king, but he discovers Canada instead

1550

1567–1569 Álvaro de Mendaña explores the southern Pacific Ocean for Spain

1576 Martin Frobisher explores the Northwest Passage for England
1577–1580 Francis Drake sails around the world

1596–1598 Dutch navigator Willem Barents explores the Northeast Passage

1600

Aztecs and Incas

In the early 1500s two great and powerful empires dominated the Americas, the Aztecs and the Incas, while the once great Maya civilization continued to prosper in the Yucatán Peninsula. But within a few years, these empires were swept away by a handful of Spanish conquistadors (conquerors) from Europe. Hernando Cortés overwhelmed the Aztec Empire in 1519–1521, while Francisco Pizarro, with only 168 troops, did the same to the Inca Empire in 1532–1533. Both leaders took full advantage of their enemies' weaknesses. For example, diseases brought by the Spanish—such as smallpox, from which the Indigenous Americans had no immunity—soon killed thousands, making a Spanish takeover of both empires much easier to achieve.

Tenochtitlán: the Aztec capital

Aztec capital
The Aztec capital, Tenochtitlán, was built on a lake and had a population of 500,000 at the time of the Spanish conquest, much larger than most European cities.

Good food
Aztec farmers grew food on reclaimed swamplands around Lake Texcoco.

Lake Texcoco

TENOCHTITLÁN

The Spanish approach
In Aztec legend a fair-skinned, bearded god named Quetzalcóatl would one day return to his people. The Aztecs believed that Cortés was Quetzalcóatl, and so at first they refused to fight him when the Spanish came to Tenochtitlán.

Human sacrifices
The Aztecs captured prisoners from neighboring tribes to sacrifice to their sun god. In revenge many of these tribes helped the Spanish against their Aztec oppressors.

Chichén Itzá
Once the Toltec capital of the Yucatán Peninsula, Chichén Itzá remained the capital of an important Mayan state until the Spanish conquered it.

The arrival of Hernando Cortés
Cortés arrived off the east coast of the Yucatán Peninsula in April 1519. He then sailed around the coast before heading inland at Cempoala toward Tenochtitlán, the Aztec capital.

Civil war
Conflict between Mayan cities had divided their empire into 16 rival states, making it harder for the Spanish to gain control quickly.

Making cocoa
In around 1500 the Aztecs conquered the rich province of Xoconochco for its cocoa and other products.

TENOCHTITLÁN
See inset (right)

An Aztec woman making tortillas

Tula

TLAXCALA
TEOTITLÁN

This may have been a feather headdress worn by an Aztec priest

Aztec steam bath

Pacific Ocean

El Tajín
Cempoala

Gulf of Mexico

Mayapan
Chichén Itzá

NORTHERN MAYA STATES

Yucatán Peninsula

QUICHÉ MAYA

Sierra Madre

XOCONOCHCO

Coatzacoalcos

Mazatlán

Panamá

Panama City

QUITO

Tumbes

Huancabamba

Andes

Llamas, used by the Incas as pack animals

Capture
Pizarro captured the Inca emperor Atahuallpa in Cajamarca. This paralyzed the empire because no decisions could be made without the emperor's agreement.

Spanish landing
The Spanish invasion fleet led by Francisco Pizarro sailed south from Panama and landed in Tumbes in 1532. The troops then headed inland toward the Inca capital.

The Amazon rain forest

Amazon

Ucayali

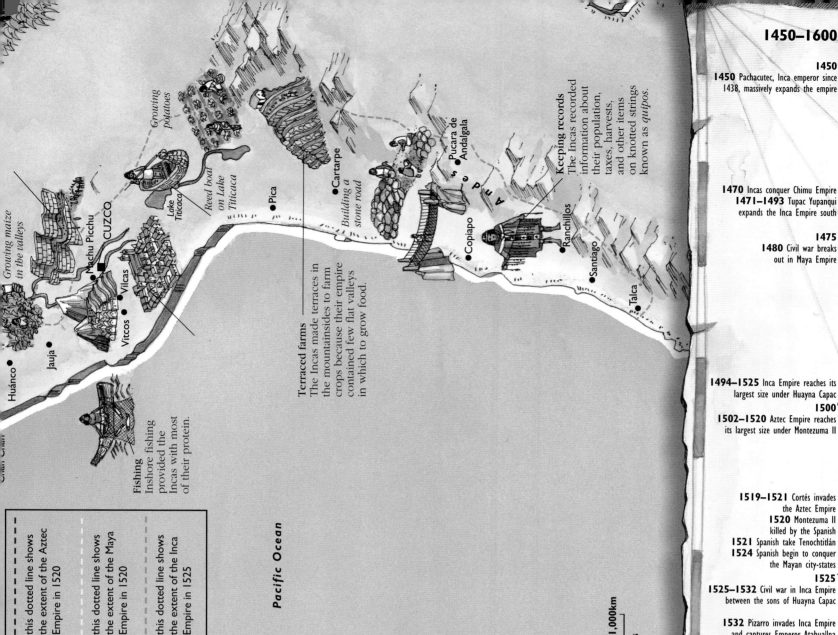

Growing potatoes

Growing maize in the valleys

Machu Picchu
CUZCO

Reed boat on Lake Titicaca

Lake Titicaca

Vilcas

Vitcos

Jauja

Huánco

Pica

Cartarpe

Building a stone road

Pucara de Andalgala

Copiapo

Ranchillos

Santiago

Talca

A n d e s

Keeping records
The Incas recorded information about their population, taxes, harvests, and other items on knotted strings known as *quipos*.

Terraced farms
The Incas made terraces in the mountainsides to farm crops because their empire contained few flat valleys in which to grow food.

Fishing
Inshore fishing provided the Incas with most of their protein.

- - - - - this dotted line shows the extent of the Aztec Empire in 1520

- - - - - this dotted line shows the extent of the Maya Empire in 1520

- - - - - this dotted line shows the extent of the Inca Empire in 1525

Pacific Ocean

0 _____ 1,000km
0 _____ 500 miles

The Spanish conquest
Although small in number, the Spanish were able to conquer the mighty Aztec, Maya, and Inca empires because they were much better armed and fought on horses, which were unknown in the Americas at that time. Most importantly, the Spanish were able to exploit their enemies' weaknesses: many local tribes hated the bloodthirsty Aztecs and fought with the Spanish against them, while the Inca Empire had not yet recovered from a lengthy civil war. Only the Mayas held out for a long period because they were divided into 16 different city-states, making it difficult for the Spanish to conquer them all at one time. This picture (above) shows Indigenous Americans receiving Christian communion from a Spanish priest.

1450 Pachacutec, Inca emperor since 1438, massively expands the empire

1450

1470 Incas conquer Chimu Empire
1471–1493 Tupac Yupanqui expands the Inca Empire south

1475

1480 Civil war breaks out in Maya Empire

1494–1525 Inca Empire reaches its largest size under Huayna Capac

1500

1502–1520 Aztec Empire reaches its largest size under Montezuma II

1519–1521 Cortés invades the Aztec Empire
1520 Montezuma II killed by the Spanish
1521 Spanish take Tenochtitlán
1524 Spanish begin to conquer the Mayan city-states

1525

1525–1532 Civil war in Inca Empire between the sons of Huayna Capac

1532 Pizarro invades Inca Empire and captures Emperor Atahuallpa
1533 Spanish execute Atahuallpa and install a "puppet" emperor, Thupu Wallpa, whom they can control

1536 Spanish take direct control of the Inca Empire

1550

1572 Last Inca resistance crushed in the mountain strongholds

1575

1600 Mayan resistance to the Spanish continues until 1697

1600

Charles V and the Hapsburg Empire
Charles V of Spain was the master of Europe. Born in 1500, he inherited the Rhineland and the Netherlands from his Hapsburg father, plus Spain and its Italian and American empires from his Spanish grandfather and mother. In 1519 he inherited Hapsburg Austria from his grandfather and was elected the Holy Roman Emperor, in effect the ruler of Germany. He abdicated (resigned) in 1556 and died in 1558.

School of Navigation
In 1416 Prince Henry the Navigator, the son of the king of Portugal, opened a navigation school in Sagres to promote exploration and discovery.

Spain and its empire

I n the early 1500s Spain, ruled by the Hapsburg family of Austria, emerged as the most powerful nation in Europe. The country and its king, Charles V, had gained a large European empire through marriage and inheritance, and then a second empire in the Americas through conquest. Spain became the major Catholic power in Europe and led the fight against the Protestant Reformation (see pages 108–109). Spanish power attracted many enemies, and the empire soon proved to be too big for one person to rule. In 1556 Charles V split his empire in two, giving Spain and its territories to his son and other lands to his brother.

The Spanish Armada
In 1588 a large fleet left La Coruña to invade England and depose the Protestant queen, Elizabeth I. The fleet was defeated by a combination of the English navy and very bad weather.

Don Quixote
The Spanish writer Miguel de Cervantes wrote the classic story *Don Quixote*. It was published in two parts, in 1605 and 1615.

The Escorial Pala
Philip II ordered huge palace to be bu outside of Madrid, fr which to govern huge Europe and Americ empi

Taking over Portugal
In 1580 Philip II of Spain defeated the Portuguese in Alcântara and seized the Portuguese throne. Spain held on to Portugal's huge empire until 1640.

Joint monarchs
In 1469 Ferdinand of Aragon married Isabella of Castile. In 1479 they both succeeded to their thrones and ruled their countries jointly, uniting Spain.

The Morisco revolt
Islamic Moors were converted to Christianity by force in 1492. They rebelled against Spanish rule 70 years later.

End of Moorish rule
Ferdinand and Isabella finally drove the Moors out of Granada in 1492, ending 781 years of Muslim rule in Spain.

Raiding parties
English privateers (pirates sent by the government) led by Francis Drake regularly raided Spanish ports to seize American treasures and disrupt shipping.

Coastal forts
The Spaniards built a series of forts along the North African coast, from which to control the western Mediterranean and fight the Ottomans.

Heading south
After 1432 Portuguese navigators began to explore the west coast of Africa, setting up trading posts as they sailed farther south.

North Africa

La Coruña
Cork tree
Douro
Ebro
PORTUGAL
MADRID ■
SPAIN
Castile
Toledo
Alcântara
Tagus
Guadiana
Toledo cathedral
LISBON
Sagres
Córdoba
Guadalquivir
Seville
Granada
Atlantic Ocean
Cadiz
Ceuta
Tangier
Melilla

0   200 km
0   100 miles

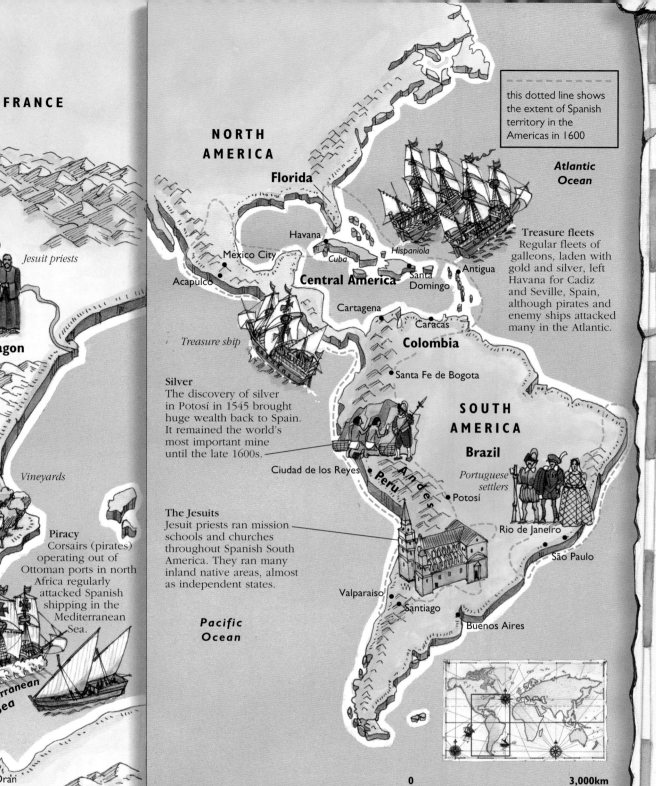

FRANCE

Navarre

Jesuit priests

Aragon

Vineyards

Piracy
Corsairs (pirates) operating out of Ottoman ports in north Africa regularly attacked Spanish shipping in the Mediterranean Sea.

Mediterranean Sea

• Oran

NORTH AMERICA

Florida

this dotted line shows the extent of Spanish territory in the Americas in 1600

Atlantic Ocean

Havana

Mexico City •   *Cuba*   *Hispaniola*   • Antigua

Acapulco •   **Central America**   Santa Domingo

Cartagena

Caracas •

Colombia

Treasure ship

• Santa Fe de Bogota

Treasure fleets
Regular fleets of galleons, laden with gold and silver, left Havana for Cadiz and Seville, Spain, although pirates and enemy ships attacked many in the Atlantic.

Silver
The discovery of silver in Potosí in 1545 brought huge wealth back to Spain. It remained the world's most important mine until the late 1600s.

SOUTH AMERICA

Brazil

Ciudad de los Reyes •

A n d e s

Peru

Portuguese settlers

The Jesuits
Jesuit priests ran mission schools and churches throughout Spanish South America. They ran many inland native areas, almost as independent states.

• Potosí

Rio de Janeiro •

São Paulo •

Valparaiso •

Santiago •

Pacific Ocean

Buenos Aires •

0   3,000km

0   1,500 miles

Spanish wealth

The gold and silver mines in Mexico and Peru brought incredible wealth to Spain. Large galleons, accompanied by armed warships, carried the bullion across the Atlantic Ocean. Despite these precautions, pirates and enemy ships, especially from England and Holland, often attacked the fleets. This wealth enabled Spain to dominate Europe because it could afford to pay for large armies, but it also caused prices to rise at home, eventually ruining the Spanish economy. This picture shows a plan of the silver mines in Potosí, in modern-day Bolivia.

1450–1600

1450

1456 Portuguese colonize Cape Verde islands, off western Africa, and head south down the west African coast

1469 Ferdinand of Aragon marries Isabella of Castile

1479 Ferdinand and Isabella begin their joint rule of Spain

1487 Portuguese sail around the Cape of Good Hope at the southern tip of Africa

1492 Spain reconquers Granada and converts the Moors to Christianity; Jews are expelled from Spain
1492 Columbus makes the first voyage to the New World
1496 Philip of Burgundy, France, marries Joanna, heiress to the Spanish throne, linking his Hapsburg family with Spain
1497 Spain builds a fort in Melilla on the North African coast
1498 Portuguese reach India

1500
1500 Birth of Charles, son of Philip and Joanna
1504 Death of Isabella; Ferdinand rules Spain with Joanna and Philip
1506 Philip dies, leaving the Rhineland and the Netherlands to Charles
1509 Spain seizes Oran in North Africa
1512 Spain conquers the kingdom of Navarre in the north of Spain
1516 Death of Ferdinand, leaving Spain to his grandson, who becomes Charles I
1517 Martin Luther's ideas for reform challenge the Catholic Church and Hapsburg power in Europe
1519 Death of Maximilian, Hapsburg ruler of Austria and Holy Roman Emperor; Charles I succeeds him as Emperor Charles V
1519–1521 Spanish capture Aztec Empire
1524 Spanish begin to take over Maya Empire
1530 Portuguese begin to colonize Brazil in South America
1532–1533 Spanish capture Inca Empire
1538 Spanish colonize Colombia in South America
1545 Silver discovered in Potosí, Peru, in South America
1548 Silver found in Mexico

1550
1556 Charles V abdicates; Philip II succeeds him in Spain; Charles's brother Ferdinand becomes the Holy Roman Emperor

1563–1584 Escorial Palace is built by the order of Philip II
1565 Spanish colonize Florida, in North America, and build a fort there to protect their gold bullion fleets
1566 Dutch begin a revolt against Spanish rule
1569–1571 Moriscos revolt in southern Spain
1571 Spanish begin to colonize the Philippines; Manila is founded
1574 Spanish lose the important port of Tunis to the Ottomans

1580–1640 Spain rules Portugal and its empire
1581 Spain makes peace with the Ottomans

1588 Spanish Armada fails to invade England

1598 Philip II dies; Philip III succeeds him

1600

PROSPETO DEL CERRO DE POTOSI

The Renaissance:
A world of new learning

The Renaissance—a French word meaning "rebirth"—was an artistic, cultural, and intellectual movement that influenced all of the arts and sciences. Renaissance artists and scholars looked back to the art and education of classical Rome and Greece for their inspiration, reviving the past in order to develop and explore new ideas and methods. This new approach became known as "humanism" because it encouraged people to achieve things for themselves, rather than simply to accept what they were taught to be true. The Renaissance began in Italy during the 1300s and reached its height during the 1400s and 1500s, spreading across all of western and northern Europe.

Scientific invention
A "Renaissance man" or "universal man" was someone who could do many things. One such person was Leonardo da Vinci (1452–1519), who, as well as being an artist and a sculptor, drew plans for a helicopter (above), a flying machine, and a tank. He also dissected human bodies to find out more about how we move and function.

Renaissance art
Renaissance artists depicted people and landscapes in a very natural way, studying anatomy and perspective to make their paintings look more realistic. Michelangelo (1475–1564) was perhaps the greatest Renaissance artist, creating lifelike sculptures, such as his *David* (left), and huge paintings such as the ceiling of the Sistine Chapel in Rome, Italy.

Astronomy
The Renaissance encouraged scientists to explore new ideas and to challenge existing beliefs. In 1543 the Polish astronomer Nicolaus Copernicus (1473–1543) proposed that the Sun was at the center of the solar system and that all of the planets revolved around it. This shocked many people because their religious teachings had always insisted that Earth was at the center of the universe. The chart above shows the arrangement that was suggested by Copernicus.

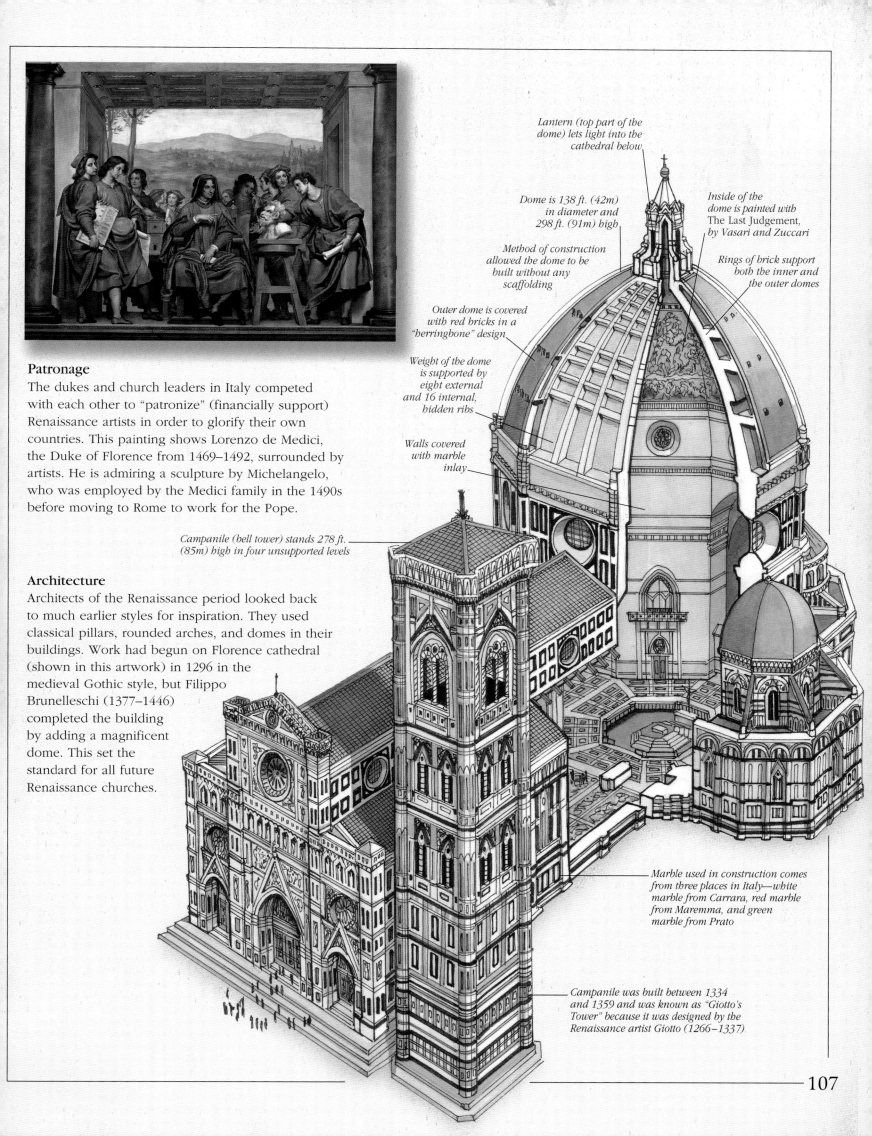

Patronage

The dukes and church leaders in Italy competed with each other to "patronize" (financially support) Renaissance artists in order to glorify their own countries. This painting shows Lorenzo de Medici, the Duke of Florence from 1469–1492, surrounded by artists. He is admiring a sculpture by Michelangelo, who was employed by the Medici family in the 1490s before moving to Rome to work for the Pope.

Architecture

Architects of the Renaissance period looked back to much earlier styles for inspiration. They used classical pillars, rounded arches, and domes in their buildings. Work had begun on Florence cathedral (shown in this artwork) in 1296 in the medieval Gothic style, but Filippo Brunelleschi (1377–1446) completed the building by adding a magnificent dome. This set the standard for all future Renaissance churches.

Lantern (top part of the dome) lets light into the cathedral below

Dome is 138 ft. (42m) in diameter and 298 ft. (91m) high

Inside of the dome is painted with The Last Judgement, by Vasari and Zuccari

Method of construction allowed the dome to be built without any scaffolding

Rings of brick support both the inner and the outer domes

Outer dome is covered with red bricks in a "herringbone" design

Weight of the dome is supported by eight external and 16 internal, hidden ribs

Walls covered with marble inlay

Campanile (bell tower) stands 278 ft. (85m) high in four unsupported levels

Marble used in construction comes from three places in Italy—white marble from Carrara, red marble from Maremma, and green marble from Prato

Campanile was built between 1334 and 1359 and was known as "Giotto's Tower" because it was designed by the Renaissance artist Giotto (1266–1337)

The Reformation

For more than 1,000 years, every Christian in western Europe belonged to the Roman Catholic Church, but some began to accuse the Church of abusing its powers. In 1517 a German monk named Martin Luther nailed a list onto the door of his church. The list contained 95 proposals for reforming the Catholic Church. This was soon printed and distributed, beginning a widespread revolt against Catholicism. The Catholic Church condemned Luther as a heretic (someone whose beliefs go against those of the Church) in 1521, so he set up his own "Lutheran Church." Those who followed Luther became known as Protestants because they "protested" their new faith against Catholicism. The reformation of the Christian Church led to years of warfare and division in Europe.

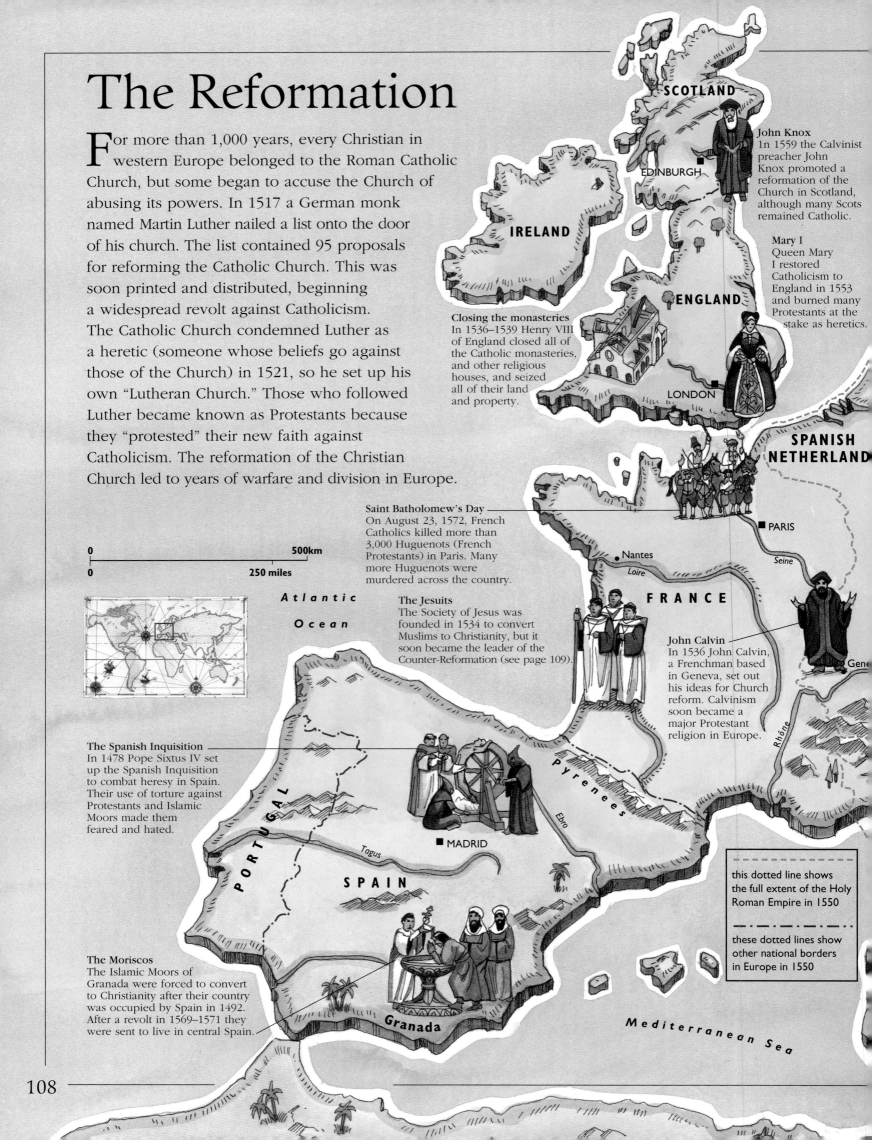

John Knox
In 1559 the Calvinist preacher John Knox promoted a reformation of the Church in Scotland, although many Scots remained Catholic.

Mary I
Queen Mary I restored Catholicism to England in 1553 and burned many Protestants at the stake as heretics.

Closing the monasteries
In 1536–1539 Henry VIII of England closed all of the Catholic monasteries, and other religious houses, and seized all of their land and property.

Saint Batholomew's Day
On August 23, 1572, French Catholics killed more than 3,000 Huguenots (French Protestants) in Paris. Many more Huguenots were murdered across the country.

The Jesuits
The Society of Jesus was founded in 1534 to convert Muslims to Christianity, but it soon became the leader of the Counter-Reformation (see page 109).

John Calvin
In 1536 John Calvin, a Frenchman based in Geneva, set out his ideas for Church reform. Calvinism soon became a major Protestant religion in Europe.

The Spanish Inquisition
In 1478 Pope Sixtus IV set up the Spanish Inquisition to combat heresy in Spain. Their use of torture against Protestants and Islamic Moors made them feared and hated.

The Moriscos
The Islamic Moors of Granada were forced to convert to Christianity after their country was occupied by Spain in 1492. After a revolt in 1569–1571 they were sent to live in central Spain.

0 ———————— 500km
0 ———————— 250 miles

this dotted line shows the full extent of the Holy Roman Empire in 1550

these dotted lines show other national borders in Europe in 1550

SCOTLAND
EDINBURGH
IRELAND
ENGLAND
LONDON
SPANISH NETHERLAND
PARIS
Nantes
Loire
Seine
FRANCE
Gene
Atlantic Ocean
PORTUGAL
Tagus
MADRID
SPAIN
Ebro
Pyrenees
Rhône
Granada
Mediterranean Sea

North Sea

NORWAY

DENMARK

SWEDEN

Baltic Sea

Gutenberg's printing press, developed in the 1440s

German Catholic church in flames

Radical preachers

Elbe

Wittenberg

Saxony

Germany

Worms

Rhine

HOLY ROMAN EMPIRE

SWISS CONFEDERATION

Augsburg

Zürich

Danube

Bavaria

Council of Trent
Catholic officials met in Trent three times after 1545.

Trent

Austria

POLAND

HUNGARY

OTTOMAN EMPIRE

VENICE

Po

PAPAL STATES

■ **ROME**

St. Peter's Basilica in Rome, Italy

Martin Luther

Martin Luther (1483–1546), pictured here in dark robes, was an Augustinian friar and professor of theology at Wittenberg University in Saxony. He objected to many aspects of Catholic beliefs and practices, but he at first wanted to reform the Church, not divide it. When this proved to be impossible, he set up his own reformed church.

Copernicus

In 1531 Copernicus, a Polish astronomer, demonstrated that the planets move around the Sun, and not around Earth. This went against the teachings of the Catholic Church.

The 95 Theses

In 1517 Martin Luther nailed 95 proposals for Catholic reform to the door of his church in Wittenberg, Saxony.

Expelling Protestants

In the late 1550s Protestants were thrown out of Bavaria and Austria as the Catholic Church regained its control. Poland had also become Catholic again.

The Pope

As a result of the Reformation, Rome's role as the headquarters of the Christian Church was reduced, but the Pope remained an important figure in Europe for many years.

The Counter-Reformation

From 1545 to 1563, the Roman Catholic Church met in Trent, in the Italian Alps, to reform the Church and to help it fight back against Protestantism. The Counter-Reformation saw great changes in practice, and religious buildings in the new Baroque style of architecture—such as Saint Peter's Basilica in Rome, Italy (above)—helped attract people back into the Catholic Church.

1510–1600

1510

1517 Martin Luther nails 95 proposals for Catholic reform to the door of his church in Wittenberg, Saxony

1520

1521 Luther presents his ideas for reform to the Holy Roman Emperor at the Diet (council) of Worms
1523 In Zürich Ulrich Zwingli proposes 67 reforms to the Catholic Church
1524 Religious warfare breaks out in Germany as peasants rise up in revolt
1525 Lutheranism is the state religion of Saxony and many other German states

1530

1531 Copernicus suggests the Sun, not Earth, is at the center of the universe
1534 Society of Jesus (Jesuits) forms
1534 Henry VIII of England breaks away from the Catholic Church when it refuses to grant him a divorce
1536 John Calvin sets out his ideas for religious reforms in his book, *Institutes*
1536–1539 Henry VIII closes monasteries

1540

1541 John Calvin begins to organize a strict Protestant church in Geneva

1544 Sweden converts to Lutheranism
1545–1563 The Roman Catholic Church meets three times in Trent, in the Alps, to launch the Counter-Reformation against Protestant Churches

1550

1553–1558 England briefly becomes Catholic again under Mary I
1555 After years of war Holy Roman Emperor agrees to the Peace of Augsburg, giving each ruler within the empire the right to choose their own state religion
1558 Elizabeth I comes to the throne and restores Protestantism to England

1560

1560 Scottish Parliament declares Scotland to be a Protestant nation
1562–1580 French wars of religion divide the country

1566 Dutch Protestants rise up in revolt against Spanish Catholic rulers

1570

1572 Thousands of French Huguenots (Protestants) are massacred by Catholics

1580

1589 The Huguenot Henry Navarre becomes Henry IV of France
1590

1593 Henry IV of France becomes a Catholic

1598 Edict of Nantes grants religious tolerance to Huguenots in France

1600

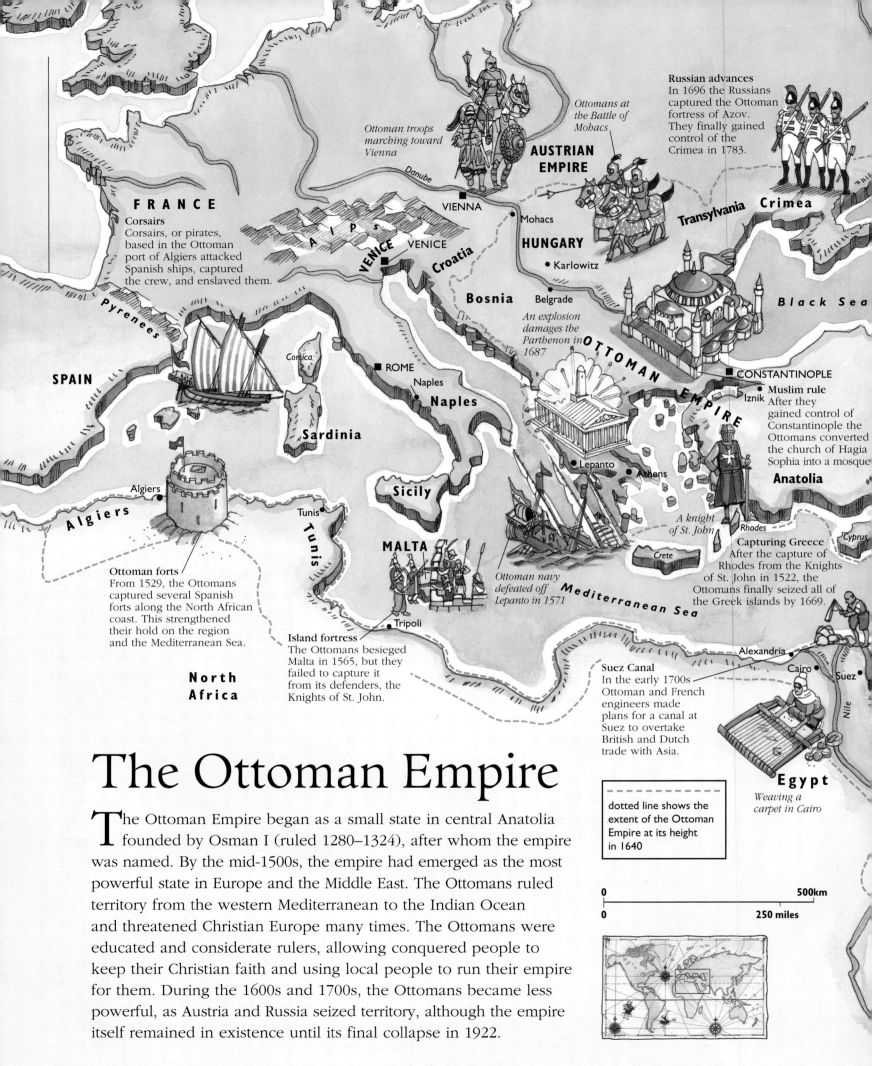

Russian advances
In 1696 the Russians captured the Ottoman fortress of Azov. They finally gained control of the Crimea in 1783.

Ottomans at the Battle of Mohacs

Ottoman troops marching toward Vienna

AUSTRIAN EMPIRE

Danube

VIENNA

Mohacs

Transylvania

Crimea

F R A N C E

Corsairs
Corsairs, or pirates, based in the Ottoman port of Algiers attacked Spanish ships, captured the crew, and enslaved them.

HUNGARY

• Karlowitz

Croatia

VENICE VENICE

Bosnia

Belgrade

Black Sea

Pyrenees

An explosion damages the Parthenon in 1687

O
T
T
O
M
A
N

CONSTANTINOPLE

Iznik

SPAIN

Corsica

■ ROME

Naples

Naples

E
M
P
I
R
E

Muslim rule
After they gained control of Constantinople the Ottomans converted the church of Hagia Sophia into a mosque

• Lepanto

• Athens

Anatolia

Sardinia

Sicily

A knight of St. John

Rhodes

Cyprus

Algiers

Tunis •

MALTA

Crete

Capturing Greece
After the capture of Rhodes from the Knights of St. John in 1522, the Ottomans finally seized all of the Greek islands by 1669.

A l g i e r s

Ottoman forts
From 1529, the Ottomans captured several Spanish forts along the North African coast. This strengthened their hold on the region and the Mediterranean Sea.

T
u
n
i
s

Ottoman navy defeated off Lepanto in 1571

Mediterranean Sea

• Tripoli

North Africa

Island fortress
The Ottomans besieged Malta in 1565, but they failed to capture it from its defenders, the Knights of St. John.

Suez Canal
In the early 1700s Ottoman and French engineers made plans for a canal at Suez to overtake British and Dutch trade with Asia.

Alexandria

Cairo •

• Suez

Nile

The Ottoman Empire

The Ottoman Empire began as a small state in central Anatolia founded by Osman I (ruled 1280–1324), after whom the empire was named. By the mid-1500s, the empire had emerged as the most powerful state in Europe and the Middle East. The Ottomans ruled territory from the western Mediterranean to the Indian Ocean and threatened Christian Europe many times. The Ottomans were educated and considerate rulers, allowing conquered people to keep their Christian faith and using local people to run their empire for them. During the 1600s and 1700s, the Ottomans became less powerful, as Austria and Russia seized territory, although the empire itself remained in existence until its final collapse in 1922.

Egypt

Weaving a carpet in Cairo

dotted line shows the extent of the Ottoman Empire at its height in 1640

| 0 | 500km |

| 0 | 250 miles |

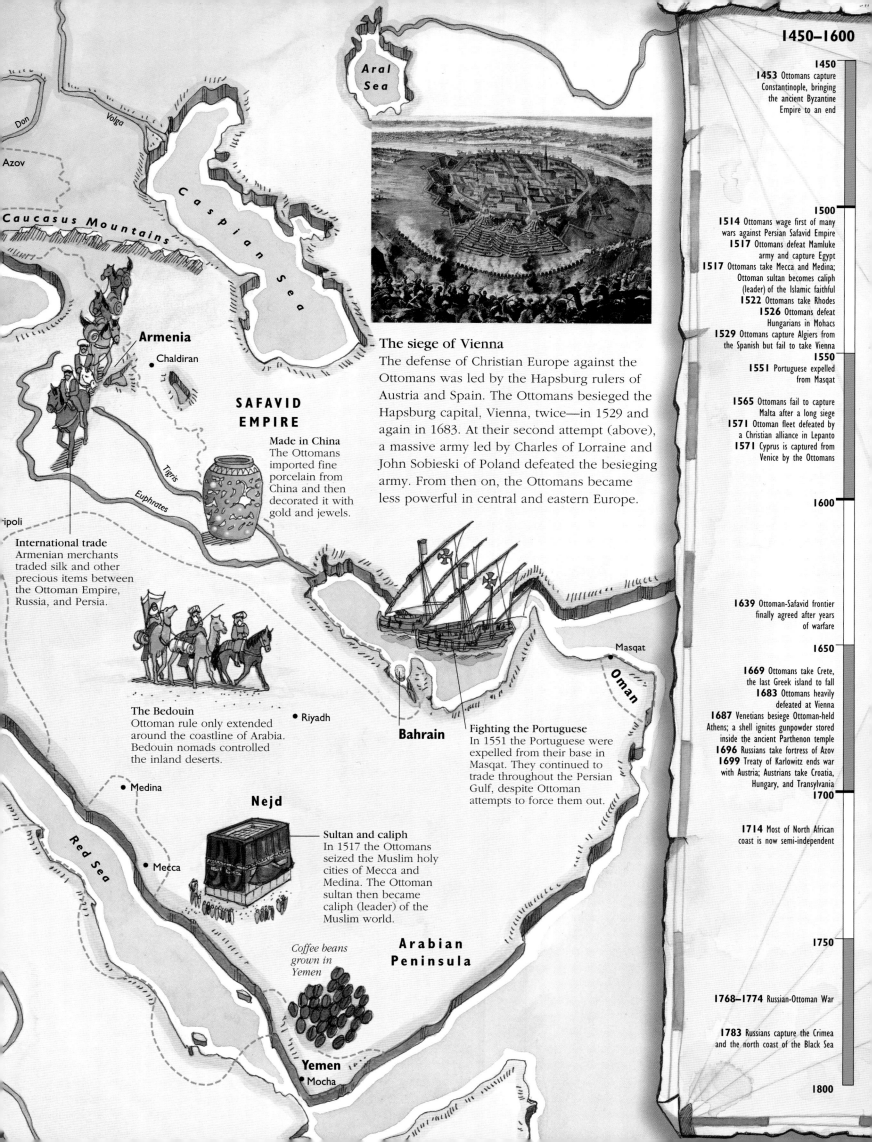

Aral
Sea

Don

Volga

Azov

Caucasus Mountains

Caspian Sea

Armenia

• Chaldiran

SAFAVID
EMPIRE

Tigris

Euphrates

ripoli

Made in China
The Ottomans
imported fine
porcelain from
China and then
decorated it with
gold and jewels.

International trade
Armenian merchants
traded silk and other
precious items between
the Ottoman Empire,
Russia, and Persia.

The Bedouin
Ottoman rule only extended
around the coastline of Arabia.
Bedouin nomads controlled
the inland deserts.

• Riyadh

• Medina

Nejd

Red Sea

• Mecca

Sultan and caliph
In 1517 the Ottomans
seized the Muslim holy
cities of Mecca and
Medina. The Ottoman
sultan then became
caliph (leader) of the
Muslim world.

*Coffee beans
grown in
Yemen*

**Arabian
Peninsula**

Yemen
• Mocha

The siege of Vienna
The defense of Christian Europe against the
Ottomans was led by the Hapsburg rulers of
Austria and Spain. The Ottomans besieged the
Hapsburg capital, Vienna, twice—in 1529 and
again in 1683. At their second attempt (above),
a massive army led by Charles of Lorraine and
John Sobieski of Poland defeated the besieging
army. From then on, the Ottomans became
less powerful in central and eastern Europe.

Masqat

Oman

Bahrain

Fighting the Portuguese
In 1551 the Portuguese were
expelled from their base in
Masqat. They continued to
trade throughout the Persian
Gulf, despite Ottoman
attempts to force them out.

1450–1600

1450
1453 Ottomans capture
Constantinople, bringing
the ancient Byzantine
Empire to an end

1500
1514 Ottomans wage first of many
wars against Persian Safavid Empire
1517 Ottomans defeat Mamluke
army and capture Egypt
1517 Ottomans take Mecca and Medina;
Ottoman sultan becomes caliph
(leader) of the Islamic faithful
1522 Ottomans take Rhodes
1526 Ottomans defeat
Hungarians in Mohacs
1529 Ottomans capture Algiers from
the Spanish but fail to take Vienna
1550
1551 Portuguese expelled
from Masqat

1565 Ottomans fail to capture
Malta after a long siege
1571 Ottoman fleet defeated by
a Christian alliance in Lepanto
1571 Cyprus is captured from
Venice by the Ottomans

1600

1639 Ottoman-Safavid frontier
finally agreed after years
of warfare

1650

1669 Ottomans take Crete,
the last Greek island to fall
1683 Ottomans heavily
defeated at Vienna
1687 Venetians besiege Ottoman-held
Athens; a shell ignites gunpowder stored
inside the ancient Parthenon temple
1696 Russians take fortress of Azov
1699 Treaty of Karlowitz ends war
with Austria; Austrians take Croatia,
Hungary, and Transylvania
1700

1714 Most of North African
coast is now semi-independent

1750

1768–1774 Russian-Ottoman War

1783 Russians capture the Crimea
and the north coast of the Black Sea

1800

The Mogul Empire

In the late 1400s the Moguls—descendants of the famous Mongol leader Timur—were driven out of central Asia by the Mongol Tatars. They moved south and began to raid India, mounting a full-scale invasion in 1526. They soon conquered northern India, and by 1600, they were advancing south into the Deccan. One hundred years later they controlled everything except the far south. The Moguls were good administrators; although Muslim, they allowed their Hindu and Sikh subjects to worship freely. In the 1700s the Mogul Empire came under attack from the Hindu Marathas of the west coast, while the French and British also gained territory. By 1800, the British had defeated the French and dominated Mogul India.

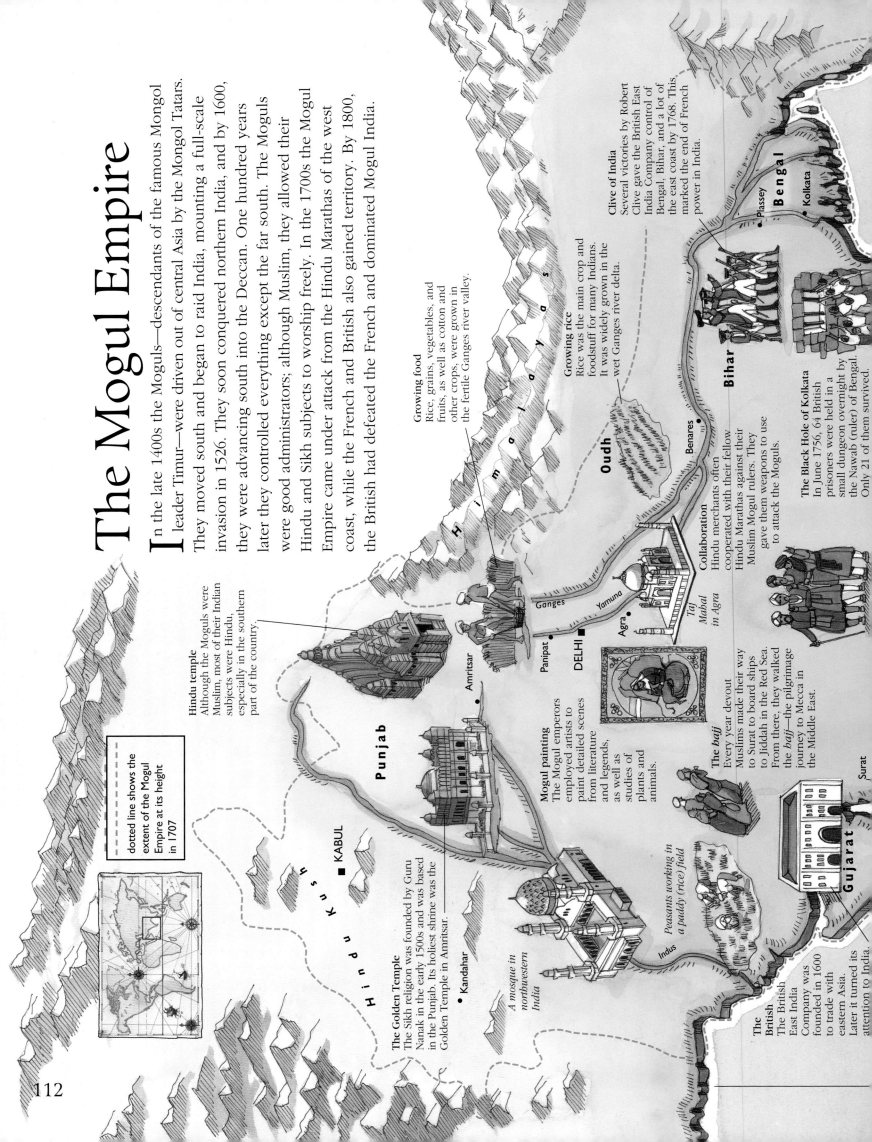

dotted line shows the extent of the Mogul Empire at its height in 1707

Hindu temple
Although the Moguls were Muslim, most of their Indian subjects were Hindu, especially in the southern part of the country.

The Golden Temple
The Sikh religion was founded by Guru Nanak in the early 1500s and was based in the Punjab. Its holiest shrine was the Golden Temple in Amritsar.

A mosque in northwestern India

Mogul painting
The Mogul emperors employed artists to paint detailed scenes from literature and legends, as well as studies of plants and animals.

Peasants working in a paddy (rice) field

The hajj
Every year devout Muslims made their way to Surat to board ships to Jiddah in the Red Sea. From there, they walked the *hajj*—the pilgrimage journey to Mecca in the Middle East.

The British
The British East India Company was founded in 1600 to trade with eastern Asia. Later it turned its attention to India.

Growing food
Rice, grains, vegetables, and fruits, as well as cotton and other crops, were grown in the fertile Ganges river valley.

Growing rice
Rice was the main crop and foodstuff for many Indians. It was widely grown in the wet Ganges river delta.

Collaboration
Hindu merchants often cooperated with their fellow Hindu Marathas against their Muslim Mogul rulers. They gave them weapons to use to attack the Moguls.

Taj Mahal in Agra

Clive of India
Several victories by Robert Clive gave the British East India Company control of Bengal, Bihar, and a lot of the east coast by 1768. This marked the end of French power in India.

The Black Hole of Kolkata
In June 1756, 64 British prisoners were held in a small dungeon overnight by the Nawab (ruler) of Bengal. Only 21 of them survived.

Hindu Kush

KABUL

Kandahar

Punjab

Amritsar

Indus

Gujarat

Surat

Himalayas

Panipat

DELHI

Agra

Yamuna

Ganges

Oudh

Benares

Bihar

Bengal

Plassey

Kolkata

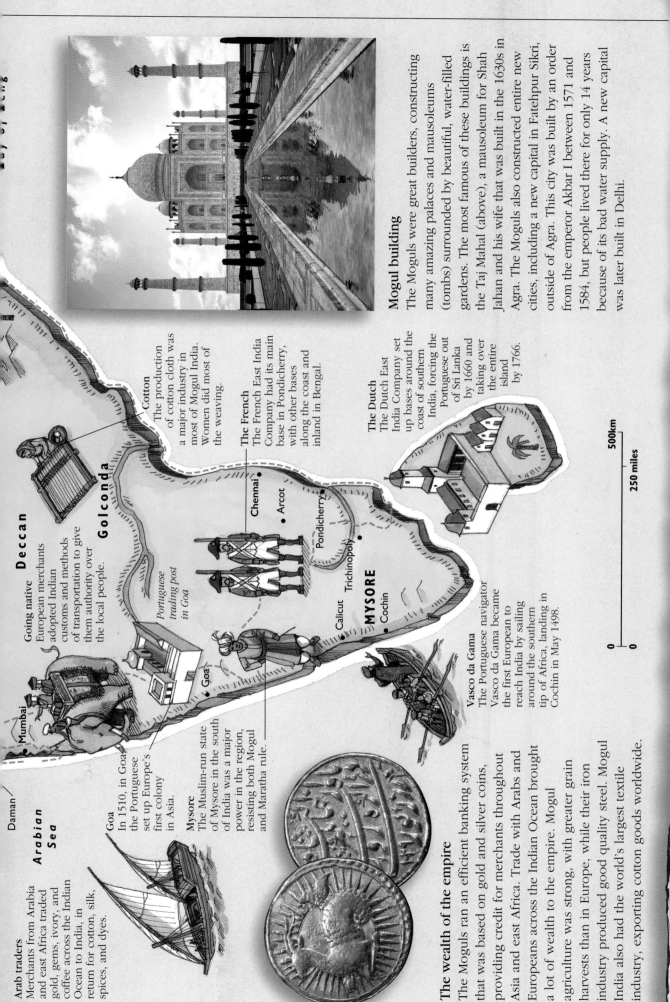

Mogul building

The Moguls were great builders, constructing many amazing palaces and mausoleums (tombs) surrounded by beautiful, water-filled gardens. The most famous of these buildings is the Taj Mahal (above), a mausoleum for Shah Jahan and his wife that was built in the 1630s in Agra. The Moguls also constructed entire new cities, including a new capital in Fatehpur Sikri, outside of Agra. This city was built by an order from the emperor Akbar I between 1571 and 1584, but people lived there for only 14 years because of its bad water supply. A new capital was later built in Delhi.

Going native
European merchants adopted Indian customs and methods of transportation to give them authority over the local people.

Cotton
The production of cotton cloth was a major industry in most of Mogul India. Women did most of the weaving.

The French
The French East India Company had its main base in Pondicherry, with other bases along the coast and inland in Bengal.

The Dutch
The Dutch East India Company set up bases around the coast of southern India, forcing the Portuguese out of Sri Lanka by 1660 and taking over the entire island by 1766.

Deccan

Golconda

Portuguese trading post in Goa

MYSORE

Chennai
• Arcot
Pondicherry
Trichinopoly
Calicut
Cochin
• Goa

Daman
Arabian Sea
Mumbai

Arab traders
Merchants from Arabia and east Africa traded gold, gems, ivory, and coffee across the Indian Ocean to India, in return for cotton, silk, spices, and dyes.

Goa
In 1510, in Goa, the Portuguese set up Europe's first colony in Asia.

Mysore
The Muslim-run state of Mysore in the south of India was a major power in the region, resisting both Mogul and Maratha rule.

Vasco da Gama
The Portuguese navigator Vasco da Gama became the first European to reach India by sailing around the southern tip of Africa, landing in Cochin in May 1498.

500km
250 miles
0
0

The wealth of the empire
The Moguls ran an efficient banking system that was based on gold and silver coins, providing credit for merchants throughout Asia and east Africa. Trade with Arabs and Europeans across the Indian Ocean brought a lot of wealth to the empire. Mogul agriculture was strong, with greater grain harvests than in Europe, while their iron industry produced good quality steel. Mogul India also had the world's largest textile industry, exporting cotton goods worldwide.

1500
1501–1530 Reign of Babur, the first Mogul emperor
1504 Moguls conquer the region around Kabul
1510 Portuguese set up a trading post in Goa, with others in Diu and Daman
1519 Moguls' first raid on India
1526 Full-scale Mogul invasion of India

1539–1556 Suri Afghans of Bihar rebel and reclaim a lot of territory from the Moguls

1550

1556–1605 Reign of Akbar I

1572 Moguls conquer Gujarat, giving them access to the sea
1576 Moguls conquer Bengal, India's wealthiest territory

1600
1600 British East India Co. is founded
1602 Dutch East India Co. is founded
1605 Moguls advance south into the Deccan
1612 British East India Co. defeats a Portuguese fleet in Surat

1628–1658 Reign of Shah Jahan, who ordered the building of the Taj Mahal
1639–1648 New capital city constructed by the order of Shah Jahan in Shahjahanabad (Delhi)
1647–1680 Led by Sivaji, Hindu Marathas raid Mogul India

1650

1655–1660 Dutch seize bases in Sri Lanka from the Portuguese
1658–1707 Reign of Aurangzeb: Mogul Empire at its largest size
1661 British East India Co. establishes a base in Mumbai
1664 French East India Co. is set up

1687 Moguls capture the southern state of Golconda

1700

1708 Marathas begin to conquer the Deccan

1739 Persian troops ransack the Mogul capital of Delhi
1740 War between Marathas and Moguls in southern India brings in the French and the British

1750
1751–1752 British under the command of Robert Clive score decisive victories against the French in Arcot and Trichinopoly
1757 Clive defeats Mogul Nawab (ruler) of Bengal in Plassey
1761 Maratha power ends after a massive defeat outside of Delhi by an Afghan army that later withdraws from India
1761 British seize Pondicherry, ending French power in India
1775 British control all of Bengal and Bihar
by 1800, Mogul Empire survives in name only
1800

The Tudors and Stuarts

Years of warfare in England between rival royal houses ended in 1485 when Henry VII became the first Tudor king. The Tudors were strong rulers who brought peace and prosperity to the country. Under King Henry VIII, England broke away from Rome and the Catholic Church and became increasingly Protestant. In 1603 the last Tudor monarch, Queen Elizabeth I, died. Elizabeth was succeeded by the Scottish king, James VI, from the Stuart family, who united England and Scotland for the first time. But the Stuarts were weak kings. One of them, King Charles I, was executed after a civil war, and another, King James II (James VII of Scotland), was driven into exile because he was a Catholic. Overseas trade, however, was slowly making Britain one of the wealthiest nations in Europe.

The English Civil War: a war of three kingdoms

Charles I was the king of England, Scotland, and Ireland. Each country had its own parliament, church, and laws. Charles believed that he had a "divine right to rule," which was given to him by God, but his religious policies attracted opposition. A rebellion broke out in Scotland in 1639 and then in Ireland in 1641, before the king and Parliament clashed in England in 1642. Civil war raged in all three kingdoms before Charles was executed by the English Parliament in 1649 for waging war on his people. From 1649 to 1660, Britain was a republic (a nation without a monarch) for the only time in its history.

The Spanish Armada
Defeated in August 1588 (see page 115), the Spanish Armada was forced to sail around the rocky north and west coasts of Ireland and Scotland, where many ships were wrecked in storms.

Union of the crowns
In 1603 the Stuart king of Scotland, James VI, became King James I of England. This united the two crowns, but both nations remained independent.

Irish rebellions
Ireland was the only part of the British Isles that remained Catholic. This led to many rebellions against Ireland's Protestant and English rulers.

Suspicious murder
Lord Darnley, the husband of Mary, Queen of Scots, was killed in an explosion in Edinburgh, Scotland, in 1567. Mary was accused of being involved, but nothing was proved.

Flodden Field
The English defeat of the Scots at Flodden Field in 1513 weakened Scotland greatly and put it at the mercy of the English for the rest of the century.

Atlantic Ocean

North Sea

SCOTLAND

■ EDINBURGH

Tweed

● Flodden

● Londonderry

Ulster

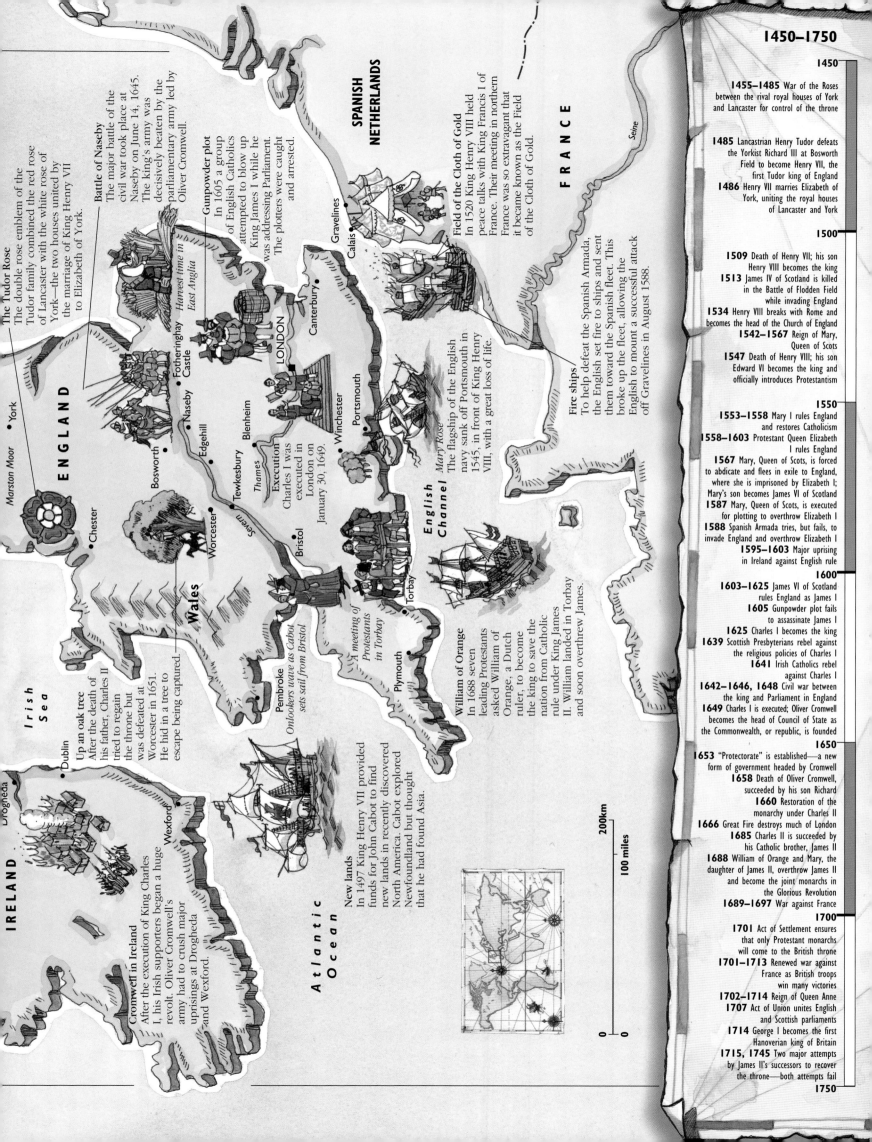

The Tudor Rose
The double rose emblem of the Tudor family combined the red rose of Lancaster with the white rose of York—the two houses united by the marriage of King Henry VII to Elizabeth of York.

Battle of Naseby
The major battle of the civil war took place at Naseby on June 14, 1645. The king's army was decisively beaten by the parliamentary army led by Oliver Cromwell.

Gunpowder plot
In 1605 a group of English Catholics attempted to blow up King James I while he was addressing Parliament. The plotters were caught and arrested.

Field of the Cloth of Gold
In 1520 King Henry VIII held peace talks with King Francis I of France. Their meeting in northern France was so extravagant that it became known as the Field of the Cloth of Gold.

Harvest time in East Anglia

SPANISH NETHERLANDS

F R A N C E

Seine

Gravelines
Calais
Canterbury
LONDON

Fire ships
To help defeat the Spanish Armada, the English set fire to ships and sent them toward the Spanish fleet. This broke up the Spanish fleet, allowing the English to mount a successful attack off Gravelines in August 1588.

Execution
Charles I was executed in London on January 30, 1649.

Mary Rose
The flagship of the English navy sank off Portsmouth in 1545, in front of King Henry VIII, with a great loss of life.

Marston Moor
• York

E N G L A N D

• Chester

Bosworth •
Fotheringhay Castle •
• Naseby
Edgehill •
• Tewkesbury
• Blenheim
• Winchester
• Portsmouth
Thames
Severn
• Worcester
• Bristol

Wales

English Channel

Up an oak tree
After the death of his father, Charles II tried to regain the throne but was defeated at Worcester in 1651. He hid in a tree to escape being captured.

Irish Sea

• Dublin

Drogheda

I R E L A N D

Wexford

Cromwell in Ireland
After the execution of King Charles I, his Irish supporters began a huge revolt. Oliver Cromwell's army had to crush major uprisings at Drogheda and Wexford.

Onlookers wave as Cabot sets sail from Bristol
Pembroke

A meeting of Protestants in Torbay

Torbay
• Plymouth

William of Orange
In 1688 seven leading Protestants asked William of Orange, a Dutch ruler, to become the king to save the nation from Catholic rule under King James II. William landed in Torbay and soon overthrew James.

New lands
In 1497 King Henry VII provided funds for John Cabot to find new lands in recently discovered North America. Cabot explored Newfoundland but thought that he had found Asia.

Atlantic Ocean

200km
100 miles

100 miles
0
0

1450

1455–1485 War of the Roses between the rival royal houses of York and Lancaster for control of the throne

1485 Lancastrian Henry Tudor defeats the Yorkist Richard III at Bosworth Field to become Henry VII, the first Tudor king of England
1486 Henry VII marries Elizabeth of York, uniting the royal houses of Lancaster and York

1500

1509 Death of Henry VII; his son Henry VIII becomes the king
1513 James IV of Scotland is killed in the Battle of Flodden Field while invading England
1534 Henry VIII breaks with Rome and becomes the head of the Church of England
1542–1567 Reign of Mary, Queen of Scots
1547 Death of Henry VIII; his son Edward VI becomes the king and officially introduces Protestantism

1550

1553–1558 Mary I rules England and restores Catholicism
1558–1603 Protestant Queen Elizabeth I rules England
1567 Mary, Queen of Scots, is forced to abdicate and flees in exile to England, where she is imprisoned by Elizabeth I; Mary's son becomes James VI of Scotland
1587 Mary, Queen of Scots, is executed for plotting to overthrow Elizabeth I
1588 Spanish Armada tries, but fails, to invade England and overthrow Elizabeth I
1595–1603 Major uprising in Ireland against English rule

1600

1603–1625 James VI of Scotland rules England as James I
1605 Gunpowder plot fails to assassinate James I
1625 Charles I becomes the king
1639 Scottish Presbyterians rebel against the religious policies of Charles I
1641 Irish Catholics rebel against Charles I
1642–1646, 1648 Civil war between the king and Parliament in England
1649 Charles I is executed; Oliver Cromwell becomes the head of Council of State as the Commonwealth, or republic, is founded

1650

1653 "Protectorate" is established—a new form of government headed by Cromwell
1658 Death of Oliver Cromwell, succeeded by his son Richard
1660 Restoration of the monarchy under Charles II
1666 Great Fire destroys much of London
1685 Charles II is succeeded by his Catholic brother, James II
1688 William of Orange and Mary, the daughter of James II, overthrow James II and become the joint monarchs in the Glorious Revolution
1689–1697 War against France

1700

1701 Act of Settlement ensures that only Protestant monarchs will come to the British throne
1701–1713 Renewed war against France as British troops win many victories
1702–1714 Reign of Queen Anne
1707 Act of Union unites English and Scottish parliaments
1714 George I becomes the first Hanoverian king of Britain
1715, 1745 Two major attempts by James II's successors to recover the throne—both attempts fail

1750

Divided Europe

After the religious turmoil of the Reformation a brief period of peace descended on Europe in the 1550s. However, the differences between Protestants and Catholics continued to divide the continent, causing civil war in France and a revolt in the Netherlands against Spanish rule. A major conflict also broke out for control of the Baltic Sea. In 1618 Protestant-Catholic rivalries in Germany led to a war that soon spread across the rest of Europe. By the end of the war, Germany was devastated; Spain lost its leadership of Catholic Europe to France; Sweden dominated northern Europe and the Baltic; and the Dutch were independent and wealthy.

dotted lines show the borders between European countries in 1648

Dutch domination
Dutch merchants controlled trade in both the North and Baltic seas. By 1650, Dutch businessmen dominated Europe's entire economy.

Reclaiming the sea
The Dutch built dykes (flood barriers) and used windmills to reclaim land from the sea. They lived on this land and grew food there.

Civil war
England, Scotland, and Ireland were all involved in civil wars from 1639–1651, keeping them out of the European conflicts.

Frost fairs
The River Thames froze over during most winters as a mini ice age engulfed Europe. Many Londoners sold their wares on the ice.

Henry IV
The conversion of the French king Henry IV from Protestantism to Catholicism, in 1593, led to the end of the wars of religion in France.

La Rochelle
French Protestant Huguenots rose up in revolt again in 1620, but they were crushed when their stronghold in La Rochelle was successfully besieged.

Peace of Westphalia
The Thirty Years' War ended in 1648, when a peace treaty was signed in the German state of Westphalia.

Cardinal Richelieu
From 1624–1642, Cardinal Richelieu ran the government for Louis XIII. He crushed the Huguenots and built up French military strength against Spain.

Portugal in revolt
Spain took control of Portugal by force in 1580. Sixty years later the Portuguese rose up in revolt and, with help from the French, won back their independence.

Escorial Palace
The huge Escorial Palace outside of Madrid was built for Philip II in 1563–1584. He ruled his large European and American empire from there.

Catalonia
In 1640 the French supported a revolt in Catalonia against Spanish rule. The region came under the protection of Louis XIII until the revolt was crushed in the 1650s.

SCOTLAND

IRELAND

ENGLAND

LONDON

North Sea

NORWAY

Emden

UNITED PROVINCES

AMSTERDAM

Dutch delft pottery

Westphali

Antwerp

SPANISH NETHERLANDS

Rocroi

Seine

PARIS

Nantes

Loire

FRANCE

La Rochelle

SWITZERLAND

Atlantic Ocean

Douro

Ebro

MADRID

LISBON

Tagus

PORTUGAL

SPAIN

Catalonia

Sardin

Guadalquivir

Mediterranean Sea

0   500km

0   250 miles

STOCKHOLM

SWEDEN

Baltic Sea

Swedish trade
After 1561 Sweden controlled most of the coast with its wealthy trade in timber, amber, and other goods.

COPENHAGEN

• Memel

Stralsund

Lübeck

• Königsberg

Danzig

PRUSSIA

Magdeburg
The ransacking of Magdeburg by Catholic forces in 1631 led to savage acts of retaliation across Germany.

Brandenburg
Magdeburg

Oder

POLAND

Germany   **Saxony**

Breitenfeld

Lützen

Elbe

Bohemia

Prague

HOLY ROMAN EMPIRE

Danube

• Nordlingen

Austria

VIENNA

Spanish intervention
Spanish troops from Italy regularly fought French and Protestant forces in Germany during the Thirty Years' War.

HUNGARY

OTTOMAN EMPIRE

Adriatic Sea

ROME

Naples

NAPLES

Ionian Sea

Tyrrhenian Sea

The Spanish Mediterranean
Throughout this period, Naples, Sicily, and Sardinia were part of Spain, despite French-inspired revolts against Spanish troops in 1647.

Sicily

The Dutch revolt

As converts to Calvinism, the Dutch came into conflict with their Spanish Catholic rulers. In 1568 they revolted, and in 1581 they declared their independence as the United Provinces. Supported by the French and the English, they fought with Spain until a 12-year truce was declared in 1609. Spain finally recognized their independence in 1648. An example of Dutch prosperity can be seen in this grand area of Amsterdam (above), developed by wealthy Dutch merchants in the 1600s.

Thrown out!
The Thirty Years' War began in 1618, when Bohemian Protestants threw two Austrian imperial officials out of a window in Prague Castle.

Dual crown
The Hapsburg rulers of Austria also ran the Holy Roman Empire and were in charge of the imperial forces against France, Sweden, and the Protestants.

The Thirty Years' War

In 1618 Protestants in Bohemia rose up against their Catholic Austrian rulers. Protestant and Catholic states across Germany soon joined in the fighting. After 1625 the war became more about territorial power than about religion, as Denmark and then Sweden joined the war on the Protestant side to expand their power in the Baltic. This painting (above) shows the king of Sweden leading a cavalry charge in the Battle of Lützen in 1632.

1550

1555 The Peace of Augsburg agreement brings religious stability to Germany
1556 Charles V abdicates, splitting the huge Hapsburg Empire between Spain and Austria
1556–1598 Philip II rules Spain
1557–1629 Russia, Sweden, and Poland fight for land around the eastern Baltic Sea

1560

1568–1609 Dutch revolt against Spanish rule

1570

1580
1580 Philip II of Spain seizes the Portuguese throne
1581 Dutch declare independence from Spain and elect William of Orange as their governor

1590

1593 Henry IV of France converts to Catholicism

1598 Henry IV issues the Edict of Nantes, granting religious tolerance to French Huguenots (Protestants)
1598 Religious wars end in France

1600

1609–1621 Twelve-year truce agreed between the Dutch and the Spanish

1610

1618–1648 Thirty Years' War started by a Protestant revolt in Bohemia

1620

1620 Bohemian revolt ended by Catholic troops
1620–1628 Huguenot revolt in France ends with the capture of La Rochelle
1621–1625 Spain renews war against the Dutch
1624–1642 Cardinal Richelieu runs France
1625 Denmark enters Thirty Years' War
1628 France and Spain are at war

1630
1630 Sweden enters Thirty Years' War
1632 Swedish king Gustavus Adolphus dies in the Battle of Lützen

1635 France enters Thirty Years' War

1639–1651 Civil wars engulf England, Scotland, and Ireland
1640
1640 France supports revolts against Spain in Catalonia and Portugal; Portuguese win back independence
1643 French victory over Spanish in Rocroi
1647 Southern Italy revolts against Spanish rule
1648 Peace of Westphalia agreement ends Thirty Years' War; Dutch gain independence

1650

The expansion of Russia

Over the course of 300 years, the small, poor, landlocked state of Muscovy expanded to become Russia—one of the major nations in Europe. In order to do this, it had to overcome huge problems—a small population, huge distances between towns, a terrible climate, and large areas of empty land in which hostile armies could easily hide. The main driving force behind Russia's success was Peter the Great, who modeled Russia on the western countries of Europe and almost single-handedly modernized the nation. Victories over Sweden, by 1721, gave Russia access to the Baltic Sea, paving the way for future Russian success and territorial gains during the 1700s.

The Ural Mountains
The Ural Mountains form the border between Europe and Asia. During the late 1500s, the Russians crossed these mountains and built many new towns in Siberia.

Polar bear roaming the Arctic tundra

Metal working
Many new state-owned iron and copper works were built in the Ural Mountains to exploit the great mineral wealth of the mountains.

Close shave
To make his country more like those in the West, Peter the Great ordered all of his lords and nobles to shave off their beards and dress in Western clothing.

Building St. Petersburg
In 1703 work began on a new capital city, which gave access to the Baltic Sea.

Moscow
After the fall of Constantinople to the Muslim Ottomans in 1453, Moscow became the center of Orthodox Christianity in Europe.

International trade
Russian merchants traded silk, tea, and gems from China and textiles from Persia and central Asia. Sugar, tobacco, and wine were imported from Europe.

Russian navy
Peter the Great studied shipbuilding in England, returning home in 1698 to create a great navy.

Fur trading
During the 1600s, in order to develop the local fur trade, a series of fortified trading stations were built along the main trade route to China.

Serfs (peasants) working on a farm

Controlling the Caspian
In 1723 Russian troops occupied the western and southern coasts of the Caspian Sea, but the Persians forced them to give up these areas in 1732.

SWEDEN
Karelia
Ingria
ST PETERSBURG
Narva
Estonia
Pskov
Novgorod
Livonia
Baltic Sea
Moscow
Smolensk
POLAND
Kyiv
Dnieper
Poltava
Don
KHANATE OF CRIMEA
Sevastopol
Black Sea
Constantinople
Caucasus Mountains
OTTOMAN EMPIRE
Caspian Sea
SAFAVID EMPIRE
Astrakhan
Azov
Kazan
Ural Mountains
RUSSIA
Siberia
Tobolsk
Tomsk
Yeniseysk
Krasnoyarsk
Irkutsk
Kyakht

The city of Peter the Great

Peter the Great wanted to give Russia "a window on the West" so that it could trade ideas, goods, and technology with western Europe. In 1703 he ordered the construction of a new city—St. Petersburg—on marshland next to the Neva river at the eastern end of the Baltic Sea. Many thousands of workers died building the city, which includes the Winter Palace (left) and other grand buildings. St. Petersburg became the national capital of Russia in 1712, as well as one of the leading cultural and diplomatic cities in Europe.

Arctic Ocean

Fur trapping
Siberian tribesmen hunted bears and other animals for their meat and fur. They traded these goods with Russian merchants in return for guns and other items.

Felling trees for timber

Alaska

Bering Strait

Crossing to North America
Russian traders crossed the Bering Strait into Alaska, and in 1784 they established the first Russian settlement there. Alaska was sold to the U.S. in 1867.

Amur

Amur

CHINA

Fortifying the border
In 1650 Russian troops occupied the Amur region, north of China and built forts along the Amur river border. The region was returned to China in 1689.

Pacific Ocean

- - - - - - - -
dotted line shows the extent of Russian territory in 1783

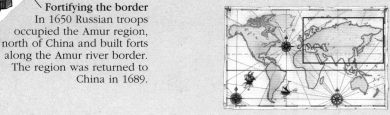

| 0 | | 500km |
| 0 | | 250 miles |

1450–1800

1450

1478 Led by Ivan III, "the Great," Muscovy conquers its main rival, Novgorod
1480 Muscovy becomes independent of Mongol Tatar rule

1500
1501 Ivan III expands his territory west, toward Poland

1533–1584 Reign of Ivan IV, "the Terrible"

1547 Ivan IV is crowned the first czar (emperor) of Russia

1550
1552 Russia begins to conquer Tatar khanates north of the Caspian Sea

1581 Russia begins to expand over the Ural Mountains and into Siberia
1582 Poland and Sweden prevent Russia from gaining access to the Baltic Sea

1600

1613–1645 Reign of Mikhail I, the first czar of the Romanov family

1637 Russian explorers reach the Pacific coast of Siberia for the first time

1650
1650–1689 Russian occupation of the Amur region, north of China

1682–1725 Reign of Peter I, "the Great"

1696 Russia captures Azov from the Ottomans, giving it access to the Black Sea
1697–1698 Peter I travels around western Europe, studying new ideas on how to modernize his country
1700
1700–1721 Great Northern War with Sweden brings Russia land around the Baltic Sea
1703 Construction of St. Petersburg begins

1712 National capital moved from Moscow to St. Petersburg

1750
1762–1792 Reign of Catherine II, "the Great"
1768–1774 War against the Ottomans brings gains around the Black Sea
1772 First Partition of Poland: Russia, Austria, and Prussia seize Polish territory; Russian frontier extends west
1783 Russia captures the Crimea
1784 Russians establish their first settlement in Alaska

1800

China and Japan

In 1368 the Chinese Ming dynasty replaced the foreign-born Mongols as the rulers in the region. In 1644 the Ming dynasty was replaced by another foreign dynasty, the Manchus, who came from the northern region of Manchuria. This was the Qing dynasty. The Manchus turned China into a dynamic, efficient state of incredible power and wealth. Neighboring states, such as Korea, came under the control of the Chinese. Japan remained independent, ruled in name by an emperor but ruled in reality by powerful shoguns (military warlords). European contact with China and Japan was very limited.

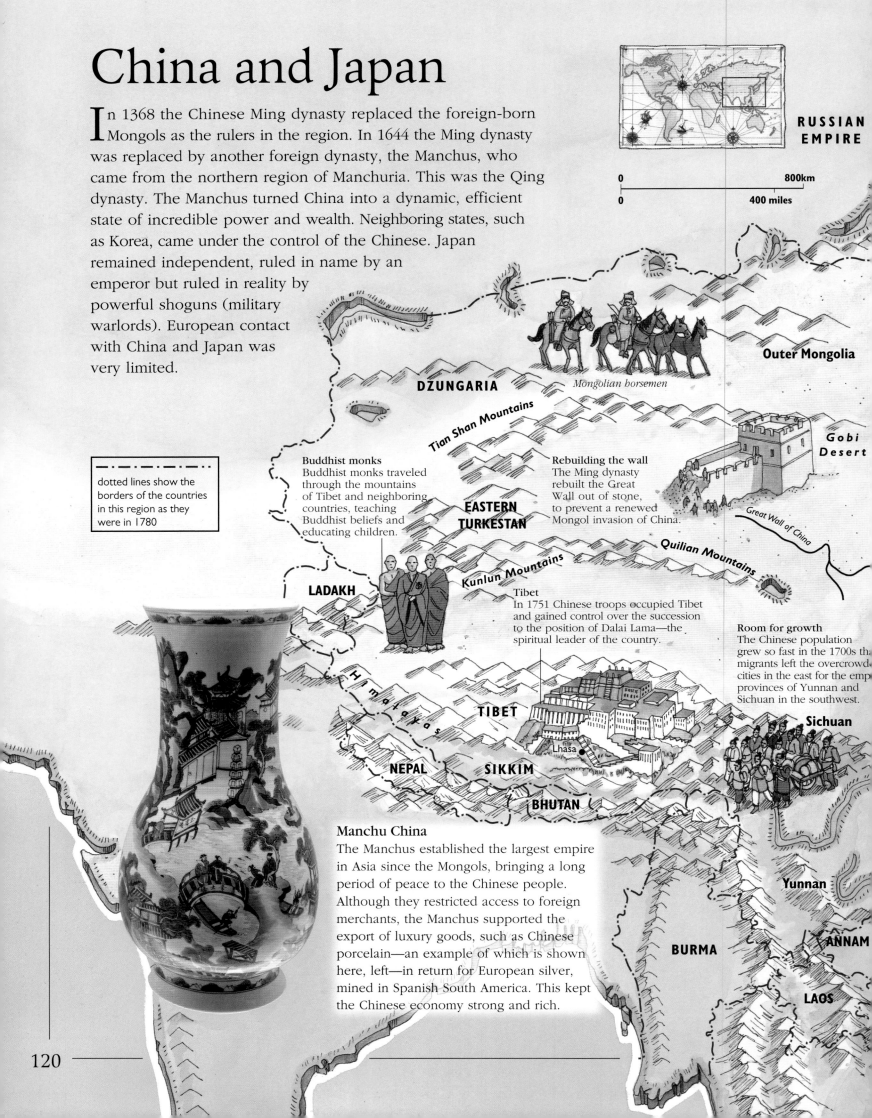

RUSSIAN EMPIRE

0   800km
0   400 miles

dotted lines show the borders of the countries in this region as they were in 1780

Outer Mongolia

Mongolian horsemen

DZUNGARIA

Tian Shan Mountains

Gobi Desert

Buddhist monks
Buddhist monks traveled through the mountains of Tibet and neighboring countries, teaching Buddhist beliefs and educating children.

EASTERN TURKESTAN

Rebuilding the wall
The Ming dynasty rebuilt the Great Wall out of stone, to prevent a renewed Mongol invasion of China.

Great Wall of China

Quilian Mountains

Kunlun Mountains

LADAKH

Tibet
In 1751 Chinese troops occupied Tibet and gained control over the succession to the position of Dalai Lama—the spiritual leader of the country.

Room for growth
The Chinese population grew so fast in the 1700s tha migrants left the overcrowd cities in the east for the emp provinces of Yunnan and Sichuan in the southwest.

Himalayas

TIBET

Lhasa

Sichuan

NEPAL   **SIKKIM**

BHUTAN

Yunnan

Manchu China
The Manchus established the largest empire in Asia since the Mongols, bringing a long period of peace to the Chinese people. Although they restricted access to foreign merchants, the Manchus supported the export of luxury goods, such as Chinese porcelain—an example of which is shown here, left—in return for European silver, mined in Spanish South America. This kept the Chinese economy strong and rich.

BURMA

ANNAM

LAOS

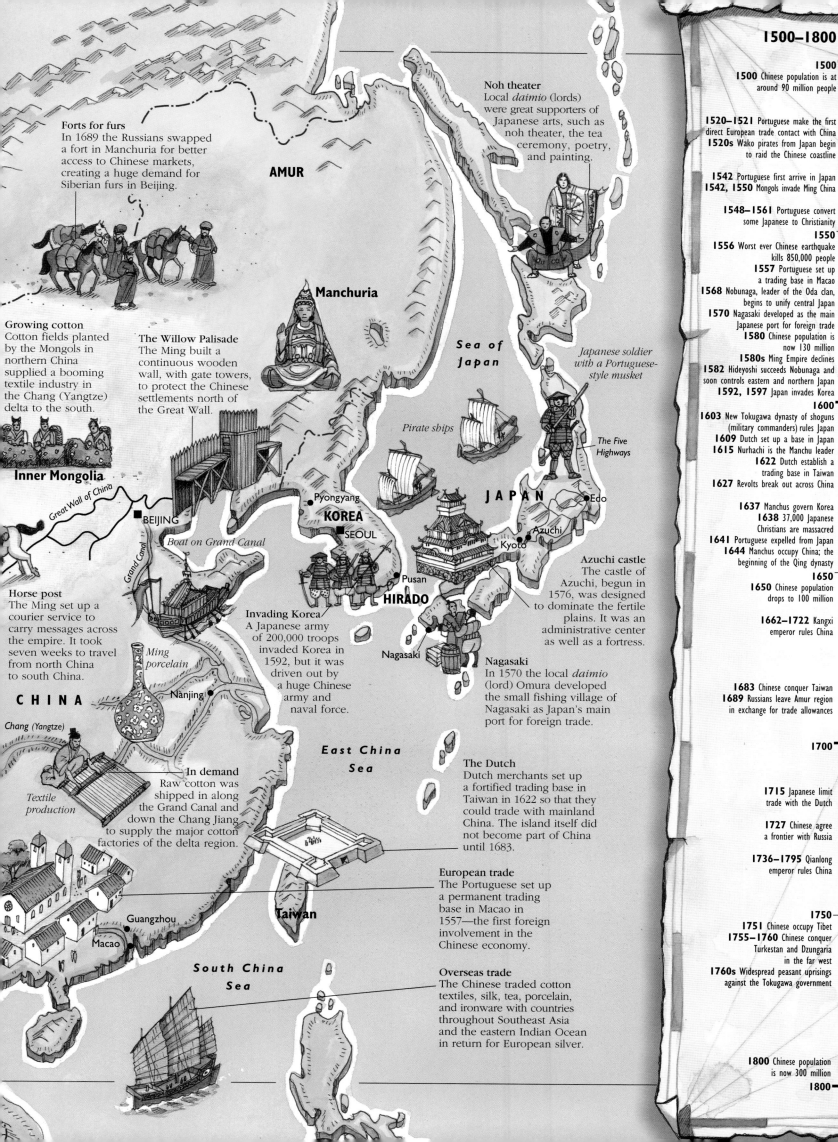

Noh theater
Local *daimio* (lords) were great supporters of Japanese arts, such as noh theater, the tea ceremony, poetry, and painting.

Forts for furs
In 1689 the Russians swapped a fort in Manchuria for better access to Chinese markets, creating a huge demand for Siberian furs in Beijing.

AMUR

Manchuria

Japanese soldier with a Portuguese-style musket

Sea of Japan

Growing cotton
Cotton fields planted by the Mongols in northern China supplied a booming textile industry in the Chang (Yangtze) delta to the south.

Inner Mongolia

The Willow Palisade
The Ming built a continuous wooden wall, with gate towers, to protect the Chinese settlements north of the Great Wall.

Pirate ships

J A P A N

The Five Highways

Great Wall of China

BEIJING

Boat on Grand Canal

KOREA

Pyongyang

SEOUL

Kyoto

Azuchi

Edo

Horse post
The Ming set up a courier service to carry messages across the empire. It took seven weeks to travel from north China to south China.

Grand Canal

Ming porcelain

HIRADO

Pusan

Azuchi castle
The castle of Azuchi, begun in 1576, was designed to dominate the fertile plains. It was an administrative center as well as a fortress.

C H I N A

Nanjing

Invading Korea
A Japanese army of 200,000 troops invaded Korea in 1592, but it was driven out by a huge Chinese army and naval force.

Nagasaki

Chang (Yangtze)

Textile production

In demand
Raw cotton was shipped in along the Grand Canal and down the Chang Jiang to supply the major cotton factories of the delta region.

East China Sea

Nagasaki
In 1570 the local *daimio* (lord) Omura developed the small fishing village of Nagasaki as Japan's main port for foreign trade.

The Dutch
Dutch merchants set up a fortified trading base in Taiwan in 1622 so that they could trade with mainland China. The island itself did not become part of China until 1683.

Guangzhou

Macao

Taiwan

European trade
The Portuguese set up a permanent trading base in Macao in 1557—the first foreign involvement in the Chinese economy.

South China Sea

Overseas trade
The Chinese traded cotton textiles, silk, tea, porcelain, and ironware with countries throughout Southeast Asia and the eastern Indian Ocean in return for European silver.

1500–1800

1500

1500 Chinese population is at around 90 million people

1520–1521 Portuguese make the first direct European trade contact with China
1520s Wako pirates from Japan begin to raid the Chinese coastline

1542 Portuguese first arrive in Japan
1542, 1550 Mongols invade Ming China

1548–1561 Portuguese convert some Japanese to Christianity

1550

1556 Worst ever Chinese earthquake kills 850,000 people
1557 Portuguese set up a trading base in Macao
1568 Nobunaga, leader of the Oda clan, begins to unify central Japan
1570 Nagasaki developed as the main Japanese port for foreign trade
1580 Chinese population is now 130 million
1580s Ming Empire declines
1582 Hideyoshi succeeds Nobunaga and soon controls eastern and northern Japan
1592, 1597 Japan invades Korea

1600

1603 New Tokugawa dynasty of shoguns (military commanders) rules Japan
1609 Dutch set up a base in Japan
1615 Nurhachi is the Manchu leader
1622 Dutch establish a trading base in Taiwan
1627 Revolts break out across China

1637 Manchus govern Korea
1638 37,000 Japanese Christians are massacred
1641 Portuguese expelled from Japan
1644 Manchus occupy China; the beginning of the Qing dynasty

1650

1650 Chinese population drops to 100 million

1662–1722 Kangxi emperor rules China

1683 Chinese conquer Taiwan
1689 Russians leave Amur region in exchange for trade allowances

1700

1715 Japanese limit trade with the Dutch

1727 Chinese agree a frontier with Russia

1736–1795 Qianlong emperor rules China

1750

1751 Chinese occupy Tibet
1755–1760 Chinese conquer Turkestan and Dzungaria in the far west
1760s Widespread peasant uprisings against the Tokugawa government

1800 Chinese population is now 300 million

1800

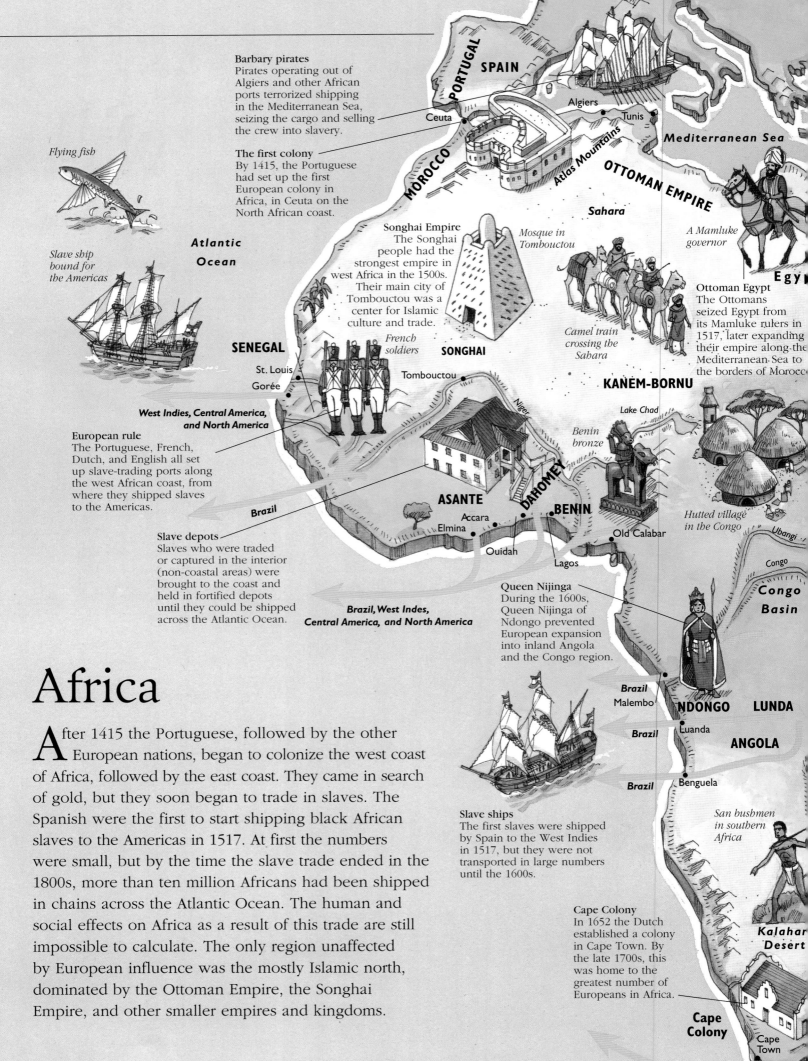

Barbary pirates
Pirates operating out of Algiers and other African ports terrorized shipping in the Mediterranean Sea, seizing the cargo and selling the crew into slavery.

The first colony
By 1415, the Portuguese had set up the first European colony in Africa, in Ceuta on the North African coast.

Flying fish

Atlantic Ocean

Slave ship bound for the Americas

Songhai Empire
The Songhai people had the strongest empire in west Africa in the 1500s. Their main city of Tombouctou was a center for Islamic culture and trade.

Mosque in Tombouctou

A Mamluke governor

Egy

Ottoman Egypt
The Ottomans seized Egypt from its Mamluke rulers in 1517, later expanding their empire along the Mediterranean Sea to the borders of Morocc

Camel train crossing the Sahara

French soldiers

SENEGAL
St. Louis
Gorée

West Indies, Central America, and North America

European rule
The Portuguese, French, Dutch, and English all set up slave-trading ports along the west African coast, from where they shipped slaves to the Americas.

Slave depots
Slaves who were traded or captured in the interior (non-coastal areas) were brought to the coast and held in fortified depots until they could be shipped across the Atlantic Ocean.

Tombouctou

KANEM-BORNU

Lake Chad

Benin bronze

ASANTE
Accara
Elmina
Ouidah

DAHOMEY
Lagos

BENIN
Old Calabar

Hutted village in the Congo

Ubangi

Congo

Congo Basin

Brazil

Queen Nijinga
During the 1600s, Queen Nijinga of Ndongo prevented European expansion into inland Angola and the Congo region.

Brazil, West Indes, Central America, and North America

Brazil
Malembo
NDONGO   **LUNDA**

Brazil
Luanda
ANGOLA

Brazil
Benguela

San bushmen in southern Africa

Africa

After 1415 the Portuguese, followed by the other European nations, began to colonize the west coast of Africa, followed by the east coast. They came in search of gold, but they soon began to trade in slaves. The Spanish were the first to start shipping black African slaves to the Americas in 1517. At first the numbers were small, but by the time the slave trade ended in the 1800s, more than ten million Africans had been shipped in chains across the Atlantic Ocean. The human and social effects on Africa as a result of this trade are still impossible to calculate. The only region unaffected by European influence was the mostly Islamic north, dominated by the Ottoman Empire, the Songhai Empire, and other smaller empires and kingdoms.

Slave ships
The first slaves were shipped by Spain to the West Indies in 1517, but they were not transported in large numbers until the 1600s.

Cape Colony
In 1652 the Dutch established a colony in Cape Town. By the late 1700s, this was home to the greatest number of Europeans in Africa.

Kalahari Desert

Cape Colony
Cape Town

Cape of Good Ho

The Portuguese east coast

In 1498 the Portuguese navigator Vasco da Gama sailed around the Cape of Good Hope on his way to India. This opened up a new trade route between Europe and India across the Indian Ocean. The Portuguese soon set up a series of trading bases along the east coast of Africa, such as in Kilwa (left). These bases stretched from Delagoa Bay in the south to the island of Socotra, at the mouth of the Red Sea, in the north.

Jesuit conversions
Jesuit missionaries arrived in Ethiopia in 1557 to convert the Ethiopians from the Coptic Church to the Roman Catholic Church.

Arab traders
Arab dhows (sailing boats) traded goods with India, the Arabian Peninsula, and the Persian Gulf, often in competition and conflict with their Portuguese rivals.

Christians united
The Portuguese sent an army to help their fellow Christian Ethiopians defeat an invading Adali army in Waina Dega in 1543.

Portuguese trade
After 1505 the Portuguese set up a series of trading bases along the east African coast. From there, they traded gold, ivory, and spices across the Indian Ocean.

Gold
The Shona and Makua people mined and panned for gold close to Lake Nyasa. They traded it for guns, textiles, and other goods with Arab and Portuguese merchants along the coast.

these arrows show the direction and destinations of the slave ships that sailed across the Atlantic Ocean from African ports

India

Arabian Sea

Arabian Peninsula

Socotra

Indian Ocean

Cairo

Nile

ETHIOPIA

Waina Dega

ADAL

Lake Turkana

Rift Valley

Mogadishu

Lake Victoria

SULTANATE OF ZANZIBAR

Rift

Malindi
Mombasa
Zanzibar

Lake Tanganyika

Kilwa

Great Mosque in Kilwa

Lake Nyasa

Valley

Mozambique

Zambezi

Madagascar

MWENEMUTAPA

Limpopo

Delagoa Bay

Brazil

0		2,000km
0		1,000 miles

1450

1482 Portuguese establish a fortress in Elmina in west Africa to protect their gold trade
1488 Portuguese navigator Bartolomeu Dias becomes the first European to sail around Africa into the Indian Ocean
1498 Vasco da Gama opens up a sea route from Europe, around Africa, to India

1500

1505 Portuguese begin to colonize Mozambique and the rest of the east African coast
1517 Spanish begin shipping slaves to the West Indies
1517 Ottomans conquer Egypt
1527–1543 Islamic Adal kingdom attacks Ethiopia
1529 Songhai Empire is at its largest size

1550

1557 Jesuit missionaries arrive in Ethiopia
1570 King Idris III Aloma creates a powerful Islamic state in Kanem-Bornu
1575 Portuguese begin to colonize Angola

1591 Moroccan force overthrows the Songhai Empire
1592 British first ship slaves to the Americas
1598 Portuguese colonize Mombasa

1600

1600 East African kingdom of Mwenemutapa is at its largest size
1624–1643 Queen Nijinga rules Ndongo
1626 French begin to colonize Senegal and Madagascar
1626–1632 Roman Catholicism becomes the official religion of Ethiopia
1637 Dutch capture Elmina from the Portuguese

1650

1652 Omanis from the Arabian Peninsula attack Zanzibar, the first major threat to Portuguese trade in east Africa
1652 Dutch establish Cape Town

1698 Omanis set up the Sultanate of Zanzibar and expel the Portuguese from the east coast

1700

1700 Kingdoms of Asante and Dahomey dominate the west African coast
1705–1714 North Africa becomes semi-independent from the Ottoman Empire
1713 Britain gains 30-year control over the shipping of African slaves to Spanish America
1724 Dahomey provides slaves for European slave traders

1750

1750s Powerful Lunda Empire emerges in central Africa

1758–1783 British and French fight for control of Senegal

1800

The slave trade:
The terrible trade in humans

Slavery has existed throughout human history, but in the 1500s a new and terrible chapter in the story began. In 1502 a Portuguese ship transported west African slaves to the Americas. Regular shipments then started up in 1517. At first this trade was slow, but the increasing demand for labor on the new sugar plantations and in the mines outgrew the supply of Indigenous Americans. So Africans were brought across the Atlantic Ocean to fill the gap. The trade flourished during the 1600s and 1700s, with approximately ten million Africans enslaved before the trade ended in the 1800s. The human cost of slavery was huge, and while it brought great wealth to European traders and North American landowners, it devastated Africa.

Trading in lives

Slaves who were captured during warfare between rival African kingdoms or enslaved by their own leaders were taken to the coast and sold to European slavers (slave traders). The picture above shows a man buying slaves in Gorée, a French island off Senegal on the west African coast. There the slaves were branded (marked with hot irons) and imprisoned in slave depots until a ship arrived to take them to the Americas.

On the plantation

Life on the plantations, such as this sugar plantation in Antigua in the West Indies, was harsh. Slaves were the property of the plantation owner and had no rights of their own. They worked long hours, often from sunrise until sunset, and were often whipped to make them work harder. They did not earn any money but were given enough food to keep them alive.

Male and female slaves hoed the land in a line, making it ready for planting sugar cane

Even young slave children were forced to work on the land

The overseer made sure that the slaves worked hard for their master

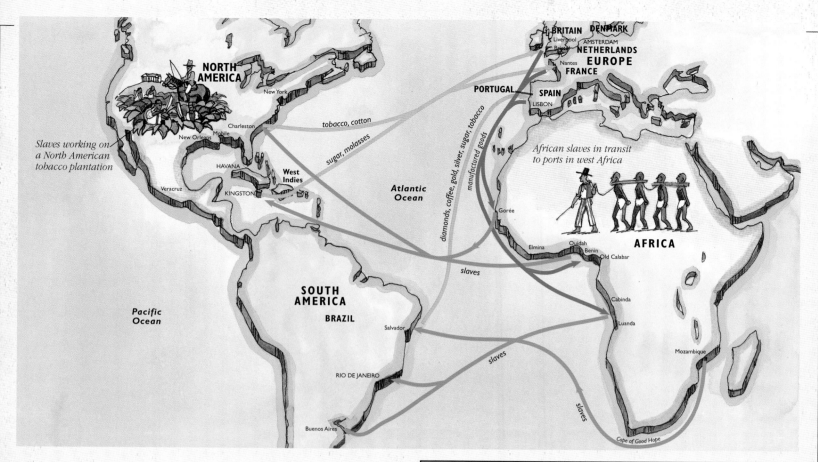

Slaves working on a North American tobacco plantation

African slaves in transit to ports in west Africa

The slave trade triangle

As shown in this map (above), the path of slave ships formed a triangular pattern across the Atlantic Ocean. Ships carrying manufactured goods, such as guns and cotton cloth, sailed from western European ports to the west African coast. There, the cargo was traded for slaves, who were then shipped across to Brazil, the West Indies, Central America, and North America. The slaves were sold to the plantation owners, and the ships returned home with a rich cargo of sugar, rum, tobacco, cotton, coffee, and sometimes silver and precious stones.

KEY TO MAP: THE "TRIANGULAR TRADE"

Ships carry manufactured goods from Europe to Africa

The Middle Passage: Slaves are taken across the Atlantic Ocean

Ships return home with raw materials from the Americas

Remembering the past

Slavery ended during the 1800s, but its impact is still with us today. The economy and social structure of much of Africa has never recovered from the removal of so many young men and women as slaves, while the free descendants of slaves, especially in the U.S., still sometimes face unfair treatment and discrimination. This statue (right) is a memorial to those who were slaves in Barbados, a British island in the West Indies.

The Middle Passage

The voyage across the Atlantic Ocean from Africa to the Americas—known as the Middle Passage—took up to 16 weeks. Conditions onboard were appalling. Hundreds of slaves were tightly packed into the hold, as this painting shows (above). They were all chained together to stop them from jumping overboard. As many as four out of every ten slaves died making the journey across.

Colonizing North America

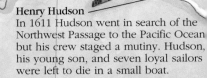

When Europeans first arrived in North America, the land puzzled them. The early explorers thought that it was Asia and did not realize that it was a continent in its own right, while Spanish conquistadors (conquerors) expected to discover gold-filled cities just like they had found earlier in Mexico and Peru. None of them realized just how big or potentially rich and fertile this continent was. But, slowly, Europeans began to colonize this new world—the French and English trapping and trading furs in the north, while farmers from all nations settled in colonies along the east coast. Once the barrier of the Appalachian Mountains was crossed in 1671, the way was clear for pioneer settlers to exploit this fertile land to the full.

Henry Hudson
In 1611 Hudson went in search of the Northwest Passage to the Pacific Ocean but his crew staged a mutiny. Hudson, his young son, and seven loyal sailors were left to die in a small boat.

Lake Winnipeg

Canada

The Great Lakes

Hudson's Bay Company
After 1670 the English Hudson's Bay Company set up bases around Hudson Bay to trade furs with the Indigenous Cree people. The French captured all of the bases in 1686.

Hunting buffalo
The Plains Indians hunted herds of buffalo for their meat, skins, and bones.

Rocky Mountains

Buffalo grazing

New Mexico
The Spaniards set up a permanent base in Santa Fe in 1609, but their settlement in the region was limited by the harsh climate.

Great Plains

Mississippi

Tents of the Plains Indians

The first settlers

The first European settlers, such as those shown in this painting (above), inhabited the eastern coastline of North America— the Spaniards in the south, the English, Dutch, Deutsch and Swedes in the center, and the French in the north and along the Saint Lawrence river. Many of the settlers had fled religious or political persecution in Europe and hoped to create a new life in a new world. They survived by growing their own crops and raising livestock, as well as by trading with the local Indigenous Americans. They also received some supplies by ship from Europe.

• Santa Fe

Spanish pueblo village in the southwest

In search of gold
From 1539 to 1543, the Spaniard Hernando de Soto led an expedition up the Mississippi river in search of gold, inflicting great cruelty on the Indigenous Americans he met on his way.

Down river
In 1682 Robert de la Salle became the first person to canoe down the Mississippi river. He was disappointed to find that it ended up in the Gulf of Mexico, and not in the Pacific Ocean.

Louisiana

Spanish explorers
In the 1500s Spain mounted huge military expeditions from Mexico and the Caribbean into North America in search of gold, as well as to convert the Indigenous to Christianity. They did not succeed.

Mexico

Hudson Bay

French exploration
The French explored the Great Lakes region between 1613 and 1740, opening up the area for fur trappers to use.

Jacques Cartier
In 1534 Cartier explored the Gulf of Saint Lawrence for the king of France, returning the following year to sail up the Saint Lawrence river.

John Cabot
In 1497 Cabot left England in search of the Northwest Passage to Asia. He landed in Newfoundland, thinking that it was Asia.

Newfoundland

Cod fishing off Newfoundland

Gulf of Saint Lawrence

Saint Lawrence

General Wolfe
In 1759 the British army, led by General Wolfe, seized the French city of Québec, leading to the end of French rule in North America. Wolfe died during the battle.

Québec

Montréal

Nova Scotia

De Champlain
In 1608 Samuel de Champlain founded a settlement in modern-day Québec—the first permanent French settlement in North America.

Lake Huron

Lake Ontario

Lake Michigan

French Jesuits exploring the Great Lakes

Lake Erie

New York

Pennsylvania

Appalachian Mountains

Fertile land
Tobacco was the most important crop in Virginia and South Carolina. Rice was grown in South Carolina and Georgia.

New Hampshire

Massachusetts

Cape Cod

Plymouth

The Pilgrims
In 1620, 101 Puritans (Calvinists from England) sailed across the Atlantic Ocean to found a settlement in Plymouth.

Connecticut
New Amsterdam

New Jersey

Delaware

Maryland

Dutch owned
In 1626 Dutch merchants purchased Manhattan Island from the local Algonquians, establishing New Amsterdam on the site of modern-day New York City.

Atlantic Ocean

Virginia

Jamestown

Roanoke Island

Jamestown
The first permanent English settlement in the New World was established in 1607 in Jamestown, named after the English king, James I.

North Carolina

South Carolina

Growing rice in Georgia

Georgia

Roanoke Island
In 1584 Walter Raleigh set up an English colony on Roanoke Island. The colony was resettled in 1587, but by 1590, it had been abandoned.

Saint Augustine

Spanish forts
The Spaniards first landed in Florida in 1513 and explored farther inland 30 years later. Their first permanent settlement was set up in Saint Augustine in 1565.

Slave ships
The first black African slaves in North America arrived with the Spaniards in Florida, in 1526. The direct slave trade from west Africa to North America did not begin until the next century.

Gulf of Mexico

Florida

0 ——— 1,000km
0 ——— 500 miles

1450

1492 Columbus lands in the Caribbean
1497 Italian navigator John Cabot reaches North America, landing in Newfoundland

1500

1513 Ponce de Léon explores the Florida coast for Spain
1524 Giovanni da Verrazano explores the Atlantic coast of North America for France
1526 Spanish bring first black slaves in North America into Florida
1534–1535 Jacques Cartier explores the Saint Lawrence river in Canada
1539–1542 Hernando de Soto explores Florida region for Spain
1540–1542 Major Spanish expedition into New Mexico

1550

1565 Spanish establish their first base in Saint Augustine, Florida, to defend gold bullion ships returning to Spain

1584–1587 English establish a colony on Roanoke Island

1600

1607 Jamestown is founded
1608 Samuel de Champlain founds Québec
1610–1611 Henry Hudson fails to find the Northwest Passage to the Pacific Ocean
1613 French begin fur trading around the Great Lakes
1619 Dutch import the first 20 African slaves to Virginia
1620 Pilgrims arrive at Plymouth
1626 Dutch buy Manhattan Island
1630–1670 French Jesuits explore the Great Lakes

1650

1664 British acquire New Amsterdam from the Dutch and rename it New York
1670 English set up Hudson's Bay Co. to trade furs in northern Canada
1671 English explorers Batts and Fallam are the first Europeans to cross the Appalachian Mountains into the Ohio river valley
1681–1682 Robert de la Salle canoes down the full length of the Mississippi river
1681–1682 William Penn founds Pennsylvania
1686–1690 Spanish explore Texas

1700

1713 Britain gains Nova Scotia and Newfoundland from France

1731 French start fur trade around Lake Winnipeg

1750

1755–1763 French and Indian War against the British
1759 General Wolfe seizes Québec
1760 Baron Amherst seizes Montréal, ending French control of Canada
1763 Treaty of Paris gives French Canada to Britain and Louisiana to Spain

1800

The age of absolutism

In the mid-1600s a series of strong monarchs emerged in Europe. They held complete control and believed in "absolutism," the idea that the power of the state was embodied in the king, who did not have to answer to anyone. The greatest of these monarchs was Louis XIV of France, who famously said, *"L'état, c'est moi"* ("I am the state"). Under Louis XIV, France fought a series of wars against the Hapsburgs of Spain and Austria to become the most powerful state in Europe by 1715. To the east, Prussia began to emerge as the strongest state in Germany, while Austria fought off its many enemies to become the leading state in central Europe by 1750.

```
0                           500km
0              250 miles
```

London's burning
A great fire engulfed the city of London in 1666, destroying most of the historic city, including the medieval Saint Paul's Cathedral.

Under water
William of Orange stopped the French invasion of the Netherlands in 1672 by ordering the dykes to be opened, flooding most of the country.

The Huguenots
In 1685 Louis XIV of France revoked the Edict of Nantes, which gave religious tolerance to Huguenots. Almost 200,000 skilled workers fled abroad with their families.

Merchant shipping
French merchant ships brought in goods from the colonies and trading posts in North America, the Caribbean, and India.

Louis XIV
Louis XIV was only five when he became the king, in 1643.

Spanish art
Spanish power declined during the 1600s, but the country enjoyed a golden age of painting and architecture, with artists such as Velázquez and Zurbarán in high demand for their lifelike portraits and still-life works.

Tidal wave
In 1755 a massive earthquake caused a tidal wave to engulf the Portuguese capital, Lisbon, killing thousands of people.

Gibraltar
The British seized the Rock of Gibraltar from Spain in 1704. Britain has held it ever since, despite constant requests from Spain to hand it back.

The French navy
Operating out of Toulon, the French navy played a major role in attacking the Hapsburg lands in Spain and Italy.

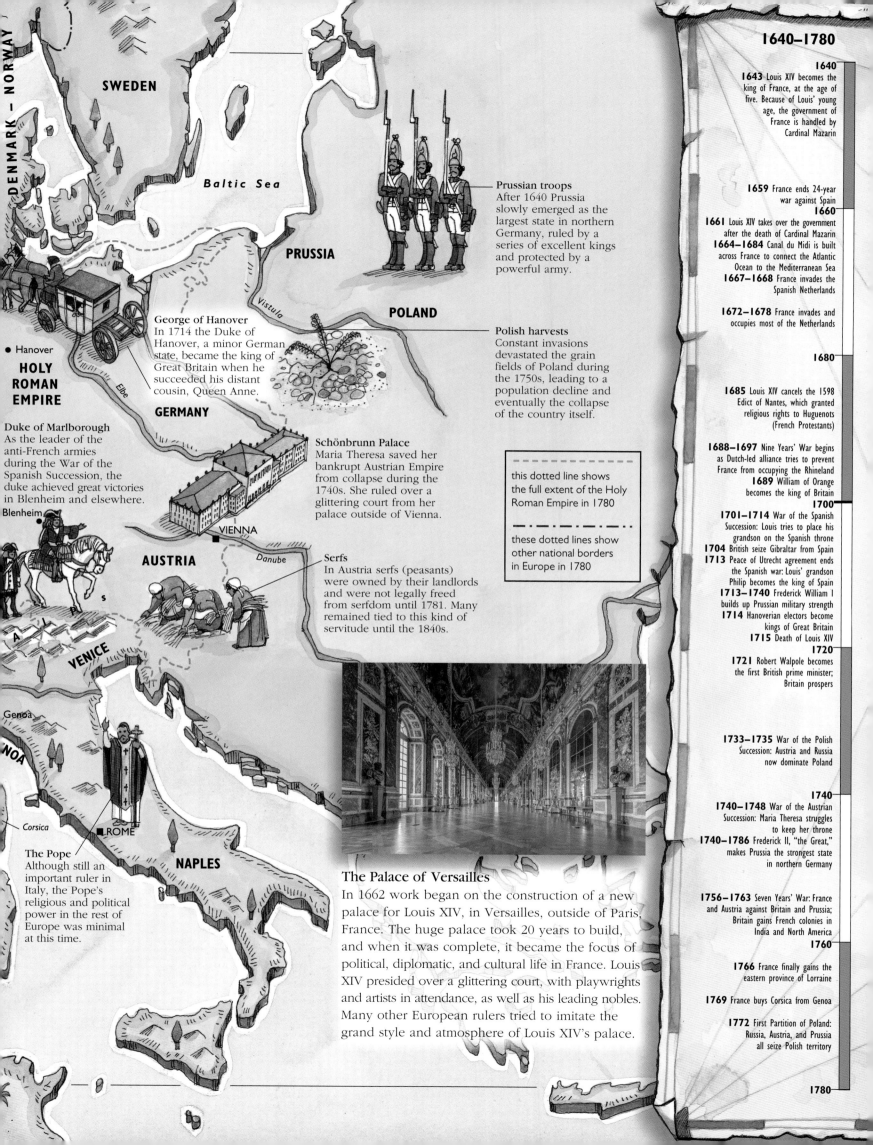

SWEDEN

DENMARK – NORWAY

Baltic Sea

PRUSSIA

Prussian troops
After 1640 Prussia slowly emerged as the largest state in northern Germany, ruled by a series of excellent kings and protected by a powerful army.

Vistula

POLAND

George of Hanover
In 1714 the Duke of Hanover, a minor German state, became the king of Great Britain when he succeeded his distant cousin, Queen Anne.

• Hanover

HOLY ROMAN EMPIRE

Polish harvests
Constant invasions devastated the grain fields of Poland during the 1750s, leading to a population decline and eventually the collapse of the country itself.

Elbe

GERMANY

Duke of Marlborough
As the leader of the anti-French armies during the War of the Spanish Succession, the duke achieved great victories in Blenheim and elsewhere.

Blenheim

Schönbrunn Palace
Maria Theresa saved her bankrupt Austrian Empire from collapse during the 1740s. She ruled over a glittering court from her palace outside of Vienna.

VIENNA

AUSTRIA

Danube

—————— this dotted line shows the full extent of the Holy Roman Empire in 1780

—·—·—·— these dotted lines show other national borders in Europe in 1780

Serfs
In Austria serfs (peasants) were owned by their landlords and were not legally freed from serfdom until 1781. Many remained tied to this kind of servitude until the 1840s.

VENICE

Genoa

GENOA

Corsica

ROME

The Pope
Although still an important ruler in Italy, the Pope's religious and political power in the rest of Europe was minimal at this time.

NAPLES

The Palace of Versailles

In 1662 work began on the construction of a new palace for Louis XIV, in Versailles, outside of Paris, France. The huge palace took 20 years to build, and when it was complete, it became the focus of political, diplomatic, and cultural life in France. Louis XIV presided over a glittering court, with playwrights and artists in attendance, as well as his leading nobles. Many other European rulers tried to imitate the grand style and atmosphere of Louis XIV's palace.

1640–1780

1640

1643 Louis XIV becomes the king of France, at the age of five. Because of Louis' young age, the government of France is handled by Cardinal Mazarin

1659 France ends 24-year war against Spain
1660

1661 Louis XIV takes over the government after the death of Cardinal Mazarin
1664–1684 Canal du Midi is built across France to connect the Atlantic Ocean to the Mediterranean Sea
1667–1668 France invades the Spanish Netherlands

1672–1678 France invades and occupies most of the Netherlands

1680

1685 Louis XIV cancels the 1598 Edict of Nantes, which granted religious rights to Huguenots (French Protestants)

1688–1697 Nine Years' War begins as Dutch-led alliance tries to prevent France from occupying the Rhineland
1689 William of Orange becomes the king of Britain
1700

1701–1714 War of the Spanish Succession: Louis tries to place his grandson on the Spanish throne
1704 British seize Gibraltar from Spain
1713 Peace of Utrecht agreement ends the Spanish war: Louis' grandson Philip becomes the king of Spain
1713–1740 Frederick William I builds up Prussian military strength
1714 Hanoverian electors become kings of Great Britain
1715 Death of Louis XIV
1720

1721 Robert Walpole becomes the first British prime minister; Britain prospers

1733–1735 War of the Polish Succession: Austria and Russia now dominate Poland

1740

1740–1748 War of the Austrian Succession: Maria Theresa struggles to keep her throne
1740–1786 Frederick II, "the Great," makes Prussia the strongest state in northern Germany

1756–1763 Seven Years' War: France and Austria against Britain and Prussia; Britain gains French colonies in India and North America
1760

1766 France finally gains the eastern province of Lorraine

1769 France buys Corsica from Genoa

1772 First Partition of Poland: Russia, Austria, and Prussia all seize Polish territory

1780

The intellectual revolution:

An enlightened view of the world

During the mid-1600s, a new way of looking at the world began to flourish in Europe. This movement is known as the Enlightenment because it was a time of new ideas based on human logic and reason, rather than on the old religious beliefs of the Christian Church. The Enlightenment had a huge impact not just on philosophy and politics, but also on science and invention. The Enlightenment movement was opposed by the Catholic Church, but some rulers supported these new ideas, setting up universities and scientific societies and granting religious and political freedom to their subjects.

Politics

The Enlightenment changed political thinking and influenced the French Revolution of 1789. In 1791–1792 the English pamphlet-writer Thomas Paine (1737–1809, right) wrote *The Rights of Man* in support of the revolution, but he was forced to flee to France. There he wrote *The Age of Reason* (1795), attacking Christianity, and was almost executed by guillotine. Paine also inspired the American Revolution with his pamphlet, *Common Sense*, which was published in January 1776.

Philosophy

The French philosopher René Descartes (1596–1650, left) is often seen as the founder of modern philosophy, putting logic and reason at the center of his thinking. He summed up his beliefs in the phrase, "I think, therefore I am." Around 100 years later Voltaire (1694–1778) wrote a series of witty pamphlets, novels, and plays that were read by people all across Europe, making the new ideas of the Enlightenment very popular.

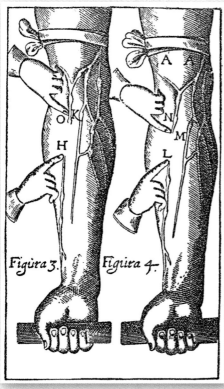

Physics

The English scientist Isaac Newton (1642–1727, right) demonstrated that white light is made up of a spectrum of colors. He did this by "refracting" the light through a glass prism. Most importantly, he defined the three laws of motion and the law of universal gravitation—the invisible force of attraction between objects.

Anatomy

In 1628 William Harvey published *De Motu Cordis*—"On the Motion of the Heart"—in which he suggested that blood is pumped by the heart and that it is constantly circulating around the body. His explanations overturned medical beliefs that had been followed since the Greeks, 1,400 years earlier.

Eyepiece lens turns image the right way up

Lenses magnify subject around 21 times, which allowed Galileo to see only one-third of the Moon at a time

Object lens magnifies subject but turns it upside down

Astronomy

Both Galileo Galilei (1564–1642) and Johannes Kepler (1571–1630) developed the basic ideas of Nicolaus Copernicus (see page 106). Galileo invented a telescope for studying the movement of the planets. Kepler discovered that the planets move around the Sun in ellipses (ovals) rather than in circles and that they move fastest when they are closest to the Sun.

Galileo used this telescope to view the sky in 1609. The telescope gives a restricted view because the lenses are small.

Microscopy

Robert Hooke (1635–1703) developed a powerful "compound," or multilens, microscope (left) for studying very small organisms. He was the first person to use the word "cell" to describe the tiny units out of which all living things are made.

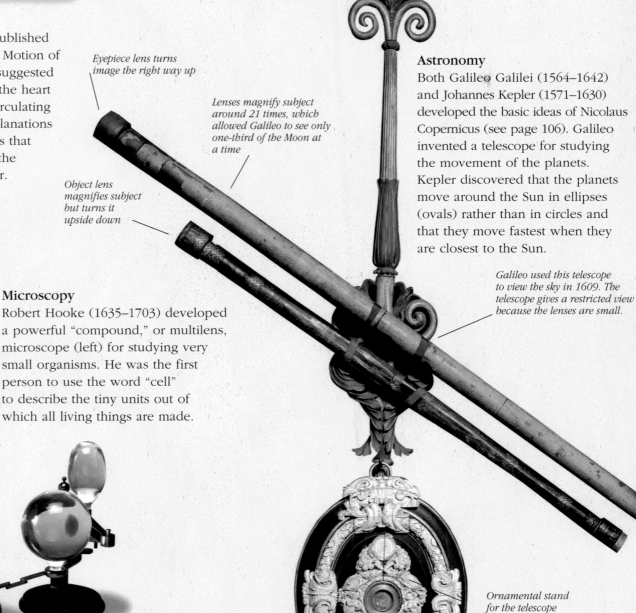

Ornamental stand for the telescope

Exploring the Pacific

The first Europeans entered the Pacific Ocean in the 1500s, looking for a new sea route to Asia and its riches. In the 1600s merchants came to set up trading posts throughout the East Indies (Indonesia). Many islands in the Pacific remained unknown to Europeans, as did Australia, until 1606 when Dutch navigator Willem Janszoon first landed on the island. He and other Dutch navigators explored the west and south sides of the island, and it wasn't until 1770 that Captain Cook landed at Botany Bay on Australia's east coast. Eighteen years later, 750 British convicts became the first permanent European settlers in Australia.

KEY TO VOYAGES

Ferdinand Magellan	→	1519–1521
Alvaro de Mendaña	→	1567–1569
Abel Tasman		1642–1643
James Cook: 1st voyage	→	1768–1771

Crossing the Pacific Ocean
Magellan took four months to cross the Pacific Ocean. He landed in Guam and then eventually reached the Philippines, where he was killed in a skirmish with local people.

Silk trade
Portuguese merchants based in Macao supplied fine Chinese silk to the Spanish in the Philippines.

Macao

CHINA

PHILIPPINES

Manila

Guam

Spanish Catholic church

South China Sea

Mining tin

Gold ore

Indigenous people in Borneo

Ternate

Cloves

Polynesians fishing

Pacific trade
Spanish galleons regularly crossed the Pacific Ocean, taking silver from Acapulco, Mexico, and returning from Manila, in the Philippines, with Chinese silk.

Malay Peninsula

Malacca

Pepper

EAST INDIES

Sumatra

Moluccas Islands

Amboina

Banda Islands

New Guinea

Tasman trading

SOLOMON ISLANDS

Cannibals
Mendaña sent some of his crew ashore in the Solomon Islands to find fresh water. They were attacked by cannibals.

Indian Ocean

BATAVIA

Sugar

Solor

Kupang

Coffee

Java

Timor

Nutmeg

Batavia
Batavia was the headquarters of the Dutch East Indies Company, a trading organization that dominated the spice trade in the region.

Reefed
Captain Cook ran his ship *Endeavour* aground on the Great Barrier Reef. He and his crew had to stop to repair the large hole in the ship's hull.

FIJI

TONGA

Malacca
The Portuguese built a large fort in Malacca so that they could dominate the sea route between the Indian Ocean and the South China Sea.

AUSTRALIA

Indigenous Australians
Around 750,000 Indigenous peoples lived in Australia before the Europeans arrived. Their numbers dropped after foreign settlement began, caused by diseases and violence brought in by the settlers.

Great Barrier Reef

Botany Bay
The first 750 British convicts landed in Botany Bay in 1788 to serve their prison sentences in Australia. 160,000 more followed until this practice was stopped in 1868.

Botany Bay

A ship from Abel Tasman's fleet

North Island

Tasmania

South Island

NEW ZEALAND

Tasmania
Tasman sent a carpenter ashore to plant a flag on what he called Van Diemen's Land, named after the governor-general of Dutch Batavia. The island is now called Tasmania, after Tasman himself.

Brutal welcome
When Captain Cook landed on the North Island of New Zealand, he and his crew were attacked by the Maori people. In the skirmish several Maori were shot.

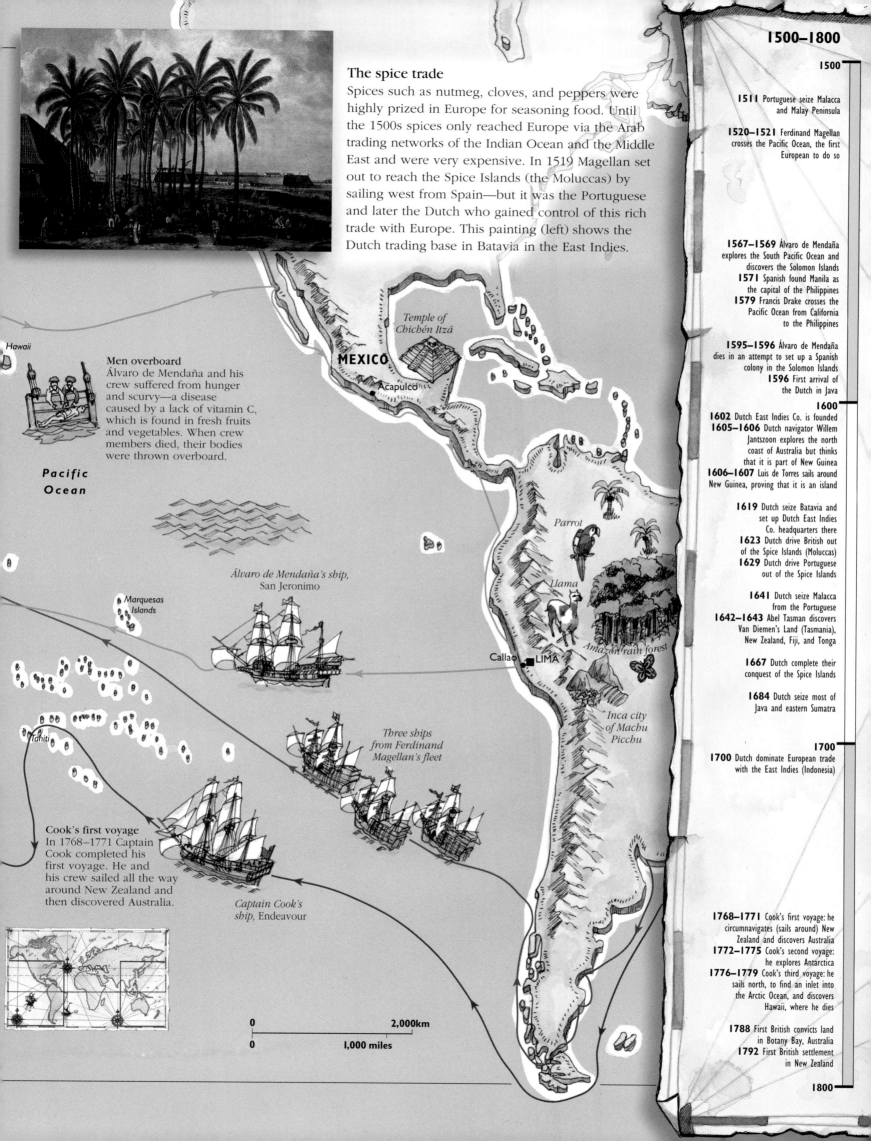

The spice trade

Spices such as nutmeg, cloves, and peppers were highly prized in Europe for seasoning food. Until the 1500s spices only reached Europe via the Arab trading networks of the Indian Ocean and the Middle East and were very expensive. In 1519 Magellan set out to reach the Spice Islands (the Moluccas) by sailing west from Spain—but it was the Portuguese and later the Dutch who gained control of this rich trade with Europe. This painting (left) shows the Dutch trading base in Batavia in the East Indies.

Hawaii

Men overboard
Álvaro de Mendaña and his crew suffered from hunger and scurvy—a disease caused by a lack of vitamin C, which is found in fresh fruits and vegetables. When crew members died, their bodies were thrown overboard.

Pacific Ocean

Álvaro de Mendaña's ship, San Jeronimo

Marquesas Islands

Tahiti

Cook's first voyage
In 1768–1771 Captain Cook completed his first voyage. He and his crew sailed all the way around New Zealand and then discovered Australia.

Captain Cook's ship, Endeavour

Three ships from Ferdinand Magellan's fleet

Temple of Chichén Itzá

MEXICO

Acapulco

Parrot

Llama

Amazon rain forest

Callao ■ **LIMA**

Inca city of Machu Picchu

| 0 | 2,000km |
| 0 | 1,000 miles |

1500–1800

1500

1511 Portuguese seize Malacca and Malay Peninsula

1520–1521 Ferdinand Magellan crosses the Pacific Ocean, the first European to do so

1567–1569 Álvaro de Mendaña explores the South Pacific Ocean and discovers the Solomon Islands
1571 Spanish found Manila as the capital of the Philippines
1579 Francis Drake crosses the Pacific Ocean from California to the Philippines

1595–1596 Álvaro de Mendaña dies in an attempt to set up a Spanish colony in the Solomon Islands
1596 First arrival of the Dutch in Java

1600

1602 Dutch East Indies Co. is founded
1605–1606 Dutch navigator Willem Jantszoon explores the north coast of Australia but thinks that it is part of New Guinea
1606–1607 Luis de Torres sails around New Guinea, proving that it is an island

1619 Dutch seize Batavia and set up Dutch East Indies Co. headquarters there
1623 Dutch drive British out of the Spice Islands (Moluccas)
1629 Dutch drive Portuguese out of the Spice Islands

1641 Dutch seize Malacca from the Portuguese
1642–1643 Abel Tasman discovers Van Diemen's Land (Tasmania), New Zealand, Fiji, and Tonga

1667 Dutch complete their conquest of the Spice Islands

1684 Dutch seize most of Java and eastern Sumatra

1700

1700 Dutch dominate European trade with the East Indies (Indonesia)

1768–1771 Cook's first voyage: he circumnavigates (sails around) New Zealand and discovers Australia
1772–1775 Cook's second voyage: he explores Antarctica
1776–1779 Cook's third voyage: he sails north, to find an inlet into the Arctic Ocean, and discovers Hawaii, where he dies

1788 First British convicts land in Botany Bay, Australia
1792 First British settlement in New Zealand

1800

The American Revolution

In 1775 all 13 of the British colonies in North America rose up in revolt. They protested against British attempts to restrict their freedom and to tax them without giving them any representation in Parliament. Led by George Washington, and later supported by the French, the colonists declared their independence in 1776 and won a series of military victories before the war ended in 1783. This victory gave birth to a new nation, the United States of America, which initially stretched only as far inland as the Mississippi river. Eventually, it extended all the way across the continent, to the Pacific Ocean in the west.

George Washington
George Washington (1732–1799) was a colonial farmer in Virginia who fought for the British against the French in the 1750s. He was the ideal person to command the American forces against the British and led them to victory in 1781. As the first president of the newly independent United States, from 1789 to 1797, he led the nation with great skill and determination.

The Boston Tea Party
Colonists who were upset by the British government's tax on imported tea dumped a cargo of tea into Boston Harbor in 1773.

Loyalists
Americans from New York and South Carolina who were loyal to the British crown fled north to Canada along with the Mohawks who had fought for the British. They settled in Ontario and the provinces close to the sea.

Paul Revere
On April 18, 1775, silversmith Paul Revere rode through the night to warn people that British troops were coming to capture military supplies in Concord.

Saratoga
A British attempt to isolate the New England colonies from the rest of America was defeated in Saratoga in 1777.

The legend of Betsy Ross
Betsy Ross was asked to make the first American flag using six-pointed stars, but she said that five-pointed stars "would look better."

Crossing the Delaware
On Christmas Day in 1776 George Washington led his recently defeated army across the icy Delaware river, surprising the British and winning a crucial battle in Trenton.

A new capital
In 1791 the decision was made to build a new national capital on the Potomac river. It was named Washington in honor of the first president, George Washington.

CANADA

Québec

Montréal

Ontario

Lake Superior

Lake Huron

Lake Michigan

Lake Erie

Lake Ontario

UNITED STATES OF AMERICA

Mississippi

Appalachian Mountains

New Hampshire

Concord
Bunker Hill
Lexington
Boston

Massachusetts

Rhode Island

Connecticut

New York

New York

Hudson

Saratoga

Princeton
Trenton

Pennsylvania
Philadelphia
Brandywine

Delaware

New Jersey

WASHINGTON
Baltimore

1760

1763 Direct British taxation is imposed in American colonies for the first time

1765 British impose the Stamp Act, taxing all newspapers and legal documents
1766 Stamp Act is abolished after widespread opposition
1766 Declaratory Act affirms the British right to legislate (make laws) in the American colonies

1770

1770 British troops kill five in Boston
1774 First Continental Congress: colonists meet in Philadelphia to decide on strategy
April 1775 Fighting breaks out at Lexington and Concord, close to Boston
June 1775 Second Continental Congress sets up an army under George Washington
June 1775 British win the first major battle at Bunker Hill
May 1776 Americans fail to capture Quebec from the British and leave Canada
July 1776 Second Continental Congress adopts the Declaration of Independence
Sept. 1776 British take New York
Dec. 1776 Washington wins a decisive battle at Trenton
1777 Congress adopts the Articles of Confederation, setting up the United States
Oct. 1777 British surrender in Saratoga
1778 French enter war on the American side
1779 Spanish enter war on the American side

1780

May 1780 British capture Charleston
July 1780 First French troops arrive to strengthen the American army
Sept. 1781 French defeat British naval fleet off Virginia Capes
Oct. 1781 Combined American and French force, led by Washington, achieve a major victory over the British at Yorktown

1783 Treaty of Paris: British recognize American independence

1787 Constitutional Convention draws up a new constitution (set of laws and rights)
1788 New constitution becomes law
1789 George Washington is elected as the first president; John Adams is the vice-president; Thomas Jefferson is the secretary of state

1790

1791 National bank is set up; site of the new capital city is decided
1792 National mint is established for issuing coins and bank notes
1792 Washington is reelected as president

1797 Washington retires; John Adams becomes the president

1800

Virginia Capes

Merchant ship heading for Europe

French support
The French navy proved to be decisive in the war, defeating a British fleet off the Virginia Capes in 1781 and blockading the British in Yorktown. The British force that was there had no choice but to surrender.

Atlantic Ocean

Virginia

Yorktown

Mount Vernon
George Washington was an important landowner in Virginia, running his large estate from his home in Mount Vernon. He retired there after leaving the presidency in 1797.

North Carolina

Yorktown
The British suffered a major defeat in Yorktown in October 1781.

Camden

Charleston

South Carolina

British victories
The British captured the important southern towns of Savannah, in 1778, and Charleston, in 1780. But they were unable to defeat the enemy army in the south.

Savannah

Georgia

Spanish involvement
Spain declared war against Britain in 1779 and reclaimed its former colony of Florida, which had been lost to the British in 1763.

East Florida

Ohio

New flag
The new American flag, first used in 1777, had 13 stripes and stars, one for each of the 13 colonies that were fighting against the British for independence.

Slaves cutting down sugar cane

West Florida

Mississippi

Gulf of Mexico

500km
250 miles

0
0

- - - - - dotted line shows the border of the United States of America in 1783

The Constitution of the United States

The Constitution of 1787 created a democratic government with three branches: (1) The legislative (an elected Senate and House of Representatives to create laws); (2) The Judiciary (an appointed Supreme Court to uphold the law); and (3) The executive (an indirectly elected presidency to propose and enforce new laws). A system of checks and balances prevented any one branch from becoming too powerful. It also created a federal government, with all power divided between the national and state governments.

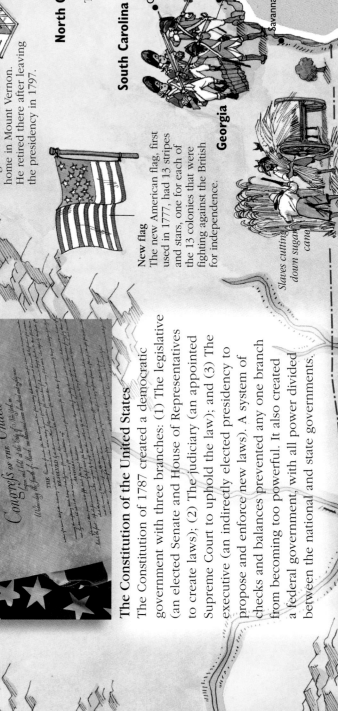

Congress of the United States

The French Revolution

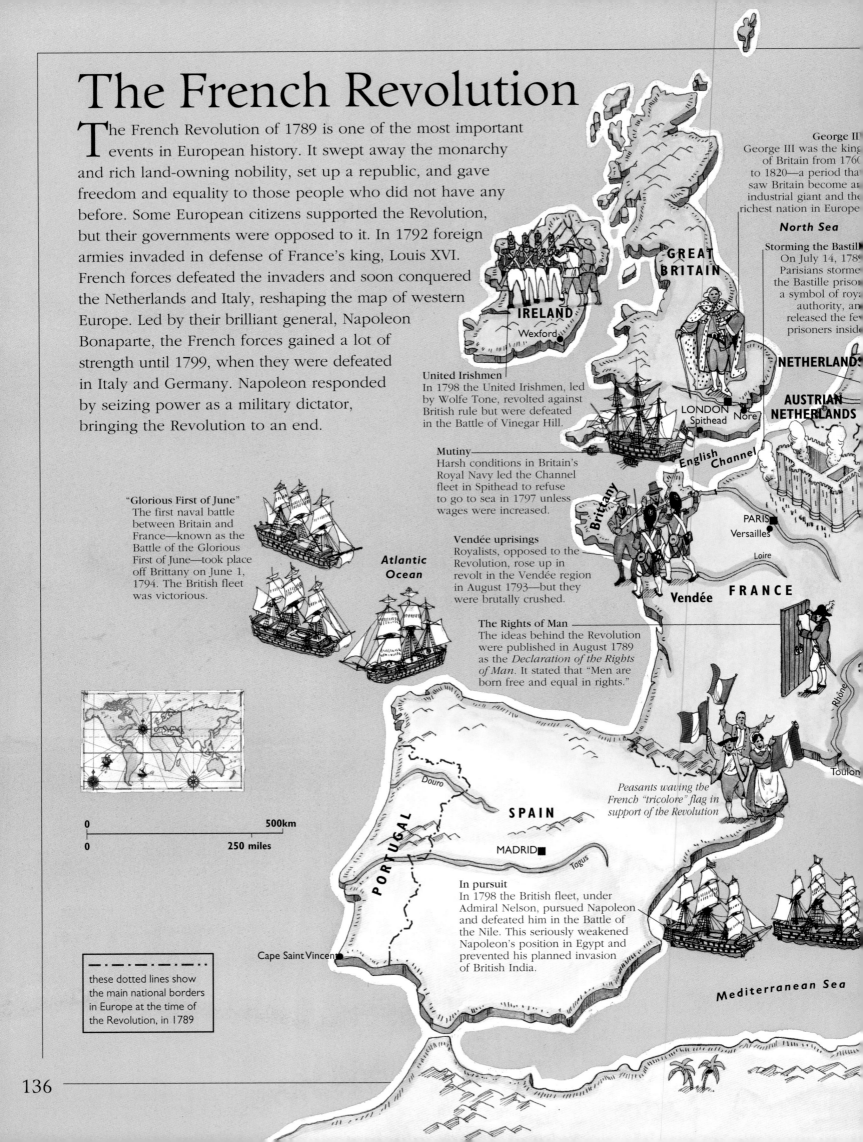

The French Revolution of 1789 is one of the most important events in European history. It swept away the monarchy and rich land-owning nobility, set up a republic, and gave freedom and equality to those people who did not have any before. Some European citizens supported the Revolution, but their governments were opposed to it. In 1792 foreign armies invaded in defense of France's king, Louis XVI. French forces defeated the invaders and soon conquered the Netherlands and Italy, reshaping the map of western Europe. Led by their brilliant general, Napoleon Bonaparte, the French forces gained a lot of strength until 1799, when they were defeated in Italy and Germany. Napoleon responded by seizing power as a military dictator, bringing the Revolution to an end.

George III
George III was the king of Britain from 1760 to 1820—a period that saw Britain become an industrial giant and the richest nation in Europe.

North Sea

Storming the Bastille
On July 14, 1789 Parisians stormed the Bastille prison, a symbol of royal authority, and released the few prisoners inside.

GREAT BRITAIN

IRELAND
Wexford

United Irishmen
In 1798 the United Irishmen, led by Wolfe Tone, revolted against British rule but were defeated in the Battle of Vinegar Hill.

LONDON
Spithead Nore

NETHERLANDS

AUSTRIAN NETHERLANDS

English Channel

Mutiny
Harsh conditions in Britain's Royal Navy led the Channel fleet in Spithead to refuse to go to sea in 1797 unless wages were increased.

Brittany

PARIS
Versailles

Loire

"Glorious First of June"
The first naval battle between Britain and France—known as the Battle of the Glorious First of June—took place off Brittany on June 1, 1794. The British fleet was victorious.

Atlantic Ocean

Vendée uprisings
Royalists, opposed to the Revolution, rose up in revolt in the Vendée region in August 1793—but they were brutally crushed.

Vendée **FRANCE**

The Rights of Man
The ideas behind the Revolution were published in August 1789 as the *Declaration of the Rights of Man*. It stated that "Men are born free and equal in rights."

Rhône

Peasants waving the French "tricolore" flag in support of the Revolution

Toulon

0 ———————— 500km
0 ———————— 250 miles

Douro

PORTUGAL

SPAIN

MADRID

Tagus

In pursuit
In 1798 the British fleet, under Admiral Nelson, pursued Napoleon and defeated him in the Battle of the Nile. This seriously weakened Napoleon's position in Egypt and prevented his planned invasion of British India.

Cape Saint Vincent

Mediterranean Sea

— · — · — · — · —
these dotted lines show the main national borders in Europe at the time of the Revolution, in 1789

RUSSIA

Baltic Sea

Prussia
Prussia emerged in the 1700s as the most powerful state in northern Europe. Along with Austria, it declared war on revolutionary France in 1792 in order to restore the French monarchy.

PRUSSIA

Elbe

BERLIN

Vistula

POLAND

Dividing Poland
Three times—in 1772, 1793, and 1795—Prussia, Russia, and Austria divided up Poland between them. The Poles did not regain their independence until 1918.

Germany

Rhine

Danube

AUSTRIAN EMPIRE

VIENNA

Marie Antoinette
Marie Antoinette, the daughter of the Austrian empress, was married to the French king Louis XVI at the age of 14. She was executed for treason in 1793.

Commander-in-chief
Napoleon emerged as the leading French commander, owing to his incredible campaigns and victories in Italy in 1796–1797.

Sava

VENICE

GENOA

OTTOMAN EMPIRE

Corsica

ROME

Sardinia

Island home
Napoleon Bonaparte was born on August 15, 1769, on the French island of Corsica, which, until the previous year, had been part of the Italian state of Genoa.

Sicily

MALTA

Beheading the king and queen

Because of the monarchy's rising debts, Louis XVI was forced to summon the Estates-General (parliament) in May 1789 to raise taxes. The ministers of the Third Estate (representing the commoners) were angered by this and soon broke away to form a national assembly. Their demands for political reform led to the Revolution, which broke out in July 1789 and reached its peak with Louis' execution in January 1793. The queen of France, Marie Antoinette, was also beheaded in October of the same year (above).

1789
May 1789 Estates-General meets but soon collapses
June 1789 Third Estate of commoners sets up the National Assembly
July 1789 Parisians storm Bastille prison
Aug. 1789 Declaration of the Rights of Man is published

1790

1791
June 1791 French king Louis XVI and his queen, Marie Antoinette, try to flee Paris

1792
July 1792 France declares war on Prussia
Sept. 1792 France abolishes monarchy and becomes a republic
Nov. 1792 French defeat Austrians and seize the Austrian Netherlands

1793
Jan. 1793 Louis XVI executed by guillotine
Jan. 1793 Second Partition of Poland
Feb.–Mar. 1793 France declares war on Britain and Dutch republic
Feb. 1793 First Coalition of European powers formed against France
Mar.–Oct. 1793 Royalist uprising in the Vendée

1794
June 1793–July 1794 Maximilien Robespierre leads a reign of terror against enemies of the Revolution

June 1794 British defeat French fleet in the Battle of the Glorious First of June

1795
Jan. 1795 French conquer Dutch republic
April 1795 France and Prussia make peace
Oct. 1795 Directory takes power in France
Oct. 1795 Third Partition of Poland: partition of country between Austria, Prussia, and Russia ends Polish independence

1796
Feb. 1796 British naval victory over Spain (a French ally) off Cape Saint Vincent
April Napolean Bonaparte commands French forces against Austrians in Italy

1797
April, May 1797 British Royal Navy mutinies twice over pay and service conditions

Oct. 1797 British defeat Dutch fleet in Camperdown off the Dutch coast
Oct. 1797 Austria and France make peace

1798
June 1798 United Irishmen fail to win independence from Britain
July 1798 Napoleon defeats Egyptians in the Battle of the Pyramids
Aug. 1798 Nelson defeats Napoleon in the Battle of the Nile

1799
Mar. 1799 Austria declares war on France
Mar., April 1799 French forces defeated in Germany and Italy
June 1799 Britain, Austria, and Russia form the Second Coalition
Nov. 1799 Napoleon Bonaparte overthrows Directory and sets up a three-man Consulate

1800

MODERN WORLD

Illustrated by Kevin Maddison

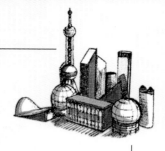

CONTENTS

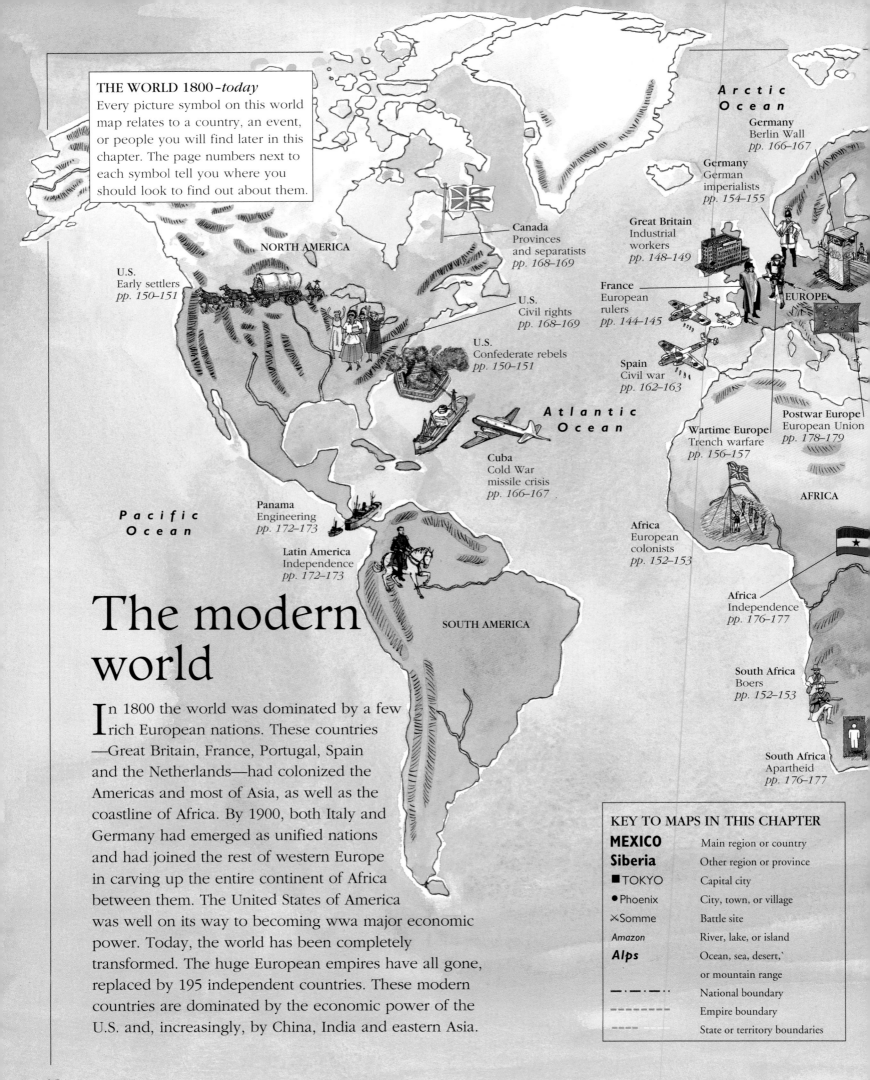

THE WORLD 1800-*today*
Every picture symbol on this world map relates to a country, an event, or people you will find later in this chapter. The page numbers next to each symbol tell you where you should look to find out about them.

Arctic Ocean

NORTH AMERICA

U.S.
Early settlers
pp. 150–151

Canada
Provinces
and separatists
pp. 168–169

U.S.
Civil rights
pp. 168–169

U.S.
Confederate rebels
pp. 150–151

Germany
Berlin Wall
pp. 166–167

Germany
German
imperialists
pp. 154–155

Great Britain
Industrial
workers
pp. 148–149

France
European
rulers
pp. 144–145

EUROPE

Spain
Civil war
pp. 162–163

Atlantic Ocean

Cuba
Cold War
missile crisis
pp. 166–167

Wartime Europe
Trench warfare
pp. 156–157

Postwar Europe
European Union
pp. 178–179

AFRICA

Pacific Ocean

Panama
Engineering
pp. 172–173

Africa
European
colonists
pp. 152–153

Latin America
Independence
pp. 172–173

SOUTH AMERICA

Africa
Independence
pp. 176–177

South Africa
Boers
pp. 152–153

South Africa
Apartheid
pp. 176–177

The modern world

In 1800 the world was dominated by a few rich European nations. These countries —Great Britain, France, Portugal, Spain and the Netherlands—had colonized the Americas and most of Asia, as well as the coastline of Africa. By 1900, both Italy and Germany had emerged as unified nations and had joined the rest of western Europe in carving up the entire continent of Africa between them. The United States of America was well on its way to becoming wwa major economic power. Today, the world has been completely transformed. The huge European empires have all gone, replaced by 195 independent countries. These modern countries are dominated by the economic power of the U.S. and, increasingly, by China, India and eastern Asia.

KEY TO MAPS IN THIS CHAPTER

MEXICO	Main region or country
Siberia	Other region or province
■TOKYO	Capital city
●Phoenix	City, town, or village
✕Somme	Battle site
Amazon	River, lake, or island
Alps	Ocean, sea, desert, or mountain range
—·—·—	National boundary
– – – – –	Empire boundary
– – – – –	State or territory boundaries

Russia
Revolutionaries
pp. 158–159

Russia
Freed serfs
pp. 154–155

Russia
Space travel
pp. 158–159

ASIA

Middle East
Oil wealth
pp. 174–175

China
Communists
pp. 170–171

Japan
Kamikaze pilots
pp. 164–165

India
Independence
pp. 176–177

Vietnam
Vietnam War
pp. 176–177

Pacific
Ocean

Indian Ocean

AUSTRALIA

Australia
European settlers
pp. 148–149

LOCATOR MAP
You will find a world map like
this along with every map in the
chapter. This allows you to see
exactly which part of the world
the main map is showing you.

POLITICAL MOVEMENTS
The following definitions may help
you when reading this chapter:

CAPITALISM: An economic system based
on private ownership, in which there is
usually a free market to buy and sell goods.

COMMUNISM: A classless society in
which private ownership is abolished.
The means of production and subsistence
belong to the community as a whole,
although this system is often under the
control of the state.

FASCISM: An extreme political movement

based on nationalism (loyalty
to one's country) and authority—often
military—which aims to unite a country's
people into a disciplined force under
an all-powerful leader or dictator.

FUNDAMENTALISM: A movement that
favors a very strict interpretation of any
one religion and its scriptures or laws.

MARXISM: A movement based on the ideas
of the philosopher Karl Marx (1818–83),
often known as the "father of communism."

NAZISM: A very extreme form of fascism,
often involving highly racist policies.

The world since 1800:
An endlessly changing world

The pace of changes over the past 200 years has probably been greater than at any other time during human history. In 1800 the population of the world was around 930 million, and most of these people lived and worked on the land. Today, the world is home to around 7.9 billion people, the vast majority of whom live and work in increasingly crowded towns and cities. New industrial techniques, mass communication, and inventions such as the airplane and the computer have transformed the lives of almost everyone today, while few people have been able to escape the effects of the wars and conflicts that have raged around the globe during the past century.

Industrial change

The Industrial Revolution began in Great Britain in the late 1700s and spread throughout Europe and across to the United States during the 1800s. Millions of people who had previously worked on the land or in small workshops now lived and worked in large industrial towns. They worked long hours in factories, iron and steel works, and shipyards—as in New York City (above)—where the working conditions were often difficult and dangerous.

Into space

The first human-made satellite to orbit Earth, *Sputnik 1*, was launched in 1957. Twelve years later astronauts landed on the Moon, and by the end of the century, they lived and worked in space for months at a time in space stations that orbited far above Earth's surface (below). Unmanned spacecraft have now explored the farthest planets, sending back remarkable photographs of our solar system and beyond.

The impact of war

The 1900s was one of the most brutal periods in all of human history. Two major world wars and several other conflicts killed millions of people and transformed the lives of millions more. For example, women worked in jobs that had been previously undertaken only by men, such as in heavy industrial plants (left). In many countries women also gained the right to vote and to be treated as equals to men for the first time.

The International Space Station (ISS) is made up of separate modules, which have been launched into space individually since 1998.

Space shuttle astronauts perform spacewalks to connect the different modules.

Communication

The development of the telegraph, postal services, mass printing techniques, the telephone, radio, television, and the Internet have transformed communication over the past 200 years. This also means that we have a huge volume of historical evidence to tell us about this period—photographs, printed material such as newspapers, and film and sound recordings. Today, information can be spread around the world in seconds via satellite technology, while computers have totally transformed the way we work, study and entertain ourselves.

*Television set
from the 1960s*

*Early 20th-century
telephone*

*Modern laptop
computer*

*Newspapers are still an important source
of up-to-date information. They are now
printed and distributed at great speed, and
in huge quantities, thanks to automated
printing presses such as this one (above).*

*Smartphone with digital
camera and Internet access*

Napoleonic Europe

In 1804 Napoleon Bonaparte, the ruler of France since 1799 and the most successful military leader of his time, crowned himself Emperor Napoleon I. A series of incredible victories gained him control of a large part of Europe, with only a few other powers able to resist him. In 1812 he invaded Russia in a final attempt to end Russian opposition to his rule. Although he seized the capital, Moscow, he was forced to retreat because of the fierce Russian winter. Victories turned to defeats, and in 1815 a joint British and Prussian force finally overcame Napoleon at Waterloo.

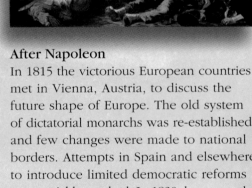

After Napoleon

In 1815 the victorious European countries met in Vienna, Austria, to discuss the future shape of Europe. The old system of dictatorial monarchs was re-established, and few changes were made to national borders. Attempts in Spain and elsewhere to introduce limited democratic reforms were quickly crushed. In 1830, however, the people of Paris, France, rose up in revolt (above) against the dictatorial Charles X, setting up a new, more liberal monarchy.

these dotted lines show the borders between European countries in 1815

Battle of Trafalgar
The British navy under Lord Nelson won a victory against the French at Trafalgar in 1805, ending the threat of an invasion of Great Britain.

Industrial Revolution
A revolution in the production of coal, iron, cotton, and wool textiles turned Great Britain into the "workshop of the world" by 1815.

Battle of Waterloo
Napoleon was finally defeated at Waterloo in 1815 by the British and the Prussians.

The Great Reform Act
The British parliament was reformed in 1832 to make it more fair and less corrupt.

Sent far away
After his defeat at Waterloo, Napoleon was sent into exile on the southern Atlantic island of Saint Helena, 5,000 miles away.

Self-crowning
Napoleon became emperor of France in 1804, crowning himself at his coronation.

Napoleon is triumphant
In 1800 Napoleon crossed the Alps, soon to be the master of Europe.

rural workers in the fields

The Peninsular War
The Spanish rose up in revolt against Napoleon in 1808.

Temporary exile
In 1814 Napoleon was sent into exile by Great Britain and its allies to the island of Elba. He soon escaped back to France.

Fighting tyranny
In 1820 the Spanish army revolted against the brutal rule of King Ferdinand VII, but it was crushed by the French in 1823.

French North Africa
In 1830 the French occupied the city of Algiers, the beginnings of a huge empire in North Africa.

Scotland

North Sea

Ireland

Dublin •

GREAT BRITAIN

LONDON ■

Boulogne •

Waterloo

• Amiens

DENMARK

NETHERLAN

GERMAN STATES

Atlantic Ocean

PARIS ■

FRANCE

Ulm

SWITZERLAND

A

Vitoria ✕

PORTUGAL

MADRID ■ SPAIN

LISBON ■

Sardinia

Balearic Islands

■ ALGIERS

Trafalgar ✕

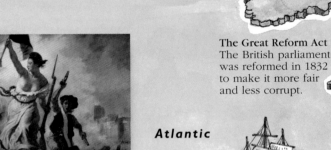

Moscow burning
In 1812, Napoleon's army arrived to capture Moscow, but soon after their arrival, the city had been set on fire.

■ MOSCOW
✕ Borodino

Retreat from Moscow
The severe Russian winter forced Napoleon's army to retreat from Russia in 1812, suffering massive losses as the troops headed home.

SWEDEN

openhagen

Tilsit

✕ Friedland

RUSSIAN EMPIRE

Berlin PRUSSIA

Leipzig

Battle of Austerlitz
Napoleon defeated the Russians and the Austrians at Austerlitz on December 2, 1805.

Austerlitz ✕
✕ Wagram
■ VIENNA

ARIA

AUSTRIAN EMPIRE

Moldavia

Serbs revolt
The Serbs revolted against their Ottoman rulers, winning home rule in 1817.

Wallachia

Serbia

Danube

OTTOMAN EMPIRE

CONSTANTINOPLE ■

Black Sea

Ottoman Empire
Although this empire was in decline, the sultan still ruled much of southeast Europe, North Africa, and the Middle East.

PAPAL
TATES

Naples

NGDOM
OF THE
O SICILIES

Young Italy
The Young Italy movement, founded in 1831, fought for a united republic of Italy.

Greeks rebel
The Greeks rose up in revolt against their Ottoman rulers in 1821. They gained independence in 1832.

■ ATHENS

GREECE

Navarino

Battle of Navarino
A combined British, French, and Russian fleet destroyed an Ottoman fleet at Navarino in 1827, helping the Greeks win their independence.

Mediterranean Sea

0 ⎯⎯⎯⎯⎯ 500km
0 ⎯⎯⎯⎯⎯ 250 miles

1800

1802 Great Britain and France sign the peace treaty of Amiens
1803 Great Britain and France go to war again; Napoleon prepares to invade Great Britain
1804 Napoleon becomes the emperor of Europe; he applies the "Code Napoléon" (French civil law) across Europe
1805 The Austrians and Russians are beaten at Austerlitz; the British navy defeats the French at Trafalgar, ending the threat of invasion

1807 The Russians and Prussians are defeated at Friedland
1808 Peninsular War begins in Spain—a lengthy conflict is fought by the Spanish and British against French occupation

1810

1812 Napoleon invades Russia, but the harsh winter forces troops to retreat
1813 The British under Wellington defeat the French at Vitoria, Spain, ending the Peninsular War; Napoleon is defeated by Russians, Austrians, and Prussians at the "Battle of the Nations" in Leipzig
1814 As enemies threaten Paris, France, Napoleon is forced to abdicate and is exiled to Elba
1815 Napoleon escapes from Elba but is finally defeated at Waterloo and is sent into exile again
1815 Congress of Vienna redraws the maps of Europe and restores previous kingdoms: Norway is united with Sweden and Belgium with the Netherlands

1817 Serbia wins home rule from Ottoman Empire

1820

1820 Revolutions are crushed in Portugal and Naples
1820–1823 Spanish revolt against Ferdinand VII is ended by the French
1821 Napoleon dies on Saint Helena in the southern Atlantic Ocean
1821 The Greeks begin war of independence against Ottoman rule

1827 Anglo-French-Russian fleet defeats Ottoman-Egyptian fleet at Navarino

1829 Moldavia and Wallachia win home rule from the Ottoman Empire

1830

1830 Revolution in France: King Charles X is overthrown and replaced by Louis-Philippe
1830 French occupy Algiers
1830–1831 Revolutions are crushed in Italy and Poland
1830–1839 Belgian revolt against Dutch rule leads to Belgian independence
1831 Young Italy movement is founded
1832 Great Reform Act is passed in Great Britain
1832 Greece becomes an independent monarchy

1840

Industrial Revolution:
Steam, iron, and steel

An industrial revolution began in Great Britain during the 1760s. New machines, driven by steam and water, were used to manufacture textiles and other products in factories that were manned by hundreds of workers. Steam engines hauled coal and iron out of mines and powered railroad engines to transport raw materials and finished goods. New technologies transformed the production of iron, steel, and chemicals. The revolution transformed Great Britain—and later the rest of Europe and the U.S.—from a mostly rural society into an urban one. New industrial towns, where the workers lived, were often squalid. Before long, people began to campaign for social and political reforms to improve these living conditions.

The railroads
The need to move raw materials to factories and take away their finished products led to a revolution in transportation. A network of canals was built in Great Britain after the 1760s, but it was the invention of the railroads in the early 1800s that led to the biggest changes. The first American steam railroad opened in 1830. Fifty years later there were more railroads in the U.S. (above) than in all of Europe.

Industrial towns
The development of factories led to the rapid growth of many towns such as Leeds in northern England (shown below). Living conditions in these towns were often terrible, as new houses for the workers were built back-to-back and close to the factories, mills, and mines where they worked.

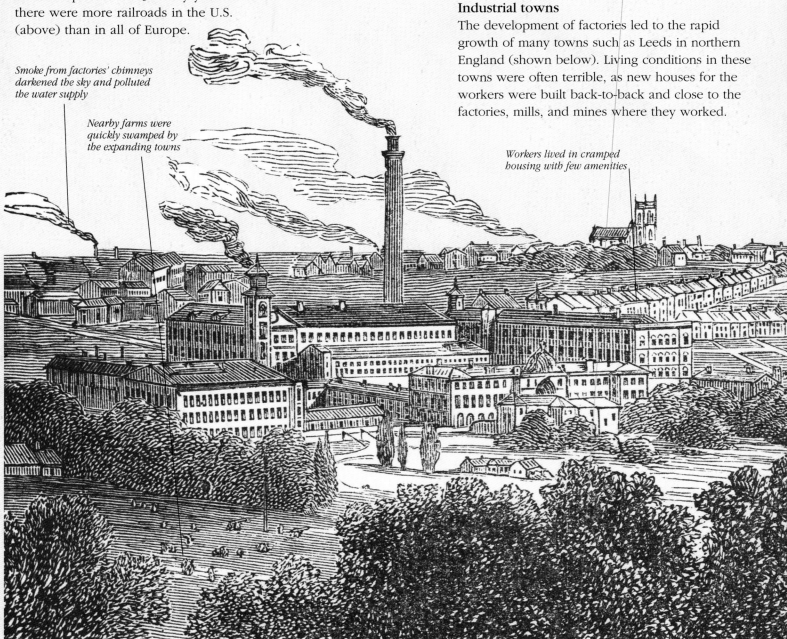

Smoke from factories' chimneys darkened the sky and polluted the water supply

Nearby farms were quickly swamped by the expanding towns

Workers lived in cramped housing with few amenities

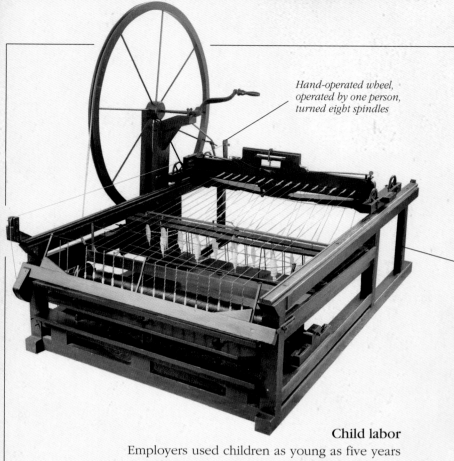

Hand-operated wheel, operated by one person, turned eight spindles

Wooden frames were later replaced by iron and then steel

New machinery

Cotton was the first textile industry to be mechanized, since cotton could easily be spun and woven by a machine. In 1764 James Hargreaves invented the spinning jenny (left), a machine that spun eight reels of thread at one time. Later, water- and steam-driven machines led to the mass production of textiles. This new technology quickly crossed the Atlantic Ocean: a power-driven cotton mill began operating in Rhode Island in 1791.

Child labor

Employers used children as young as five years old in their factories, mills, and mines because they were able to work in small spaces and their tiny hands could repair and operate machinery. The dangerous conditions meant that many children died or were injured. In Great Britain the 1833 Factory Act banned children under nine years old from working in textile mills (right). Another law in 1842 banned children under ten years old from working in mines.

Great engineers

Intelligent engineers and inventors helped power the Industrial Revolution. In Great Britain the engineer Isambard Kingdom Brunel built railroads, stations, rail and road bridges, tunnels, and ships. Here (right), Brunel is standing in front of the launching chains of his ship, the SS *Great Eastern*.

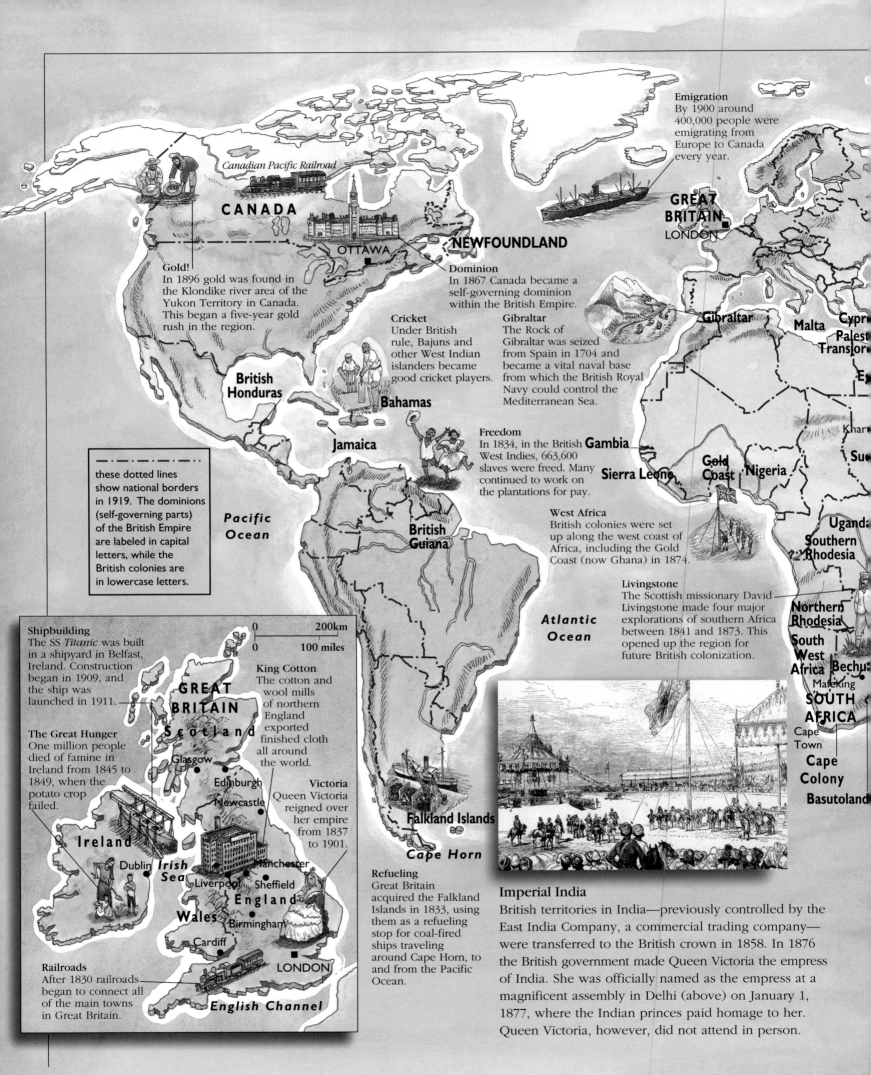

Canadian Pacific Railroad

CANADA

OTTAWA

NEWFOUNDLAND

Gold!
In 1896 gold was found in the Klondike river area of the Yukon Territory in Canada. This began a five-year gold rush in the region.

Dominion
In 1867 Canada became a self-governing dominion within the British Empire.

Cricket
Under British rule, Bajuns and other West Indian islanders became good cricket players.

British Honduras

Bahamas

Jamaica

these dotted lines show national borders in 1919. The dominions (self-governing parts) of the British Empire are labeled in capital letters, while the British colonies are in lowercase letters.

Pacific Ocean

British Guiana

Gibraltar
The Rock of Gibraltar was seized from Spain in 1704 and became a vital naval base from which the British Royal Navy could control the Mediterranean Sea.

Freedom
In 1834, in the British West Indies, 663,600 slaves were freed. Many continued to work on the plantations for pay.

West Africa
British colonies were set up along the west coast of Africa, including the Gold Coast (now Ghana) in 1874.

Livingstone
The Scottish missionary David Livingstone made four major explorations of southern Africa between 1841 and 1873. This opened up the region for future British colonization.

Atlantic Ocean

Gibraltar **Malta** Cypr... Palest... Transfor...

Gambia

Sierra Leone **Gold Coast** **Nigeria**

Khar...

Su...

Uganda

Southern Rhodesia

Northern Rhodesia

South West Africa **Bechua...** Mafeking **SOUTH AFRICA**

GREAT BRITAIN
LONDON

Emigration
By 1900 around 400,000 people were emigrating from Europe to Canada every year.

Cape Town **Cape Colony** **Basutoland**

Falkland Islands

Cape Horn

Refueling
Great Britain acquired the Falkland Islands in 1833, using them as a refueling stop for coal-fired ships traveling around Cape Horn, to and from the Pacific Ocean.

Inset: Great Britain

Shipbuilding
The SS *Titanic* was built in a shipyard in Belfast, Ireland. Construction began in 1909, and the ship was launched in 1911.

The Great Hunger
One million people died of famine in Ireland from 1845 to 1849, when the potato crop failed.

King Cotton
The cotton and wool mills of northern England exported finished cloth all around the world.

Victoria
Queen Victoria reigned over her empire from 1837 to 1901.

0   200km
0   100 miles

GREAT BRITAIN
Scotland
Glasgow
Edinburgh
Newcastle
Ireland
Dublin
Irish Sea
Manchester
Liverpool Sheffield
England
Birmingham
Wales
Cardiff
LONDON
English Channel

Railroads
After 1830 railroads began to connect all of the main towns in Great Britain.

Imperial India

British territories in India—previously controlled by the East India Company, a commercial trading company—were transferred to the British crown in 1858. In 1876 the British government made Queen Victoria the empress of India. She was officially named as the empress at a magnificent assembly in Delhi (above) on January 1, 1877, where the Indian princes paid homage to her. Queen Victoria, however, did not attend in person.

1800–1940

1800
1800 Great Britain gains Malta

1814 Great Britain gains Cape Colony from the Dutch

1819 Sir Stamford Raffles founds Singapore

1820

1830 World's first public railroad opens
between Liverpool and Manchester, England
1833 Great Britain gains the Falkland Islands
1834 Slaves are freed throughout
the British Empire
1837 Victoria becomes the queen
1839–1842 Great Britain fails
to subdue Afghanistan

1840
1840 Treaty of Waitangi between
British and Maori in New Zealand
1841 Great Britain acquires Hong Kong
1845–1849 Great Hunger kills
one million people in Ireland
1853–1899 Great Britain establishes
protectorates in the Gulf states
1854 Gold miners demand
the vote in South Australia
1857–1858 Mutiny breaks out in India
1858 East India Company is dismantled;
India transferred to the British crown
1860
1861 Nigerian coast becomes a British colony

1867 Canada becomes a self-governing dominion
1868 Last convicts are shipped to Australia

1874 Gold Coast becomes a British colony
1875 Great Britain gains control of the
Suez Canal
1877 Victoria is proclaimed the empress of India

1880
1882 Egypt becomes a British protectorate
1884 European nations begin
to scramble for African colonies
1888 Great Britain gains Rhodesia (Zimbabwe)

1893 New Zealand women gain the vote
1894–1895 Uganda and Kenya
become British colonies
1896 Rubber is first cultivated in Malay Peninsula

1899–1902 British crush the
Boers in South Africa
1900
1901 Victoria dies; Edward VII becomes the king
1901 Australian colonies unite to form
the Commonwealth of Australia
1907 New Zealand becomes a dominion
1910 Union of South Africa is created
1910 George V becomes the king

1917–1934 Newfoundland is a dominion

1919 Great Britain, Australia, and New Zealand
gain German colonies in Africa and Oceania
1920
1920 Great Britain gains Jordan and Iraq and
Palestine become governed by Britain
1922 Ireland becomes a Free
State within the British Empire
1922 Egypt becomes independent
1931 Statute of Westminster makes dominions
independent and equal to Great Britain and
creates the British Commonwealth of Nations
1936 George VI becomes the king after
his brother, Edward VIII, abdicates
1939 Empire joins Great Britain in World War II
against Germany, Italy, and, in 1941, Japan

1940

The Suez Canal
Great Britain acquired 40 percent of the Suez Canal shares from the khedive (ruler) of Egypt in 1875, giving it control of the waterway.

Protectorates
Great Britain gained several bases along the southern shore of the Gulf to help stamp out piracy and slavery in the region.

Afghan victories
In 1839–1842 and 1878–1880 the British fought two disastrous wars against the Afghans and failed to bring them under their control.

Mutiny!
A mutiny by sepoys (Indian soldiers) almost ended British rule of the subcontinent in 1857.

Hong Kong
Great Britain acquired Hong Kong from the Chinese in 1841 and soon turned it into a major trading port and commercial center.

Rubber
Rubber was first grown commercially in the Malay Peninsula in 1896, with plants that were originally from South America and cultivated in England.

The Sudan
The British general Charles Gordon was killed when Islamic Mahdist forces overran Khartoum in 1886.

Singapore
Britain founded Singapore in 1819. It soon became the major commercial port in the region.

Indian arrivals
During the mid to late 1800s, Great Britain imported Indian laborers to work on the plantations of South Africa and build railroads in East Africa.

Gold strikers
In 1854 gold miners in Australia rose up to demand democratic rights in the mining areas, but they were defeated by British troops in Ballarat.

Cape Colony
The acquisition of the Cape Colony from the Netherlands in 1814 gave Great Britain control of shipping in and out of the Indian Ocean.

Anzac troops
Australia and New Zealand sent large numbers of troops to fight for Great Britain during World War I.

Himalayas
British gunboat
railroad in Bombay
growing tea in Sri Lanka

Iraq
Kuwait
Oman
Aden
British Somaliland
Delhi
Lucknow
India
Mumbai
Myanmar
Hong Kong
Sri Lanka
Malay States
Singapore
North East New Guinea
Territory of Papua
Solomon Islands
New Hebrides (Great Britain and France)
Uluru
AUSTRALIA
Ballarat
Melbourne
NEW ZEALAND
Pacific Ocean
Indian Ocean

The British Empire

Between 1800 and 1920, Great Britain carved out the largest empire the world has ever seen. At its peak, the empire covered around one-fifth of the globe—with colonies on every continent—and contained 410 million people, one-fifth of the world's population. The British built the empire in order to provide raw materials for their industries—such as cotton, silk, sugar, gold, and diamonds—and a ready market for finished goods. Pride in British values, as well as a desire to convert local people to Christianity, were also the reasons for the creation of the empire, but not everyone liked, agreed with, or benefitted from this way of life.

Convicts
From 1788 to 1868, Great Britain shipped thousands of convicts out to Australia to serve their sentences in penal colonies.

Taking control
The British signed a treaty with the Maori in 1840, which gave Great Britain control of New Zealand.

The U.S. in the 1800s

In just over 100 years, the United States of America transformed itself. It grew from a narrow strip of newly independent colonies along the coast of the Atlantic Ocean to a continental power that stretched out across the Pacific Ocean and up toward the Arctic. However, most of this new land was already occupied by Indigenous Americans, who fought fiercely to survive and keep their ancient heritage alive. By the end of the 1800s, the Indigenous Americans were confined to special reservations, and the U.S. was on its way to becoming the richest and most powerful country in the world.

The U.S. Civil War

The southern states of the U.S. allowed white citizens to keep black slaves to work on their cotton plantations and in their homes. However, other states were against slavery. The argument between the two sides erupted in 1861, when 11 southern states left the Union and set up the independent Confederacy. A vicious civil war broke out that lasted for four years and killed at least 600,000 people. This picture shows Confederate fortifications close to Petersburg, Virginia, in 1865. The Union, led by President Abraham Lincoln, eventually won the war and abolished slavery.

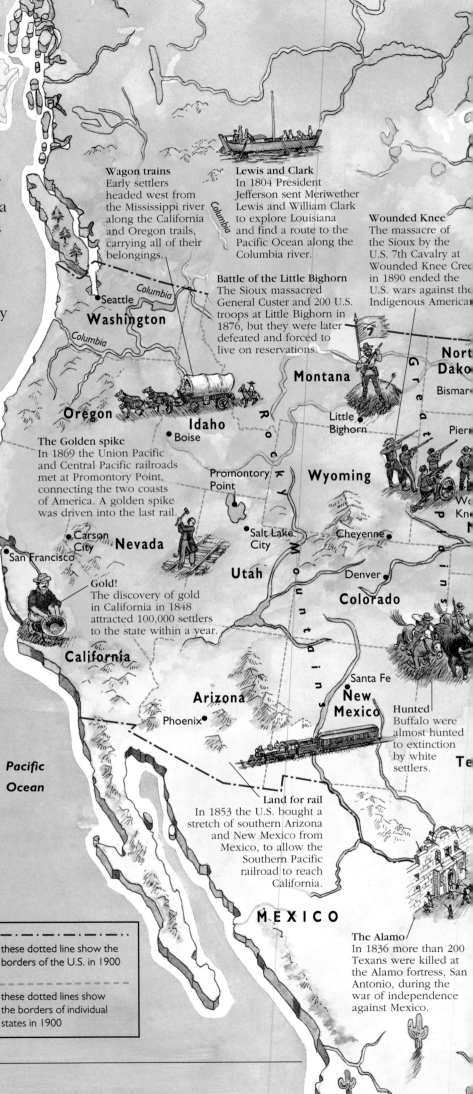

Wagon trains
Early settlers headed west from the Mississippi river along the California and Oregon trails, carrying all of their belongings.

Lewis and Clark
In 1804 President Jefferson sent Meriwether Lewis and William Clark to explore Louisiana and find a route to the Pacific Ocean along the Columbia river.

Battle of the Little Bighorn
The Sioux massacred General Custer and 200 U.S. troops at Little Bighorn in 1876, but they were later defeated and forced to live on reservations.

Wounded Knee
The massacre of the Sioux by the U.S. 7th Cavalry at Wounded Knee Creek in 1890 ended the U.S. wars against the Indigenous Americans.

The Golden spike
In 1869 the Union Pacific and Central Pacific railroads met at Promontory Point, connecting the two coasts of America. A golden spike was driven into the last rail.

Gold!
The discovery of gold in California in 1848 attracted 100,000 settlers to the state within a year.

Hunted
Buffalo were almost hunted to extinction by white settlers.

Land for rail
In 1853 the U.S. bought a stretch of southern Arizona and New Mexico from Mexico, to allow the Southern Pacific railroad to reach California.

The Alamo
In 1836 more than 200 Texans were killed at the Alamo fortress, San Antonio, during the war of independence against Mexico.

Pacific Ocean

Seattle — Washington — Columbia — Oregon — Idaho — Boise — Montana — Little Bighorn — Nort Dako — Bismar — Pier — Carson City — Nevada — San Francisco — Promontory Point — Salt Lake City — Wyoming — Cheyenne — Wo Kne — N — Utah — Denver — Colorado — California — Arizona — Phoenix — New Mexico — Santa Fe — Te

MEXICO

- - - - these dotted line show the borders of the U.S. in 1900

– – – these dotted lines show the borders of individual states in 1900

0		1,000km
0		500 miles

KEY TO EAST COAST STATES

1	Maine	7	Connecticut
2	Vermont	8	Pennsylvania
3	New Hampshire	9	New Jersey
4	New York	10	Delaware
5	Massachusetts	11	Maryland
6	Rhode Island	12	Virginia

CANADA

Skyscrapers
The Reliance Building, the world's first steel-frame skyscraper, was built in Chicago in 1895.

Model-T Ford
The first Model-T rolled off the Ford production line in 1908. Its low cost made car ownership possible for millions of people for the first time.

Lake Superior

Lake Huron

Lake Ontario

immigrants arriving in New York in the 1890s

Minnesota
South Dakota
St Paul

Wisconsin

Michigan
Lansing
Madison
Detroit

farming on the plains

Iowa
Des Moines

Lake Michigan

Chicago

Lake Erie

Ohio
Columbus

Indiana
Indianapolis

New York

Philadelphia

Illinois
Springfield

Lincoln

Kansas City
Missouri
Jefferson City
Topeka
Kansas

Abilene

slaves on southern plantations

Indian Territory
Oklahoma City

West Virginia

WASHINGTON, D.C.

Burning the capital
In 1814 British troops burned down the White House during its war with the U.S.

Kentucky

Appomattox

Hampton Roads

Surrender
The Civil War reached its end when Confederate commander Robert E. Lee surrendered his army at the Appomattox Court House, Virginia, in April 1865.

Nashville
Tennessee
Memphis

North Carolina

South Carolina

Arkansas
Little Rock

Alabama
Atlanta
Charleston

Mississippi
Jackson

Georgia

Fort Sumter

Atlantic Ocean

Louisiana
Baton Rouge

New Orleans

jazz musicians in New Orleans

Austin
San Antonio

FLORIDA

Outbreak of war
The U.S. Civil War began when southern Confederate troops bombarded Fort Sumter (a Union fort) in Charleston, South Carolina, in April 1861.

Oil wells
Oil was first discovered in Spindletop, Texas, in 1901, giving birth to a massive oil industry.

Forced removal
During the 1830s, more than 100,000 Indigenous Americans were forced to move from the eastern U.S. to the Indian Territory (now Oklahoma) to make room for white settlers.

Driving cattle
Cattle were driven north every year from Texas to Abilene for transportation by railroad to slaughterhouses in Kansas City and Chicago.

Gulf of Mexico

Appalachian Mountains

Mississippi

Rocky Mountains

1800
1800 U.S. consists of only 16 states
1803 Louisiana is purchased from France, doubling the size of the country
1804–1806 Lewis and Clark explore Louisiana territory

1812–1815 Anglo-American war is caused by British attempts to prevent the U.S. from trading with Napoleonic France

1819 Spain gives Florida to the U.S.
1820
1820 Missouri Compromise allows for equal numbers of slave states and free (antislavery) states to join the Union

1830 Indian Removal Act forces Indigenous Americans (then called Indians) to move to the Indian Territory

1836 Texas gains independence from Mexico

1840
1845 U.S. annexes (takes control of) the Republic of Texas
1846 Great Britain and the U.S. agree to divide Oregon
1846–1848 U.S. goes to war with Mexico over its border with Texas
1848 U.S. gains California and other western states from Mexico
1848 Gold discovered in California

1853 U.S. buys southern New Mexico and Arizona from Mexico

1860
1860 South Carolina leaves the Union, followed by ten more proslavery states
1861–1865 Civil War between Union and Confederate states
1865 13th Amendment to the U.S. Constitution formally abolishes slavery
1867 U.S. buys Alaska from Russia for $7.2 million and acquires Midway Island, its first Pacific Island territory
1869 First Transcontinental Railroad is completed
1870 U.S. population is now at 40 million

1876 Battle of Little Bighorn
1880

1890 Sioux massacred at Wounded Knee Creek
1892 Ellis Island begins to admit immigrants
1895 First skyscraper is built in Chicago

1898 Spain loses Puerto Rico, Guam, and the Philippines to the U.S.
1898 U.S. gains Hawaiian Islands in the Pacific Ocean
1899 U.S. acquires Samoa in the south Pacific Ocean
1900
1901 Oil is found in Texas
1905 One million immigrants enter the U.S. each year

1908 First Model-T Ford car is produced in Detroit

1910 U.S. population is now at 92 million

1917 U.S. enters World War I

1920 U.S. consists of 48 states
1920

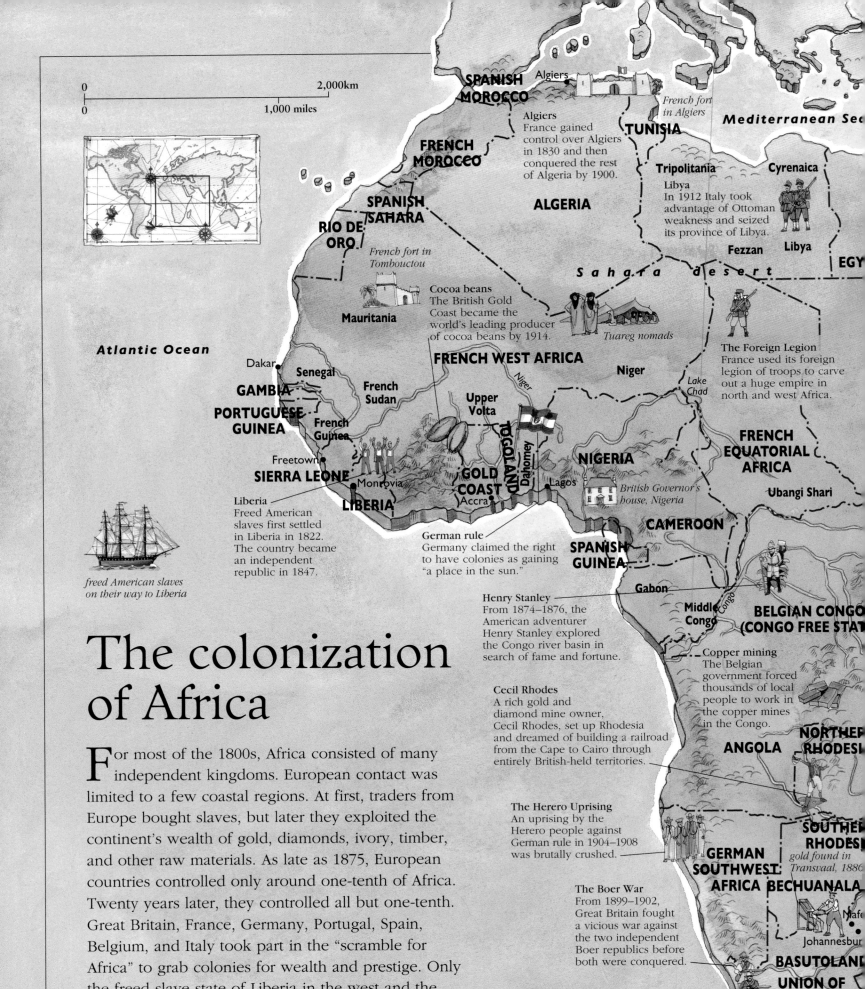

The colonization of Africa

For most of the 1800s, Africa consisted of many independent kingdoms. European contact was limited to a few coastal regions. At first, traders from Europe bought slaves, but later they exploited the continent's wealth of gold, diamonds, ivory, timber, and other raw materials. As late as 1875, European countries controlled only around one-tenth of Africa. Twenty years later, they controlled all but one-tenth. Great Britain, France, Germany, Portugal, Spain, Belgium, and Italy took part in the "scramble for Africa" to grab colonies for wealth and prestige. Only the freed slave state of Liberia in the west and the empire of Ethiopia in the east—the sole African state to defeat a European nation—remained independent.

SPANISH MOROCCO

FRENCH MOROCCO

TUNISIA

Algiers
France gained control over Algiers in 1830 and then conquered the rest of Algeria by 1900.

French fort in Algiers

Tripolitania **Cyrenaica**

Libya
In 1912 Italy took advantage of Ottoman weakness and seized its province of Libya.

Fezzan **Libya**

ALGERIA

EGY

Mediterranean Sea

SPANISH SAHARA

RIO DE ORO

French fort in Tombouctou

Mauritania

Cocoa beans
The British Gold Coast became the world's leading producer of cocoa beans by 1914.

Tuareg nomads

Sahara desert

FRENCH WEST AFRICA

Niger

The Foreign Legion
France used its foreign legion of troops to carve out a huge empire in north and west Africa.

Atlantic Ocean

Dakar

Senegal

French Sudan

GAMBIA

PORTUGUESE GUINEA

French Guinea

Upper Volta

Niger

TOGOLAND

Dahomey

NIGERIA

FRENCH EQUATORIAL AFRICA

Lagos

Ubangi Shari

Freetown

SIERRA LEONE

Monrovia

GOLD COAST

Accra

British Governor's house, Nigeria

Liberia
Freed American slaves first settled in Liberia in 1822. The country became an independent republic in 1847.

LIBERIA

German rule
Germany claimed the right to have colonies as gaining "a place in the sun."

CAMEROON

SPANISH GUINEA

freed American slaves on their way to Liberia

Gabon

Henry Stanley
From 1874–1876, the American adventurer Henry Stanley explored the Congo river basin in search of fame and fortune.

Middle Congo

BELGIAN CONGO (CONGO FREE STAT

Cecil Rhodes
A rich gold and diamond mine owner, Cecil Rhodes, set up Rhodesia and dreamed of building a railroad from the Cape to Cairo through entirely British-held territories.

Copper mining
The Belgian government forced thousands of local people to work in the copper mines in the Congo.

ANGOLA

NORTHER RHODESI

The Herero Uprising
An uprising by the Herero people against German rule in 1904–1908 was brutally crushed.

GERMAN SOUTHWEST AFRICA

SOUTHER RHODES

gold found in Transvaal, 1886

BECHUANALA

The Boer War
From 1899–1902, Great Britain fought a vicious war against the two independent Boer republics before both were conquered.

Johannesbur

BASUTOLAND

The Great Trek
Boer farmers escaped from British rule in the Cape Colony by moving north in the Great Trek of 1834–1848. They settled in what became the Orange Free State and Transvaal.

UNION OF SOUTH AFRICA

Cape Town

Cape Colony

0 _____ 2,000km
0 _____ 1,000 miles

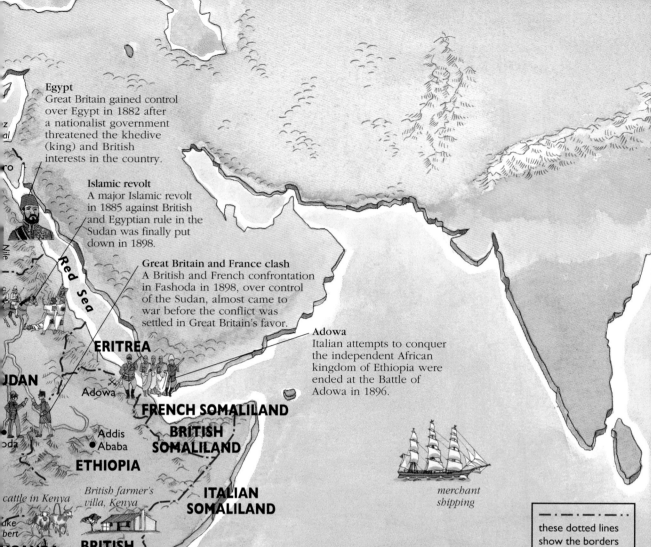

Egypt
Great Britain gained control over Egypt in 1882 after a nationalist government threatened the khedive (king) and British interests in the country.

Islamic revolt
A major Islamic revolt in 1885 against British and Egyptian rule in the Sudan was finally put down in 1898.

Great Britain and France clash
A British and French confrontation in Fashoda in 1898, over control of the Sudan, almost came to war before the conflict was settled in Great Britain's favor.

Adowa
Italian attempts to conquer the independent African kingdom of Ethiopia were ended at the Battle of Adowa in 1896.

Red Sea

ERITREA

Adowa

FRENCH SOMALILAND

Addis Ababa

BRITISH SOMALILAND

ETHIOPIA

cattle in Kenya

British farmer's villa, Kenya

ITALIAN SOMALILAND

UGANDA
Entebbe
Lake Victoria

BRITISH EAST AFRICA
Nairobi

Indian immigrants
Laborers were brought from British-run India to build a railroad from Mombasa on the coast up to Entebbe in Uganda.

Lake Tanganyika

Mombasa

Slave trade
The slave market in Zanzibar exported slaves to the Arab world until the British closed it down in 1873.

GERMAN EAST AFRICA
Zanzibar

Lake Malawi

German Africa
German rule in Africa was ended during World War I, when Great Britain, France, and South Africa occupied all of its colonies.

YASALAND

MOZAMBIQUE

MADAGASCAR

isbury

Ulundi

The Zulu Wars
Conflict between the British and the Zulu kingdom finally ended in a Zulu defeat at Ulundi in 1879.

WATINI

merchant shipping

Indian Ocean

these dotted lines show the borders between states in Africa in 1914

The Zulus

Shaka, leader of the Zulus of southern Africa from 1816–1828, was an excellent military leader. He replaced the old thrown spear of his warriors with an *assegai*, or short stabbing spear, turning them into the most feared army in the region. The Zulus resisted all attempts by the Boers and British to take over their lands but were finally defeated by the British at Ulundi in 1879. Unusually, the British allowed them to keep their lands because of the respect that they held for these warrior people.

Stopover port
Merchant ships carrying tea and other products from Asia to Europe stopped off for supplies in Cape Town.

1807 British end their involvement in the transatlantic slave trade

1814 Great Britain gains Cape Colony from the Dutch

1822 First freed slaves settle in Liberia

1825
1826 Great Britain begins to take over the Gold Coast

1830 France invades Algiers
1830–1900 France conquers Algeria

1834–1848 Boers move north in the Great Trek

1840–1873 David Livingstone explores central Africa

1847 Liberia becomes an independent republic

1850

1852–1854 Boers establish the republics of Orange Free State and Transvaal
1854 France takes over Senegal
1855 Emperor Tewedros begins to modernize Ethiopia

1861 Great Britain begins to colonize Nigeria

1873 British end the slave market in Zanzibar
1874–1876 Henry Stanley explores the Congo river region
1875
1879 British finally conquer the Zulu kingdom
1882 British take control of Egypt
1884–1885 European powers divide up Africa at the Berlin Conference
1885 Leopold II of Belgium makes the Congo his personal possession
1885–1898 Islamic revolt by the Mahdi against British rule in Sudan
1886 Gold discovered in the Transvaal
1888 British establish Rhodesia
1889 Italy gains Eritrea and Somaliland
1894 Great Britain occupies Uganda
1895 Great Britain occupies Kenya
1896 Italians fail to conquer Ethiopia
1898 Great Britain retakes Sudan
1899–1902 British defeat the Boers in South Africa

1900

1904 Great Britain and France settle their colonial disputes in Africa
1904–1908 Herero Uprising against German rule in southwest Africa
1906 Morocco is split between France and Spain
1908 Belgium takes control of the Congo

1910 Union of South Africa gains independence from Great Britain

1914–1918 Germany loses its African colonies during World War I

1925

Imperial Europe

In the years after 1848 the map of Europe changed significantly. Germany and Italy emerged as unified countries, and Austria-Hungary became a dual monarchy. France became an empire again and then, after 1871, a republic, while Russia slowly began to reform itself. Great Britain, the most powerful and richest country in the world, avoided most European entanglements and developed a huge overseas empire. In the Balkans the Ottoman (Turkish) Empire continued to fall apart, losing almost all of its European land by 1913. The Industrial Revolution that had begun in Great Britain led to new industries and railroads in most countries, creating new industrial towns and a large working class population.

Atlantic Ocean

The unification of Germany

In 1848 Germany consisted of 39 separate states, dominated by Prussia and Austro-Hungary. Otto von Bismarck became the prime minister of Prussia in 1862. He defeated Denmark and Austria, set up a North German Confederation, excluding Austria, and took over Hanover and other German states. In 1871 Prussia defeated France and took its two eastern provinces of Alsace and Lorraine. King Wilhelm I of Prussia was then proclaimed the emperor of Germany (shown above), uniting the remaining 25 German states under Prussian rule.

Gunboat diplomacy
In 1911 Germany sent a gunboat to protect its interests in Morocco, causing a major diplomatic conflict with France.

HMS *Dreadnought*
The battleship *Dreadnought* outclassed every other warship when she was launched in 1906, starting a naval arms race between Great Britain and Germany.

Queen Victoria
Queen from 1837 to 1901, Victoria was related to almost every European monarch.

North Sea

Bismarck
With a series of excellent diplomatic and military victories, Otto von Bismarck unified Germany in 1864–1871.

coal mine in the Ruhr valley, Germany

free trade in northern Germany

armaments factory in Pilsen

Karl Marx
The communist revolutionary Karl Marx fled Germany and took refuge in London in 1848.

Revolution
In 1848 the unpopular King Louis-Philippe was overthrown, and France became a republic, a country not governed by a monarch.

a barricade erected in Paris

Napoleon III
The nephew of Napoleon Bonaparte, Louis Napoleon, became the president of France in 1848 before seizing power and becoming the emperor in 1851.

French farmers

Emmanuel II
King of Sardinia since 1849, Victor Emmanuel II became the king of a united Italy in 1860.

NORWAY
OSLO

COPENHAGEN
DENMARK
Schleswig Holstein

GERMAN EM...
BER...

GREAT BRITAIN
LONDON

NETHERLANDS

BELGIUM
Sedan Frankfurt

LUXEMBOURG
Alsace-Lorraine

SWITZERLAND ALPS

FRANCE

Rhine
Elbe

Pil...

ITALY
ROME

Corsica

Sardinia

Sicily

PORTUGAL

Pyrenees

MADRID

SPAIN

Balearic Islands

Mediterranean Sea

MOROCCO

0   500km
0   250 miles

Industrial Revolution
In the second half of the 1800s, Russia industrialized very quickly, opening many new coal mines, steel works, and factories.

Sadowa
In the Seven Weeks' War of 1866, Prussia defeated Austria at Sadowa and ended the country's influence in Germany.

MOSCOW

Trans-continental railroad
The Trans-Siberian Railroad linking Moscow to Vladivostok, on the Pacific coast, was begun in 1891 but not finished until 1916.

Freedom
Serfs (peasants) in Russia received their freedom from their owners in 1861.

The Dual Monarchy
In 1867 the Austrian empire split into a two-monarch state called Austria-Hungary. United by its Hapsburg rulers, it had a common army and currency.

RUSSIAN EMPIRE

Ukraine
The Ukraine was the "breadbasket of Russia," as well as its major industrial area.

wheat being harvested in the Ukraine

Potemkin
Revolution broke out in Russia in 1905 and spread to the armed forces. The crew of the Russian battleship *Potemkin* mutinied and fled to Romania.

DEN
STOCKHOLM

owa
(öniggrätz)

VIENNA

AUSTRO-HUNGARIAN EMPIRE

Danube

Odessa

Black Sea

ROMANIA
Ploiesti
BUCHAREST

Romanian oil
Before the development of Middle Eastern oil, most European oil came from the oil wells of Ploiesti.

Bosnia **SERBIA**
Balkans
BULGARIA
MONTENEGRO SOFIA

Constantinople

OTTOMAN EMPIRE

Albania

The Balkan Wars
Two wars in the Balkans in 1912–1913 saw the Ottoman Turks almost expelled from Europe, while Serbia emerged as a major Balkan country.

GREECE

ATHENS

Rhodes

Cyprus

Crete

The Royal Navy
The British Royal Navy commanded the Mediterranean Sea, protecting British sea routes to India.

Garibaldi
In 1859–1860 the Italian nationalist Giuseppe Garibaldi invaded Sicily and Naples with 1,000 troops and forced them to unify with the rest of Italy.

Mediterranean Sea

These dotted lines show the borders between European countries in 1912

EGYPT

1840

1848 Revolutions in France, Italy, Germany, and Austria against conservative rule
1848 Karl Marx flees to London
1849 Attempts to set up a German National Assembly end in failure

1850

1851 Napoleon III seizes power in France and restores the French Empire

1859–1860 Italian kingdoms united as one country under Victor Emmanuel II

1860

1861 Russian serfs (peasants) are liberated
1862 Bismarck becomes the prime minister of Prussia
1863–1864 Prussia defeats Denmark to gain two northern duchies
1866 Seven Weeks' War
1866 Italy gains Venice from Austria
1867 Creation of North German Confederation under Prussian rule
1867 Creation of Austro-Hungary

1870

1870 Italy takes over the Papal States to complete its unification
1870–1871 Franco-Prussian war ends in French defeat; creation of German Empire
1871 Third Republic is established in France
1878 Romania gains independence from the Ottoman Empire
1878 Great Britain gains Cyprus from Ottomans
1879–1882 Triple Alliance of Germany, Austro-Hungary, and Italy

1880

1883 Death of Karl Marx

1888 Wilhelm II becomes the emperor of Germany

1890

1890 Bismarck resigns

1894 Franco-Russian military alliance

1900

1901 Death of Queen Victoria

1904 Entente Cordiale ("friendly understanding") agreement between Great Britain and France
1906 HMS Dreadnought is launched; naval arms race begins in Europe
1908 Austria-Hungary takes over Bosnia
1908 Bulgaria becomes independent

1910

1912–1913 Two Balkan wars redraw the map of southeast Europe
1913 Albania becomes an independent nation
1914 World War I breaks out in Europe

1920

World War I

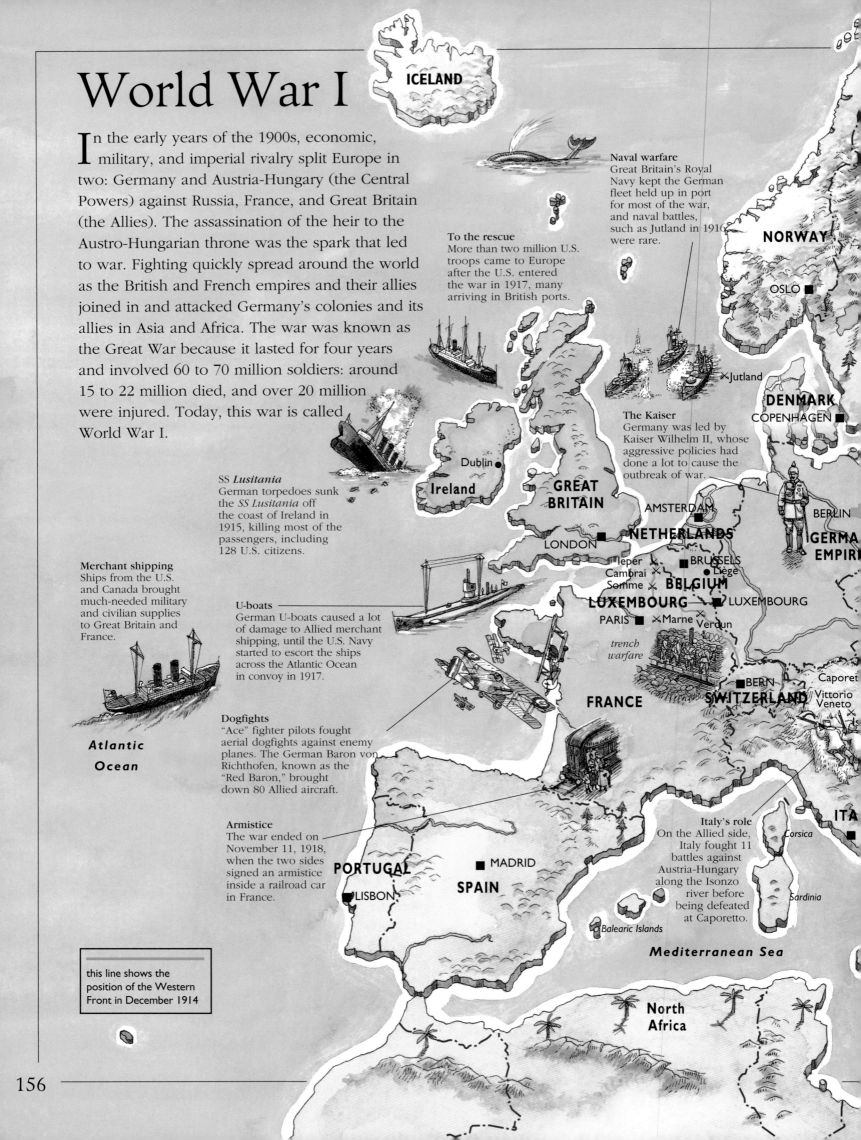

In the early years of the 1900s, economic, military, and imperial rivalry split Europe in two: Germany and Austria-Hungary (the Central Powers) against Russia, France, and Great Britain (the Allies). The assassination of the heir to the Austro-Hungarian throne was the spark that led to war. Fighting quickly spread around the world as the British and French empires and their allies joined in and attacked Germany's colonies and its allies in Asia and Africa. The war was known as the Great War because it lasted for four years and involved 60 to 70 million soldiers: around 15 to 22 million died, and over 20 million were injured. Today, this war is called World War I.

ICELAND

Naval warfare
Great Britain's Royal Navy kept the German fleet held up in port for most of the war, and naval battles, such as Jutland in 1916, were rare.

To the rescue
More than two million U.S. troops came to Europe after the U.S. entered the war in 1917, many arriving in British ports.

NORWAY

OSLO

×Jutland

DENMARK
COPENHAGEN

The Kaiser
Germany was led by Kaiser Wilhelm II, whose aggressive policies had done a lot to cause the outbreak of war.

Dublin

Ireland

GREAT BRITAIN

AMSTERDAM

BERLIN

GERMAN EMPIRE

SS Lusitania
German torpedoes sunk the SS *Lusitania* off the coast of Ireland in 1915, killing most of the passengers, including 128 U.S. citizens.

NETHERLANDS

LONDON

Ieper ×
Cambrai ×
Somme ×

BRUSSELS
Liège

BELGIUM

LUXEMBOURG
× LUXEMBOURG

PARIS
×Marne

Verdun

Merchant shipping
Ships from the U.S. and Canada brought much-needed military and civilian supplies to Great Britain and France.

U-boats
German U-boats caused a lot of damage to Allied merchant shipping, until the U.S. Navy started to escort the ships across the Atlantic Ocean in convoy in 1917.

trench warfare

BERN

Caporet

FRANCE

SWITZERLAND

Vittorio
Veneto

Atlantic Ocean

Dogfights
"Ace" fighter pilots fought aerial dogfights against enemy planes. The German Baron von Richthofen, known as the "Red Baron," brought down 80 Allied aircraft.

Armistice
The war ended on November 11, 1918, when the two sides signed an armistice inside a railroad car in France.

ITA

Corsica

Italy's role
On the Allied side, Italy fought 11 battles against Austria-Hungary along the Isonzo river before being defeated at Caporetto.

PORTUGAL

■ MADRID

SPAIN

Sardinia

■ LISBON

Balearic Islands

Mediterranean Sea

this line shows the position of the Western Front in December 1914

North Africa

Czar
The Russian czar Nicholas II was a poor military leader who lost the support of his people during the war. He was overthrown in the revolution of 1917.

DEN
Finland
HELSINKI
TOCKHOLM
SAINT PETERSBURG (PETROGRAD)

Moscow

The Eastern Front
Unlike the stalemate in the west, the war in the east was very mobile, with large-scale battles and troops advancing over hundreds of miles.

RUSSIAN EMPIRE

Masurian Lakes
Tannenberg

Russians marching into Austria-Hungary

Peace treaty
After two revolutions in 1917, the new Bolshevik (communist) rulers of Russia made peace with Germany in Brest-Litovsk.

Brest-Litovsk

War production
Both sides of the war produced huge amounts of shells and other armaments in munitions factories placed far behind the front line.

STRO-HUNGARIAN EMPIRE
BUDAPEST

ROMANIA
BUCHAREST
BELGRADE
Sarajevo
SERBIA
BULGARIA
SOFIA
MONTENEGRO
TIRANË
ALBANIA
GREECE
ATHENS

Trench warfare
The worst fighting took place along the Western Front in western Europe. Each side dug a long line of defensive trenches facing the enemy. They regularly bombarded the opposing side and launched attacks over the top of the trenches, with a huge loss of human life. Neither side made any real progress until late in 1918, when fresh American troops and improved artillery bombardment gave the Allies the advantage.

0   500km
0   250 miles

Black Sea

Genocide
During 1915, the Ottomans deported Armenians from their homeland to stop them from helping the Russians. Up to 1.3 million were killed.

Armenia

CONSTANTINOPLE

Gallipoli

OTTOMAN EMPIRE

Lawrence of Arabia
In 1916 the Arabs rose up in revolt against their Ottoman rulers, supported by the British officer T. E. Lawrence, in the hope of winning their independence.

Assassination
The assassination of Archduke Franz Ferdinand, heir to the Austrian throne, by Serb nationalist Gavrilo Princip sparked the outbreak of the war.

Gallipoli
Allied landings on the Gallipoli peninsula in the Ottoman Empire were a disaster, and the troops were forced to withdraw.

Cyprus
Crete

Mediterranean Sea

1914

June 1914 Archduke Franz Ferdinand is assassinated in Sarajevo; Austro-Hungary declares war on Serbia
Aug. 1914 Germany invades neutral Belgium to attack France; Great Britain, France, and Russia now at war with the Central Powers of Germany and Austro-Hungary
Aug. 1914 Germans defeat the invading Russian army at Tannenberg
Aug. 1914 Allies attack German colonies in Africa, Asia, and the Pacific Ocean
Sept. 1914 Germans advance into France
Oct. 1914 Ottoman Empire enters war on the Central Powers side
Nov. 1914 Trenches built along the length of the Western Front

1915

Feb. 1915 Germans begin submarine blockade of Great Britain
April 1915 Germans use poison gas on the Western Front for the first time
April 1915–Jan., 1916 Allied troops seize Gallipoli but fail to capture Constantinople
May 1915 German torpedoes sink the SS Lusitania off the Irish coast
May 1915 Italy enters the war on the Allied side
May 1915 Ottoman genocide against Armenians
June 1915–Aug., 1917 Italy fights 11 battles against Austro-Hungary
Oct. 1915 Central Powers invade Serbia

1916

Jan. 1916 Serbia is defeated
Feb.–Dec. 1916 Germans try but fail to break the French resolve at the Siege of Verdun
May–June 1916 British Royal Navy wins the Battle of Jutland in the North Sea
June 1916 Arabs rise up in revolt against their Ottoman rulers
July–Nov. 1916 Massive British losses at the Battle of the Somme

1917

Feb. 1917 Germans begin submarine warfare in the Atlantic Ocean, hitting U.S. shipping
March 1917 Russian revolution overthrows Czar Nicholas II
April 1917 U.S. enters the war on the Allied side
July–Nov. 1917 Bloody battle at Ieper (Passchendaele)
Nov.–Dec. 1917 British use massed tanks for the first time at Cambrai, France
Nov. 1917 Bolsheviks seize power in Russia
Dec. 1917 Austro-Hungarians win the Battle of Caporetto against the Italians

1918

March 1918 Germany and Russia make peace at Brest-Litovsk
March 1918 Massive German advance into France
July–Aug. 1918 Germans halted at the Second Battle of the Marne, near the Marne river in France
Aug. 1918 Germans pushed back on the Western Front by the Allies
Oct. 1918 Italy defeats Austro-Hungarians at Vittorio Veneto
Oct. 1918 Ottoman Empire makes peace with the Allies
Nov. 1918 German fleet mutinies; Kaiser Wilhelm II abdicates and flees into exile
Nov. 1918 Armistice ends the war

1919

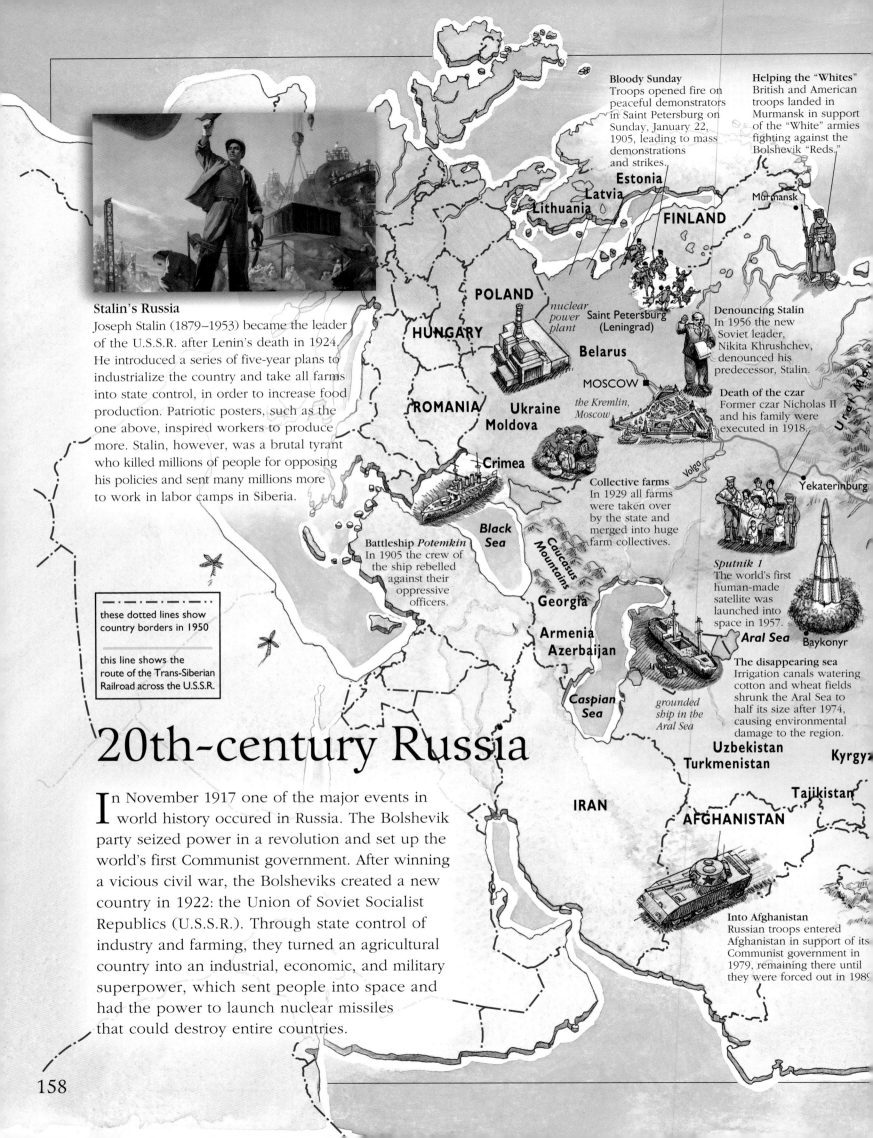

Stalin's Russia

Joseph Stalin (1879–1953) became the leader of the U.S.S.R. after Lenin's death in 1924. He introduced a series of five-year plans to industrialize the country and take all farms into state control, in order to increase food production. Patriotic posters, such as the one above, inspired workers to produce more. Stalin, however, was a brutal tyrant who killed millions of people for opposing his policies and sent many millions more to work in labor camps in Siberia.

- – · – · – · these dotted lines show country borders in 1950

— — — this line shows the route of the Trans-Siberian Railroad across the U.S.S.R.

20th-century Russia

In November 1917 one of the major events in world history occured in Russia. The Bolshevik party seized power in a revolution and set up the world's first Communist government. After winning a vicious civil war, the Bolsheviks created a new country in 1922: the Union of Soviet Socialist Republics (U.S.S.R.). Through state control of industry and farming, they turned an agricultural country into an industrial, economic, and military superpower, which sent people into space and had the power to launch nuclear missiles that could destroy entire countries.

Bloody Sunday
Troops opened fire on peaceful demonstrators in Saint Petersburg on Sunday, January 22, 1905, leading to mass demonstrations and strikes.

Helping the "Whites"
British and American troops landed in Murmansk in support of the "White" armies fighting against the Bolshevik "Reds."

Estonia
Latvia
Lithuania
FINLAND
Murmansk

POLAND
HUNGARY
ROMANIA

nuclear power plant
Saint Petersburg (Leningrad)

Belarus

MOSCOW
the Kremlin, Moscow

Ukraine
Moldova

Crimea

Black Sea

Caucasus Mountains

Battleship *Potemkin*
In 1905 the crew of the ship rebelled against their oppressive officers.

Georgia

Armenia
Azerbaijan

Caspian Sea

grounded ship in the Aral Sea

Denouncing Stalin
In 1956 the new Soviet leader, Nikita Khrushchev, denounced his predecessor, Stalin.

Death of the czar
Former czar Nicholas II and his family were executed in 1918.

Collective farms
In 1929 all farms were taken over by the state and merged into huge farm collectives.

Yekaterinburg

Ural Mou...

Volga

Sputnik 1
The world's first human-made satellite was launched into space in 1957.

Aral Sea
Baykonyr

The disappearing sea
Irrigation canals watering cotton and wheat fields shrunk the Aral Sea to half its size after 1974, causing environmental damage to the region.

Uzbekistan
Turkmenistan
Kyrgyz...

Tajikistan

IRAN

AFGHANISTAN

Into Afghanistan
Russian troops entered Afghanistan in support of its Communist government in 1979, remaining there until they were forced out in 1989

Industrial growth
After 1925, major new towns were built close to the Ural Mountains to exploit the region's huge reserves of coal and iron ore.

The "Gulag"
Stalin sent millions of Russians, including criminals and opponents of the government, to the "Gulag"—"corrective labor camps" in the far north and east of the country.

Changing leaders
These traditional Russian *matrioshka* stacking dolls have been updated to show the changing leadership of the U.S.S.R.

Promoting the Revolution
Posters of Lenin and other Bolshevik leaders were used to promote the Bolshevik cause after 1917.

The Red Flag
The Communist red flag, with the hammer and sickle logo, was flown everywhere in the Soviet Union (U.S.S.R.).

U.S.S.R.

Ob

Siberia

Japanese Siberia
Japanese troops entered Siberia in 1918 in support of the "Whites." They declared an independent republic before they were forced to retreat in 1922.

Cross-country
The 5,786 (9,311-km) Trans-Siberian Railroad, from Moscow in the west to Vladivostok in the east, was finished in 1916.

Lake Baikal

akhstan

The "virgin lands" campaign
Khrushchev tried to turn the steppes of Kazakhstan into rolling wheat fields, but overfarming led to soil erosion and poor harvests.

MONGOLIA

Missile sites
Missile bases were built throughout Siberia, from which the U.S.S.R. could have launched nuclear ICBM—intercontinental ballistic missiles—against its enemy, the U.S.

Vladivostok

KOREA

CHINA

Tsushima Straits
The Russian Baltic fleet sailed halfway around the world to attack Japan, but it was heavily defeated in the Tsushima Straits in 1905. This forced Russia to make peace with Japan.

0		1,000km
0	500 miles	

1900–1990

1900

1904–1905 Russia is heavily defeated by Japan and loses land in the east
1905 Revolution breaks out across Russia

1910

1914 Russia enters World War I against Germany and Austro-Hungary
1917 Czar Nicholas II abdicates in March
1917 Bolsheviks seize power in November
1918 Treaty of Brest-Litovsk ends war for Russia
1918–1921 Civil war between "Reds" and "Whites"; western troops help "Whites"
1918 Bolsheviks murder Nicholas II and his family

1920

1920–1922 Peasant revolts occur across Russia
1921 "New economic policy" reintroduces free trade to encourage food production
1922 Union of Soviet Socialist Republics (U.S.S.R.) is set up
1924 Death of Lenin; Stalin takes over as leader
1928 First "five-year plan" is introduced to industrialize the country
1929 Collectivization of farms begins

1930

1932–1933 Massive famine in the Ukraine and central Asia as a result of collectivization
1934 Stalin begins show trials and "purges" to get rid of opponents

1938 Stalin's purges at their worst
1939 Nazi-Soviet Pact with Adolf Hitler

1940

1941 Germany invades the U.S.S.R. during World War II

1945 Soviet troops enter Berlin at the end of World War II

1949 U.S.S.R. explodes its first atomic bomb

1950

1953 Death of Stalin; Khrushchev takes over as leader
1954 "Virgin lands" policy is launched to grow more crops
1956 Khrushchev denounces (fiercely criticizes) Stalin in a secret speech
1957 U.S.S.R. launches Sputnik I, the world's first human-made satellite, into space

1960

1961 Soviet cosmonaut Yuri Gagarin becomes the first person in space

1964 Khrushchev is ousted; Leonid Brezhnev takes over as leader

1970

1972 U.S. president Nixon visits the U.S.S.R.

1979 Russian troops enter Afghanistan

1980

1982 Death of Brezhnev; Yuri Andropov and then Konstantin Chernenko succeed him

1985 Mikhail Gorbachev becomes the leader of the U.S.S.R. and begins reforms

1990

The U.S. and the Great Depression:
Economic boom and bust

The U.S. economic boom of the 1920s ended when the New York Stock Exchange crashed in October 1929. As prices and profits collapsed and banks failed, the U.S.—and then the rest of the world—entered a decade-long economic slump. Millions of people lost their jobs or had their incomes reduced, while world trade was cut by almost two thirds between 1929 and 1932. In the U.S., President Roosevelt's New Deal tried to tackle the problem, but it was the threat of war in Europe and Asia and the need to make more weapons that finally produced the jobs that got unemployed people back into work.

The postwar boom
The 1920s was a period of great optimism in America. The economy was booming after World War I, the country was peaceful and prosperous, and women had more freedom than ever before. New forms of entertainment, such as movies and jazz music, transformed the lives of ordinary people. The picture above shows fashionable women from the 1920s, known as flappers, who summed up the spirit of the decade. Many thought that the boom would last forever.

Hollywood
The invention of a working sound movie system in 1927 transformed the cinema, killing off silent films by 1930. Millions of people flocked to the cinema during the 1930s to see spectacular films, such as *The Wizard of Oz* (below), to take their minds off the economic gloom of their daily lives.

Worldwide slump
The economic slump began in the U.S., but it had spread around the world by 1931. As millions lost their jobs, social and political unrest grew. In Great Britain, in 1936, 200 unemployed shipyard workers from Jarrow in northeast England marched south to London to draw attention to the poverty and lack of jobs in their town.

The New Deal

In 1933 Franklin D. Roosevelt, pictured here (right), became the U.S. president, pledging "a new deal for the American people." He reformed the banking system, gave financial support to farmers and home owners, and, through the Public Works Administration, set millions of people to work building dams, roads, bridges, schools, and other public projects.

Extreme poverty

Unemployment in the U.S. rose from two million industrial workers in 1928 to 11.6 million in 1932 and stayed high for the rest of the decade. Millions of people lost their life savings when their banks failed. They were forced to rely on soup kitchens (below) and money from the government to keep them alive. From 1934 to 1938, extreme poverty spread to the farming communities of Oklahoma, Kansas, and other Midwestern states when high winds stripped a huge area of land of its soil.

Europe between the world wars

The years after World War I were chaotic across all of Europe. Germany tried to recover from its defeat in the war. Meanwhile new countries, which had emerged from the former defeated empires, struggled to establish themselves as independent states. Economic chaos after the slump of 1931 only made matters worse, as millions of people lost their jobs. Fascist (extreme right-wing and dictatorial) parties came to power in Italy, much of eastern Europe, and, in 1933, Germany. This divided the continent between democracies, dictatorships, and the U.S.S.R., which was a dictatorship as well as the world's only communist state.

Atlantic Ocean

The Spanish Civil War

In 1936 the Spanish army, led by the Nationalist General Francisco Franco, rose up in revolt against the democratic Republican government. The civil war that followed lasted three years and involved several international forces: the U.S.S.R. sent arms to the Republicans; Germany and Italy sent troops and planes to the Nationalist rebels; volunteers from around the world fought on both sides; while Great Britain and France remained neutral. The war ended with a Nationalist victory in 1939, starting 36 years of authoritarian government in Spain.

Free Ireland
After hundreds of years of British rule, most of Ireland became an independent country in 1921.

Television
The first regular TV broadcasts in Europe were made by the British Broadcasting Corporation (BBC) in 1936.

Hyper inflation
German economic collapse in 1923 caused such massive inflation that trillions of German marks were needed just to buy simple groceries.

Jews fleeing from the Nazis

"Peace in our time"
In 1938 the British prime minister, Neville Chamberlain, returned from Germany believing that he had reached a peace settlement with Hitler.

Versailles
The leaders of the four victorious Allied powers met in Versailles, outside of Paris, to agree to a peace settlement with Germany after World War I.

Guernica
In April 1937 German bombers destroyed the ancient Basque capital during the Spanish Civil War.

Unemployed
The huge rise in unemployment after the 1931 worldwide economic slump led to massive social unrest.

Two dictators
Hitler and Mussolini agreed to an alliance—the Rome-Berlin Axis—in 1936. Other countries joined the axis during World War II.

Civil war
Around 500,000 people lost their lives during the Spanish Civil War.

North Sea

NORW

OSL

DENM

GREAT BRITAIN

DUBLIN

IRISH FREE STATE

AMSTERDAM

NETHERLANDS

LONDON

BRUSSELS

BELGIUM

Rhine

Rhineland

PARIS

Nuremberg Rally

SWITZERLAND

BERN

FRANCE

Guernica

Basque Country

SPAIN

MADRID

PORTUGAL

LISBON

Sardinia

Balearic Islands

Mediterranean Sea

FINLAND

HELSINKI

WEDEN

STOCKHOLM

TALLINN

ESTONIA

RIGA

LATVIA

LITHUANIA

The U.S.S.R.
As the world's only Communist state, the U.S.S.R. under Stalin mostly stayed out of European politics. It watched the rise of Hitler with alarm, before allying with him in 1939.

MOSCOW

U.S.S.R.

ENHAGEN

East Prussia

GDANSK (DANZIG)

ERLIN

The Polish Corridor
The thin strip of land giving Poland access to the Baltic Sea contained many Germans and was a source of tension between the two countries.

WARSAW

Starvation
Under Joseph Stalin, millions of peasants starved as their farms were taken under state control.

etenland

AGUE

CZECHOSLOVAKIA

VIENNA

Communist Hungary
The Communists under Béla Kun seized power in Hungary in 1919 but were quickly forced out by an invading Romanian army.

POLAND

TRIA

BUDAPEST

HUNGARY

German troops in Austria

Union
In March 1938 Germany occupied Austria, causing the *Anschluss*—the annexation of Austria.

ROMANIA

BUCHAREST

Danube

Black Sea

BELGRADE

YUGOSLAVIA

BULGARIA

SOFIA

LY

Atatürk
Kemal Atatürk, a World War I hero, abolished the Turkish sultanate in 1922 and set up an independent republic in 1923.

OME

TIRANË

ALBANIA

TURKEY

Greek immigration
More than one million Greeks were forced to flee from Asia Minor when Turkey occupied some Greek cities in 1922.

GREECE

ATHENS

Sicily

Yugoslavia
Yugoslavia became one country in 1919, merging the Serb, Croat, and Slovene peoples into one state.

Cyprus

Crete

Mediterranean Sea

Mussolini
Mussolini and his Fascist Party took power in Italy in 1922 and soon crushed all opposition to their rule.

| 0 | 500km |
| 0 | 250 miles |

1918 World War I ends with the defeat of Germany and Austro-Hungary
1919–1920 Treaty of Versailles, and other peace treaties, are signed in France to draw up the postwar borders of Europe

1919 Yugoslavia, Hungary, Czechoslovakia, Poland, Finland, and three Baltic states (Estonia, Latvia, and Lithuania) emerge from the ruins of the Austro-Hungarian and Russian empires

1920
1920 Communists try to take power in Germany
1920–1921 Poland wins war against the U.S.S.R.
1921 Irish Free State is established within the British Empire

1922 Mussolini takes power in Italy
1922 Greeks expelled from Asia Minor
1922 Germany and the U.S.S.R. sign an economic treaty

1923 Turkish republic is set up under Kemal Atatürk

1926 General Strike in Great Britain

1928 Kellogg-Briand Pact is signed in Paris: all countries agree to renounce war

1929 Beginning of the Great Depression

1930

1931 Worldwide economic slump
1931 Spain becomes a republic

1933 Adolf Hitler comes to power in Germany
1934 Greece, Romania, Turkey, and Yugoslavia sign the Balkan Pact against Germany and the U.S.S.R.
1935–1936 Italy invades Abyssinia (Ethiopia)
1936 British Broadcasting Corporation (BBC) begins regular TV broadcasts
1936 Germany reoccupies the demilitarized Rhineland
1936 Germany and Italy agree to the Rome-Berlin Axis alliance
1936–1939 Spanish Civil War

1938 Germany takes over Austria
1938 Germany takes Sudetenland from Czechoslovakia after Great Britain, France, and Italy agree to terms with Germany in Munich
1939 Germany takes over the rest of Czechoslovakia
1939 Italy occupies Albania
1939 Nazi-Soviet pact: Germany and Russia agree to partition (split up) Poland
1939 Germany invades Poland, beginning World War II

1940

The war in Europe

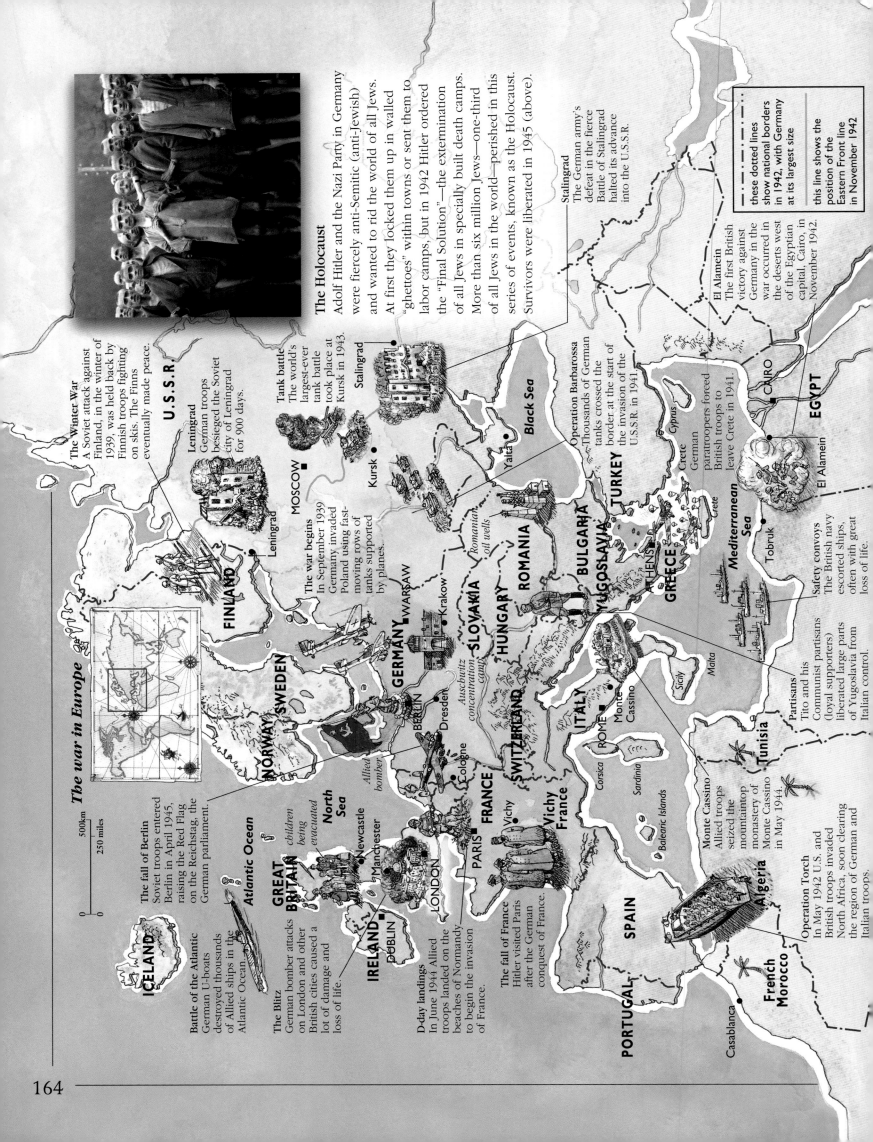

500km
250 miles
0

The Holocaust

Adolf Hitler and the Nazi Party in Germany were fiercely anti-Semitic (anti-Jewish) and wanted to rid the world of all Jews. At first they locked them up in walled "ghettoes" within towns or sent them to labor camps, but in 1942 Hitler ordered the extermination—the "Final Solution"—the extermination of all Jews in specially built death camps. More than six million Jews—one-third of all Jews in the world—perished in this series of events, known as the Holocaust. Survivors were liberated in 1945 (above).

ICELAND

The fall of Berlin
Soviet troops entered Berlin in April 1945, raising the Red Flag on the Reichstag, the German parliament.

Battle of the Atlantic
German U-boats destroyed thousands of Allied ships in the Atlantic Ocean.

Atlantic Ocean

The Blitz
German bomber attacks on London and other British cities caused a lot of damage and loss of life.

GREAT BRITAIN

children being evacuated

North Sea

Newcastle
Manchester

IRELAND
DUBLIN
LONDON

D-day landings
In June 1944 Allied troops landed on the beaches of Normandy, to begin the invasion of France.

The fall of France
Hitler visited Paris after the German conquest of France.

PARIS
FRANCE

Vichy France
Vichy

PORTUGAL

SPAIN

French Morocco
Casablanca

Algeria

Operation Torch
In May 1942 U.S. and British troops invaded North Africa, soon clearing the region of German and Italian troops.

NORWAY
SWEDEN
FINLAND

The Winter War
A Soviet attack against Finland, in the winter of 1939, was held back by Finnish troops fighting on skis. The Finns eventually made peace.

U.S.S.R.

Leningrad
German troops besieged the Soviet city of Leningrad for 900 days.
Leningrad

MOSCOW
Moscow

The war begins
In September 1939 Germany invaded Poland using fast-moving rows of tanks supported by planes.

Tank battle
The world's largest-ever tank battle took place at Kursk in 1943.
Kursk

Stalingrad
The German army's defeat in the fierce Battle of Stalingrad halted its advance into the U.S.S.R.

GERMANY
WARSAW
Krakow
BERLIN
Dresden
Cologne

Allied bomber

Auschwitz concentration camp

SLOVAKIA
HUNGARY
ROMANIA
Romanian oil wells

SWITZERLAND

ITALY
ROME
Monte Cassino

Monte Cassino
Allied troops seized the mountaintop monastery of Monte Cassino in May 1944.

Corsica
Sardinia
Balearic Islands
Sicily
Malta

Tunisia

YUGOSLAVIA

Partisans
Tito and his Communist partisans (loyal supporters) liberated large parts of Yugoslavia from Italian control.

BULGARIA
GREECE
ATHENS
Crete

Crete
German paratroopers forced British troops to leave Crete in 1941.

TURKEY
Black Sea
Yalta
Cyprus

Mediterranean Sea

EGYPT
CAIRO

El Alamein
The first British victory against Germany in the war occurred in the deserts west of the Egyptian capital, Cairo, in November 1942.

Tobruk
El Alamein

Safety convoys
The British navy escorted ships, often with great loss of life.

Operation Barbarossa
Thousands of German tanks crossed the border at the start of the invasion of the U.S.S.R. in 1941.

— — — these dotted lines show national borders in 1942, with Germany at its largest size

——— this line shows the position of the Eastern Front line in November 1942

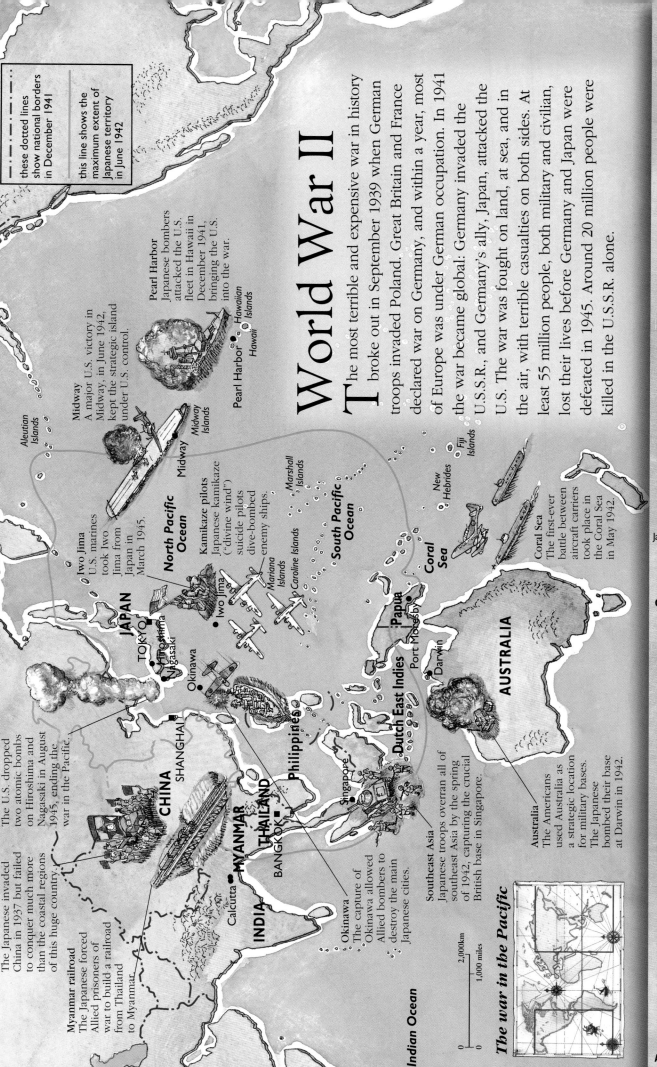

World War II

The most terrible and expensive war in history broke out in September 1939 when German troops invaded Poland. Great Britain and France declared war on Germany, and within a year, most of Europe was under German occupation. In 1941 the war became global: Germany invaded the U.S.S.R., and Germany's ally, Japan, attacked the U.S. The war was fought on land, at sea, and in the air, with terrible casualties on both sides. At least 55 million people, both military and civilian, lost their lives before Germany and Japan were defeated in 1945. Around 20 million people were killed in the U.S.S.R. alone.

these dotted lines show national borders in December 1941

this line shows the maximum extent of Japanese territory in June 1942

Pearl Harbor
Japanese bombers attacked the U.S. fleet in Hawaii in December 1941, bringing the U.S. into the war.

Hawaiian Islands

Pearl Harbor • Hawaii

Midway
A major U.S. victory in Midway, in June 1942, kept the strategic island under U.S. control.

Midway Islands

Midway

Aleutian Islands

Iwo Jima
U.S. marines took Iwo Jima from Japan in March 1945.

North Pacific Ocean

Kamikaze pilots
Japanese kamikaze ("divine wind") suicide pilots dive-bombed enemy ships.

Marshall Islands

Mariana Islands

Caroline Islands

South Pacific Ocean

Fiji Islands

New Hebrides

Coral Sea
The first-ever battle between aircraft carriers took place in the Coral Sea in May 1942.

Coral Sea

Iwo Jima

JAPAN

TOKYO

Hiroshima
Nagasaki

Okinawa

Papua
Port Moresby

Hiroshima
The U.S. dropped two atomic bombs on Hiroshima and Nagasaki in August 1945, ending the war in the Pacific.

Okinawa
The capture of Okinawa allowed Allied bombers to destroy the main Japanese cities.

Southeast Asia
Japanese troops overran all of southeast Asia by the spring of 1942, capturing the crucial British base in Singapore.

SHANGHAI

CHINA

China
The Japanese invaded China in 1937 but failed to conquer much more than the coastal regions of this huge country.

Myanmar railroad
The Japanese forced Allied prisoners of war to build a railroad from Thailand to Myanmar.

Calcutta • **MYANMAR**

INDIA

THAILAND
BANGKOK

Philippines

Singapore

Dutch East Indies

Darwin

AUSTRALIA

Australia
The Americans used Australia as a strategic location for military bases. The Japanese bombed their base at Darwin in 1942.

Indian Ocean

The war in the Pacific

0   2,000km
0   1,000 miles

1939–1946

1939
Sept. 1939 Germany invades Poland; Great Britain, and France declare war—start of World War II
Nov. 1939 U.S.S.R. invades Finland

1940
April 1940 Germany invades Denmark and Norway
May 1940 Germany invades the Low Countries and France
June 1940 Italy enters war on Germany's side
July–Oct. 1940 Battle of Britain: the British air force defeats the German Luftwaffe (air force)
Sept. 1940 Blitz against British cities begins
Sept. 1940 Italians invade Egypt
Oct. 1940 Italians invade Greece
Oct. 1940 Hungary, Romania, and Bulgaria join Germany and Italy

1941
April 1941 Germany invades Yugoslavia and Greece
May 1941 British are forced out of Crete
June 1941 Operation Barbarossa: Germany invades the U.S.S.R.
Sept. 1941 Siege of Leningrad begins
Dec. 1941 Japan attacks Pearl Harbor; the U.S. enters the war
Dec. 1941 German advance is stopped outside of Moscow

1942
Jan. 1941 Hitler orders extermination of all Jews
Feb.–March 1942 Japanese bomb Darwin; Japanese take Malaya, Singapore, and Dutch East Indies
April–May 1942 Battle of the Coral Sea halts the Japanese advance
May 1942 Japanese take the Philippines
May 1942 First British area bombing campaign against Cologne
Oct.–Nov. 1942 British victory in El Alamein
Nov. 1942 Operation Torch: Allied invasion of North Africa
Nov. 1942 Germans occupy Vichy, France

1943
Feb. 1943 Germans surrender in Stalingrad
April 1943 Jewish uprising in Warsaw, Poland
May 1943 Battle of the Atlantic ends
May 1943 German and Italian troops surrender in Tunisia
June–Aug. 1943 Soviets defeat German tanks in Kursk
July 1943 Allies invade Italy

1944
Jan. 1944 Siege of Leningrad ends
June 1944 D-day: Allied troops invade France
June 1944 Allies begin their bombing of southern Japan from Chinese bases
July 1944 Soviet troops enter Poland
Aug. 1944 Allied troops liberate Paris
Oct. 1944 British troops liberate Greece
Oct. 1944 Battle of Leyte Gulf in the Philippines ends Japanese naval power
Nov. 1944 First Japanese kamikaze attacks on Allied ships

1945
March 1945 Allied troops cross the Rhine river
March 1945 U.S. marines take Iwo Jima in the Pacific
April 1945 Soviet troops enter Berlin
April 1945 Hitler commits suicide
May 1945 Italy and Germany surrender: peace in Europe
May 1945 U.S. marines take Okinawa and begin to bomb Japan
May 1945 Allied firestorm devastates Tokyo
Aug. 1945 U.S. drops atomic bombs on Hiroshima and Nagasaki; Soviets attack Japan
Sept. 1945 Japanese surrender: the war ends

1946

The Cold War

The U.S. and U.S.S.R. emerged victorious at the end of World War II, but political differences between them soon erupted into a "cold" war—one that never reached an all-out military conflict, despite the ever-present threat of war. By 1949, the world was roughly divided between pro-Western and pro-communist states. Allies of the two sides fought wars on their behalf, such as in Korea and Vietnam, while both the U.S.S.R. and U.S. built up huge arsenals of nuclear and other weapons. Attempts to achieve an understanding between the two sides failed in the 1970s. By the late 1980s, the U.S. had outspent the U.S.S.R. and forced it toward financial ruin. The collapse of communism brought the Cold War to an end in 1991.

CANADA

Reykjavik

WEST GERMAN

BRITAIN

The United Nations
Many of the Cold War diplomatic meetings took place at the UN headquarters in New York City.

Greenham Common

LONDON

PAR
Gene

FRANC

American firepower
In the 1980s the U.S. was able to outspend the U.S.S.R. on nuclear weaponry, leading to a series of arms reduction agreements in 1988 and 1991.

Fulton

New York

WASHINGTON, D.C.

SPA

Greenham Common
The decision to place U.S. nuclear missiles in Great Britain, in 1982, led to huge protests at the Greenham Common base. The missiles were removed in 1989.

UNITED STATES
OF AMERICA

The Cuban missile crisis
In 1962 the U.S.S.R. stationed nuclear missiles in Cuba, bringing the world to the brink of nuclear war before they agreed to remove them.

Guatemala
In 1954 the U.S. backed a counterrevolution in Guatemala to overthrow the socialist government and install a pro-U.S., military government.

CUBA

GUATEMALA

NICARAGUA

Atlantic Ocean

Grenada
In 1983 U.S. troops overthrew the left-wing (socialist) government of Grenada because of its growing ties with communist Cuba.

GRENADA

Nicaragua
In 1978 the radical Sandinista rebels overthrew the military government and introduced many social reforms. This led to a lengthy civil war until peace was declared in 1990.

these dotted lines show the borders between countries in 1949

Chile
In 1973 a U.S.-backed military coup overthrew President Allende, the world's first democratically elected Marxist head of state.

CHILE

0   4,000km

0   2,000 miles

SANTIAGO

The end of the Cold War
After 1985 the new leader of the U.S.S.R., Mikhail Gorbachev, wanted to reduce military spending and improve the living conditions of Soviet citizens. In 1988 he pulled Soviet troops out of eastern Europe. Without Soviet support, the communist governments there could not survive. One by one, democratically elected governments replaced them. In 1989 a hated symbol of the Cold War, the Berlin Wall (left), was torn down. One year later Germany was reunited as one country. By then the U.S.S.R. was collapsing and was replaced by 15 independent countries in 1991.

The Berlin Wall
In 1961 communist authorities in East Berlin erected a wall to prevent its citizens from fleeing to freedom in the west.

The U.S.–U.S.S.R. arms race
The development of intercontinental ballistic missiles in the 1960s led to an expensive race to build up arms.

Mikhail Gorbachev
In 1985 Gorbachev became the leader of the U.S.S.R. and introduced much-needed social and economic reforms.

Divided Korea
In 1950 communist North Korea invaded capitalist South Korea. A ceasefire was agreed, but the peninsula remains divided.

■MOSCOW

UNION OF SOVIET SOCIALIST REPUBLICS

EAST GERMANY
■WARSAW
PRAGUE
CZECHOSLOVAKIA
■BUDAPEST

The "Prague Spring"
An attempt to soften the communist rule in Czechoslovakia was crushed by Soviet and other troops in 1968.

Chairman Mao
Mao Zedong led communist China from 1949 until his death in 1976.

HUNGARY
SYRIA
LEBANON
IRAQ
ISRAEL
IRAN
EGYPT
JORDAN

AFGHANISTAN
CHINA
NORTH KOREA

INDIA

SOUTH KOREA

VIETNAM

Hungary
In 1956 Soviet tanks crushed Hungary's attempt to pull out of the pro-Soviet Warsaw Pact.

The Vietnam War
In the war of 1954–1975, the U.S. supported South Vietnam. The U.S.S.R. and China supported communist North Vietnam, the eventual victor.

Arab–Israeli wars
In these frequent Middle East conflicts, the U.S. increasingly supported Israel while the U.S.S.R. supported the Arab states.

Afghanistan
The Soviet invasion of Afghanistan in 1979, to support its communist government, caused a breakdown in relations between the U.S. and U.S.S.R.

SOMALIA

CAMBODIA
MALAYA PENINSULA

ETHIOPIA

Somalia
After Somalia invaded Ethiopia, in 1977, the U.S.S.R. supported Ethiopia while the U.S. supported the Somalis.

Nehru of India
Prime Minister Nehru was one of the main leaders of the Non-Aligned Movement, whose members did not take either side in the Cold War.

Indian Ocean

Civil war in Angola
After 1975, Cuban- and Soviet-backed forces fought U.S.- and South African-backed forces for control of the country.

ANGOLA

Malay Peninsula
In 1948 communist forces attacked European settlers in the Malay Peninsula. Twelve years of jungle warfare followed before British troops crushed the communist units in 1960.

Cambodia
In 1970 U.S. planes secretly bombed Cambodia to prevent supplies from reaching communists in South Vietnam. This dragged Cambodia into a decade of warfare.

AUSTRALIA

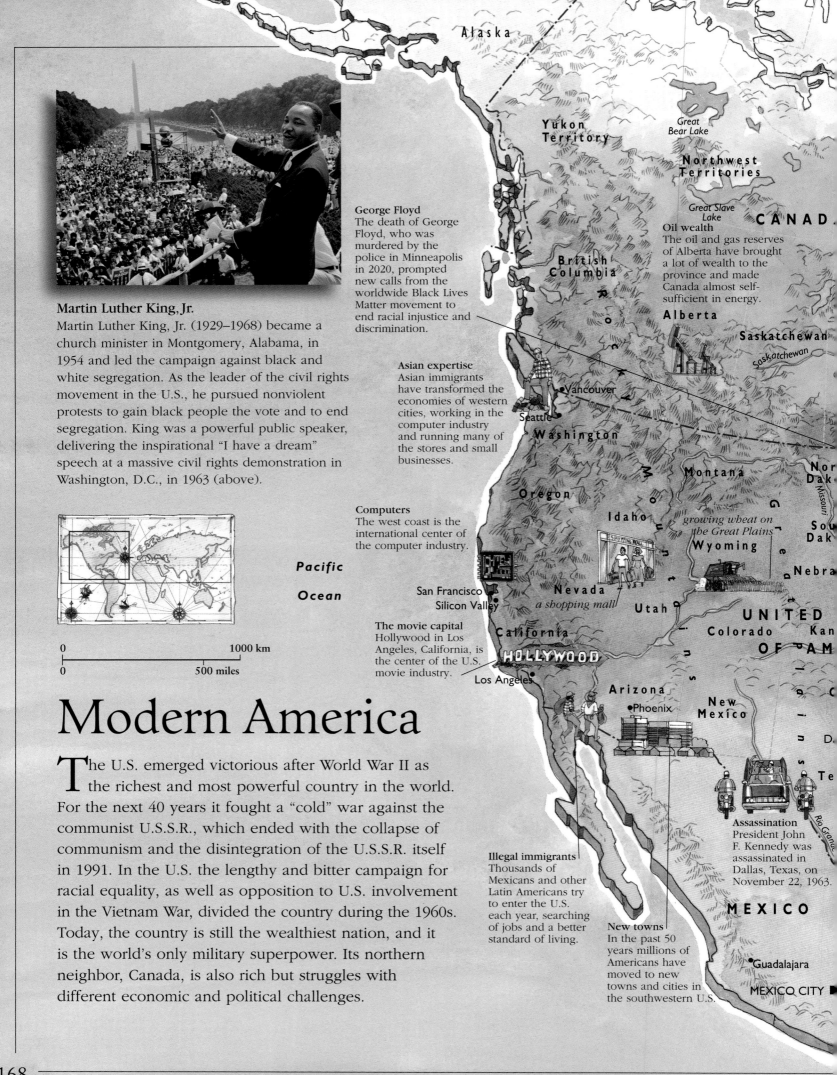

Martin Luther King, Jr.
Martin Luther King, Jr. (1929–1968) became a church minister in Montgomery, Alabama, in 1954 and led the campaign against black and white segregation. As the leader of the civil rights movement in the U.S., he pursued nonviolent protests to gain black people the vote and to end segregation. King was a powerful public speaker, delivering the inspirational "I have a dream" speech at a massive civil rights demonstration in Washington, D.C., in 1963 (above).

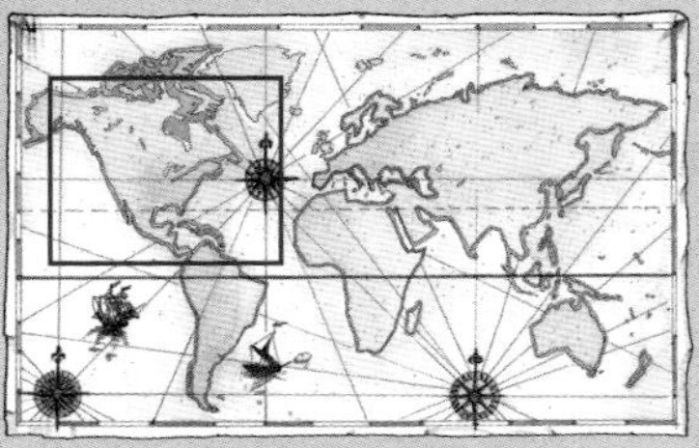

0 1000 km
0 500 miles

George Floyd
The death of George Floyd, who was murdered by the police in Minneapolis in 2020, prompted new calls from the worldwide Black Lives Matter movement to end racial injustice and discrimination.

Asian expertise
Asian immigrants have transformed the economies of western cities, working in the computer industry and running many of the stores and small businesses.

Computers
The west coast is the international center of the computer industry.

The movie capital
Hollywood in Los Angeles, California, is the center of the U.S. movie industry.

Modern America

The U.S. emerged victorious after World War II as the richest and most powerful country in the world. For the next 40 years it fought a "cold" war against the communist U.S.S.R., which ended with the collapse of communism and the disintegration of the U.S.S.R. itself in 1991. In the U.S. the lengthy and bitter campaign for racial equality, as well as opposition to U.S. involvement in the Vietnam War, divided the country during the 1960s. Today, the country is still the wealthiest nation, and it is the world's only military superpower. Its northern neighbor, Canada, is also rich but struggles with different economic and political challenges.

Alaska
Yukon Territory
Great Bear Lake
Northwest Territories
Great Slave Lake
CANAD
British Columbia
Alberta
Saskatchewan
Saskatchewan
Vancouver
Seattle
Washington
Montana
Oregon
Idaho
growing wheat on the Great Plains
Wyoming
Nevada
a shopping mall
Utah
San Francisco
Silicon Valley
California
HOLLYWOOD
Los Angeles
Colorado
UNITED
OF AM
Arizona
Phoenix
New Mexico
MEXICO
Guadalajara
MEXICO CITY
Rio Grande
Missouri
Pacific
Ocean

Oil wealth
The oil and gas reserves of Alberta have brought a lot of wealth to the province and made Canada almost self-sufficient in energy.

Illegal immigrants
Thousands of Mexicans and other Latin Americans try to enter the U.S. each year, searching of jobs and a better standard of living.

New towns
In the past 50 years millions of Americans have moved to new towns and cities in the southwestern U.S.

Assassination
President John F. Kennedy was assassinated in Dallas, Texas, on November 22, 1963.

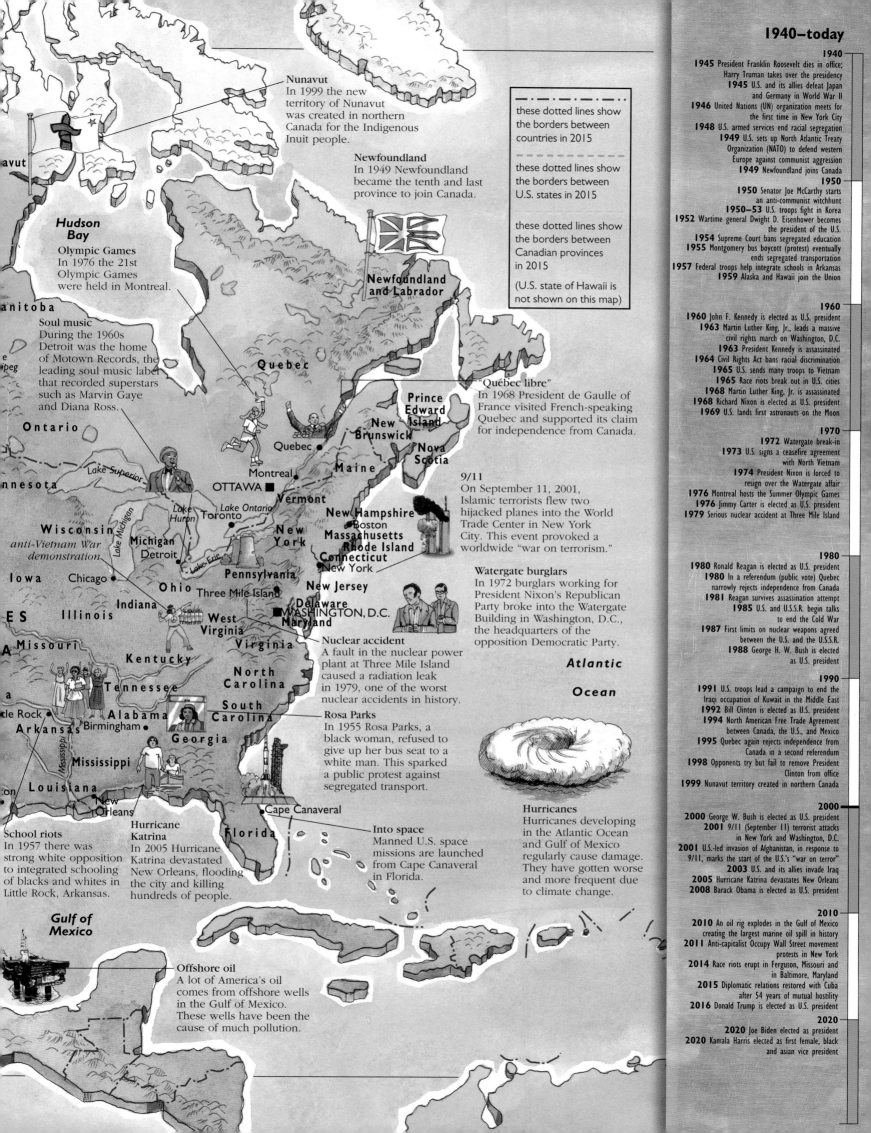

Nunavut
In 1999 the new territory of Nunavut was created in northern Canada for the Indigenous Inuit people.

Newfoundland
In 1949 Newfoundland became the tenth and last province to join Canada.

these dotted lines show the borders between countries in 2015

these dotted lines show the borders between U.S. states in 2015

these dotted lines show the borders between Canadian provinces in 2015

(U.S. state of Hawaii is not shown on this map)

Hudson Bay

Olympic Games
In 1976 the 21st Olympic Games were held in Montreal.

Soul music
During the 1960s Detroit was the home of Motown Records, the leading soul music label that recorded superstars such as Marvin Gaye and Diana Ross.

"Québec libre"
In 1968 President de Gaulle of France visited French-speaking Quebec and supported its claim for independence from Canada.

9/11
On September 11, 2001, Islamic terrorists flew two hijacked planes into the World Trade Center in New York City. This event provoked a worldwide "war on terrorism."

Watergate burglars
In 1972 burglars working for President Nixon's Republican Party broke into the Watergate Building in Washington, D.C., the headquarters of the opposition Democratic Party.

Atlantic

Ocean

Nuclear accident
A fault in the nuclear power plant at Three Mile Island caused a radiation leak in 1979, one of the worst nuclear accidents in history.

Rosa Parks
In 1955 Rosa Parks, a black woman, refused to give up her bus seat to a white man. This sparked a public protest against segregated transport.

Hurricanes
Hurricanes developing in the Atlantic Ocean and Gulf of Mexico regularly cause damage. They have gotten worse and more frequent due to climate change.

School riots
In 1957 there was strong white opposition to integrated schooling of blacks and whites in Little Rock, Arkansas.

Hurricane Katrina
In 2005 Hurricane Katrina devastated New Orleans, flooding the city and killing hundreds of people.

Into space
Manned U.S. space missions are launched from Cape Canaveral in Florida.

Gulf of Mexico

Offshore oil
A lot of America's oil comes from offshore wells in the Gulf of Mexico. These wells have been the cause of much pollution.

Map labels: Nunavut, Ontario, Manitoba, Minnesota, Iowa, Wisconsin, Michigan, Illinois, Indiana, Missouri, Kentucky, Tennessee, Alabama, Arkansas, Mississippi, Louisiana, Quebec, New Brunswick, Prince Edward Island, Nova Scotia, Newfoundland and Labrador, Maine, Vermont, New Hampshire, Massachusetts, Rhode Island, Connecticut, New York, New Jersey, Pennsylvania, Ohio, West Virginia, Virginia, Delaware, Maryland, North Carolina, South Carolina, Georgia, Florida; Lake Superior, Lake Huron, Lake Michigan, Lake Erie, Lake Ontario; Chicago, Detroit, Toronto, Montreal, Quebec, Ottawa, Boston, New York, Three Mile Island, Washington, D.C., Birmingham, New Orleans, Little Rock, Cape Canaveral; Mississippi; *anti-Vietnam War demonstration*

1940–today

1940

1945 President Franklin Roosevelt dies in office; Harry Truman takes over the presidency
1945 U.S. and its allies defeat Japan and Germany in World War II
1946 United Nations (UN) organization meets for the first time in New York City
1948 U.S. armed services end racial segregation
1949 U.S. sets up North Atlantic Treaty Organization (NATO) to defend western Europe against communist aggression
1949 Newfoundland joins Canada

1950

1950 Senator Joe McCarthy starts an anti-communist witchhunt
1950–53 U.S. troops fight in Korea
1952 Wartime general Dwight D. Eisenhower becomes the president of the U.S.
1954 Supreme Court bans segregated education
1955 Montgomery bus boycott (protest) eventually ends segregated transportation
1957 Federal troops help integrate schools in Arkansas
1959 Alaska and Hawaii join the Union

1960

1960 John F. Kennedy is elected as U.S. president
1963 Martin Luther King, Jr., leads a massive civil rights march on Washington, D.C.
1963 President Kennedy is assassinated
1964 Civil Rights Act bans racial discrimination
1965 U.S. sends many troops to Vietnam
1965 Race riots break out in U.S. cities
1968 Martin Luther King, Jr. is assassinated
1968 Richard Nixon is elected as U.S. president
1969 U.S. lands first astronauts on the Moon

1970

1972 Watergate break-in
1973 U.S. signs a ceasefire agreement with North Vietnam
1974 President Nixon is forced to resign over the Watergate affair
1976 Montreal hosts the Summer Olympic Games
1976 Jimmy Carter is elected as U.S. president
1979 Serious nuclear accident at Three Mile Island

1980

1980 Ronald Reagan is elected as U.S. president
1980 In a referendum (public vote) Quebec narrowly rejects independence from Canada
1981 Reagan survives assassination attempt
1985 U.S. and U.S.S.R. begin talks to end the Cold War
1987 First limits on nuclear weapons agreed between the U.S. and the U.S.S.R.
1988 George H. W. Bush is elected as U.S. president

1990

1991 U.S. troops lead a campaign to end the Iraqi occupation of Kuwait in the Middle East
1992 Bill Clinton is elected as U.S. president
1994 North American Free Trade Agreement between Canada, the U.S., and Mexico
1995 Quebec again rejects independence from Canada in a second referendum
1998 Opponents try but fail to remove President Clinton from office
1999 Nunavut territory created in northern Canada

2000

2000 George W. Bush is elected as U.S. president
2001 9/11 (September 11) terrorist attacks in New York and Washington, D.C.
2001 U.S.-led invasion of Afghanistan, in response to 9/11, marks the start of the U.S.'s "war on terror"
2003 U.S. and its allies invade Iraq
2005 Hurricane Katrina devastates New Orleans
2008 Barack Obama is elected as U.S. president

2010

2010 An oil rig explodes in the Gulf of Mexico creating the largest marine oil spill in history
2011 Anti-capitalist Occupy Wall Street movement protests in New York
2014 Race riots erupt in Ferguson, Missouri and in Baltimore, Maryland
2015 Diplomatic relations restored with Cuba after 54 years of mutual hostility
2016 Donald Trump is elected as U.S. president

2020

2020 Joe Biden elected as president
2020 Kamala Harris elected as first female, black and asian vice president

China in the 1900s

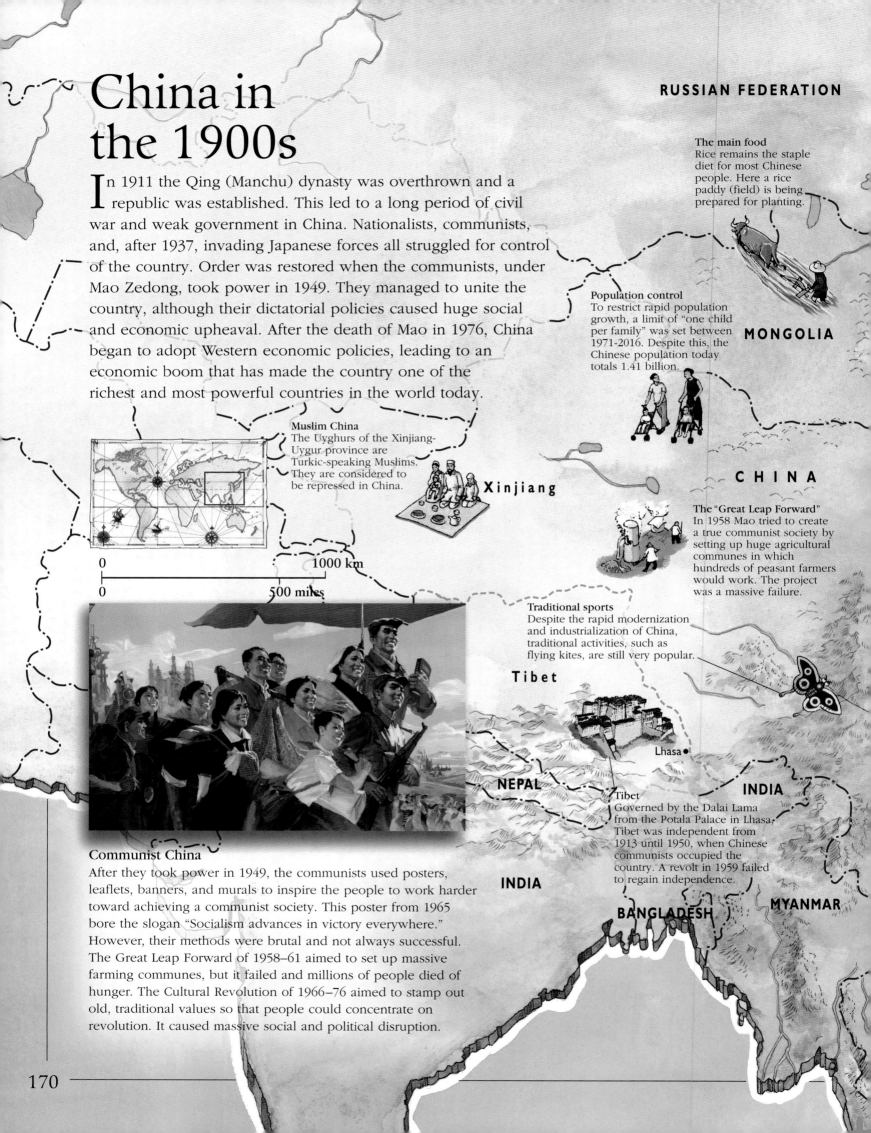

In 1911 the Qing (Manchu) dynasty was overthrown and a republic was established. This led to a long period of civil war and weak government in China. Nationalists, communists, and, after 1937, invading Japanese forces all struggled for control of the country. Order was restored when the communists, under Mao Zedong, took power in 1949. They managed to unite the country, although their dictatorial policies caused huge social and economic upheaval. After the death of Mao in 1976, China began to adopt Western economic policies, leading to an economic boom that has made the country one of the richest and most powerful countries in the world today.

RUSSIAN FEDERATION

The main food
Rice remains the staple diet for most Chinese people. Here a rice paddy (field) is being prepared for planting.

MONGOLIA

Population control
To restrict rapid population growth, a limit of "one child per family" was set between 1971-2016. Despite this, the Chinese population today totals 1.41 billion.

Muslim China
The Uyghurs of the Xinjiang-Uygur province are Turkic-speaking Muslims. They are considered to be repressed in China.

Xinjiang

CHINA

The "Great Leap Forward"
In 1958 Mao tried to create a true communist society by setting up huge agricultural communes in which hundreds of peasant farmers would work. The project was a massive failure.

0	1000 km
0	500 miles

Traditional sports
Despite the rapid modernization and industrialization of China, traditional activities, such as flying kites, are still very popular.

Tibet

Lhasa●

NEPAL

Tibet
Governed by the Dalai Lama from the Potala Palace in Lhasa, Tibet was independent from 1913 until 1950, when Chinese communists occupied the country. A revolt in 1959 failed to regain independence.

INDIA

INDIA

BANGLADESH

MYANMAR

Communist China

After they took power in 1949, the communists used posters, leaflets, banners, and murals to inspire the people to work harder toward achieving a communist society. This poster from 1965 bore the slogan "Socialism advances in victory everywhere." However, their methods were brutal and not always successful. The Great Leap Forward of 1958–61 aimed to set up massive farming communes, but it failed and millions of people died of hunger. The Cultural Revolution of 1966–76 aimed to stamp out old, traditional values so that people could concentrate on revolution. It caused massive social and political disruption.

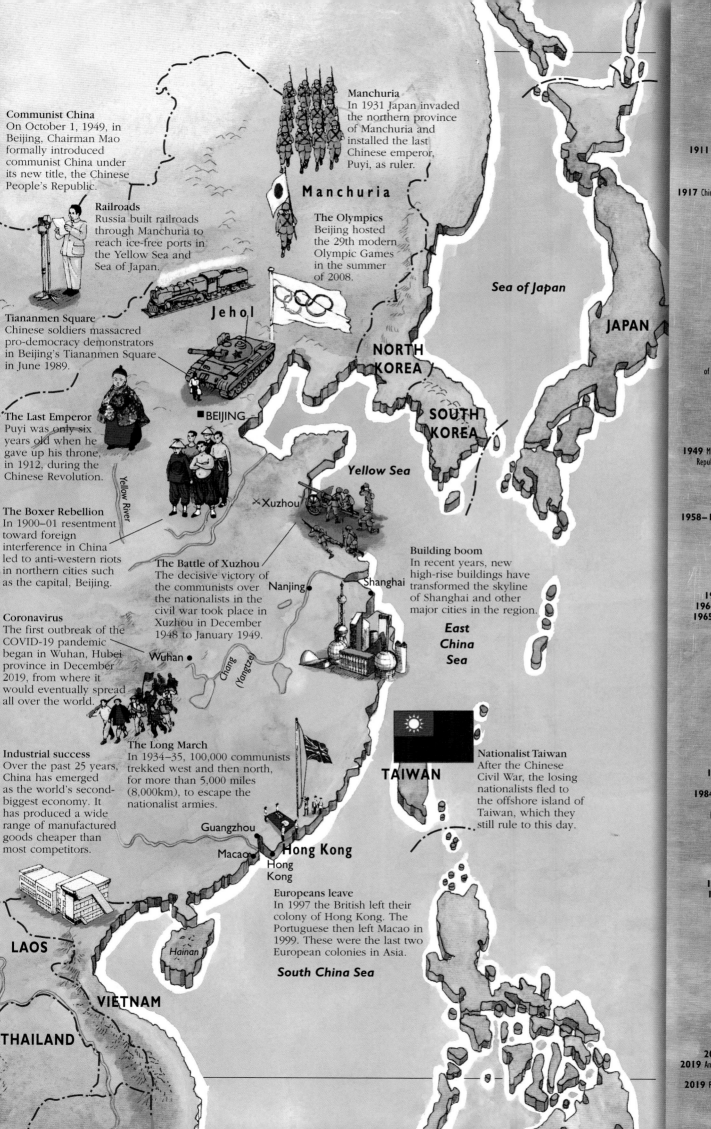

Communist China
On October 1, 1949, in Beijing, Chairman Mao formally introduced communist China under its new title, the Chinese People's Republic.

Railroads
Russia built railroads through Manchuria to reach ice-free ports in the Yellow Sea and Sea of Japan.

Tiananmen Square
Chinese soldiers massacred pro-democracy demonstrators in Beijing's Tiananmen Square in June 1989.

The Last Emperor
Puyi was only six years old when he gave up his throne, in 1912, during the Chinese Revolution.

The Boxer Rebellion
In 1900–01 resentment toward foreign interference in China led to anti-western riots in northern cities such as the capital, Beijing.

Coronavirus
The first outbreak of the COVID-19 pandemic began in Wuhan, Hubei province in December 2019, from where it would eventually spread all over the world.

Industrial success
Over the past 25 years, China has emerged as the world's second-biggest economy. It has produced a wide range of manufactured goods cheaper than most competitors.

Manchuria
In 1931 Japan invaded the northern province of Manchuria and installed the last Chinese emperor, Puyi, as ruler.

The Olympics
Beijing hosted the 29th modern Olympic Games in the summer of 2008.

Manchuria

Jehol

BEIJING

Yellow River

✕ Xuzhou

The Battle of Xuzhou
The decisive victory of the communists over the nationalists in the civil war took place in Xuzhou in December 1948 to January 1949.

Nanjing

Shanghai

Wuhan

Chang (Yangtze)

The Long March
In 1934–35, 100,000 communists trekked west and then north, for more than 5,000 miles (8,000km), to escape the nationalist armies.

Guangzhou

Macao

Hong Kong

Hong Kong

Europeans leave
In 1997 the British left their colony of Hong Kong. The Portuguese then left Macao in 1999. These were the last two European colonies in Asia.

Hainan

LAOS

VIETNAM

THAILAND

Sea of Japan

JAPAN

NORTH KOREA

SOUTH KOREA

Yellow Sea

Building boom
In recent years, new high-rise buildings have transformed the skyline of Shanghai and other major cities in the region.

East China Sea

TAIWAN

Nationalist Taiwan
After the Chinese Civil War, the losing nationalists fled to the offshore island of Taiwan, which they still rule to this day.

South China Sea

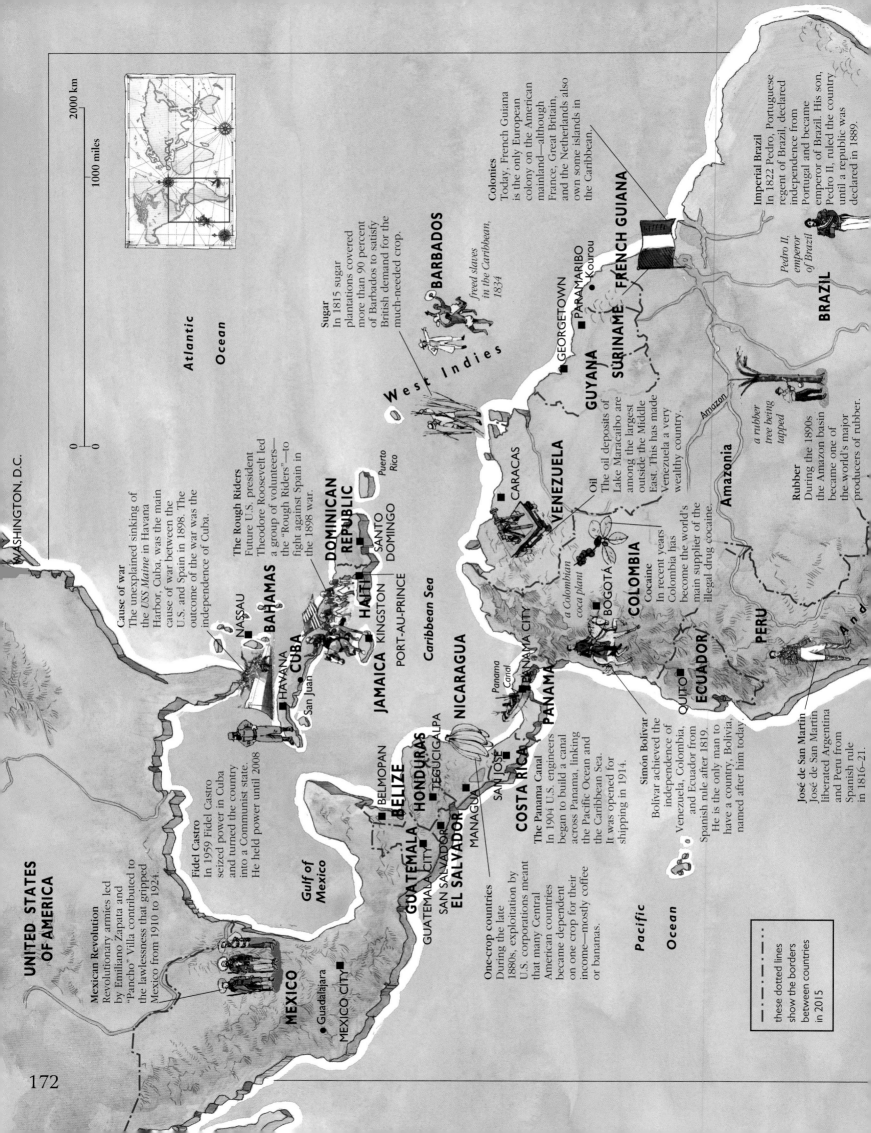

2000 km

1000 miles

0

0

WASHINGTON, D.C.

Atlantic

Ocean

**UNITED STATES
OF AMERICA**

Mexican Revolution
Revolutionary armies led
by Emiliano Zapata and
"Pancho" Villa contributed to
the lawlessness that gripped
Mexico from 1910 to 1924.

MEXICO

• Guadalajara

MEXICO CITY ■

**Gulf of
Mexico**

Cause of war
The unexplained sinking of
the *USS Maine* in Havana
Harbor, Cuba, was the main
cause of war between the
U.S. and Spain in 1898. The
outcome of the war was the
independence of Cuba.

The Rough Riders
Future U.S. president
Theodore Roosevelt led
a group of volunteers—
the "Rough Riders"—to
fight against Spain in
the 1898 war.

Fidel Castro
In 1959 Fidel Castro
seized power in Cuba
and turned the country
into a Communist state.
He held power until 2008

NASSAU ■

BAHAMAS

CUBA
• HAVANA

• San Juan

*Puerto
Rico*

**DOMINICAN
REPUBLIC**

SANTO
DOMINGO ■

HAITI KINGSTON
PORT-AU-PRINCE

JAMAICA

Caribbean Sea

West Indies

BARBADOS

*freed slaves
in the Caribbean,
1834*

Sugar
In 1815 sugar
plantations covered
more than 90 percent
of Barbados to satisfy
British demand for the
much-needed crop.

One-crop countries
During the late
1880s, exploitation by
U.S. corporations meant
that many Central
American countries
became dependent
on one crop for their
income—mostly coffee
or bananas.

GUATEMALA
GUATEMALA
CITY ■

BELMOPAN ■

BELIZE

HONDURAS
■ TEGUCIGALPA

SAN SALVADOR ■
EL SALVADOR

■ MANAGUA

NICARAGUA

SAN JOSÉ ■
COSTA RICA

The Panama Canal
In 1904 U.S. engineers
began to build a canal
across Panama, linking
the Pacific Ocean and
the Caribbean Sea.
It was opened for
shipping in 1914.

*Panama
Canal*

PANAMA CITY ■
PANAMA

**Pacific

Ocean**

Colonies
Today, French Guiana
is the only European
colony on the American
mainland—although
France, Great Britain,
and the Netherlands also
own some islands in
the Caribbean.

GEORGETOWN ■
GUYANA

PARAMARIBO ■
SURINAME

Kourou •
FRENCH GUIANA

Imperial Brazil
In 1822 Pedro, Portuguese
regent of Brazil, declared
independence from
Portugal and became
emperor of Brazil. His son,
Pedro II, ruled the country
until a republic was
declared in 1889.

*Pedro II,
emperor
of Brazil*

BRAZIL

■ CARACAS
VENEZUELA

Oil
The oil deposits of
Lake Maracaibo are
among the largest
outside the Middle
East. This has made
Venezuela a very
wealthy country.

*a Colombian
coca plant*

Cocaine
In recent years
Colombia has
become the world's
main supplier of the
illegal drug cocaine.

■ BOGOTÁ
COLOMBIA

Simón Bolívar
Bolívar achieved the
independence of
Venezuela, Colombia,
and Ecuador from
Spanish rule after 1819.
He is the only man to
have a country, Bolivia,
named after him today.

QUITO ■
ECUADOR

PERU

José de San Martín
José de San Martín
liberated Argentina
and Peru from
Spanish rule
in 1816–21.

Amazon

Amazonia

*a rubber
tree being
tapped*

Rubber
During the 1890s
the Amazon basin
became one of
the world's major
producers of rubber.

■ ......■

these dotted lines
show the borders
between countries
in 2015

Latin America

Charismatic liberators such as Simón Bolívar helped Latin America to win independence from Spain in the early 1800s. The empire of Brazil also gained its independence from Portugal before becoming a republic. All of these new countries were politically unstable and were often governed by dictators. During the 1900s, social divisions between the rich and the poor led to long periods of military rule and revolutionary upheaval. The U.S. supported the continent's independence from European rule, but often treated Central American nations as its backyard, controlling their economies and intervening when their elected governments threatened U.S. interests.

The end of slavery

The trade in African slaves across the Atlantic, to work in the plantations of Central and South America, was ended by Great Britain in 1807 and France in 1815—but a variety of traders continued to supply slaves to Brazil and Cuba until the 1860s. The institution of slavery itself was abolished in all British colonies in 1834, but survived in Brazil until 1888. A lack of alternative work, however, meant that many former slaves were forced to continue working on the plantations as paid laborers.

Che Guevara
The revolutionary leader Che Guevara was killed in Bolivia in 1967 while trying to encourage the tin miners to revolt.

Bernardo O'Higgins
The liberator of Chile was the son of an Irishman who spent his childhood in Europe. He returned to Chile to lead the independence struggle after 1813.

Allende
In 1973 a U.S.-backed military coup overthrew President Salvador Allende of Chile, the world's first democratically elected Marxist head of state.

Brasília
The capital of Brazil was moved from the overcrowded Rio de Janeiro to the new, inland city of Brasília in 1960.

Oil war
The lure of oil in the Gran Chaco region caused war between Bolivia and Paraguay in 1932–1935, although no oil was ever found there.

Evita
Juan Perón and his wife Eva (Evita) became hugely popular leaders in Argentina after 1946.

Immigration
From the mid-1850s, more than 4.5 million immigrants from southern Europe arrived in Argentina. This was followed by 115,000 Jews fleeing oppression in Russia after 1881.

Gauchos
Cowboys known as gauchos tended the huge cattle ranches in the pampas regions of northern Argentina and Uruguay.

The Falklands
In March 1982 Argentine forces invaded the British-owned Falkland Islands. Three months later they were defeated by British forces.

Falkland Islands

BRASÍLIA • Rio de Janeiro
São Paulo •
PARAGUAY • ASUNCIÓN
Gran Chaco
BOLIVIA LA PAZ
URUGUAY • MONTEVIDEO
CHILE BUENOS AIRES •
Andes
ARGENTINA
SANTIAGO •
Pacific Ocean
Ayacucho

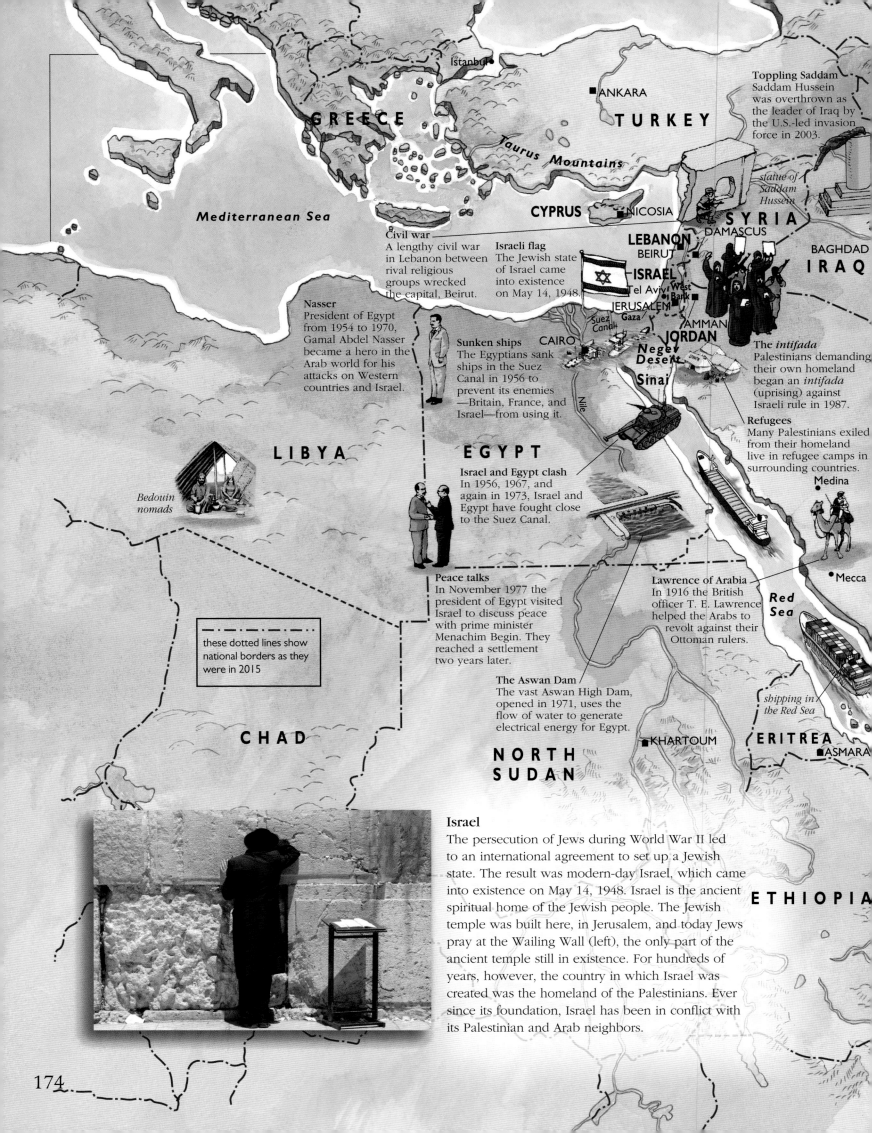

GREECE

TURKEY

Istanbul

ANKARA

Taurus Mountains

Toppling Saddam
Saddam Hussein was overthrown as the leader of Iraq by the U.S.-led invasion force in 2003.

statue of Saddam Hussein

Mediterranean Sea

CYPRUS NICOSIA

SYRIA
DAMASCUS

BAGHDAD

IRAQ

Civil war
A lengthy civil war in Lebanon between rival religious groups wrecked the capital, Beirut.

Israeli flag
The Jewish state of Israel came into existence on May 14, 1948.

LEBANON
BEIRUT

ISRAEL
Tel Aviv West Bank

JERUSALEM
Gaza

AMMAN

JORDAN

Nasser
President of Egypt from 1954 to 1970, Gamal Abdel Nasser became a hero in the Arab world for his attacks on Western countries and Israel.

Sunken ships
The Egyptians sank ships in the Suez Canal in 1956 to prevent its enemies —Britain, France, and Israel—from using it.

CAIRO

Suez Canal

Negev Desert

Sinai

The *intifada*
Palestinians demanding their own homeland began an *intifada* (uprising) against Israeli rule in 1987.

Refugees
Many Palestinians exiled from their homeland live in refugee camps in surrounding countries.

Medina

LIBYA

Bedouin nomads

EGYPT

Israel and Egypt clash
In 1956, 1967, and again in 1973, Israel and Egypt have fought close to the Suez Canal.

Nile

Lawrence of Arabia
In 1916 the British officer T. E. Lawrence helped the Arabs to revolt against their Ottoman rulers.

Red Sea

Mecca

these dotted lines show national borders as they were in 2015

Peace talks
In November 1977 the president of Egypt visited Israel to discuss peace with prime minister Menachim Begin. They reached a settlement two years later.

shipping in the Red Sea

CHAD

The Aswan Dam
The vast Aswan High Dam, opened in 1971, uses the flow of water to generate electrical energy for Egypt.

KHARTOUM

NORTH SUDAN

ERITREA
ASMARA

Israel

The persecution of Jews during World War II led to an international agreement to set up a Jewish state. The result was modern-day Israel, which came into existence on May 14, 1948. Israel is the ancient spiritual home of the Jewish people. The Jewish temple was built here, in Jerusalem, and today Jews pray at the Wailing Wall (left), the only part of the ancient temple still in existence. For hundreds of years, however, the country in which Israel was created was the homeland of the Palestinians. Ever since its foundation, Israel has been in conflict with its Palestinian and Arab neighbors.

ETHIOPIA

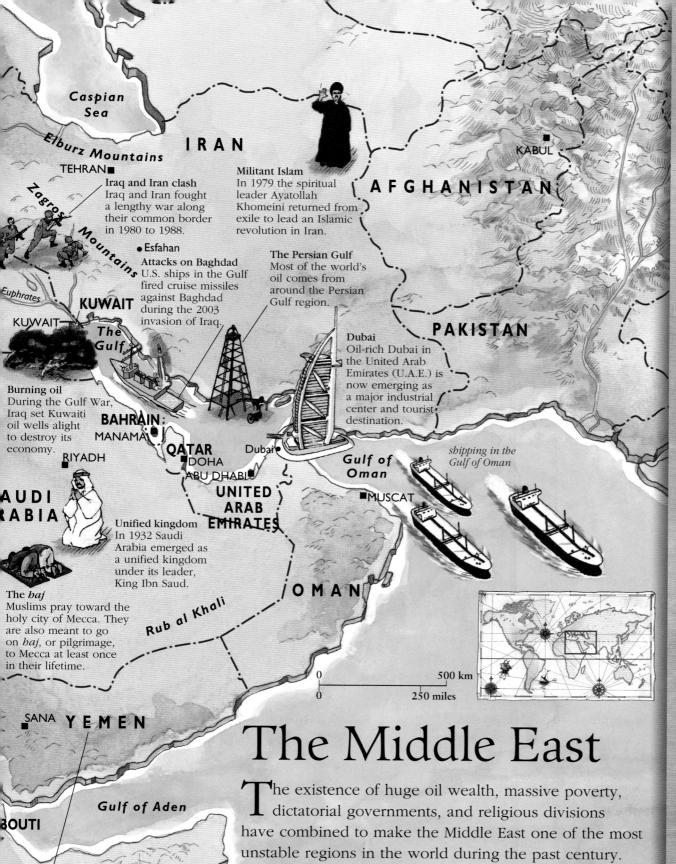

Caspian Sea

Elburz Mountains

TEHRAN ■

IRAN

Zagros Mountains

Iraq and Iran clash
Iraq and Iran fought a lengthy war along their common border in 1980 to 1988.

● Esfahan

Militant Islam
In 1979 the spiritual leader Ayatollah Khomeini returned from exile to lead an Islamic revolution in Iran.

KABUL ■

AFGHANISTAN

Attacks on Baghdad
U.S. ships in the Gulf fired cruise missiles against Baghdad during the 2003 invasion of Iraq.

The Persian Gulf
Most of the world's oil comes from around the Persian Gulf region.

Euphrates

KUWAIT

KUWAIT ■

The Gulf

PAKISTAN

Dubai
Oil-rich Dubai in the United Arab Emirates (U.A.E.) is now emerging as a major industrial center and tourist destination.

Burning oil
During the Gulf War, Iraq set Kuwaiti oil wells alight to destroy its economy.

RIYADH ■

BAHRAIN

MANAMA ■

QATAR

DOHA ■

ABU DHABI ■

Dubai ●

Gulf of Oman

shipping in the Gulf of Oman

SAUDI ARABIA

UNITED ARAB EMIRATES

Unified kingdom
In 1932 Saudi Arabia emerged as a unified kingdom under its leader, King Ibn Saud.

■ MUSCAT

The haj
Muslims pray toward the holy city of Mecca. They are also meant to go on haj, or pilgrimage, to Mecca at least once in their lifetime.

OMAN

Rub al Khali

0 ——— 500 km
0 ——— 250 miles

SANA ■ **YEMEN**

Gulf of Aden

DJIBOUTI

Civil War
War broke out in Yemen in 2014 when rebel Houthis overthrew the government. Saudi Arabia and the United Arab Emirates were drawn into the fighting, which has wrecked the country.

The Middle East

The existence of huge oil wealth, massive poverty, dictatorial governments, and religious divisions have combined to make the Middle East one of the most unstable regions in the world during the past century. The creation of the Jewish state of Israel, in 1948, in land that had been previously occupied by the Palestinians has added to the instability. There have been four major wars between Israel and its Arab neighbors, creating millions of Palestinian refugees in neighboring countries. In recent years, the rise of fundamentalist Islam in Iran and elsewhere has created massive tensions between the Arab world and the West, notably the U.S.

1910–today

1910
1914 Ottoman Turks control most of the region
1916 Arabs revolt against Ottoman rule
1917 Great Britain issues the Balfour Declaration, promising Jews a homeland in Palestine
1918 Ottoman Empire collapses at the end of World War I

1920
1920 Great Britain takes over Palestine and Iraq; France takes over Syria and Lebanon
1922 Egypt gains independence from Great Britain

1930
1932 Kingdom of Saudi Arabia founded
1932 Iraq gains independence from Great Britain
1938 Saudi Arabia begins to export oil

1940
1946 Jordan gains independence from Great Britain
1946 Syria and Lebanon gain full independence from France
1948 Israel founded; first war between Israel and its Arab neighbors

1950
1952 Political coup in Egypt overthrows the king
1954 Nasser becomes president of Egypt
1956 Israel invades Egypt in association with Great Britain and France

1960
1961 Kuwait gains independence
1964 Palestinian Liberation Organization (PLO) founded
1967 Six-Day War: Israel defeats Arab armies and occupies the West Bank, Gaza, and Golan Heights

1970
1971 Great Britain withdraws from the Persian Gulf; the United Arab Emirates are formed
1973 Egypt and Syria attack Israel
1975–89 Civil war in Lebanon
1977 Peace talks between Egypt and Israel
1979 Egypt and Israel sign a peace treaty
1979 Islamic revolution in Iran
1979 Saddam Hussein is president of Iraq
1980
1980–88 Iran-Iraq War caused by Iraqi invasion of neighboring Iran
1982–2000 Israel invades and occupies southern Lebanon
1987 Palestinians begin an "intifada" (uprising) against Israel

1990
1990 Unification of Yemen
1990–91 Gulf War: Iraq invades Kuwait but is expelled after international intervention
1993 Israel recognizes the PLO as representatives of the Palestinians
1998 First limited rule for Palestinians in Israel

2000
2003 U.S.-led force invades and occupies Iraq and overthrows Saddam Hussein
2005 Israel withdraws from Gaza
2008 The three-week Gaza War breaks out between Israel and the Palestinians
2009 Protests erupt in Iran after the re-election of Mahmoud Ahmadinejad as president

2010
2010 The Arab Spring sparks revolutions in Tunisia, Libya, Egypt, Yemen, and Syria
2011 Civil war erupts in Syria
2014 Islamic State, an armed Islamist movement, begins an offensive across northern Iraq
2014 Israel launches air strikes on Gaza
2014 Civil war breaks out in Yemen

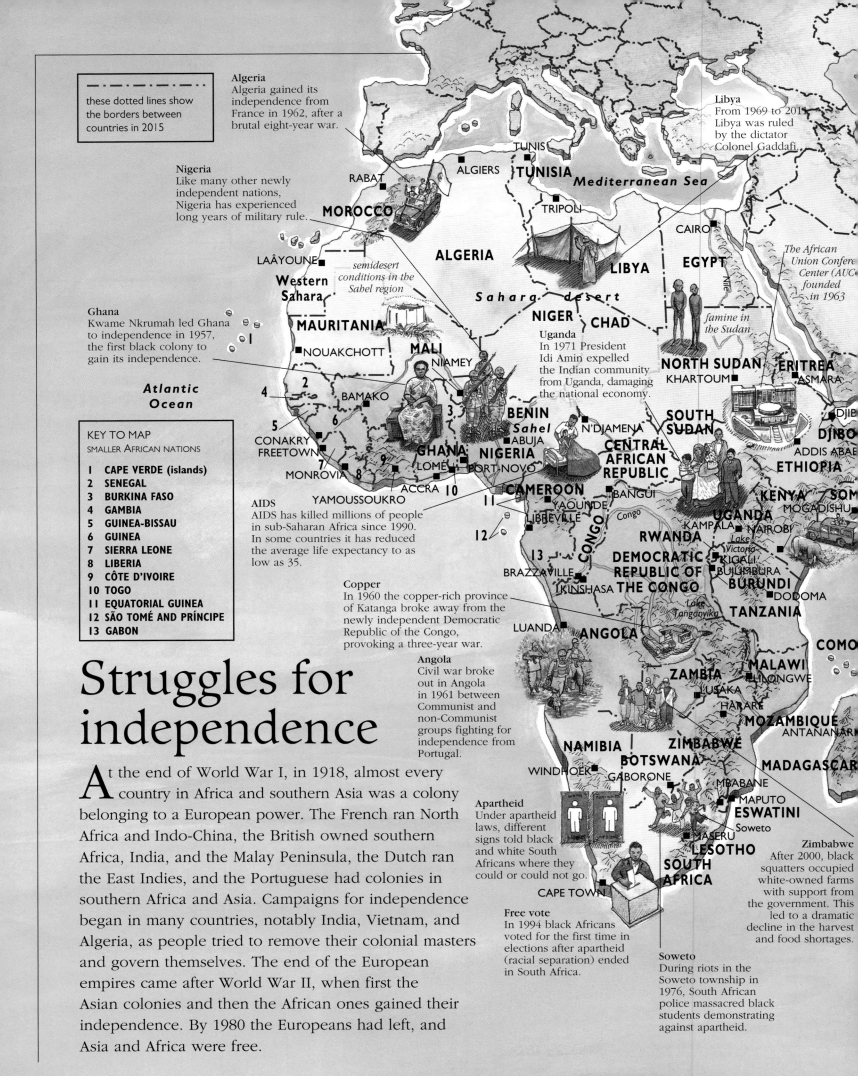

Algeria
Algeria gained its independence from France in 1962, after a brutal eight-year war.

Libya
From 1969 to 2011 Libya was ruled by the dictator Colonel Gaddafi.

Nigeria
Like many other newly independent nations, Nigeria has experienced long years of military rule.

Ghana
Kwame Nkrumah led Ghana to independence in 1957, the first black colony to gain its independence.

The African Union Conference Center (AUC) founded in 1963

Uganda
In 1971 President Idi Amin expelled the Indian community from Uganda, damaging the national economy.

semidesert conditions in the Sahel region

famine in the Sudan

KEY TO MAP
SMALLER AFRICAN NATIONS

I   CAPE VERDE (islands)
2   SENEGAL
3   BURKINA FASO
4   GAMBIA
5   GUINEA-BISSAU
6   GUINEA
7   SIERRA LEONE
8   LIBERIA
9   CÔTE D'IVOIRE
10   TOGO
11   EQUATORIAL GUINEA
12   SÃO TOMÉ AND PRÍNCIPE
13   GABON

AIDS
AIDS has killed millions of people in sub-Saharan Africa since 1990. In some countries it has reduced the average life expectancy to as low as 35.

Copper
In 1960 the copper-rich province of Katanga broke away from the newly independent Democratic Republic of the Congo, provoking a three-year war.

Angola
Civil war broke out in Angola in 1961 between Communist and non-Communist groups fighting for independence from Portugal.

Struggles for independence

At the end of World War I, in 1918, almost every country in Africa and southern Asia was a colony belonging to a European power. The French ran North Africa and Indo-China, the British owned southern Africa, India, and the Malay Peninsula, the Dutch ran the East Indies, and the Portuguese had colonies in southern Africa and Asia. Campaigns for independence began in many countries, notably India, Vietnam, and Algeria, as people tried to remove their colonial masters and govern themselves. The end of the European empires came after World War II, when first the Asian colonies and then the African ones gained their independence. By 1980 the Europeans had left, and Asia and Africa were free.

Apartheid
Under apartheid laws, different signs told black and white South Africans where they could or could not go.

Zimbabwe
After 2000, black squatters occupied white-owned farms with support from the government. This led to a dramatic decline in the harvest and food shortages.

Free vote
In 1994 black Africans voted for the first time in elections after apartheid (racial separation) ended in South Africa.

Soweto
During riots in the Soweto township in 1976, South African police massacred black students demonstrating against apartheid.

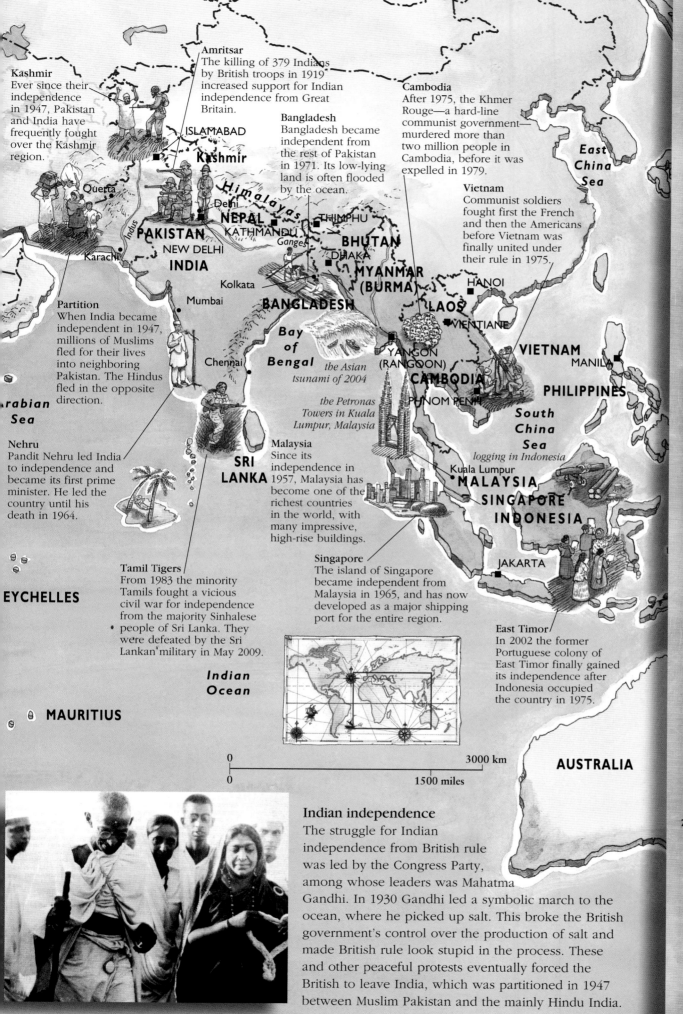

Kashmir
Ever since their independence in 1947, Pakistan and India have frequently fought over the Kashmir region.

Amritsar
The killing of 379 Indians by British troops in 1919 increased support for Indian independence from Great Britain.

Cambodia
After 1975, the Khmer Rouge—a hard-line communist government—murdered more than two million people in Cambodia, before it was expelled in 1979.

Bangladesh
Bangladesh became independent from the rest of Pakistan in 1971. Its low-lying land is often flooded by the ocean.

Vietnam
Communist soldiers fought first the French and then the Americans before Vietnam was finally united under their rule in 1975.

ISLAMABAD
Kashmir
Quetta
Delhi
Himalayas
THIMPHU
NEPAL
KATHMANDU
BHUTAN
PAKISTAN
NEW DELHI
Ganges
DHAKA
INDIA
Karachi
MYANMAR (BURMA)
Kolkata
HANOI
Mumbai
BANGLADESH
LAOS
VIETNAM
VIENTIANE
MANILA
Bay of Bengal
the Asian tsunami of 2004
YANGON (RANGOON)
CAMBODIA
PHILIPPINES
Chennai
the Petronas Towers in Kuala Lumpur, Malaysia
PUNOM PENH
South China Sea
*ba*bian Sea

Partition
When India became independent in 1947, millions of Muslims fled for their lives into neighboring Pakistan. The Hindus fled in the opposite direction.

Nehru
Pandit Nehru led India to independence and became its first prime minister. He led the country until his death in 1964.

Malaysia
Since its independence in 1957, Malaysia has become one of the richest countries in the world, with many impressive, high-rise buildings.

logging in Indonesia
Kuala Lumpur
MALAYSIA
SINGAPORE
INDONESIA

SRI LANKA

EYCHELLES

Tamil Tigers
From 1983 the minority Tamils fought a vicious civil war for independence from the majority Sinhalese people of Sri Lanka. They were defeated by the Sri Lankan military in May 2009.

Singapore
The island of Singapore became independent from Malaysia in 1965, and has now developed as a major shipping port for the entire region.

JAKARTA

East Timor
In 2002 the former Portuguese colony of East Timor finally gained its independence after Indonesia occupied the country in 1975.

Indian Ocean

☖ **MAURITIUS**

0 ———————— 3000 km
0 ———————— 1500 miles

AUSTRALIA

Indian independence
The struggle for Indian independence from British rule was led by the Congress Party, among whose leaders was Mahatma Gandhi. In 1930 Gandhi led a symbolic march to the ocean, where he picked up salt. This broke the British government's control over the production of salt and made British rule look stupid in the process. These and other peaceful protests eventually forced the British to leave India, which was partitioned in 1947 between Muslim Pakistan and the mainly Hindu India.

East China Sea

1910–today

1910
1918 World War I ends
1918 Most of Africa, southern, and southeast Asia are under European colonial rule
1920 Britain, France, and South Africa take over former German colonies in Africa
1922 Egypt gains independence from Great Britain
1926 Morocco revolts against French rule

1930
1935–36 Italy invades Abyssinia (Ethiopia)
1940–41 Japan occupies French Indo-China
1941 Great Britain occupies Italian East African colonies and frees Abyssinia
1941 Ho Chi Minh forms nationalist Viet Minh guerilla group in Vietnam
1941–42 Japan occupies southeast Asia
1946 Philippines independent of the U.S.
1946–54 French fight for control of Vietnam
1947 Great Britain grants independence to India and Pakistan
1948 Britain grants independence to Myanmar and Sri Lanka
1949 Dutch grant Indonesia independence

1950
1951 Libya becomes independent
1954 France leaves Indo-China; Laos and Cambodia become independent
1955 Sudan gains independence from joint British-Egyptian rule
1956 France grants independence to Morocco and Tunisia
1957 Great Britain grants the Malay Peninsula independence
1957–62 Most of sub-Saharan Africa gains independence
1962 France grants Algeria independence
1964–75 U.S. supports South Vietnam against communist North Vietnam
1965 Singapore independent of Malaysia

1970
1971 Bangladesh breaks away from Pakistan
1975 Indonesia occupies the Portuguese colony of East Timor
1975 Vietnam is reunited under Communist rule
1975 Portuguese colonies in Africa win independence, but civil war continues in Angola
1975–79 Khmer Rouge military regime kills millions in Cambodia
1980 Zimbabwe, Great Britain's last remaining colony in Africa, wins independence
1983 Tamil Tiger guerillas begin their fight for independence in Sri Lanka

1990
1990 Namibia gains independence from South Africa
1993 Eritrea gains independence from Ethiopia
1994 Apartheid comes to an end in South Africa
1994 Genocide (mass extermination of an ethnic group) in Rwanda by extremist militia groups
2002 East Timor gains independence from Indonesia
2002 Civil war ends in Angola
2009 Sri Lankan military defeats Tamil Tiger rebels
2009 Boko Haram, an extreme Islamist group, begins an uprising in northern Nigeria

2010
2010 China replaces U.S. as Africa's biggest trading partner
2011 South Sudan wins independence from Sudan
2011 A civilian government replaces military rule in Myanmar
2013 In Mali, Tuareg rebels seize power; France, the former colonial ruler, sends troops
2013 Ebola breaks out in West Africa, the worst outbreak of the disease in history
2015 The idea of an independent Kurdish state gains momentum as Kurds resist the spread of Islamic State in Syria and Iraq

2020
2020 War breaks out in Ethiopia between the government and the rebel Tigray province

Modern Europe

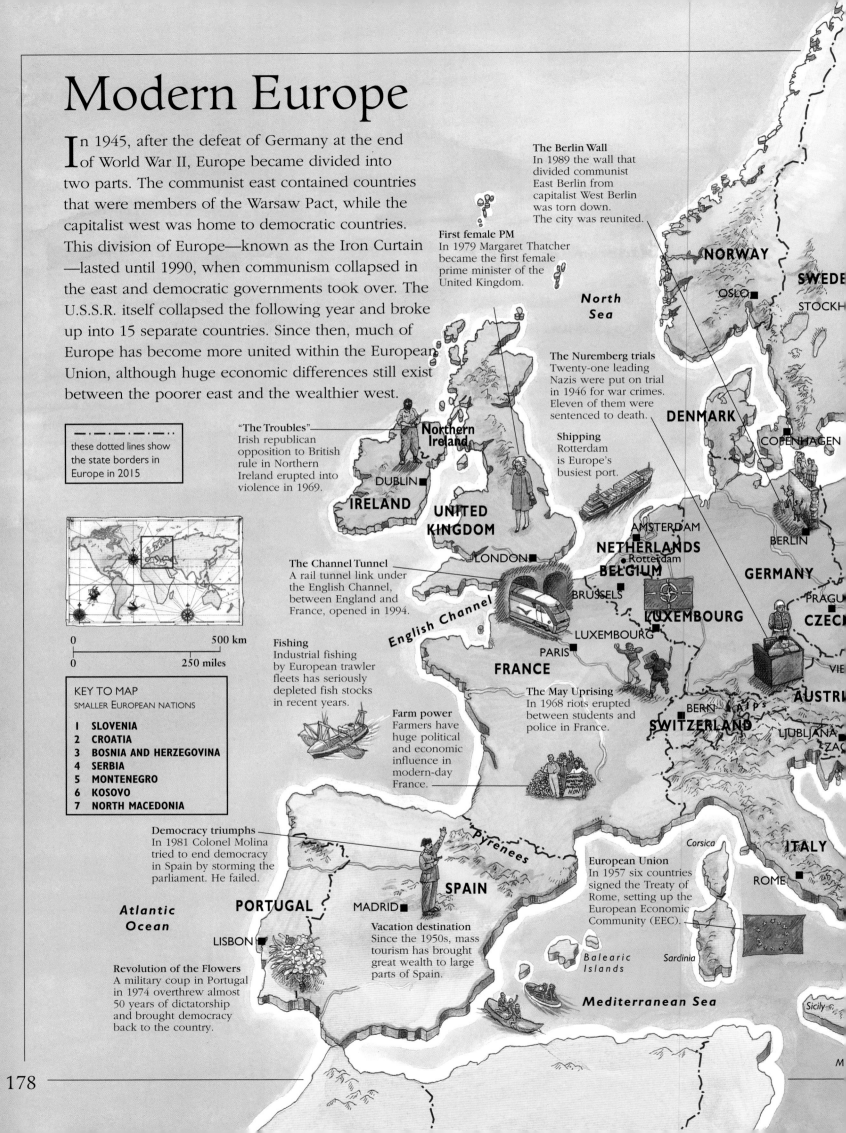

In 1945, after the defeat of Germany at the end of World War II, Europe became divided into two parts. The communist east contained countries that were members of the Warsaw Pact, while the capitalist west was home to democratic countries. This division of Europe—known as the Iron Curtain —lasted until 1990, when communism collapsed in the east and democratic governments took over. The U.S.S.R. itself collapsed the following year and broke up into 15 separate countries. Since then, much of Europe has become more united within the European Union, although huge economic differences still exist between the poorer east and the wealthier west.

these dotted lines show the state borders in Europe in 2015

0 ———— 500 km
0 ———— 250 miles

KEY TO MAP
SMALLER EUROPEAN NATIONS

1 SLOVENIA
2 CROATIA
3 BOSNIA AND HERZEGOVINA
4 SERBIA
5 MONTENEGRO
6 KOSOVO
7 NORTH MACEDONIA

The Berlin Wall
In 1989 the wall that divided communist East Berlin from capitalist West Berlin was torn down. The city was reunited.

First female PM
In 1979 Margaret Thatcher became the first female prime minister of the United Kingdom.

North Sea

The Nuremberg trials
Twenty-one leading Nazis were put on trial in 1946 for war crimes. Eleven of them were sentenced to death.

Shipping
Rotterdam is Europe's busiest port.

"The Troubles"
Irish republican opposition to British rule in Northern Ireland erupted into violence in 1969.

The Channel Tunnel
A rail tunnel link under the English Channel, between England and France, opened in 1994.

Fishing
Industrial fishing by European trawler fleets has seriously depleted fish stocks in recent years.

Farm power
Farmers have huge political and economic influence in modern-day France.

The May Uprising
In 1968 riots erupted between students and police in France.

Democracy triumphs
In 1981 Colonel Molina tried to end democracy in Spain by storming the parliament. He failed.

European Union
In 1957 six countries signed the Treaty of Rome, setting up the European Economic Community (EEC).

Vacation destination
Since the 1950s, mass tourism has brought great wealth to large parts of Spain.

Revolution of the Flowers
A military coup in Portugal in 1974 overthrew almost 50 years of dictatorship and brought democracy back to the country.

NORWAY
SWEDE
OSLO
STOCKH
DENMARK
COPENHAGEN
BERLIN
Northern Ireland
DUBLIN
IRELAND
UNITED KINGDOM
LONDON
AMSTERDAM
NETHERLANDS
Rotterdam
BELGIUM
BRUSSELS
GERMANY
PRAGU
CZECH
LUXEMBOURG
LUXEMBOURG
PARIS
FRANCE
VIE
AUSTRI
BERN
SWITZERLAND
LJUBLJANA
ZAG
English Channel
Pyrenees
PORTUGAL
LISBON
SPAIN
MADRID
Atlantic Ocean
Corsica
ITALY
ROME
Balearic Islands
Sardinia
Mediterranean Sea
Sicily

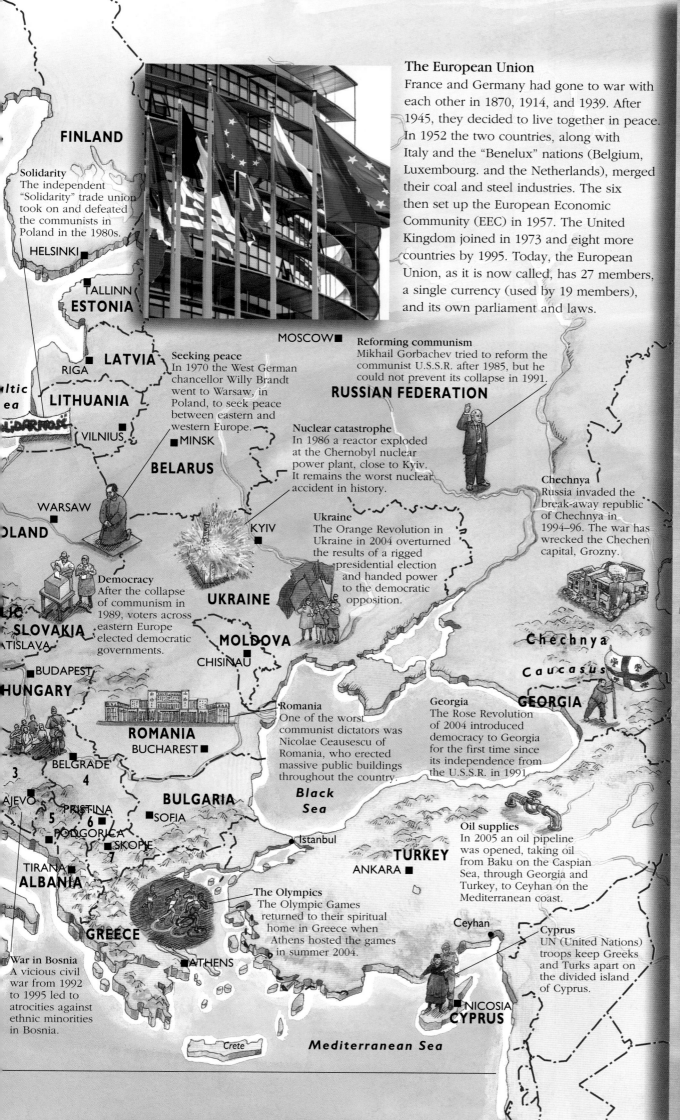

FINLAND

Solidarity
The independent "Solidarity" trade union took on and defeated the communists in Poland in the 1980s.

HELSINKI

TALLINN
ESTONIA

LATVIA
RIGA

Baltic Sea

LITHUANIA

VILNIUS

MINSK

BELARUS

WARSAW

POLAND

SLOVAKIA
BRATISLAVA

BUDAPEST
HUNGARY

Democracy
After the collapse of communism in 1989, voters across eastern Europe elected democratic governments.

Seeking peace
In 1970 the West German chancellor Willy Brandt went to Warsaw, in Poland, to seek peace between eastern and western Europe.

MOSCOW

Reforming communism
Mikhail Gorbachev tried to reform the communist U.S.S.R. after 1985, but he could not prevent its collapse in 1991.

RUSSIAN FEDERATION

Nuclear catastrophe
In 1986 a reactor exploded at the Chernobyl nuclear power plant, close to Kyiv. It remains the worst nuclear accident in history.

KYIV

Ukraine
The Orange Revolution in Ukraine in 2004 overturned the results of a rigged presidential election and handed power to the democratic opposition.

UKRAINE

MOLDOVA
CHISINAU

Chechnya
Russia invaded the break-away republic of Chechnya in 1994–96. The war has wrecked the Chechen capital, Grozny.

Chechnya

Caucasus

GEORGIA

Georgia
The Rose Revolution of 2004 introduced democracy to Georgia for the first time since its independence from the U.S.S.R. in 1991.

Romania
One of the worst communist dictators was Nicolae Ceausescu of Romania, who erected massive public buildings throughout the country.

ROMANIA
BUCHAREST

BELGRADE

3
4

SARAJEVO
5 PRISTINA 6
PODGORICA
1
SKOPJE
7

TIRANA
ALBANIA

BULGARIA
SOFIA

Black Sea

Istanbul

Oil supplies
In 2005 an oil pipeline was opened, taking oil from Baku on the Caspian Sea, through Georgia and Turkey, to Ceyhan on the Mediterranean coast.

TURKEY
ANKARA

Ceyhan

Cyprus
UN (United Nations) troops keep Greeks and Turks apart on the divided island of Cyprus.

The Olympics
The Olympic Games returned to their spiritual home in Greece when Athens hosted the games in summer 2004.

GREECE
ATHENS

War in Bosnia
A vicious civil war from 1992 to 1995 led to atrocities against ethnic minorities in Bosnia.

NICOSIA
CYPRUS

Crete

Mediterranean Sea

The European Union

France and Germany had gone to war with each other in 1870, 1914, and 1939. After 1945, they decided to live together in peace. In 1952 the two countries, along with Italy and the "Benelux" nations (Belgium, Luxembourg. and the Netherlands), merged their coal and steel industries. The six then set up the European Economic Community (EEC) in 1957. The United Kingdom joined in 1973 and eight more countries by 1995. Today, the European Union, as it is now called, has 27 members, a single currency (used by 19 members), and its own parliament and laws.

The world today:
Looking toward the future

The world in the third decade of the new millennium is a remarkably challenging place. Rapid population growth—there are at least 7.7 billion people squashed onto the planet today—and industrial development are straining the world's resources and leading to environmental disasters. Millions of people have left their homes as refugees from war, or in search of better lives, which has positive and negative impacts on both the countries they have left and those where they have settled. Tensions exist between rich and poor, and between people of different religions. But there are also many ways in which human beings are meeting these challenges, and solving the many problems of the modern world.

Multiculturalism

In the past 50 years, large numbers of people left poverty and often oppression in poorer parts of the world and moved to the rich nations of Europe, North America, and Australia in search of work and a better life. These migrants have taken their own religions and cultures with them, turning their host cities into vibrant multicultural, multiethnic places. While some migrants benefit economically, many migrants face racial hatred and social isolation in their new countries. This picture (above) shows school children taking part in a cricket match at a One Day International between England and Australia.

A large percentage of the world's population now lives in heavily built-up urban environments. This sprawling new district is in Mumbai, India.

Disease awareness

During the 1980s a new disease—AIDS, or Acquired Immune Deficiency Syndrome—spread around the world. The disease struck parts of Africa especially severely. By 2013, however, health workers were successfully treating sufferers with drugs that reduce the symptoms. Other diseases remain dangerous. There is still no simple cure for Ebola, which affected West Africa in 2014–2015. Every year about a million people die of malaria, a disease spread by the humble mosquito, and 2019 saw the beginning of the Covid-19 global pandemic, which has already killed millions.

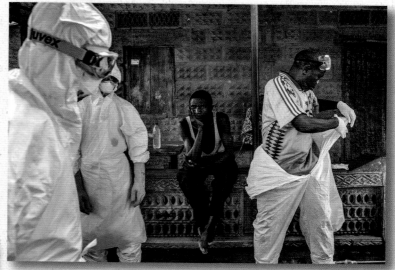

An aid worker in Sierra Leone, West Africa, feeds a child infected with the Ebola virus. During a deadly outbreak in 2014–2015, more than 11,000 people died.

Sustainable development

The huge increase in the world's population over the past 50 years, and the rapid economic growth of previously poor countries such as India and China, have together put a strain on the world's natural resources, such as oil, gas, and water. Environmentalists, scientists, and economists are now looking at ways in which economic development can sustain rather than exploit these resources for the benefit of future generations.

This is an architect's design for a complex of "farmscrapers" to be built in the city of Shenzen, China. Each building rises to 111 floors and combines homes and offices.

Alternative energy sources

It has become obvious that humans are having a harmful impact on the world's climate. Pollution from cars, airplanes, and industry have contributed to a steady rise in temperatures and the destruction of many habitats, making increasing numbers of animal species extinct each year. Extreme weather is becoming more dangerous, and appearing more frequently than before. More "renewable" forms of energy, such as wind power (below), are being used, because they do not produce any of the "greenhouse gases" that contribute to global warming.

Huge rows of wind turbines are now a common sight in isolated or mountainous locations such as the Tehachapi Pass in California. Wind farms have been generating electricity in this region since the early 1980s.

Index

This index lists the main peoples, places and topics that you will find in the text in this book. It is not a full index of all the place names and physical features to be found on the maps.

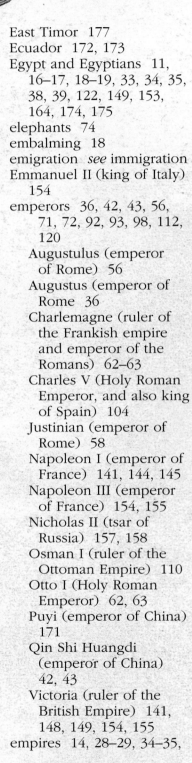

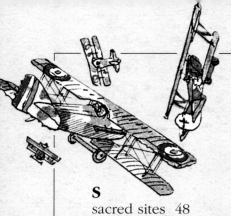

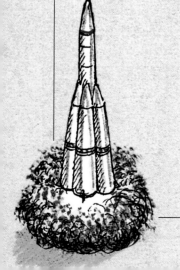

Acknowledgments

The publisher would like to thank the following for permission to reproduce their material.

b = bottom, *c* = center, *l* = left, *r* = right, *t* = top

Cover all images Shutterstock, background map http://mapsof.net; Pages 1 and 3 (globe and scroll artwork) Mark Bergin.

THE ANCIENT WORLD:
Pages 10tr Alamy/Lanmas; 10b Alamy/eye35; 11tl Shutterstock/Dima Moroz; 11tr Shutterstock/SL-Photography; 11bl Shutterstock/cl2004lhy; 11br Getty/David Silverman; 13tr Shutterstock/faber1893; 15tr Alamy/Art Collection 3; 17bl Alamy/GRANGER; 18tr Alamy/robertharding; 18bl Alamy/Heritage Image Partnership Ltd; 19tl Alamy/The Print Collector; 18-19b Shutterstock/WitR; 21tc Shutterstock/LouieLea; 23bc Alamy/Suzuki Kaku; 25tc Shutterstock/Pecold; 27tc Alamy/www.BibleLandPictures.com; 29tl Shutterstock/ Ekaterina Khudina; 31tc Alamy/agefotostock; 32tr Shutterstock/Paul Picone; 32b Shutterstock/Waj; 33cr Shutterstock/CPQ; 33bl Alamy/Azoor Photo; 35tl Shutterstock/Pabkov; 36tr Alamy Azoor Photo; 36bl Alamy/Malcolm Fairman; 36-37b Shutterstock/Art of Life; 37cl Alamy/dpa picture alliance; 38bl Getty/DEA/G.DAGLI ORTI; 41t Alamy/GRANGER; 41b Shutterstock/chetansoni; 42cl Alamy/CPA Media Pte Ltd; 45br Shutterstock/Sopotnicki; 47c Alamy/J.Enrique Molina; 47bl Shutterstock/javarman; 49cr Alamy/WorldFoto

THE MEDIEVAL WORLD:
50 (globe artwork) Katherine Baxter; 54tr Shutterstock/Mikhail Pogosov; 54-55b Shutterstock/JaySi; 55tl Alamy/Jeff Morgan 13; 55tc Alamy/imageBROKER; 55tr Alamy/ClassicStock; 55br Alamy/Paul Springett B; 57tc Alamy/Album; 59c Alamy/INTERFOTO; 60tl iStock/naumoid; 60tr Shutterstock/orxy; 60cr Alamy/Garden Photo World; 61tr Shutterstock/gopixgo; 62c Alamy/imageBROKER; 62bl Alamy/Album/British Library; 65bl Alamy/Xinhua; 66tr Alamy/Sonia Halliday Photo Library; 66cl Shutterstock/Sergey Melnikov; 66br Alamy/Everett Collection Historical; 67tl Alamy/Robert Murray; 68bl Shutterstock/Renu V Nair; 70cr Alamy/Album/British Library; 72cl Shutterstock/Phraisohn Siripool; 75tc Alamy/Roy Garner; 77tc Shutterstock/Lisa Strachan; 78bl Alamy/PRISMA ARCHIVO; 80c Alamy/World History Archive; 80bl Alamy/Keith Corrigan; 82bl Shutterstock/Tanja Midgardson; 83tl Alamy/Science History Images; 85bc Alamy/Photo12; 86bc Alamy/The Picture Art Collection; 89bl Alamy/Classic Image; 90tl Alamy/Chris Hellier; 90c Shutterstock/BorisVetshev; 90bl Alamy/Art Collection 2; 91tl Alamy/agefotostock; 93bl Shutterstock/Mila Bedoya; 93c Alamy/Photo 12

KINGFISHER
LONDON & NEW YORK

Copyright © Macmillan Publishers International Ltd 2008, 2022
First published in 2022 in the United States by Kingfisher,
120 Broadway, New York, NY 10271
Kingfisher is an imprint of Macmillan Children's Books, London.
All rights reserved.

Distributed in the U.S. and Canada by Macmillan,
120 Broadway, New York, NY 10271

EU representative: Macmillan Publishers Ireland Ltd, 1st Floor,
The Liffey Trust Centre, 117-126 Sheriff Street Upper, Dublin 1, D01 YC43

Consultant (2022 edition): Philip Steele

Material previously published in *The Kingfisher Atlas of World History* (2008).

ISBN: 978-0-7534-7813-4

Libraray of Congress Cataloging-in-Publication data has been applied for.

Kingfisher books are available for special promotions and premiums.
For details contact: Special Markets Department, Macmillan,
120 Broadway, New York, NY 10271.

For more information, please visit www.kingfisherbooks.com

Printed in Thailand
1 3 5 7 9 8 6 4 2
1TR/0422/RRD/UG/128MA

FSC
www.fsc.org

MIX
Paper from
responsible sources
FSC® C116313